ENHANCING SELF-ESTEEM

ENHANCING SELF-ESTEEM

Third Edition

C. Jesse Carlock, Ph.D.
Editor

USA	Publishing Office:	ACCELERATED DEVELOPMENT *A member of the Taylor & Francis Group* 325 Chestnut Street Philadelphia, PA 19106 Tel: (215) 625-8900 Fax: (215) 625-2940
	Distribution Center:	ACCELERATED DEVELOPMENT A member of the Taylor & Francis Group 47 Runway Road, Suite G Levittown, PA 19057-4700 Tel: (215) 269-0400 Fax: (215) 269-0363
UK		ACCELERATED DEVELOPMENT *A member of the Taylor & Francis Group* 1 Gunpowder Square London EC4A 3DE Tel: +44 171 583 0490 Fax: +44 171 583 0581

ENHANCING SELF-ESTEEM: Third Edition

1 2 3 4 5 6 7 8 9 0 GHB 98

Printed by Edwards Brothers, Ann Arbor, MI, 1998.

A CIP catalog record for this book is available from the British Library.
∞The paper in this publication meets the requirements of the ANSI Standard Z39.48-1984 (Permanence of Paper).

Library of Congress Cataloging-in-Publication Data
Carlock, C. Jesse
Enhancing self-esteem / C. Jesse Carlock. — 3rd ed.
p. cm.
Rev. ed. of: Enhancing self-esteem / Diane Frey. 2nd ed. ©1989.
Includes bibliographical references and index.
ISBN 1-56032-396-5 (pbk. : alk. paper)
1. Self-esteem. 2. Self-esteem — Problems, exercises, etc.
I. Frey, Diane. Enhancing self-esteem. II. Title.
BF697.5.S46F73 1998
158.1—dc21 98-26790
CIP

ISBN: 1-56032-396-5 (paper)

TABLE OF CONTENTS

List of Tables and Figures

DEDICATION

This book is dedicated to all the "Bridge People" who believe in me when I doubt myself, help me laugh at my foibles, and inspire me to reach for my wildest dreams ...

PREFACE

I have been in practice for 22 years. Whenever I begin working with people, I always ask them to describe what problems or difficulties brought them to me. Over the years, I have found that a high percentage describe one of their central concerns as problems with self-esteem.

Sometimes I can see the pain in people's faces, appearance, and demeanor; it clearly conveys the devastation low self-esteem has had on their lives. In others, the damage is well-masked and detected only over time, as cracks begin to show in the facade or a tiny leak occurs here and there.

But despite all the damage they may unveil to me, I rest secure in knowing there is a core in people that remains unsullied. And if I can earn enough trust, I know they will open the door to the deepest part of themselves and, through that opening–through authentic, rich contact–I can kindle hope. Hope activates that precious core, which then begins to glow and radiate beams throughout the self.

Through that relationship I know that I can become one of the "bridge people" I talk about in this book: people who can guide others to a new, more positive way of experiencing themselves. This book will introduce you to maps, books, and resources that can help you in this venerable mission.

This book is about hope. It is about people being willing to learn how to emotionally touch themselves and each other. I invite you to summon your curiosity and explore through the following pages a multitude of avenues for enhancing your own self-esteem. For people can change, as Virginia Satir proclaimed often, "it's just a question of when and in what context."

INTRODUCTION

When, midstream through revising *Enhancing Self-Esteem* for its third edition, I was offered the opportunity to take on the project of revising and updating the book as the sole author, I was caught by surprise. I had completed my half of the book, and I was relieved that the bulk of my work was done. Facing the prospect of writing the other half was daunting. I am not an expert in all the areas the text covered in prior editions.

But then I began viewing the project differently. If I took not only responsibility for but also authority of the book, I could design it any way I liked. My excitement built as I began to take ownership and think about what I wanted to include in the other half of the book and how I could accomplish that. I invited four colleagues whom I respect highly to join me, each contributing a chapter on a topic in which he or she has expertise and excitement. It has been a delightful collaborative arrangement. You, the reader, will undoubtedly benefit from these contributors' fresh ideas and perspectives.

Part I describes the heart of my model to enhance self-esteem. Chapter 1 explains the basic terms used throughout the book, such as self-esteem, self, and self-concept; briefly outlines the development of the self and self-concept; and sketches a comprehensive process for enhancing self-esteem that includes attention to emotional, cognitive, physical, and interpersonal dimensions.

In chapter 2, Dr. Norman Shub brings into sharp focus three elements he believes are pivotal in creating high self-esteem: developing and assimilating positive beliefs, revising or eliminating negative beliefs, and forming beliefs to meet essential emotional needs. Dr. Shub presents his model in a creative and down-to-earth manner, providing many examples and exercises to help the reader.

In chapter 3, I describe how to work with competing forces in the self: the drive toward self-improvement and the force toward self-consistency and stability. If we are to achieve enhanced self-esteem, we must value and attend to both ends of this polarity. The chapter includes several concepts related to self-regulation, with examples provided. With increased awareness of internal mechanisms, perspectives, and dynamics from an observer or "control tower" position, we can learn to strategically manage our change process in a way that limits threat to the integrity of the self.

Chapter 4 addresses the crucial role of other people and our skill in relating to others in creating, changing, and maintaining high self-esteem. A healthy support network and good interpersonal skills are essential to high self-esteem. Identifying the sources of our self-view, correcting distortions, and sorting out others' projections are indispensable in developing an accurate self-picture.

In chapter 5, I examine the physical dimension of the self-esteem change process from several vantage points: the impact on self-esteem of our cultural preoccupation with weight and our narrow standards of beauty; the importance of being centered, grounded, and supported by our breathing; and the critical skills of sensation and awareness in identifying and meeting needs.

Part II is devoted to exploring special self-esteem issues and interventions relating to gender, children, parents, and life transitions. This section also includes a practical discussion of self-esteem assessment. At the request of many readers, I have added a special resource list that includes educational videotapes, audio cassettes, full-length feature films, and children's books that may be helpful to teachers, trainers, and leaders of psychoeducational groups.

Chapter 6 represents a major revision of the first edition of this book: It updates material on women's self-esteem and has been broadened to include issues related to men's self-esteem. In it, I explore the challenges of breaking free from prescribed gender roles while maintaining high self-esteem. While stretching the boundaries of gender role behavior provides us with more options for better coping, richer relationships, and self-expression, running counter to cultural expectations often triggers adverse reactions from those who measure our worth on the basis of how well we meet those role demands.

In chapter 7 Dr. Antoinette Cordell brings her many years of clinical experience to the critical topic of children and self-esteem. She reviews clinically relevant literature, offers clinical vignettes, and details strategies she has found effective in enhancing self-esteem in children. Dr. Cordell also addresses specific problems of children with special needs, such as gifted children, children of divorce, those with ADHD or learning disabilities, and those from diverse cultural backgrounds.

Parenting is one of the most important roles in our culture, and the impact of parenting on self-esteem can be substantial. In chapter 8, Nancy King looks at this often-neglected topic, pointing out chief challenges to parents' self-esteem during their children's infancy, childhood, adolescence, and young adulthood, as well as difficulties encountered in parenting the parent. Her clinical experience and her own parenting experience bring the chapter to life. Ms. King offers insights and suggestions to help parents negotiate the tasks of parenting with more awareness and confidence.

From birth to death, we continually face transitions in life. And although these transitions offer opportunities for growth, they can be rocky and scary times. In chapter 9, I discuss the types of transitions we face throughout our lives, outline the phases of the change process, and offer practical suggestions to help cushion these inevitable periods so that self-esteem is least compromised.

In chapter 10 Dr. Kathleen Glaus reviews some of the more familiar and usable instruments for measuring self-esteem and makes recommendations useful in clinical and educational settings. Dr. Glaus also looks at issues of gender, racial, and cultural bias in self-esteem assessment.

Enhancing Self-Esteem offers a balance of current theory and research on the topic of self-esteem as well as an array of practical exercises for each topic presented. Whether you are looking to strengthen yourself or are wishing to locate resources to help others, I trust you will find a rich assortment of tools to help you. Most people I have known who have purchased prior editions report that their books are sufficieintly "dog-eared," providing evidence of their frequent use and utility. This won't be a book that gathers dust on the shelf!

PART I

Model to Enhance Self-Esteem

Chapter 1

ENHANCING SELF-ESTEEM: A MODEL FOR CHANGE

C. Jesse Carlock

WHAT IS SELF-ESTEEM?

"Self-esteem" has been a common buzzword for at least a couple of decades now. The term is thrown about so glibly it has almost lost its meaning. That is not to say self-esteem is unimportant. Low self-esteem has been linked strongly with depression and poor relationship choice and tangentially associated with many other symptoms. Conversely, high self-esteem is associated with happiness, serenity, success, and fulfillment. But singing the praises of children (or adults) without grounding that praise in objective data will not build high self-esteem. Ungrounded praise only creates an unrealistic and skewed sense of self. The work of developing high self-esteem requires more involvement and precise work in identifying a realistic base.

When someone says, "I have problems with self-esteem," it is only a starting place. You know the ballpark at this point—and it's a huge one. Mapping the person's problem areas and strengths in concrete terms is the next step.

Simply stated, self-esteem is the way you feel about yourself. Most people have a global feeling about themselves that runs along a continuum from high to low, good to bad. If 10 represents high self-esteem, and 1 represents low self-esteem, where would you fall? Anyone can judge where they usually fall along the continuum. But you may have no way of knowing where to begin to help raise your own or another's self-esteem.

When directed, most people can become more specific in identifying self-aspects and rating their self-esteem in each of these areas (see chapter 10 for information on assessment). However, they may need guidance in the process. Satir's (1981) self-mandala is a useful tool for partializing the different aspects of self. The mandala she created consists of the following parts (starting from the center, "I," and moving out in a series of concentric circles):

I: the center; that which you call self; your overall sense of worth

physical self: appearance, health, posture, touch needs; body conditioning, hair care, and clothing (see chapter 5)

intellectual self: your mind, cognitive abilities, planning, problem solving, and ability to use good judgment (see chapter 3)

emotional self: your ability to experience the full range of emotions, regulate your emotions, express them appropriately, and use them in coping (see chapter 3)

sensual self: your ability to use all of your senses (visual, auditory, tactile, olfactory, gustatory, and kinesthetic) in making contact with yourself and the world (see chapter 5)

interactional self: your ability to make contact with others—to relate professionally, socially, or intimately; includes your ability to say what you think and feel, and ask for what you want and need; encompasses your style of relating to others and your communication skills (see chapter 4)

contextual self: your awareness of and use of time, space, color, light, and environmental factors; your view of your history, ground, and field of your life; your need for a calm or stimulating environment

nutritional self: your attention to how you nourish yourself—the foods, liquids, and substances you put into your body (see chapter 5)

life force: your attention to a force greater than yourself; your soul or spiritual force (see Activity 1.6)

What are your beliefs about yourself in each of these areas? How would you rate yourself? Do any of these ratings reduce your self-esteem? By making the concept of "self-esteem" more concrete, it becomes more amenable to change, allowing you to set specific, realistic goals.

WHAT IS THE BASIS OF HIGH SELF-ESTEEM?

Authors have come up with a variety of definitions of self-esteem (see Table 1.1). Borrowing bits and pieces from several theorists, let's define self-esteem as how you feel about yourself, how highly you regard yourself. That degree of regard is based on your sense of

- how lovable and special you believe you are;
- how wanted you feel and your sense of belonging;
- how special or unique you believe you are;
- how competent you feel and how well you fulfill your potential;
- how willing you are to take risks and face challenges;
- and how able you are to set goals, make choices, and fulfill your goals and dreams (Cantor & Bernay, 1992; McDowell, 1984; Satir, 1981)

According to Cantor and Bernay (1992) and Shub (1994), people with high self-esteem have positive feelings about themselves that are not shaken by challenge or adversity. In essence, their self-esteem is rock-solid. But self-esteem is not an all-or-nothing commodity. That kind of thinking can impede our ability to accurately evaluate ourselves. The self is composed of many parts, and our feelings about these parts vary. For self-esteem to be stable, it must be based on a realistic appraisal, free from distortions, not overly inflated or diminished. Because self-esteem is based on dimensions that are not black and white (such as how lovable you believe you are and how special you see yourself being), everything is a matter of degree. So the inviolability of self-esteem also is a matter of degree.

In a nutshell, high self-esteem comes from actualizing yourself: that is, claiming and cultivating your natural talents and resources, and identifying and facing your challenges (for instance, being willing to assert who you are in the face of external pressures to be different).

"I am loved and special. I am wanted."

So many of us lack a firm belief in these two core messages. It takes a healthy family to deliver them clearly, repeatedly, and believably—with ac-

TABLE 1.1
Definitions of Self-Esteem

Bednar & Peterson (1989)	Posited that an enduring sense of realistic self-appraisal, which reflects how the person views and values the self, is directly related to the degree to which the individual chooses to cope and face challenges rather than to avoid them, regardless of the outcome (similar to Allport, 1961).
Horney (1992, 1994)	Believed that each person is born with unique potential, and that self-esteem derives from achieving that potential. High self-esteem comes from cultivating one's talents, yet the self only flourishes with interpersonal recognition, affirmation, validation, encouragement, and support.
James (1890)	Defined self-esteem as the degree to which one can achieve one's goals and aspirations, or the ratio between one's accomplishments and one's supposed potentialities.
Josephs (1992, p. 91)	Stated that self-esteem "refers to how highly one regards oneself." Saw two dimensions of self-esteem: self-acceptance in belonging and pride in individuality.
May (1973)	Regarded autonomy as crucial to self-esteem. Stressed the inevitable anxiety that comes from asserting one's individuality in the face of external pressures to be different. If one can withstand that pressure, self-esteem is strengthened.
Sullivan (1953)	Viewed self-esteem as a social need to be liked and accepted, to belong, to fit in. Believed self-esteem is derived from social interaction mediated by reflected self-appraisals, and is maintained by conforming to social expectations and resisting unacceptable roles.

tions supporting words—over those essential early years of childhood and onward. Yet, the drive toward growth is so strong that many people manage to build a decent foundation out of scraps of loving messages picked up along the way. People are instinctively creative about finding what they need to piece together a quilt of loving messages from even the most tangential sources. I remember a client who was raised in an extremely abusive home, where she was emotionally neglected and sexually abused. When I asked who in her childhood had helped her survive, she remembered a stranger she had met when her family was visiting relatives. This person had shown an interest in her, smiled, asked her questions about herself, and lightly touched her in a nonthreatening and nurturing way. The imprint of this single occasion with a stranger was embedded in her memory, and she had drawn on the memory to keep the embers of her sense of worth alive over the years.

Each of us is unique: As Virginia Satir loved to remind us, "No one's finger prints are exactly the same as anyone else's." But there are degrees to which people recognize their uniqueness and specialness. Some lucky children are raised in a bed of rich soil where their needs are attended to, where feelings of being loved and special are firmly and repeatedly planted, where they are seen, and heard, and responded to. Those around them seem to delight in reflecting the miracle of their unfolding personalities. For the rest of us, the soil was probably uneven. But thankfully, even if our family environment lacked the richness required to build high self-esteem, other significant people and experiences can (to some extent) compensate for deficiencies or further enrich an otherwise healthy base. How to facilitate that process is the purpose of this book.

THE EMERGENCE OF SELF

Many theorists have tried to define the concept of *self* (see Table 1.2). I believe the self is *metamorphic*: It forms early and gradually becomes stable, but it has the ability to alter over the course of a lifetime. *It is always in process*. The self is formed through genetics, introjects (undigested messages, beliefs, and behavior patterns incorporated from significant others), and life experiences. It emerges through our actions and our interactions with others and the environment. The self's robustness is built through meeting the challenges life poses.

Through our interactions with others and the environment, we begin to organize our experiences, personal resources, talents, and abilities. Others also experience us in clusters of primary traits: For example, a person who is passive, unmotivated, and obstructionistic may be seen as having an avoiding aspect of self. Polster (1990) explained that traits which characterize us and are guiding and orienting forces in our lives become apparent, and others resonate with those traits in particular ways. He viewed the self as a small work of fic-

TABLE 1.2
Definitions of Self

Adler (1979)	Believed that people construct their own views of self, strive to make meaning out of their lives, and work toward an overarching goal of wholeness, self-actualization, and self-fulfillment ("striving for superiority").
Allport (1961)	Stressed that the concept of self is built over the course of human development through learning and choice. Emphasized the importance of self-discipline and the courage to face rather than avoid difficulties as central to self-esteem.
Cooley (1902)	Contended that the central aspect of self is the social self, which emerges through interactions with significant others. Self-concept is derived from how we imagine others define and respond to us ("looking-glass self").
James (1890)	Posited that one's concept of self includes all the parts one chooses to include (body, abilities, talents, children, possessions).
Perls, Hefferline, & Goodman (1977)	Proposed a process view of self—a fluid system of contacts with the environment—versus a structure, although they also viewed the self as having continuity over time.
Rogers (1951)	Proposed that the self develops from a combination of what one directly experiences and introjects. Believed that one's sense of self is derived from one's values and affective preferences, and that the more congruent one's ideal, real, and perceived self, the healthier one's self-esteem.

tion, the themes of which may be changed by accessing, integrating, and clustering our constituent selves (Polster, 1990, 1995).

This emergence of self can be viewed from several perspectives. For example, Harter (1983), drawing on a number of theorists, outlined the emergence of self in infancy, maintaining that the process is a gradual one. During the first five months there is no self-other differentiation (symbiotic phase)—infant and mother are one. Gradually, infants become aware that their bodily self can cause movement. Harter explained that, later, infants become aware of themselves as active agents and begin to differentiate their bodily selves from others. Further along, children begin the psychological differentiation of self from others. Appreciation of self as object follows the differentiation of other as object, as noted in visual recognition studies summarized by Harter (1983).

Mahler and Furer's (1968) work emphasized the task of developing maternal object constancy through the infant's development of representations of the mother. Other theorists have examined the nature of the attachment bond, and its critical impact on the child's developing sense of self. According to Harter (1983), the results of research in this area suggest that infants who are securely attached tend to show higher self-esteem and greater competence and confidence in interpersonal relationships.

In a fertile early environment—one in which there is recognition, support, affirmation, stimulation, validation, and encouragement—the self blooms. Less fertile environments—where there is an insecure attachment between infant and parental figures—tend to produce people with lower self-esteem. Some environments are simply barren, and the self lacks the nourishment it needs to flourish. In these cases, awareness is narrowed, and identity development may be dwarfed.

Some environments are overtly toxic, and awareness and feedback are knitted in a negative, critical, disconfirming way. In environments where family rules are rigid and constricting, the self is not able to grow in its own natural directions or express itself in other than acceptable ways. Energy and liveliness here is strangled. Needs, wants, behaviors, and feelings may be ignored or punished. In these families, the self-regulating process is disturbed.

From infancy, the seeds of the self are beginning to grow. Citing the work of Stern and Kant, Crocker (1996) pointed out that five foundational elements of the self are already in operation by the time a child is 4 months old:

- agency
- organic wholeness
- temporal continuity
- affectivity
- "I" who accompanies all experience

Crocker (1998) explained that the 4-month-old is aware of living through time, knows that "this is my thumb," and can make qualitative judgments ("I like this or that"). Crocker reminded us that even infants have a gestalt of preferences whose basis is unknown. We just prefer one thing or another. She believed this affectivity is at the core of personhood.

In outlining the shifts during childhood in the conception of self, Harter (1983) cited Sarbin (1962), who postulated that a transition occurs in the first two years of life from the somatic to the social self. Epstein (1973) described a sequence of emergence from the bodily self to the psychological self to the moral self.

Harter (1983) explained that the final stages of Epstein's continuum could not be observed until adolescence, since moral development requires a much higher level of cognitive ability.

In applying the Piagetian perspective, Harter (1983) drew from several sources to outline changes in the development of the self over time:

Preoperational period: During this time, children learn categories of behavior with which they can define themselves. There probably is no logical order to these, however, and the categories are not stable over time. At this stage children do not possess role-taking capabilities. They cannot imagine what others think of them.

Concrete operational period: During this period, children begin to consolidate and organize traits and to verify observable traits. Children have some perspective-taking skills now, allowing them to imagine what others think of them. They also have an emotional reaction to their perceptions of these evaluations or judgments. Children are now able to engage in a process of self-evaluation.

Formal operational thought: During adolescence, the capacity for introspection blossoms. Adolescents are capable of deductive reasoning and tend to deal, not only with reality, but with the hypothetical. They become increasingly aware of their feelings, thoughts, and intentions, and they begin to make generalizations based on their experiences (and sometimes overgeneralizations due to errors in their newly found skills of abstraction).

Since adolescence is a time of heightened self-consciousness—a time when the self-concept becomes more unstable—Allport (1961) emphasized that a major task of adolescence is to consolidate aspects of the self into a cohesive unit. The whole-making or synthesizing functions of self become vital at this time. As Crocker (1996) asserted,

> this synthesizing function attempts to help adolescents assimilate their experiences into a whole. If we are unable to assimilate some experiences, we accommodate by walling them off. But this walling off then blocks functioning (Crocker, 1998).

Harter (1983) stressed that we look, not only at how socialization shapes our self-concept, but also at how our ongoing life experiences form our perspectives and establish the ground for our perspectives and the meanings we attach to experiences. According to Crocker (1998), personality is an aspect of self that results from the accumulated history of the individual. This personality influences both our experiences and how we organize them.

As reported by Harter (1983), Rosenberg described these shifts in children's self-concept from ages 10 to 18 years:

- Younger children describe characteristics that can be observed, such as behavior, facts, achievements, possessions, and physical attributes.

- Trait descriptions appear next, with a focus on emotional control, aspects of character, and emotional states. Harter (1983) reported that by about age 8, children understand that they can experience two opposing feelings simultaneously. Interpersonal descriptions appear later.

- Descriptions of one's interior life appear toward age 18, when the adolescent will focus on abstract tendencies and potentials, hopes, secrets, attitudes, and emotions.

Other theorists have posited that the self continues to develop beyond the age of 18. As cited by Harter (1983), Fisher proposed that cognitive development extends into adulthood, with four levels of abstraction—each one building on the previous. Harter (1983) believed these increasingly higher levels of abstract ability might have implications on our sense of self across the life span, but research on changes throughout the life span is lacking. (For further discussion of self-concept development, see chapter 7.) Yet, we know that the range of our influence expands and contracts as we age, as do our bodily well-being and sense of control. There is no doubt these changes affect our self-esteem.

THE PROCESS OF CHANGE

I vividly remember Virginia Satir towering over me, all nearly-six feet of her, her eyes intense, her voice self-assured: "I know people can change—right down to my bones, through every cell, in every fiber in my body—I know that *people can change*. It's just a question of *when* and in *what context*."

The strength of her conviction served as a bridge for me, from doubt to the belief that I, too, could change, when almost every fiber inside of me believed that *I could not.* Virginia Satir was only one of the *"bridge people"* in my life. Miraculously, people have always appeared in my life just at the point when discouragement was about to turn to resignation—people who believed in me, believed I could change, could achieve my goals, could become happy and hopeful, when I lacked faith in myself. But despair need not be the only motivator to propel us to locate bridge people who can help us by encouraging the changes we select, noticing and reflecting the changes they see, cheerleading when we hit a slump, or simply believing in us.

Bridge people provide inspiration, encouragement, and support to take the leap from the middle ground, as we let go of what is old and familiar and move toward what is new and unknown (see chapter 9). Anyone can serve as a bridge person. Sometimes we are bridge people for others and are not even aware of our impact. Who have been the bridge people in the different phases of your life? Are there bridge people in your life now who can help facilitate changes you want to make? For whom have you been a bridge person? For whom could you be a bridge person? The process of creating self-worth is also a modeling process.

Bridge people can have even broader and deeper impact when they are aware and deliberate in the process of enhancing self-esteem. The more meaningful the relationship, the stronger the impact. Shub (1994) contended that people who are meaningful to us can help us pay closer attention and provide more valence. A chorus of bridge people is even better, especially when the chorus is composed of people from different areas of our lives (for example, teachers, colleagues, church members, community acquaintances, friends, family, therapists, support or therapy groups). While bridge people cannot prevent us from struggling and stumbling, they can hold our hands through change and provide a secure base from which we venture beyond our comfort zones. In choosing your bridge people, you should look for those who will verify your new self-concept. You will have to learn to bear the dissonance that their behavior and attitudes toward you will likely stimulate.

While there are ways that individuals working alone can transform and maintain self-esteem, involving others in the process of can be a potent addition. They can create a cocoon of support, affirmation, validation, encouragement, and stimulation to which you can retreat when you need to recharge. This kind of nurturing environment breeds both self-acceptance and change. Bridge people can provide clear reflections of who and how we are from moment to moment—simple observations, without judging good or bad.

To begin the process of changing self-esteem, we do not have to desire change, or even be committed to change. I have heard stories of people who have had a tremendously positive impact on someone's changing self-esteem simply by being who they are: naturally affirming and validating, reflecting positive personality traits and talents. We might not consciously seek out these benefactors, but we may unconsciously gravitate toward them when they appear in our lives. Most people want to feel better about themselves and will seek to meet their needs, even when they are not able to articulate that desire and have not made a conscious commitment to doing so. Of course, awareness, desire, commitment to change, and informed, deliberate efforts to change can surely propel the process.

The comprehensive model described in the next section incorporates working with self-awareness (beliefs, emotions, physical processes) and skill development to modify self-esteem.

MODEL FOR SELF-ESTEEM ENHANCEMENT

Phase I. Self-Awareness

Within each of us lies an embryo waiting to grow and be born. This is the self. With ideal parenting, this self-embryo is free to grow in its own directions with appropriate guidance. As the self-embryo grows and expresses itself, it is nurtured, and its character is carefully and accurately defined by its caregivers as well as others in the environment.

Within a secure relationship—one in which children feel loved and special and in which their uniqueness is noticed and defined as it emerges again and again—the self and self-esteem flourish. Self-esteem flourishes because, as Shub asserted, the structure of a positive self has been made firm (see chapter 2). Shub (1994) used the image of steel rods to indicate the strength of these positive self-beliefs, which brace the structure of the self in individuals with high self-esteem.

Unfortunately, many of us grow up in less than ideal conditions. We form a picture of who we are and how we feel about ourselves through our interactions with important figures in our lives, who are themselves imperfect or who lack wholeness. Some of these important figures may be outright destructive. Consequently, parts of our self-picture may be inaccurate or distorted, and huge chunks of the self may be missing or outside of awareness. Let's look now at how that distorted picture is formed.

All of us are born with certain traits, personality propensities, preferences, and other unique manifestations that express our personhood. Through interactions with the world, our traits come to light and we learn patterns of behavior that further define us. Some of who we are emerges and is reinforced; but some of what emerges is discouraged, ignored, punished, or otherwise reacted to by those in our environment. People around us, particularly those who exert power over us, help shape the self in this way. In our natural course of development, we *introject* attitudes and behavior patterns from those significant people who take care of us. Polster (1990) described this introjecting process as a "spontaneous receptivity unimpeded by the deliberate faculties of the mind." These internalized attitudes, traits, and patterns may or may not be problematic.

Sometimes, in order to avoid the loss of love (through emotional or physical abandonment, rejection, or abuse), we may not develop those self-aspects which are not approved—we may send them "underground." For example, if we continually hear the message, "Don't talk back," we may learn to stifle our anger or assertiveness. If we hear, "Don't ask so many questions," we may learn to restrain our inquisitiveness.

Sometimes, negatively viewed traits may be reinforced, such as "You're so clumsy," "You're so stubborn," or "You're always careless." These messages are called *introjects* (See chapter 3). Let's look at the impact of a single traumatic event on the beliefs of an 8-year-old boy:

> A boy runs into his house, crying, his nose bloodied, his arm bruised, shaking. He tells his father that an older boy, the neighborhood bully, beat him up and took his money.
>
> His father responds, "Don't be such a crybaby. What are you, a wimp? Look at you. You're a mess. Now wipe your face and get back out there."

What might this little boy conclude about himself? "I'm weak. I'm a coward."

He might also conclude that, in order to be accepted, he must obey the following rules:

Boys must act strong.

Boys must not cry.

Boys must not show fear.

The father's intentions may be to develop strength in his son. He may well be acting out of love, or out of a fear that his son might otherwise develop feelings of inadequacy as a man in our culture, which expects toughness from men. Learning how to be tough in certain situations is important for both girls and boys, of course, but not at the risk of obliterating sensitivity to one's own or another's feelings, needs, or self-worth (see chapter 6).

Beliefs also are strengthened by repeated, everyday occurrences. For example:

> A 10-year-old comes downstairs to make her breakfast. She is dressed and ready for school. Her parents are in the kitchen. They immediately launch into this verbal barrage: "You're not going to wear that to school, are you? Don't you have anything else to wear? I told you to put those clothes in the hamper yesterday. You need that hair cut, too. Hey, that's too much sugar on your cereal. You're getting too fat as it is. Look at your blouse. It's already gaping open."

This kind of constant criticism creates a feeling that, "I'm never good enough. I don't do anything right." In many households, interactions like this are the norm. Perception is knitted in a negative way and, while the parents may not intend to be destructive, over time the affect on the child's self-esteem is disastrous (see chapter 4). Often the parents' behavior is the product of toxic messages they received growing up, which they now project onto their own children.

So far, we've looked at some of the more problematic, toxic, or limiting beliefs we may have received from our environments. But we may receive empowering messages as well. We may hear, "You have a right to speak your feelings," "It's okay to ask for what you want," or "You can make mistakes and still be lovable." Whatever the messages are, it is important to become aware of the beliefs behind them, and to evaluate their accuracy.

In some scenarios, self-aspects that are approved may overdevelop. For example, we might see an overdeveloped sense of obedience and conformity in a child who continually hears, "You are such a good boy. You always do as you're told." And the child whose mantra is "You're doing such a great job of taking care of your brothers and sisters" may have an overdeveloped sense of responsibility. Obedience and responsibility are positive traits, but they should not be developed at the expense of a discerning mind, an ability to responsibly challenge authority when appropriate, or the time and encouragement to be a child oneself and attend to one's own needs. When traits are overdeveloped, behavior becomes patterned and the person is unable to see other options.

A distorted and unstable sense of self also may be formed from inflated feedback that does not have realistic base. For example:

> Lance is an average-looking child, but he has rather large ears. His schoolmates sometimes tease him about his appearance, which understandably hurts his feelings.
>
> His parents could help Lance develop a realistic view of his physical attributes. They could help by teaching him to emphasize his

> good features and to minimize his less attractive ones (for example, by letting his hair grow a bit longer). They could help him put his big ears into perspective by talking about other differences (acne, height, weight, nose shapes, skin color, hair) and about acceptance of differences.
>
> Instead, they simply tell Lance repeatedly how handsome he is, and that the kids who make fun of him are just jealous.

Lance's parents love him, but they do him no service by refusing to see him honestly. We see the pattern repeated when Lance does his chores or homework incompletely or sloppily, and his parents reward him, telling him what a great kid he is and what a good job he's done. Such unrealistic and general feedback is confusing. A much more helpful and valuable approach would be for Lance's parents to point out specific things he has done well, and to teach him how to improve a little bit at a time until he has mastered tasks.

The Importance of Introjects. What are introjects, and why is it important to identify them? Introjects are ideas, beliefs, attitudes, values, behaviors, styles of relating, and traditions that are internalized without discrimination. Energy is used to passively accept what is provided rather than to identify the individual's needs and wants (Fields, 1991). When unassimilated, introjects direct and determine the nature of our contact and our perceptions, and are outside of our awareness. We may project these introjects onto the environment, altering our view of the world and other people.

As Shub (1992) pointed out, some introjects that govern the regulation of our lives (*management introjects*) can be relatively harmless, unless they are too rigid and interfere with contact. Examples of beneficial management introjects would be, "Be punctual and be courteous." However, within the category of management introjects are also *introjects that govern our ability to meet our emotional needs*. These are extremely important in maintaining high self-esteem, since they regulate our ability to meet our needs for such necessities as warmth, touch, support, validation, love, understanding, respect, or solitude.

The emotional needs Shub identified can be divided into two classes: emotional and social (see chapter 2 for a complete discussion). In addition, there are several other categories of needs that are equally important: intellectual, sensual, environmental, nutritional, physical, and spiritual (see chapter 5). All of these needs are intertwined.

For example, I recently talked with a woman who owns a guest lodge in New Zealand. She frequently hosts guests who are on their way home from a research laboratory in Antarctica, where many of them have spent many months.

Antarctica is barren, covered in ice and snow, the horizon providing no perspective; everything is white. This woman described the problems she has noticed in the researchers who transition in her guest lodge. All but one have experienced severe mood problems and disorientation. The one researcher who fared best had volunteered time every day in a greenhouse, where she grew hydroponic tomatoes and other plants. This is a dramatic example of how environmental conditions can affect our mood and behavior. Other examples of the affects of one need upon another are common: the effect of sensory deprivation on mood; the effect of obesity on health, emotional well-being, and social interaction; the effect of excess sugar on mood and attention.

Being aware of what you need intellectually, sensually, environmentally, nutritionally, physically, and spiritually—and committing to meet these needs on a daily basis—is requisite for high self-esteem. By being aware of your needs, you can develop a daily plan for meeting them. For example, Satir used to say that people have a minimum daily requirement of 12 hugs. You should know what your minimum daily requirement is on all your needs, and create a daily plan to meet those needs. A few examples from my own plan are listed below:

- a low-fat, low-sugar diet
- emotional contact with a peer daily
- one hour alone every day
- vigorous exercise four or five times per week
- 7½ hours of sleep per night
- hugs and other tender physical contact several times every day
- laughing every day
- music every day

However, since none of us is perfect at this, we sometimes get off track, so it is important to develop a means to recognize when this is happening. Shub used the metaphor of the emotional dashboard to monitor warning signals that a need is not being satisfied (see chapter 2). Likewise, in chapter 3 I speak of using the "inner barometer" to monitor your feelings, thoughts, sensations, wants, and needs. Monitoring yourself for signals in each of the seven need areas can alert you that a need is not being adequately met. (For examples, see Table 1.3.)

People have their own idiosyncratic signals. Through self-awareness, you can identify your own personal signals. Once you have developed the practice

TABLE 1.3
Examples of Monitoring in the Seven Need Areas

Need Area	Signal	Problem
nutritional	rash	eating a food to which you are allergic
intellectual	boredom	not enough stimulation
social	loneliness	working too much, so have not spent enough time with friends
emotional	tearing easily	have not taken enough time to be in touch and express sadness about client's death

of listening to yourself, and have committed yourself fully to meeting the needs you identify, you have what you need to take care of yourself.

Shub (1992) identified another critical class of introjects that are core and can severely block an individual's ability to grow or expand, affecting the individual physically, socially, cognitively, sexually, spiritually, and affectively. Such introjects might comprise a life theme and, according to Shub, tend to be affectively charged.

For example, Shub (1992) identified one *life theme introject* this way: "I must take care of others." This overarching introject might subsume a number of related introjects which restrict awareness of personal needs and expression of feelings, beliefs, and needs: for example, "My needs are not important," "Always work hard," "There is no time for play," "Don't ask for help," and "I am responsible for others' feelings." In an empowering direction, another life theme might be this: "I can do almost anything I set my mind to."

Another critical class of beliefs is *identity introjects.* These introjects form part of how we define ourselves. They also may be positive or negative: for example, "I am bright, capable, curious, warm, and adventuresome" or "I am sloppy, shy, selfish, moody, and bratty." Such identity introjects may be accurate or distorted to various degrees.

If we do not evaluate and assimilate the various introjects that define us and govern our perceptions and behavior, we are left with such questions as, "Who am I really, and whose life am I leading?" Without assimilation, we may be enacting a self-definition that is faulty and that we have not evaluated and truly owned and embraced.

What does it mean to assimilate a belief? Melnick and Nevis (1992, p. 74) described assimilation as "chewing over an experience in order to drain the energy." Perls, Hefferline, and Goodman (1977, p. 223) theorized that, "What is assimilated is not taken in as a whole, but is first destroyed (destructured) completely and transformed—and absorbed selectively according to the need of the organism." So we can see that the process of assimilating an introject involves a critical analysis of the introject to see if it fits and can be absorbed, or if it must be modified or perhaps expunged altogether.

Self-awareness involves learning to observe ourselves objectively. It is the central process for developing insight about and "re-architecting" the self. Through the awareness process, we begin to identify how we define ourselves and the origins of those self-definitions. We can then decide if our beliefs are accurate or distorted and seek to change, modify, debate, or add traits that more accurately reflect our current selves.

As we relate with others and the world—as we observe our feelings, thoughts, attitudes, and behavior—introjects that have a lot of energy around them will surface, jump out with clarity, or gradually emerge as identifiable patterns. It is important when identifying our introjects to look at each phase of life development. Introjects may form during any life stage, although the *core introjects* that pervasively affect self-concept and self-esteem are formed early and reinforced repeatedly, thereby strengthening their hold.

The specific strategy we should use to shift self-esteem depends on how the different varieties of introjects are balanced, according to Shub (1994). Without a few core, assimilated positive introjects, revamping will be hampered or stalled. A positive foundation must be built for the rest of the construction to stand. Also, nurturing positive traits tends to be less threatening to the integrity of the self than trying to eradicate or diminish the strength of a troublesome self-aspect.

An exception to this is if a powerful, core, negative assimilated introject stands in the way of assimilating core positive beliefs. If this is the case, identifying and reworking this negative introject must take priority (see Phase III). Otherwise it would be like trying to lay a foundation on top of a huge tree stump. The stump, if not removed, would jeopardize the integrity of the foundation.

The main work of Phase I, then, is identifying and fleshing out the self-view, and beginning to identify the origin of the different components of that self-view. Shub (1994) included as a chief goal of this phase defining the core traits that have realistic foundations and that make us unique. We must identify what is special about ourselves. Shub insisted that the traits must be specific, accurate, and believable. We can correct and expand our self-view through careful self-observation and through feedback from others (see chapter 2).

Phase II. Assimilating Positive Traits

Catching yourself (or being caught by someone else) in the act of exhibiting a trait and identifying the data which supports that trait is quite effective in furthering the process of assimilation (Shub, 1994). Later, you can deepen your experience of the trait by tracking when you demonstrate the trait and attending to your physical/sensory expression/experience when the trait emerges (see chapter 5).

For example, if I wanted to strengthen my belief that I am a giving person, I would notice that I went out of my way to gather books and tapes for a friend who is recovering from a serious illness, and that I took an hour out of my workday to deliver them and to talk with my friend about the emotional impact of this illness on her life. I would also be aware of how I felt as I did this gathering and visiting. I would notice the pleasant sensations in my chest, the warmth in my cheeks, the softness of my eyes as we talked. I would notice the impact my actions and feelings had on my friend, and I would be aware of the positive energy generated between us. By attending in this way, I would begin to assimilate my giving nature.

As you go through the process of shifting your filter to these positive traits and seeking out information to confirm this self-view, your sense of self-consistency and predictability may be shaken (see chapter 3). You must learn to bear this middle ground (see chapter 9).

Identifying memories, relationships, life experiences, or events when you experienced or expressed these traits also facilitates assimilation. You can enlist significant others to help in this process. If your current network lacks people with optimistic attitudes and healthy levels of self-esteem, you must expand of your social network (see chapter 3). In addition, groups can be a powerful help in identifying and assimilating traits.

Phase III. Modifying or Eliminating Negative Introjects

As you relate your life story, experiences, perceptions, beliefs, and impressions, your negative *and* positive introjects will become apparent. The negative, core introjects that help form your life themes or script are the most crucial ones to reframe, integrate with other traits, weaken, alter, or discard, as these organize perception and behavior and help structure your life. Such central negative introjects can interfere with your ability to positively and freely interact with your environment. The six steps to changing introjects are as follows (adopted from Shub, 1992):

1. **Identify the negative introjects in clear and specific terms.** Note that introjects may also be conclusions we draw from experiences that run the gamut from benign to traumatic. For example:

A parent has an explosive temper and abuses his son. The son concludes he is worthless.

The youngest of five children is born with cerebral palsy. The family spends a lot of energy caring for the needs of this child. The fourth child concludes, "My needs are not important" or "I have to take care of myself."

2. **Examine the impact of each introject** on you and the impact on those around you by tracking how it operates in your day-to-day life, in your overall outlook, and in your hopes and your dreams. For example,

   When I was in my early 30s, I began noticing that, despite all my achievements and successes, I felt I was not good enough. When people gave me positive feedback, I discounted or countered the feedback with internal self-talk. I also focused on negative feedback. For example, 98% of the evaluations I received in my teaching and training were positive, but I could only focus on the 2% that were negative.

   While we should use negative feedback to improve our performance, we must be able to filter out what does not fit and keep negative feedback in perspective, so that it does not overshadow the 98% that is positive. This introject of mine was clearly core and in need of revision. Related negative introjects include, "I must be perfect," "Everybody must like me," and "Everyone has expectations as high as mine" (see chapter 4).

   By noticing sensory and motor changes, we can become aware of when our introjects are at work (see chapter 5). For example, when you are given positive feedback, do you avoid receiving it by constricting your breathing, turning your head slightly, or averting your glance? This heightening of moment-to-moment awareness helps increase our motivation to change and provides ongoing opportunities to do so. Revising or eliminating introjects requires a combination of cognitive, affective, sensory, and behavioral changes.

3. **Examine the source(s) of each introject.** Identify memories, patterns, experiences, or modeling related to each introject. Experiential activities can identify introjects and the surface and discharge effects connected with them (see Polster & Polster, 1974). In evaluating introjects it is important to examine the data on which each is based, compile contrary evidence, examine the impact of the introject on your life, and see if it presently fits for you.

4. **Decide whether you want to keep, alter, or give up each introject.** Make a clear statement of what is accurate, then decide if you want to change your belief, behavior, trait, or attitude, state the trait, behavior, belief, or attitude you want to adopt, and consider making it one of your goals (see step 5).

   If you decide to give up an introject, make a direct statement to the source using experiential methods. Assign a nickname to the introject, then use artwork or other creative means to gradually experience the introject as alien to your self (Shub, 1992). Sometimes it is important to identify the positive intention in the introject (if there is one), and to find a more effective way of accomplishing this objective.

5. **Identify the exact revision you want to assimilate.** Doing so is crucial. For example, you may want to revise an introject that says, "I'm never good enough." Your revision may be, "I am good enough. I am worthwhile. I can make mistakes and have personal faults, *and I'm still good enough.* I can just 'be' and be good enough." Now you must develop a plan to facilitate the assimilation of these beliefs (see prior discussion). As you begin to recognize these revised beliefs as active in the moment and are able to feel confidence in these beliefs, assimilation occurs (Shub, 1994).

6. **Recognize that old patterns die hard.** Inevitably, we slip back into old behavior. Using the example in step 2, even when you have done the initial work in revising an introject such as "I'm not good enough," when you receive positive feedback that contradicts that introject, you may still exhibit a somatic pattern of constricting your breathing and averting your glance. However, if the work in step 2 has been done thoroughly, you will be aware that these behaviors are artifacts of the old introject, be able to restate with self-talk "I am competent," and choose to deepen absorption by taking a full breath and looking the person in the eyes. Intervention at a systemic level may also facilitate the change process. Direct work with families, churches, groups, and organizations to shift norms can help produce more rapid and wider change.

Phase IV. Identifying and Improving Skill Deficits

Because of a lack of good modeling and narrowed experience, some people have lowered self-esteem as a result of skill deficits in a variety of areas, such as social and financial planning. For example, in the social area, people may lack skills in meeting and greeting people, small talk, reading nonverbal cues, self-disclosure, conflict resolution, and other basic communication skills (see chapter 3). Of course, introjects may be involved in skill deficits.

For example, I was raised in the New York area and, for my protection, my mother drilled into my head, "Don't talk to strangers!" I also learned not to make eye contact with strangers, since I found that even this could bring unwanted or dangerous attention. Well, let me tell you, if you follow this rule rigidly and don't revise it once you are mature enough to use judgment, it is impossible to meet new people! The rule needed to be revised and updated. There still are contexts when not talking to strangers and avoiding eye contact can help keep me safe. But now I have a choice about it. I have learned other skills like making eye contact, smiling, and simple ways to greet people and make small talk when I want contact. I did not have these skills as a young adult. My parents rarely socialized except with family. My mother had no friends with whom she socialized and was generally a quiet woman. I identified with my mother and, like her, I have a more introverted personality style. My family's world was small, and so was mine until college. I lacked basic social skills, which affected my ability to form and maintain satisfying relationships, which in turn affected my coping ability and ultimately my self-esteem.

Deficits may be caused by introjects in another way. For example, if you were taught that authorities are always right and that you must obey authorities, then skills to tactfully and effectively challenge authorities when appropriate would not be in your behavioral repertoire. This would be limiting and disempowering. Likewise, if you were encouraged always to do the "right thing," say the right thing, be passive and gentle, you would likely experience deficits in your ability to be expressive, spontaneous, assertive, and aggressive. You would need to learn how to expand in these ways and tolerate the anxiety, excitement, and liveliness these suppressed polarities would engender (see chapter 6).

Phase V. Integration

Phase V involves refining, practicing, continued awareness building, and relapse prevention. Additional areas of strength can be identified and developed, strengths deepened, and areas for improvement identified (see chapter 4). Self-esteem grows from challenges. People with high self-esteem are not rigid and brittle; they are flexible and open to feedback. They learn to tolerate and accept their shadow sides, and they come to see that even these so-called faults contain seeds of potential resources which—when transformed through either dilution, concentration, or addition of some other element—can be a tremendous asset. For example, even being rude has its place if your personal boundaries are being violated repeatedly (see chapter 4).

Finally, there is practice, practice, practice. Paying ongoing attention to the core positive introjects that organize the new self-concept will help solidify the changes and help us tolerate exposure to negative experiences and unpleasant feedback. Repetitive reinforcement of positive traits and beliefs through direct experience continues the assimilation process, so that in times of extreme stress the new pathways are strong. Continued practice of newly acquired skills and attention to nurturing expanded social networks are other elements of this phase. As we begin to realize that we have the capacity to impact others, our sense of personal agency is strengthened, and this feeling of empowerment activates further growth.

The integration phase also involves developing strategies for relapse prevention. Identifying situations that present potential challenges to your self-esteem (for example, impending job layoff or a visit to highly critical family members), anticipating and preparing for such events whenever possible, paying close attention to evidence of positive core traits and beliefs prior to the event, and bolstering self-support (e.g., breathing, centering, self-talk) and interpersonal supports are a few examples of relapse-prevention strategies.

Fully integrating new traits, skills, and beliefs can be a long process. The test of full assimilation comes when stress and anxiety are at their highest and the new traits, skills, and beliefs hold. These unavoidable "stress tests" can be helpful both in identifying areas that are still vulnerable and in further strengthening your new traits, skills, and beliefs. What kinds of supports must you develop to weather these tests and resist reverting to old feelings and toxic messages, behaviors, attitudes, and outdated beliefs?

There is no way we can move ahead without making goofs, but we can learn to have confidence in our process. Even without knowing what your self-picture will look like when you're through, you can learn to trust yourself and, with faith and hope, welcome your unfolding.

ACTIVITIES YOU CAN DO

ACTIVITY 1.1 ROOTS OF SELF-CONCEPT

Introduction: This activity helps you to understand the effect of others, especially parents, on self-concept development.

Time required: 30 to 45 minutes

Participants: Adults or children ages 9 and above

Setting: Office or classroom

Materials: None

Procedure: Answer the following questions in as much detail as you can.

1. Who in your family criticized/affirmed you? What did they criticize/affirm about you?

2. Considering your mother and father separately, how did each feel about self? Physical self? Social self? Emotional self? Intellectual self? Spiritual self?

3. How did you win recognition in your family?

4. How did your family react to your accomplishments? To your failures?

5. What did it mean to be a "good boy" or a "good girl" in your family?

6. Whose opinions counted in your family? Were your feelings/thoughts listened to? Were they valued?

7. Think of your mother and father separately. What did they expect of you? Complete this sentence in their voices: I expect you to ...

8. How did your mother and father express the four basic emotions: anger, joy, sadness, and fear?

9. Who in your family encouraged your interests? Your skills? How?

10. What are the mistakes you made that you still feel bad about?

11. What happens to you when you make a mistake? What do you feel?

12. Did your parents have a life theme, such as "drinking themselves to death," "committing suicide," "making it," "succeeding in business," or "never quite making it"?

13. How did your parents manipulate you? With guilt? Fear? Criticalness? Sweetness? False compliments? Rejection?

14. How do you copy your parents (e.g., in appearance, values, education, work, how they had fun, listening patterns, attitudes)?

15. What did you have to do or to be in order to be accepted and loved by your parents?

16. How important was it for you to do well? What was expected of you in school, in social situations, at home?

17. How important were chores, housework, jobs?

    Now make a list of the unspoken "do's and don'ts" from each parent who raised you (e.g., "Don't show your feelings," "Be smart, but not smarter than I am," "Flirt but don't be sexual," or "See me as a perfect parent").

Power Structure in the Family: Think back to childhood and consider your mother's and your father's negative traits and moods:

1. Faults
2. Weaknesses
3. Negative feelings about him- or herself, partner, and you
4. Sins of omission, what he or she did not do for you
5. Bad moods
6. Negative philosophies
7. Fears
8. Needs
9. Ways of dealing with emotions
10. Reaction to criticism
11. Bad habits
12. Chronic ailments
13. Prejudices
14. Ways of handling conflict or anger
15. Negative reactions
16. Negative slogans
17. Unfulfilled desires
18. Excuses
19. Reaction to failure
20. Complaints
21. What was sacrificed
22. Areas of incompetence
23. Ways of showing disapproval
24. Things that embarrassed him or her

    Look at which traits you adopted, rebelled against, or are totally free from (it's rare to be free of more than 10% without deliberate work).

Outcomes: Helps you gain a better understanding of the roots of self-concept.

ACTIVITY 1.2 CUTTING LOOSE FROM PARENTS

Introduction: The following activity is intended to help you become more aware of the interactional effects of parents on self-concept and self-esteem.

Time required: 15 to 30 minutes

Participants: Ages 9 or above

Setting: Office or classroom

Materials: None

Procedure: Close your eyes and sit comfortably. Imagine sitting in a room where you feel very safe. In a moment, one of your parents will walk through the door. Get relaxed, breathe slowly and deeply, as you watch your parent walk through the door and sit with you. Make some kind of contact. Pay attention to how you feel as you do this. Feel good? If not, try something different if you like.

Just sit with your parent for a while. Really look at him or her. How do you feel as you look? Tell your parent how you feel. Express all the things you've wanted so badly to say. It's time to clear your mind. It's time to finish any old business. It feels good to clear the slate. Be aware of your feelings as you do this.

Now switch and be your parent, and respond. How do you feel about what your child has said? Tell your child how you feel. Tell your child how you feel about him or her.

Outcomes: Helps you gain insight into the interactional effects of parents on your self-concept and self-esteem.

ACTIVITY 1.3 POLARITIES

Introduction: This activity helps put you in touch with the different sides of yourself.

Time required: 1 hour

Participants: Ages 9 and older

Setting: Group setting, office or classroom

Materials: Paper, pencil

Procedure: List five psychological qualities that would describe you.

Now, get in touch with the psychological opposites of each of these qualities. Are you able to own both sides?

Now, in groups of three or four, spend three minutes enacting one side and three minutes enacting the other side.

The side with the psychological opposite probably represents your "dark side," the side you disown. Identify specific situations when each of these qualities was or could be helpful to you. Now, identify specific situations when each of the qualities might be a problem for you.

List your major learnings.

Outcomes: Helps you identify parts of yourself that you have not owned.

ACTIVITY 1.4 ASSIMILATING POSITIVE TRAITS

Introduction: Your positive traits must be totally believable before they can work for you.

Time required: Unlimited

Participants: Any number or adolescents or adults

Setting: Office or classroom

Materials: Paper, pen

Procedure: List five traits that make you special. Then choose one trait to work on per week.

Notice and make note of when you display this trait. Note how you experience yourself when you display this trait. Note its impact on others. Record this.

Ask three friends, colleagues, or family members to notice and call your attention to times when you display this trait. Ask them to give you specific data as well as feedback on how this trait affects them at the moment.

Reflect on your past (recent and distant) and record times when you experienced or expressed this trait.

Outcomes: Helps you assimilate your positive traits, thereby strengthening the foundation of your self-esteem.

ACTIVITY 1.5 BRIDGE PEOPLE

Introduction: How can you positively influence a younger person? The activity puts you in touch with your personal power as a nurturer.

Time required: 20 minutes

Participants: Any number of adolescents or adults

Setting: Office or classroom

Materials: None

Procedure: Form dyads and think of a person in your life who nurtured you, cared for you, gave you a lot of affection and esteem. It could be a neighbor, aunt, grandmother, teacher, someone other than a parent. Imagine a specific time when you felt his or her positive influence on you.

Now, think of someone over whom you have the potential for such influence—someone who looks to you for guidance and love. Imagine a scene where you are a nurturing agent for this person.

Share with your partner your thoughts about the power people have to influence the lives of others, to help others feel better about themselves.

Make a contract to try to positively influence a younger person.

Outcomes: Increases your ability to nurture another, and help others to develop a more positive image of self. Enhances your awareness and use of your personal power.

Note: Activity is original. Idea initiated by Elkins (1977).

ACTIVITY 1.6 SELF-MANDALA

Introduction: This activity is intended for use in a group setting. It heightens awareness of all the various aspects of self.

Time required: 30 minutes

Participants: Group of 9 or more

Setting: A large room

Materials: None (review self-mandala concept)

Procedure: Choose someone in the group to be each part of your mandala (i.e., physical self, intellectual self). Each person representing each part is free to move around you on a track in any way he or she chooses. Acknowledge each part of yourself by saying, "You are my (*fill-in*) self" (Do this from memory.)

Be aware of those parts you do not remember. Do you deny these parts? While the other parts of you continue their movements, tell the parts you do not remember to sit on the floor. They may give you little pinches to heighten your awareness. Ask the people representing the parts how they experience you. Take charge of your parts by bringing each person to you without speaking. How do you use your parts to help you?

Give a message to your parts to move in harmony around you. Allow your parts to pick you up and support you. After putting you down, the people representing your parts encircle you and each one says to you, "I am your __________ (fill in blank) self. Will you accept me?" When you say "yes" the person puts his or her hand on your neck. This affirmation continues until all the parts have formed a necklace by putting their hands on your neck.

Finally, close your eyes and feel all the parts, recognizing the degree of acceptance you feel toward each of them. Notice also your objections to owning any of them.

Process this experience with your group. Discuss what you learned, relearned, or wonder about the various aspects of yourself.

Outcomes: Enables you to explore various aspects of self.

Note: Idea initiated by Satir (1981).

By imagining that this self-mandala can be held up in front of others, one can experience what parts of the other person shine through dramatically and what parts are in the shadows. Viewing people through the mandala aids the helper to fully experience the person and not become overly focused on symptoms or labels. The question the helper can ask him- or herself is, "How can I help tune in and turn on other parts of the mandala for this person, to enable him or her to become a more fully functioning, positive person?"

For example, in the initial helping stages, the helper might notice that a male participant is very unaware of his sensual, nutritional, and emotional self. Perhaps he is most aware of his intellectual and interactional self. Possibly he is living primarily in his thoughts about others and self to avoid feelings. The helper could then aid this man particularly in becoming more aware of these "shadow areas." The helper would choose techniques that enhance the sensual, nutritional, and emotional self in addition to helping the participant become more aware of how all these aspects of the self-mandala interact.

ACTIVITY 1.7 CIRCLE OF SUPPORT

Introduction: Supportive people in your life provide a buffer for self-esteem and offer opportunities to develop additional personal resources. This activity helps you identify some of the gifts from this tapestry of people.

Time required: 30 minutes

Participants: Adolescents and adults

Setting: Homework, classroom, group

Materials: Paper, pen, colored markers

Procedure: In the center of a sheet of paper, draw a circle about the size of a quarter. Write your name in the middle of this circle and draw a number of spokes out from it. Reflect on your life from birth until the present day, and recall all the people who show or showed you some special interest or who nurtured you (physically, emotionally, intellectually, or spiritually). Separate the people into five different groups: birth to 12; 13 to 21; 22 to 35; 36 to 50; and 51+. Include a full range of people, including neighbors, family, teachers, ministers, housekeepers, storekeepers, pets, friends, colleagues, and any others you remember as significant to you in some way. At the end of each spoke draw a small circle. Select a different color marker for each period. Within each of these smaller circles, write the name of the person and the gift that each person gave you.

Examine your wheel. How do you feel as you take in all the gifts each person has given to you? Have your resources expanded or contracted over the years? What other changes or patterns do you notice?

As you go through the next few weeks, additional people who contributed to your growth and development may occur to you. Add these to your wheel.

Now, gently close your eyes and imagine yourself in the center of a circle surrounded by these nurturing people. Imagine yourself slowly turning around and looking closely at each of them. Look into their eyes and take in their love and affection. As you turn to each one, he or she has some important but simple message to deliver. Listen carefully as they deliver their messages and lightly place one of their hands around your neck, forming a beautiful chain of love. With each breath allow yourself to take in more and more of their warmth, caring, and love.

When you are ready, allow your eyes to open. Notice how you are feeling.

Make some notes about any awarenesses you had during this experience.

Pick someone with whom you can share your wheel.

Outcomes: Increases self-worth by focusing on assets and resources; helps you knit together your survival net.

Note: Revised from an activity in Carlock and Shaw (1988). Activity based on tool invented by Satir (1981).

ACTIVITIES FOR GROUPS

ACTIVITY 1.8 "ME" PUPPETS

Introduction: This activity explores the child's view of self, and can be used to explore the impact of this self-view relationally.

Time required: 45 minutes

Participants: One or more children ages 6 to 8

Setting: Any setting

Materials: Small paper bags and a variety of simple materials that can be used to make puppets; a simple puppet stage (optional)

Procedure: Set out a wide variety of materials on a long table.

Ask the children to come up with five words to describe themselves. Brainstorm and make a list on poster board of words that address physical, social, intellectual, and emotional domains: for example, tall, caring, smart, pretty, loud, active, quiet, sad, happy, shy, talkative, funny, silly, helpful, giving. As a variation, you can ask the group to suggest other words they believe describe the child, which provides feedback to the child.

If the children contribute negative words, you can try to identify the seed of good in them. For example, if someone contributes the adjective "selfish," you might say, "The positive part of being selfish is you know how to go out and get what you want when your need is strong. That just needs to be balanced with being kind and sharing. Giving and taking are both important."

Make sure each child has identified words that are positive. Coach the children if necessary.

Have the children sit at the table with their paper bags and gather the materials they need to make "Me" puppets. Help the children if necessary.

Once they have made their puppets, have the children take turns acting out themselves with the puppets. Make a puppet yourself, and demonstrate how to do this. For example, if my words were short, plump, brainy, helpful, funny, and loving, I might make a short, squat puppet with lots of brains showing out of its head, big soft arms, and a sweet smile on its face. If I then acted out this image, I might say, "Hi, my name is Jesse. (Move the puppet around in funny ways.) We have a really great show planned for you today! (Point with the puppet's arms.) Look at this great puppet. And this one, too. Okay, gang, ready to party? Well, that's all for now. Goodbye!" (Whisk the puppet quickly behind the curtain.)

You also can have two puppets appear on stage and interact with each other. This creates all kinds of teaching opportunities about such things as getting along with others, saying what you feel, and giving feedback.

There are endless variations of this activity, depending upon your specific goal.

Outcomes: Allows children to externalize their self-view, see themselves more clearly, and see how others relate to them. During the process, distortions can be corrected, self-views can be modified or expanded, and relationship skills can be taught in a safe way.

ACTIVITY 1.9 THE "ME" BOX

Introduction: This activity facilitates self-disclosure and helps children differentiate the self shown to the world and the private self.

Time required: 45 minutes

Participants: Children ages 10 to 12

Setting: Classroom, group, individual therapy, homework

Materials: Boxes of various sizes; art materials, such as colored markers, crayons, construction paper, paste, tape, and stickers; children's magazines that can be cut up

Procedure: Show the children an example of a "Me" Box. Then have each child pick a box to represent the self.

On the outside of their boxes, ask the children to draw or paste different items to represent what they show to the world.

Inside their boxes, have them place drawings or pictures from magazines that represent their thoughts, feelings, wishes, talents, secrets, memories, and anything else that is hidden from others. Build a box for yourself and present it to the class.

Give the children an opportunity to present their boxes. First, they tell what they think others see and know about them. Give feedback, and ask the other children to give feedback as well. Note surprises, additions made, or corrections suggested.

You will likely find opportunities throughout the activity to talk about appropriate risk-taking, respecting feelings, accepting differences, dealing with fears, being sensitive to others' vulnerabilities, building trust, and other such concepts.

The boxes can be added to or changed from time to time, if your group is ongoing. Periodically give the children opportunities to talk about their boxes.

Outcomes: Increase self-awareness, trust, and self-disclosure.

ACTIVITY 1.10 MY STEEL RODS

Introduction: Identifying accurate positive beliefs about yourself is crucial to developing high self-esteem that is believable and grounded in reality.

Time required: 45 minutes

Participants: Children ages 7 to 12

Setting: Classroom, group, individual therapy, home, church, scouts, or other special activities

Materials: Poster board and colored markers

Procedure: Depending on their ages, ask the children to tell you or to write down five things that make each of them special. Help them to be as specific as possible. Instead of just settling for "nice," for example, explore how this trait shows itself. Perhaps the child is polite to others, plays well with others, or is kind and helpful to a variety of peers (children who are overweight, outgoing, withdrawn, sad). If the child is too young to write, record the trait and an example. Then help the child think of a picture he or she can draw to represent that quality.

Post these lists with the children's names around the room. Over the course of the year (if you are in an ongoing group), point out to the children when you see them displaying their special qualities. During this ongoing process, you may find that the special qualities identified need to be refined or modified. This is an important part of the process. Make additions or alterations on the poster board.

Outcomes: Identify positive, demonstrable qualities central to a child's self-concept, and reinforce the child's awareness and assimilation of these qualities.

REFERENCES

Adler, A. (1979). Superiority and social interest. (H. L. Ansbacher & R. R. Ansbacher, Eds. & Trans.). New York: Norton.

Allport, G. (1961). *Pattern and growth in personality.* New York: Holt, Rinehart & Winston.

Bednar, W., & Peterson, S. (1989). *Paradoxes and innovations in clinical theory and practice.* Washington, DC: American Psychological Association.

Cantor, D., & Bernay, T. (1992). *Women in power: The secrets of leadership.* Boston: Houghton Mifflin.

Carlock, C. J., & Shaw, C. (1988). *Self-esteem for adult children of alcoholics* (Cassette Recording). Muncie, IN: Accelerated Development.

Cooley, C. (1902). *Human nature and social order.* New York: Scribner's.

Crocker, S. (1998). *Gestalt therapy as a new paradigm.* Cleveland, OH: Gestalt Institute of Cleveland Press.

Elkins, D. (1977). *Teaching people to love themselves.* Rochester, NY: Growth Associates.

Epstein, S. (1973). The self-concept revisited or a theory of a theory. *American Psychologist, 28,* 405-416.

Fields, B. (1991). *Introjection and projection*. Cleveland, OH: Gestalt Institute of Cleveland, P.G.I.

Harter, S. (1983). Developmental perspectives on the self-system. In E. M. Hetherington (Ed.), *Handbook of child psychology: Vol. 4. Socialization, personality, and social development* (4th ed., pp. 275-385). New York: Wiley.

Horney, K. (1992). *Our inner conflicts*. New York: Norton.

Horney, K. (1994). *The neurotic personality of our time*. New York: Norton.

James, W. (1890). *Principles of psychology*. New York: Henry R. Holt.

Josephs, L. (1992). *Character structure and the organization of the self*. New York: Columbia University Press.

Mahler, M., & Furer, M. (1968). *On human symbiosis and the vicissitudes of individuation*. New York: International Universities Press.

May, R. (1973). *Man's search for himself*. New York: Dell.

McDowell, J. (1984). *Building your self-image*. Wheaton, IL: Living Books.

Melnick, J., & Nevis, S. (1992). Diagnosis: The struggle for a meaningful paradigm. In E. C. Nevis (Ed.), *Gestalt therapy: Perspectives and applications* (pp. 57-78). New York: Gardner.

Perls, F., Hefferline, R., & Goodman, P. (1977). *Gestalt therapy*. New York: Bantam.

Polster, E. (1990, December). *The self in action*. Paper presented at the Evolution of Psychotherapy Conference, Anaheim, CA. Sponsored by the Milton H. Erickson Foundation, Phoenix, AZ.

Polster, E. (1995). *A population of selves*. San Francisco: Jossey-Bass.

Polster, E., & Polster, M., (1974). *Gestalt therapy integrated*. New York: Vintage Books.

Rogers, C. (1951). *Client-centered therapy*. Boston: Houghton Mifflin.

Sarbin, T. R. (1962). A preface to a psychological analysis of the self. *Psychological Review, 59*, 11-22.

Satir, V. (1981, August). AVANTA Process Community conference. Park City, UT.

Shub, N. (1992). Gestalt therapy over time. In E. C. Nevis (Ed.), *Gestalt therapy: Perspectives and applications* (pp. 79-112). New York: Gardner.

Shub, N., (1994, October). Transcript from Developing Self-Esteem Workshop. Gestalt Institute of Central Ohio, Columbus, Ohio.

Sullivan, H. (1953). *The interpersonal theory of psychiatry*. New York: Norton.

Chapter 2

DEVELOPING HIGH SELF-ESTEEM

Norman Shub

Norman Shub, Ph.D., BCD, *is a well-known author, teacher, and psychotherapist who has led workshops around the world. He has lectured and presented at major universities, including Oxford, Trinity, and the Sorbonne. His published works are used in psychotherapy training in many countries. He is a pioneer in the area of character treatment and differential diagnosis. Norman is the founder of the nationally known therapy practice, Gestalt Associates, and is the clinical director of the Gestalt Institute of Central Ohio, which provides high-quality training in depth psychotherapy.*

Most therapists in the United States agree that self-esteem development problems constitute a national tragedy. Low self-esteem affects identity formation for young people. For adults, low self-esteem impedes the ability to develop relationships and to live and function successfully.

High self-esteem consists of having the strongest possible positive core beliefs about the self and an absence of major negative beliefs about the self. High self-esteem also consists of having clearly identified emotional needs and a commitment to meeting those needs. Whatever your age, high self-esteem maximizes your ability to experience life fully.

This chapter will help you understand both the need for high self-esteem and the self-esteem development process. It offers practical suggestions for developing high self-esteem. In addition, it should serve as a wake-up call to parents, teachers, and spouses as well as to ourselves. We need to understand how high self-esteem can help our families, our communities, and our country become more successful and functional.

According to Victor Fuchs (1995), a leading authority on child endangerment, many experts believe American children are in trouble. Not all children, certainly; but, compared with previous generations, today's youngsters perform worse in school, are more than twice as likely to commit suicide, and use more alcohol and drugs. They are twice as likely to be obese, and they show other signs of physical, mental, and emotional distress. Although experts disagree about the causes of these problems, one theme surfaces frequently: the adequacy of our investment in our children. High self-esteem in the adult requires a tremendous emotional investment in the child. Parents need to spend many years "crawling under the skin" of their children to help them discover what is special about themselves, avoid negative beliefs, and develop a commitment to care for themselves. If this investment does not occur, children are likely to grow up without high self-esteem. They must then find a way as adults to develop it, if they are interested in possessing one of the necessary ingredients for a satisfying life.

Figure 2.1 shows that self-esteem can be conceptualized as a continuum. However, graphically depicting the self-esteem development process and the degrees of self-esteem development is complicated because three factors intertwine to produce high self-esteem. Every person has some level of self-esteem. Some people have poor self-esteem, which is marked by a combination of few positive beliefs, strong negative beliefs, and an absence of beliefs about emotional need-meeting. Some people have high self-esteem, which is marked by strong positive beliefs, diminished negative beliefs, and clear beliefs about emotional needs, plus a willingness to meet them. My goal in this chapter is to encourage you to work toward the highest level of self-esteem possible. I want to help you move from your current position on the self-esteem continuum to the highest level you can achieve.

Self-esteem development begins in childhood, but self-esteem can be enhanced at any stage in life. Diane Ehrensaft's (1995) groundbreaking book on the changing roles in parenting discusses how difficult parenting is if parents lack self-esteem, and the implications of that lack for their children. According to Ehrensaft, adults with low self-esteem have trouble maximizing their functioning in daily life. They also have trouble functioning well as parents and doing all they can for their children. But the life cycle offers many opportunities for intervening to correct a self-esteem deficit. In this chapter, we'll explore how an adult can develop high self-esteem.

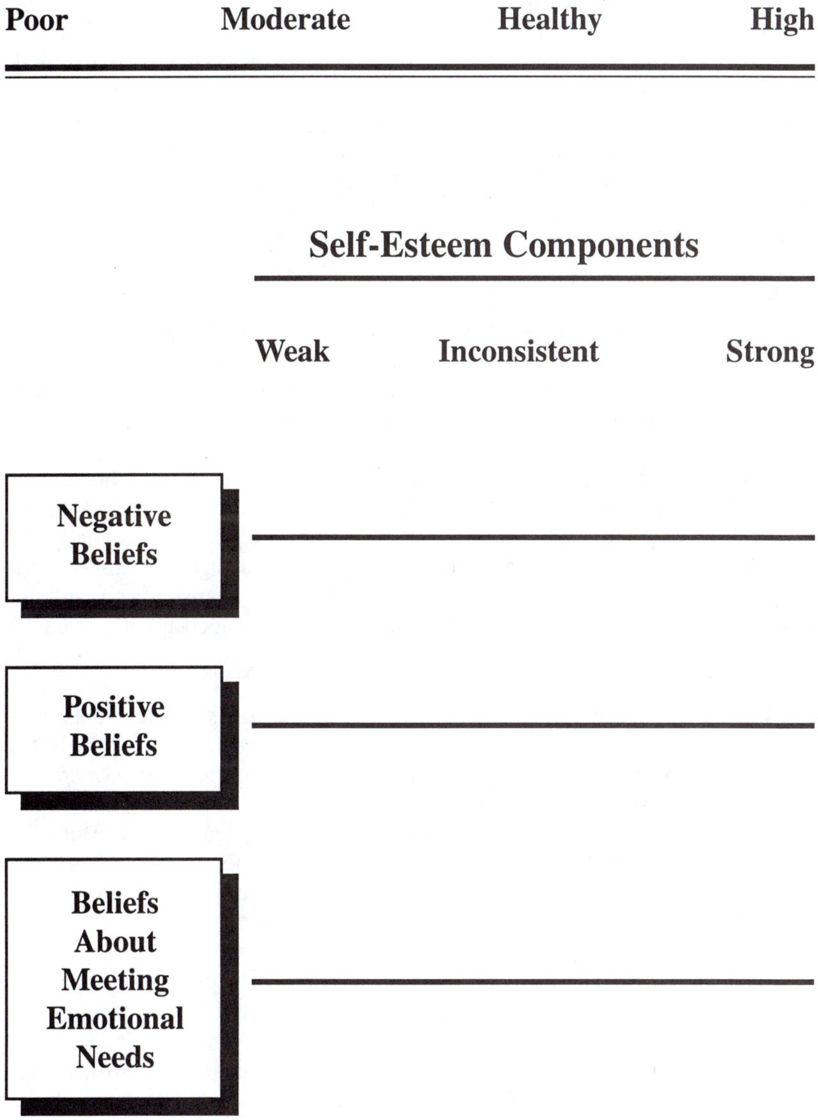

Poor **Moderate** **Healthy** **High**

Self-Esteem Components

Weak **Inconsistent** **Strong**

Negative Beliefs

Positive Beliefs

Beliefs About Meeting Emotional Needs

Figure 2.1. The self-esteem continuum.

AN AUTHORIAL VIGNETTE

Like many adults, I have suffered from low self-esteem and struggled with self-esteem issues. As recently as 10 years ago, my alarm would ring in the morning and I would roll away from my sleeping wife, stretch, groan, and walk—haggard, tired, and sleepy—to the bathroom mirror. As I stared at my reflected image, at my face, fleshy jowls, and neck, I would think unkind thoughts about myself. "I'm not proud of you and I'm not happy to see you," I would think. "You don't look that good. In fact, you don't look good at all. I'm not sure I really like you."

For many years, I felt that way about myself every morning. For me, as for anyone, life without high self-esteem was difficult. I was not proud of myself, and I could not articulate my positive aspects. I saw myself in a negative light and interpreted the events of my life through a negative lens.

My self-esteem is different now—and I'm not making that up for this chapter or to instill false hope in you. When I get up in the morning and look in the mirror, I like myself and I feel better. Even though my body is essentially the same, I accept it instead of constantly disparaging it. I have good feelings about myself, and I'm proud of who I am. My perceptions, my sense of self, and my understanding of what is special about me have all changed greatly from 10 years ago.

I share these facts about myself (as I will share facts about clients with whom I have worked over the years) to help you understand that, although it is a difficult process, you can develop high self-esteem *through your own efforts*. Self-esteem development is a process parents should begin with their infant children and continue with them until the moment they leave home. But self-esteem development does not end there. It must continue as an active process throughout your life. Developing the highest self-esteem involves a lifelong commitment to building positive core beliefs and defusing negative core beliefs about yourself, and to identifying and meeting your emotional needs. In time and with hard work, adults can create an acceptable level of self-esteem in themselves.

If you did not develop a basic positive sense of yourself while growing up, building one as an adult is difficult—sometimes extremely difficult—and you will need the help of others to do it. I will not gloss over that hard truth. But we all need positive self-esteem in order to feel good about ourselves and to maximize our potential for effective daily living. The alternative is to live lives that are not as fulfilling or enjoyable as they could be.

This chapter will define high self-esteem, break it down into its components, show the process of developing it, and provide some exercises for working on your own self-esteem. If you are one of the unfortunate people who gained little positive sense of your self while growing up and are now living your life not feeling good about yourself, not proud of the special traits you embody, and not understanding your uniqueness, this chapter can help you stand taller and be stronger.

IF YOU DIDN'T GET IT, WHERE DO YOU START?

Thomas Szasz (1994) noted that one possible cure for mental illness is not receiving professional treatment, but developing high self-esteem. How does a person grow up lacking self-esteem? The following case study demonstrates:

> Sally was a bright, attractive 22-year-old social work intern. Sally's parents cared about her, but they were extremely busy. Her physician father and her artist mother, preoccupied with their own lives, did not invest the time, patience, and sensitive caring that would have allowed Sally to learn from the inside out what was special about herself and to develop the positive core beliefs essential to high self-esteem.
>
> Sally grew up with doubts about herself. Her successful parents would make general statements about how she could do anything she wanted or become whatever she wanted—even the first woman president of the United States. They said nice things, but they did not support, validate, struggle with, care about, nurture, or involve themselves with Sally. They did not help her understand what made her unique, so she could begin to see, feel, know, believe, and never forget her specialness.
>
> Part of developing high self-esteem is coming to understand authentically what it is about you that really matters. Sally grew up with doubts. She did not know if she was special. She stared at the mirror for hours, seeing the imperfections in her face. She imagined the imperfections in her speech, her intelligence, and her sensitivity. She could not see the beauty of her existence. If boys did not ask her out, she wondered what was wrong with her, never suspecting they might be afraid of her. Sally only knew that something was wrong with her.
>
> If one of Sally's friends did something with another girl and excluded her, Sally knew it was because she was not good enough. If she saw boys laughing, she wondered if they were laughing at her looks. This intelligent, vivacious, and pretty young woman lived on a seesaw of ambivalence, never really knowing if she was okay.

> Sometimes she felt good and sometimes not, but she never developed a clear sense that she was special.

Sally grew up with low self-esteem, and her story is not unique. Many of you reading this book right now are experiencing or have experienced the same doubts. If you are like me or Sally, your discomfort, suffering, and unhappiness may be so great that you want to do something to change your self-esteem quotient.

THE IMPORTANCE OF HIGH SELF-ESTEEM

Sally's story illustrates the importance of self-esteem to human existence. The high self-esteem that begins with the development of positive core beliefs would have made Sally less ambivalent. She would have known and been proud of who she was. So, first of all, *high self-esteem makes living easier* in that each of us meets each moment understanding our specialness.

Second, *high self-esteem supports us as we live our daily lives* and encounter situations that go wrong or don't work out as expected. High self-esteem allows us to deal with life's problems and disappointments without losing our selves, without feeling bad about *"me."*

> Jim, a television producer, grew up in a difficult family, but he worked hard in therapy and learned to appreciate his sensitivity, openness, intelligence, and caring. Jim produced a somewhat avant-garde show that received negative reviews. He was upset that the critics could not see what he was trying to do—*but Jim did not lose track of who he was*. He did not start doubting his fundamental creative abilities, and he did not start feeling bad about Jim. Jim felt bad about the television show, but he did not lose track of his own value. Jim's high self-esteem helped him handle the crisis.

Third, *high self-esteem allows us to take risks and face challenges*—to put ourselves out there—because we are not afraid of losing who we are.

> Polly, a bright, articulate, and sensitive registered nurse, was highly valued by staff and patients alike. Polly saw a notice in the hospital cafeteria inviting staff members interested in attending medical school to apply for a scholarship, and she thought, "Why not?" She discussed medical school with some of her colleagues. They tried to discourage her, saying it would be too hard and that her children would suffer. The truth is, *they* did not feel good enough about *themselves*, even if they were interested, to consider accepting the challenge.

> Polly applied for and was awarded the scholarship, and she now works as a physician. Polly's high self-esteem—the fact that she possessed a group of core positive beliefs that she knew, felt, believed, and could articulate—allowed her to accept this and other challenges in her life.

Developing positive beliefs, transcending negative ones, and committing to meet one's own emotional needs are all part of high self-esteem. And high self-esteem is what allows people to take the risks necessary to continue growing throughout life. Perls (the founder of modern Gestalt therapy), Hefferline, and Goodman (1951) defined growing as the willingness to assimilate the novel. They also contended that the willingness to try the new and to rethink the familiar is part of what keeps us vital. Self-esteem is the linchpin of that process.

Fourth, *self-esteem allows us to feel good about ourselves and thus to succeed in relationships*. In his seminal book on self-actualization, Johnson (1979) argued that self-acceptance and high self-esteem are prerequisites for successful relationships. Being in a healthy relationship means valuing who we are and expecting that others will recognize our value and know that they must treat us with respect, sensitivity, and common decency because we value ourselves.

> Len was a 40-year-old divorcee, respected, bright, strong, and exciting. He asked Sarah out because he found her interesting, warm, and emotionally appealing. But Sarah had a problem with responsibility and time management. On their third date, Len waited 45 minutes in Sarah's living room before she was ready to leave. Len was furious. His sense of self said to him, "I don't deserve this. I need and want and am going to be treated with respect and sensitivity by everyone in my life; and I don't have to put up with anything else." He confronted Sarah and verbalized his concerns.
>
> Sarah immediately believed that Len was not kidding. She saw clearly that he liked himself enough to not tolerate bad treatment. His self-esteem convinced her that if she wanted to date him she had to be more respectful and timely, or she had to end the relationship. Sarah decided that she liked Len a lot. She apologized and promised herself she would not be as insensitive in this relationship as she had been in previous ones. What created the crisis and also allowed the relationship to develop was Len's sense of self. It demanded that others treat him with respect and sensitivity. It also allowed Len to be vulnerable and to offer his support to Sarah as she worked through her feelings about him.

Working to develop high self-esteem—something that Sally and I and the others I have described so far all have tried to do—is a vital aspect of making your life as meaningful as possible.

WHAT IS HIGH SELF-ESTEEM?

High self-esteem can be defined both metaphorically and in terms of its five actual components.

Steel Rods: A Metaphor for High Self-Esteem

Metaphorically, high self-esteem feels like having a group of steel rods running from your head to your feet. Those steel rods are the core positive beliefs that you know and appreciate about yourself. They are invisible, and only you know what each rod represents. The rods hold you up. They may bend or weaken, but they are the core of your being. Events may upset you, and you may temporarily lose your bearings, but the rods snap back and let you feel yourself again. When tragedy hits, you do not fall apart. When someone disturbs you, you stay intact. A trauma may upset you, but you do not crumble. In those steel rods, you have a solid core of positive self-esteem.

The Five Components of High Self-Esteem

Returning to Figure 2.1, you can see that positive beliefs lie on a continuum from very poor—which means the beliefs are weak or are only tiny buds—to very strong—the steel rods. A person can be anywhere in between for any particular belief. So if you diagram your belief system, belief by belief rather than as a whole, each of your beliefs will lie somewhere on the continuum from a positive bud that is just beginning to grow to a steel rod that is in place and will be there forever. Your goal should be to take each of your core positive beliefs and move it from a bud to a steel rod.

In nonmetaphoric terms, high self-esteem translates into five components:

Knowing: You understand clearly what each core belief is about.

Feeling: In addition to knowing each core belief, you experience it in your heart.

Believing: You are convinced, beyond the shadow of a doubt, that your five or six truly special qualities are real and will not go away.

Articulating: You can state your beliefs out loud. If you need to say who you are in a job interview or a relationship discussion, you have the knowledge, the feeling, and the belief to do so: "I have integrity. I am kind. I am sensitive."

Never completely losing: The core beliefs remain no matter what. They do not disappear when something happens, they do not crumble, they

> do not disintegrate. They may bend or weaken, but they are always there.

You know, feel, believe, and can articulate your core beliefs, and you cannot lose them. The steel rods are there to stay. Crises may hit, things may go wrong, you may make mistakes, relationships may end, and jobs may terminate—but the steel rods are abiding. So part of the process of developing high self-esteem is identifying the traits that are special about you. The beliefs come from your parents, teachers, friends, and other people in your childhood who worked hard to show you about you is special. If you did not develop your positive beliefs in childhood, then you must develop them in adulthood.

THE SELF IN SELF-ESTEEM

Now that we have explored what makes self-esteem important and have defined it, we need to look at what the self is, so that you can understand where self-esteem fits in the self. My discussion of the self will not be exhaustive, although after reading it you should understand where self-esteem lies in the self, how it works in relationship to other parts of the self, and what you need to change in your self as you develop your own high self-esteem.

Parts of the Self

Figure 2.2 illustrates that the self is bounded by the character, which is the stylistic way people interact with the world (for a more detailed discussion, see Shub, 1994a). That is, how we act and treat other people is our way of being in the world, like the skin of the physical body. Inside the character are the basic functions of the self. Therapists call these contact functions because they define the way we take information from and express information to the world through our senses—how we meet the environment and experience it through our senses.

The self also contains our system of beliefs, which is the way we feel about ourselves and the beliefs we hold about who we are. Self-esteem develops through the interaction of our belief system and the way we imagine other people see us. As Figure 2.2 demonstrates, the belief system is complicated. It contains negative beliefs, which make experiencing the world more difficult, and positive beliefs, also called *life themes*. The positive beliefs in the center of Figure 2.2 build self-esteem, while the negative ones detract from it. Other belief levels exist as well.

> Neil's father praised his efforts but always found something to criticize. When Neil turned in his homework, his father praised most of it but emphasized the part that could have been done better. When Neil painted a picture for art class, his father marveled at the com-

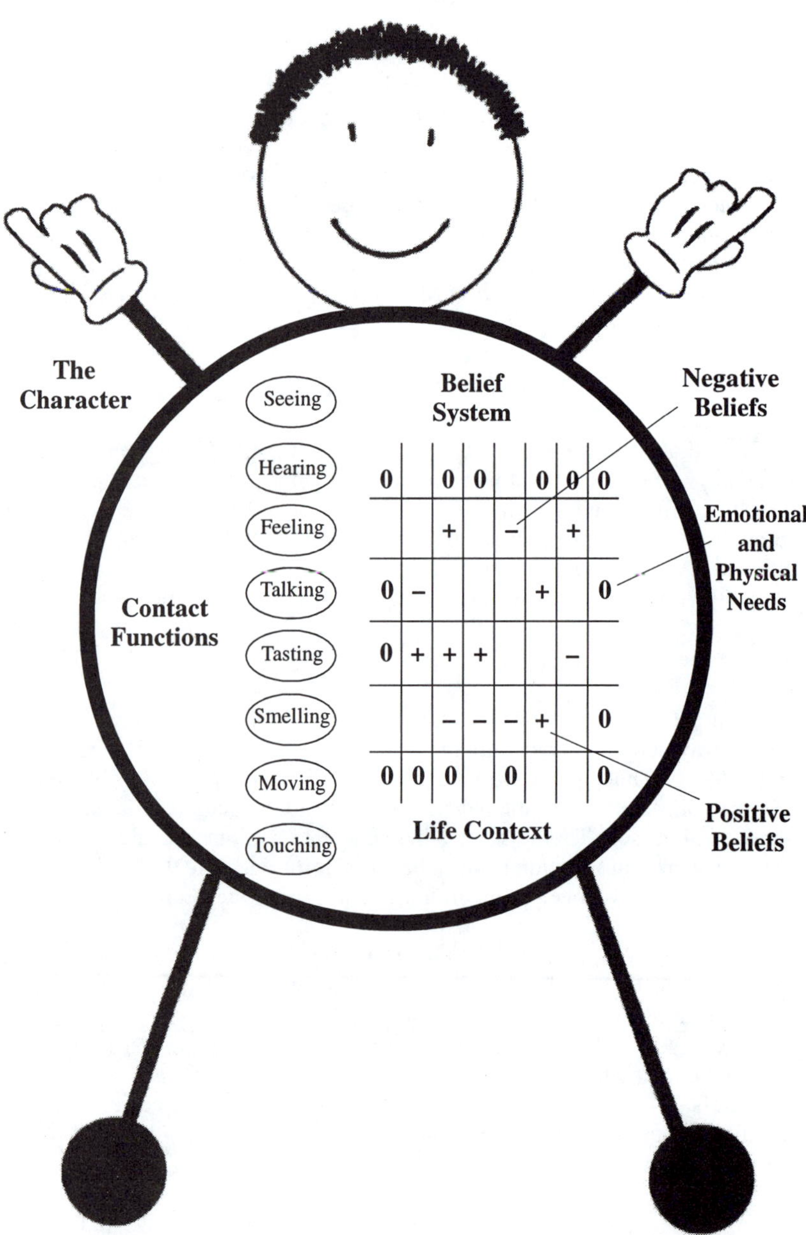

Figure 2.2. The self.

> plexities of the art, then asked if he had considered using a little more red. When Neil brought his first girlfriend home, his father liked her looks and intelligence and her success in school, but he talked to Neil about dating somebody from a wealthier family.
>
> His father's criticisms helped Neil develop a core negative belief that nothing he did would ever be good enough. As a result of that deep belief, Neil developed a number of secondary or resultant beliefs. One of them was that no really exceptional woman would want him.

Beliefs about the self that result from accepting a negative core belief are just as difficult to transcend as the deeper negative beliefs. They can profoundly affect the attempt to develop high self-esteem because they always interfere with a person's ability to experience the positive.

Management beliefs tell us to carry an umbrella when it rains; they govern our manners and the way we meet our emotional needs; and they tell us which emotional needs are important. Management beliefs are important because they support and enhance self-esteem. The most important management beliefs are those relating to emotional needs. These beliefs are developed in childhood as parents help their children experience, explore, understand, and know their emotional needs. Just as we develop our core positive beliefs or life themes in childhood, so we develop our beliefs about identifying and meeting our emotional needs.

Adult self-esteem work occurs in three parts of the self. These can be viewed as discrete, but they are actually synergistic and interactive. When I discuss working on one part of the self, keep in mind that such work affects all parts of the self.

First, I will examine negative beliefs in order to show how they interfere with high self-esteem. Then I will examine the core positive beliefs (the steel rods) that are a major part of self-esteem development. Finally, I will examine beliefs about emotional needs and the accompanying commitment to meeting those needs. This commitment helps support the experience of living in the world and being present in the moment.

The Self Can Change

To see how self-esteem develops, you first need to understand the self. Our culture currently views self in a number of ways. For a thorough discussion of some of those ways, I encourage you to read Wilber (1995), a prominent postmodern philosopher and social critic who offers an insightful exploration of various theories of the self and how they operate in American culture.

My own view is the *humanistic phenomenological or growth model*, which says that the self is constantly changing and growing. This view has its roots in classical philosophy, particularly in the work of Martin Buber, Soren Kierkegaard, and Martin Heidegger. According to Perls, Hefferline, and Goodman (1951, p. 151),

> The self is not a thing or a structure or a fixed institution but a process. The self is an organizing process which is constantly changing. It is an I in process. The self is the integrator, the artist of life. It plays the crucial role of finding and making meanings that we live and grow by.

Believing in the self as process means believing that the self constantly changes, grows, and presses forward to experience the world more fully. Rather than being a static, fixed entity, the self is always evolving, so we can change or transcend our current selves. I reject the naysayers who argue that, in terms of self-esteem, you are stuck with what you have. I know from my own work that is not true. *People can transcend and move beyond the negative beliefs that interfere with their lives.* They can develop positive beliefs and identify their emotional needs, can understand that emotional needs are an important part of self-esteem, and can develop beliefs that support meeting those emotional needs.

Emotional Needs

Clarkson and McKewan (1993, p. 42) wrote, "The person organizes his experience—his sensations, images, energy, interest and activity—around the need until he has met it. Once the need is met, the person feels satisfied. So that particular need loses interest for him and recedes." In this view of the self, needs constantly emerge, are met, and recede. This continuous cycle of need-meeting underscores the importance of having a clear commitment to meeting our emotional needs as a part of self-esteem development.

Most of us know that we must eat, sleep, drink water, and take care of our physical bodies. But many of us never understand that we must care for and nurture our emotional selves as well as our physical selves. To understand the self as process, we must learn exactly how to meet our emotional needs and be committed to meeting them. Each person's emotional needs are different, and the complexity of those needs differs from person to person. Emotional needs include validation, support, tenderness, play, friendship, solitude, and warmth. We need these experiences to feel good every day and to provide a solid foundation to anchor our steel rods. We must pay as much attention to them as we pay to our sleep, body weight, and physical health.

In my practice, I help clients understand their emotional and physical needs by extracting those needs from a clinical diagram of the self and placing them on what I call the *physical and emotional dashboards* (see Figure 2.3). An

Physical Dashboard

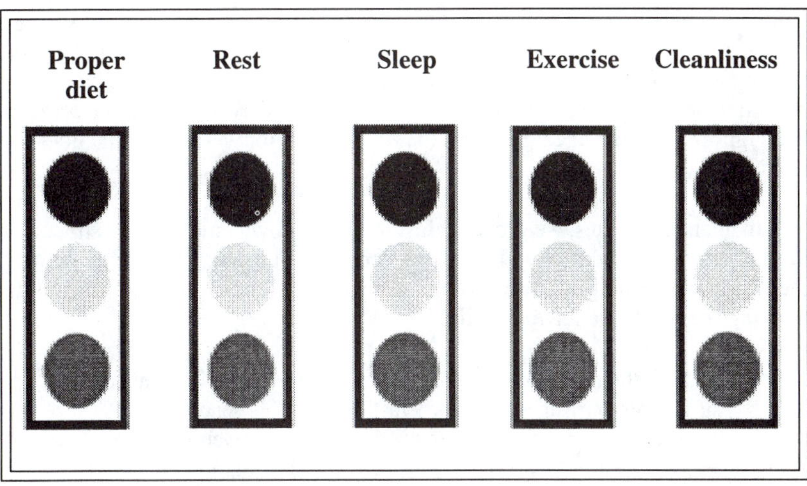

Emotional Dashboard

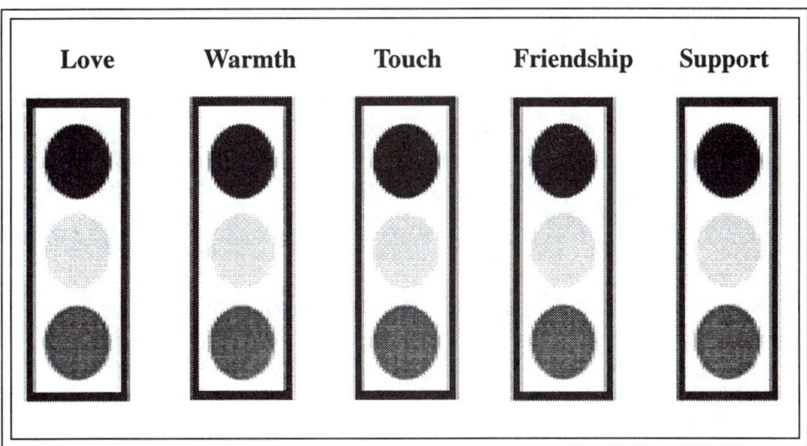

Figure 2.3. Physical and emotional dashboards.

emotional dashboard is like a car dashboard, with emotional needs listed on the top and green, yellow, and red lights underneath each one. People raised to recognize their emotional needs can identify them clearly. They also have developed beliefs that tell them exactly what they must pay attention to so they can meet those needs. When a need has been insufficiently supported, the light on their emotional dashboard turns from green to yellow; this warns them they have not been paying enough attention to that need. When they have really been ignoring a need, the light turns to red, and a major warning signal goes off inside the self.

In healthy families, we grow up developing our own emotional dashboards. We know what our emotional needs are because our parents help us identify them. They also help us develop the management beliefs that commit us to meeting the needs we have identified.

> College student Jim loved to party, spent his evenings with a variety of different girlfriends, and procrastinated on his schoolwork. At the beginning of the quarter, Jim had just returned, well-rested and excited, from a Mexican vacation. His physical dashboard lights were all green. As Jim stayed up later and drank more, his physical dashboard light relating to rest and relaxation turned yellow. Jim was tired, grouchy, and restless, but he still did not attend to the fact that his light had turned yellow.
>
> As final exams approached, Jim tried to study at night, but now he was truly exhausted. His dashboard light had turned to red. Even when Jim tried to sleep, he could not. He realized he should have attended to his yellow light when it began blinking several weeks before. Now his light was red, he was in crisis, and he regretted not paying attention to his dashboard light.

Developing management beliefs that commit us to meeting our emotional needs is what forces us to pay attention to our emotional dashboards. Had Jim developed beliefs that committed him to noticing his dashboard lights and doing something about them, he could have saved himself a horrible quarter at college.

> When Barbara's emotional dashboard light turned yellow, she became aware that something important was happening. She realized she had been working for weeks on end without seeing her friends, and that she was lonely. She stopped herself in her tracks and felt and knew that she needed to get the support she was missing.
>
> Barbara had developed and refined her emotional dashboard, she paid attention to it. When Barbara was not receiving enough fun,

validation, friendship, solitude, or support, her internal dashboard helped her, and she made meeting her needs a priority.

Many people lack an emotional dashboard because they have never defined their emotional needs. It's amazing how many people don't know they even have emotional needs. If you ask them about their emotional needs, they looked puzzled and shocked. Even if they harbor a vague notion of these needs, they have not developed the management beliefs that commit them to meeting those needs.

Identified emotional needs make up our emotional dashboards. The dashboard metaphor helps us understand and pay attention to the idea that emotional needs count. Management beliefs commit us to paying attention to the lights on the dashboard and doing something about them. Those who did not develop management beliefs in childhood must develop them in adulthood. They are a fundamental aspect of developing high self esteem.

Commitment to Growth

Having an emotional dashboard and the accompanying management beliefs helps our steel rods stay strong and anchored. In real terms, knowing our emotional needs and making a commitment to meet them creates an environment in which our positive core beliefs can remain strong because we are doing everything we can to make the moment-to-moment experience of our lives rich. The commitment to changing and to developing high self-esteem may come from reading this book, from being in therapy, or from some other source. Wherever it comes from, the truth is that *the self can change* and that, in relation to positive and negative beliefs and emotional needs, we can develop the strength and vitality we have been missing. We must be willing to work to develop this vitality; it requires a major commitment to our own growth. We must develop that commitment if it is missing.

Growth is not easy, nor is it swift. It is difficult and requires a lifelong commitment to struggling with the internal parts of the self in order to improve and enhance them. But a commitment to growth is an essential part of developing and maintaining high self-esteem. Bob and Mary Goulding (1979), pioneers in the field of changing beliefs, emphasized repeatedly that *confronting early beliefs is the central part of self-esteem development*, and that the growth process is a lifelong endeavor.

POSITIVE AND NEGATIVE BELIEFS

Joyce entered therapy at 42, upset at her inability to form a relationship with a man. As Joyce began to work on her issues, she remembered trying to talk to her mother when she was young and felt hurt,

> scared, or angry. Her mother would say, "Just keep a stiff upper lip, Joyce. Go to church more, be good, and these things will go away."
>
> Joyce realized that both her mother and her father had devalued her attempts to share her feelings, repeating the message again and again that her feelings did not count. So Joyce began to believe that feelings did not count—particularly her feelings.
>
> In relationships with men, when Joyce tried to communicate concerns about the way she was being treated, she did so haltingly and without confidence. Many people perceived that Joyce did not truly value her own emotions. Men often took advantage of Joyce and did not treat her seriously, listen to her, or respect her. Eventually Joyce was taken for granted, and her negative belief that her feelings did not count played a big part in that problem.
>
> Joyce's twin sister Paula, the family star, had the opposite experience. Like Joyce, Paula was beautiful, smart, and popular, but when Paula said anything to her parents, they listened. They hung on her every word, cherishing each communication as if it were a precious gem. Positive support and parental involvement allowed this daughter to feel good about herself and to develop a group of positive beliefs that helped her sustain herself day in and day out.
>
> The parents worked hard to make Paula feel special and to help her identify her strengths. Although Paula and Joyce shared similar attributes, the positive ones were emphasized in Paula and were not emphasized in Joyce.

These sisters illustrate how positive and negative beliefs are developed in life. *Positive beliefs are developed when parents actually see something authentic and special about their child.* As a result of their involvement, love, support, and validation, the child begins to see, feel, and believe in that special part of him- or herself. *Negative beliefs usually are alien.* They are not things we have decided about ourselves or come to see, feel, and experience. They are the result of what we have heard from teachers, friends, and mostly from our parents. We may be treated so that we come to believe things about ourselves that are not true. These negative beliefs interfere with the way we live our lives.

Redeciding, transcending, or changing negative beliefs is difficult. Negative beliefs can be very powerful; they are a part of the self. As Goulding and Goulding (1979, p. 8) noted,

> [R]edecisions or changing beliefs cannot be made solely by learning the facts. If the child attempts to talk himself into going into the

> basement by reminding himself that the facts are, there is nothing in this basement that will hurt me, he may react like the little boy in the kreplach story that is often told to graduate students of psychotherapy.

The kreplach story the authors refer to concerns a young boy who is afraid of *kreplachs* (three-cornered, meat-filled pancakes). His family sends him to a psychiatrist, who devises a fine treatment plan. The psychiatrist and the boy together shop for the kreplach ingredients, then chop and cook the meat. They prepare, roll, and cut the dough. Then they add the meat and fold the first corner of the first kreplach, then the second corner. During this process, the boy remains interested and unafraid. But as they fold the last corner, the boy screams, "Oy, kreplach!" and runs from the room in terror.

The point is that even an irrational belief can be stronger than any first-hand experience to the contrary. Adult reasoning often is insufficient, because facing the depth and power of a negative belief can be an overwhelming experience. Such beliefs gain a life of their own and are reinforced again and again in childhood. The boy's belief that a kreplach could somehow hurt him was so strong that, no matter how much reason was applied, he could not finish making the kreplach.

But if negative beliefs can be strong, so can positive beliefs—so strong they function as the steel rods that hold us up. In the next section, we'll see how positive and negative beliefs develop, and we'll examine the degree of support, tenderness, and validation required first to develop positive beliefs and then to commit to undoing negative ones.

How Positive and Negative Beliefs Develop

Positive and negative beliefs develop in various ways in childhood, as illustrated by the following case histories.

> **Rudy's Story: Developing Positive Beliefs.** In the second grade, Rudy wrote a simple composition about his parents and brought it home. Rudy's parents read this paper, talked about it with his older brothers and sisters, and put it on the refrigerator. They loved Rudy, and they were so excited about his writing that they celebrated his efforts—not just the product, but the efforts. Rudy saw, felt, and was excited by their excitement.
>
> When his teacher announced that the class was going to produce a small mimeographed newspaper, Rudy volunteered, primarily because his parents were so excited by what he accomplished before. Rudy told his parents he was going to be part of the class newspaper. Rudy's father took him to the library, where they checked out

some simple books on newspapers. Rudy's mother and father read the books with Rudy, and Rudy's excitement for the project grew.

When Rudy's teacher asked for a volunteer to edit the newspaper, Rudy raised his hand. When he brought home the first copy, his mother took him on a special tour of the local newspaper, where they met the printers, saw the papers coming off the presses, and visited the city room. Because his parents were involved and nurturing, Rudy continued to explore his interest in writing and literature.

Like a tree, every child has buds. Some buds open for just a minute. A child takes one violin lesson, hates it, and never does that again. Some buds open for a long time and then close, which may happen with Rudy's interest in writing. But some buds stay and flower for a lifetime. These are the buds—developed through nurture and involvement—that become the positive core beliefs that comprise a person's self-esteem. Parents, teachers, and other adults who interact with a child nurture what is special about that child, and the child grows excited and begins to explore the thing that is being nurtured. Eventually the child comes to know, to see in his or her own behavior, to feel in the heart, and to believe that there is something special about him her. This belief will last a lifetime. Such stories can be told about millions of children whose parents care about, support, and nurture them and who thus develop positive core beliefs.

Jean's Story: Developing Negative Beliefs. Jean's father was a self-important, busy executive who dominated his wife. Jean was a bright girl—precocious, verbal, and excited. As she grew up, whenever Jean tried to talk to her father, he said things like, "Jean, I'm busy now. Can't you see I'm on an important phone call? Can't you see that I'm writing? Can't you see that I'm tied up with the computer right now? I'm on my way to play golf. We'll do that later. I can't play with you because I'm wearing my good suit."

Jean learned, not only from her father's words but also from his actions, that she was not important. The message was loud and clear. Jean's mother saw what was happening but did not interfere because she feared her husband's anger. She told Jean how wonderful and smart she was, and what Jean could accomplish. Jean did not connect with these words, however, because she knew, from her father and from her own experience, that she made mistakes, that she could not do anything right.

No matter how hard Jean tried, her father's words echoed in her mind: This isn't good enough, that isn't good enough, this isn't right, that isn't right. Jean didn't know she had special qualities, because her mother never specifically talked about or reinforced those qualities, and her father told her again and again what was wrong with her. Jean's mother told Jean that she was great, but her father told her repeatedly that she was not. Because of this confusion and lack of authentic support, Jean could not believe she was special.

Thus Jean grew up with the belief that she was not important—a powerful negative belief that was reinforced repeatedly by her father's rejection and her mother's superficial noninvolvement. As an adult, Jean did not consciously think about this belief, but it floated around inside her. When Jean tried to do something that required her to feel important, the belief surfaced. She heard a voice in her head saying she was not important. When she began arguing with the voice, she could not concentrate on what she was doing.

In college, whenever Jean considered a major step, like running for student government, she heard a voice in her head: "Jean, I don't have time for you right now. Jean, I'm busy. Jean, you don't know what you're doing. Jean, just be quiet. Jean, don't say anything. Jean, wait until I'm done." Sometimes Jean actually heard her father's voice, but mostly the voice just repeated the words, and she never made the connection. She did not understand that she had taken in his negative words and was repeating them to herself in her voice. Whenever Jean needed to feel important and to act on that feeling, the voice emerged. It broke the surface of her awareness, and she lost track of what was happening. Throughout her life, Jean stopped herself from taking steps she needed to take because of her powerful negative belief that she was not good enough.

This belief interfered with Jean's happiness in many ways. It was like having a powerful boom box somewhere inside her body. Whenever she started to do something important, the boom box materialized in her mind and began broadcasting the negative thoughts she heard growing up. The boom box was powered by all the pain and anger that Jean could not express about all the times her father and mother hurt her.

Negative beliefs interfere in our daily functioning and with our self-esteem. That is why, in order to develop high self-esteem, we must identify the boom box inside us and see that it is not ours, that it is alien. We must hold the boom box up in the light of day and see the damage and the blackness it causes. We must turn it off and make it stop interfering with our daily life.

Billy's Story: Positive and Negative Beliefs. Billy was the only child of two loving parents. When Billy achieved something special, his parents were wonderfully supportive. Because they valued success and wanted him to be successful, they were excited about his writing, his grades, and all kinds of achievements. In many ways, Billy's parents were exemplary. They loved Billy and were involved with him. But they thought play was a waste of time. They both grew up in humorless, dry homes, and they never learned how to have fun.

Sometimes Billy would tickle his father or want to play a board game or cowboys and Indians. As he grew, he wanted to do puzzles or throw a football with his dad. His father frowned, made an excuse, had something better to do, or reminded Billy to do his homework. His mother dismissed Billy or did not take him seriously. In one way or another, his parents seemed to disapprove of having fun with him. They were good parents, but they did not know how to have fun. So Billy grew up with positive beliefs about his intelligence and competence and negative beliefs about being humorous, playful, and childlike.

As an adult, Billy had difficulty in his marriage and as a father. He was a high achiever and very successful, but when he tried to play with his kids, the negative belief about playing would emerge, and he would behave awkwardly. When Billy tried to play around with his wife and friends, the belief would emerge, and he would withdraw from the scene. One summer, Billy's family and several other families went camping at a lake. The other parents had brought squirt guns, and they began to chase and squirt their kids. The minute the squirt guns appeared, Billy grew tense. His negative belief emerged, and he heard the voice in his head saying, "It's not okay to play; it's a waste of time."

Billy could not enter into the play. He withdrew into his head, where he judged the others as foolish, although he understood that the problem was his. Billy was a devoted and caring father who worked hard to provide, was always there to help with homework, and was available for serious discussions. But his negative beliefs interfered with his ability to be emotional, playful, and childlike with his children.

Like Billy, most of us develop both positive and negative beliefs in childhood. To achieve high self-esteem, we need to strengthen the positive beliefs. We need to further reinforce the steel rods. Then we need to bring the negative beliefs out into the light of day, discharge the pain and anger that empower them, and transcend them so that they do not interfere with our daily lives anymore.

HOW AN ADULT DEVELOPS HIGH SELF-ESTEEM

Building high self-esteem is a complicated multi-step process, but it is a doable one. The first step is to develop a base line—that is, to assess where you are right now. To do that, you can use the self-esteem map, which is both an experience and a process for establishing your base line. But first, let's look at Patricia, a former client of mine. I will sketch her background for you and then take you through the process by which Patricia and I worked to build her self-esteem.

> Patricia's family did not work hard to help Patricia identify what was special about her or to understand her emotional needs and how to meet them. After she became a nurse, Patricia realized that her self-esteem problem was hurting her: She had difficulty advocating for herself, she did not value herself with men, and she did not regard herself anywhere near as positively as other people said they regarded her. When somebody said something positive to Patricia, the comment went right through her without resonance because she had undeveloped positive buds and strong negative beliefs. Her self-esteem was weak, and she could not hear people saying nice things to her.

Developing Core Positive Beliefs

As a therapist, I help adults begin the process of developing core positive beliefs by first helping them to see authentically what is special about them. Everyone has special traits: kindness, sensitivity, humor, an ability to teach, intelligence, vulnerability, warmth, strength, an ability to think through problems. They may not know, feel, believe in, or be able to articulate these traits, and they may not be able to always keep them in mind, but everyone has special traits. So the first step in helping adults develop high self-esteem is to help them see what about them is really special—a difficult step because they may not truly believe that they have any special characteristics. Once they have identified their actual positive traits, they need to listen to what other people say about them and to notice when they hear positive statements.

> As Patricia began to work on her self-esteem, she came to acknowledge that most people really did recognize four or five positive traits in her. She was warm, sensitive, bright, and funny, and she truly cared about people. These were authentic and real traits. (Self-esteem cannot be built on traits that are not authentic.)
>
> After we had identified her positive special traits, Patricia began to listen for these traits in what people said about her. She began to study her own behavior for evidence of the traits. She saw people

laugh at her stories and respond to her warmth and sincerity. She saw her patients feel cared for, and she saw them acknowledge her tenderness with cards and letters. As she began to see more clearly that her positive traits existed, Patricia began to believe in them and talk about them.

Patricia's self-esteem development process was in full swing once she truly began to believe in her own warmth, sensitivity, humor, intelligence, and concern for others. But results did not come quickly. As with childhood self-esteem development, repeated practice, work, reinforcement, and experience are needed. But the positive beliefs did develop, and Patricia began to strengthen the steel rods she needed to hold her up and to help her weather the storms of her life.

Discharging Negative Beliefs

While she worked to develop positive beliefs, Patricia began to realize that she also harbored harmful negative beliefs. As she attempted challenges in the world, she saw how she would begin feeling anxious, how the boom box noise inside her would rise to the surface. As she attempted something new, voices would say to her, "You're not good enough, you're not bright enough, you're not doing well enough." Patricia's negative beliefs had developed in her childhood because her mother, who competed with Patricia constantly, often made snide negative comments about Patricia's abilities. Patricia's sisters also constantly told her that she was not as good as other kids in terms of her intelligence, her behavior, her skills, or her accomplishments. Patricia developed the belief that she was fundamentally not good enough.

Patricia had developed three powerful negative beliefs: that she was not good enough, that she was not intelligent enough, and that she could not do well. The "not good enough" belief seriously interfered with Patricia's ability to form relationships with men and with her attempts to assert herself and be successful. When she tried to assert herself or tried activities that involved her looks—like going to the gym, dating, buying clothes, or talking with other women about make-up—the belief would surface. She would become anxious and battle it in her head. She could not concentrate, and she had difficulty feeling attractive. So Patricia wanted to begin working on these negative beliefs.

Working on negative beliefs is different from working on positive beliefs. The first step is to identify the belief. This means learning to feel the belief emerging, to feel the twist in your gut, to feel the anxiety arise.

When Patricia went out to buy make-up, she began to feel anxious as she entered the department store. She thought, "These people will think I'm not pretty. I shouldn't be doing this. Look how beautiful they are. I'm going to look stupid wearing this bright red lipstick. It won't be attractive on me." She would feel the twist in her gut that told her a negative belief was emerging.

Each of us has a body signal that tells us when a negative belief is emerging, and everyone's signal is slightly different. Patricia called her signal the "gut twist." She would feel herself getting anxious, then would hear the voice in her head. She would lose her concentration standing at the make-up counter trying to examine lipstick while she battled with herself. One part of her would say, "I need to leave. I shouldn't be talking to these people. I look stupid. This lipstick's too bright." Another part of her would say, "There's nothing wrong with this. You're okay. What are you worried about? You deserve to feel attractive. You deserve to feel special. Just buy the damn lipstick!"

The battle with the voice—the "I'm not good enough" negative belief—sometimes became so intense that Patricia could not concentrate on the lipstick and appeared rattled and uncomfortable. Of course, the person selling the make-up, sensing something wrong, would ask, "Are you okay, ma'am," which only embarrassed Patricia even more. A few times she actually ran from stores.

Tracking a negative belief means experiencing it on your own as you move into a life experience that calls it forth. You feel the body cue, sense the belief emerging, feel your anxiety rising, hear the voice in your head, and notice yourself having trouble concentrating. Then, as you conclude your business or as time passes, the belief recedes and stops interfering, and you feel better. So the first step is to identify the belief, which also means being able to say the words that the belief embodies: "I'm not pretty." "I'm stupid." "No one could ever want me." "I can never succeed." "I'm not good enough." "No one will ever love me." "My feelings don't count." Those are negative beliefs.

You want to feel the belief emerging, to identify it exactly in words, and to experience the entire process: feeling good, feeling the body sensation, feeling the belief emerge, feeling the anxiety, fighting the internal war, losing focus, moving away from whatever it is that scares you or threatens you, feeling the belief retreat, and feeling better again. This is how you learn to track a negative belief in your own life, and it is a long-term process.

The next step is finding the boom box and whatever ugly, difficult, and interfering negative beliefs it has stored inside it. The voices it broadcasts can be quite loud, so the second step is disempowering the voices: defining them, holding them up to the light of day, and stripping them of their emotional power by addressing the part of the past from which they come. This step often is difficult to accomplish on one's own without outside help. It can be done, and later I will suggest ways to work on the past on your own. But people often need outside help (counselors or therapists) when they get to this stage, because clearly understanding their negative beliefs and experiencing where in the past the beliefs came from can be difficult. Patricia chose to work on this stage independently, so she began thinking about where her negative beliefs came from.

> Patricia began imagining her mother, and one day she returned home, took a large piece of blank paper, and drew a stick-figure picture of her mother. Suddenly she found herself crying, and she began talking to her mother, saying, "Mom, I'm really angry with you. It wasn't fair. We weren't competing. I'm your daughter. I'm competent. I *am too* good enough!" Patricia began to discharge some of the pain and anger associated with her belief on her own, but after she calmed down, she realized she needed help. Eventually she called me again, and together we worked on her problems in depth.

As people explore their past, deal with negative beliefs, and take the feelings they have blamed themselves for (the pain, anger, or shame) and the voice they always thought was theirs and put them back where they belong in somebody else's cupboard, the belief weakens. In the future when it surfaces, it will be weaker than it was before. As they discharge more of their feelings and understand more about where the belief came from and how it formed in the past, the belief will grow weaker still. Eventually, if it does emerge, they can feel it coming, push it back down, and move beyond it.

> With some therapy and a lot of help from inside herself, Patricia reached the point where the belief emerged only rarely. When it did emerge, she could say, "That's not true. I'm not going to listen to you, Mom. I'm not going to think about this, and I am not incompetent. I am capable." She pushed the belief down and went on, and it no longer seriously interfered with her life.

Developing Beliefs That Support Emotional Needs

> The third step in the self-esteem development process is understanding our emotional needs. Patricia did not understand much about her emotional needs. No one had ever really talked to her about what she needed on a daily basis. She ate healthy foods, drank the required amount of fluids, worked out, and slept well, but she did not know much about taking care of her heart and soul. As she be-

gan thinking about her emotional needs, she started keeping a list. She wrote down the things she thought she needed each day or most of the time in order to feel good: solitude, support from others, friendship, validation, and warmth. She realized that she never had thought about these needs, that she was not actively working to fulfill them, and that she really did not believe they were important.

Patricia chose not to work on this aspect by herself but to work in therapy. Together we identified her emotional needs more clearly and developed core management beliefs that gave Patricia permission to meet them. Core management beliefs are those that develop around specific emotional needs. Patricia first had to identify the fact that solitude, support from others, friendship, validation, and warmth were important to her. Then she had to develop the belief that she needed to continually work to get a particular need met. Some of the management beliefs we worked on developing were these:

- Warmth is important for me, and I am going to continue to spend time making sure that I have the warmth I need.
- Friendship is important for me, and I am going to continue to spend time making sure that I have the friends and the support system I need.
- Solitude is important for me, and I am going to spend time seeking enough solitude so that I have what I need to feel emotionally balanced.

Patricia made friends and created a support system, received validation, and had fun while she worked at developing the belief that she needed to continuously monitor and try to meet her emotional needs. Those experiences met her emotional needs, strengthened her positive core beliefs, and kept the negative ones from emerging. So Patricia's self-esteem process included developing positive core beliefs, defusing negative ones, identifying her emotional needs, developing a positive belief that she needed to meet those needs, and learning how to meet them.

Beliefs about managing our emotional needs evolve from the same process as developing positive beliefs. Changing those beliefs requires exploring the past and finding out what it was that we learned about our needs in the first place. Note that I suggest working on core beliefs first; as we do so and come to appreciate ourselves more, we will feel that we are people worthy of having our needs met. Identifying our needs, believing those needs are important, and developing a commitment to meeting them will be easier because we will have developed positive beliefs about ourselves. The best process is to work on our negative beliefs first, or on our negative and positive ones concurrently. Then we can identify our emotional needs and help ourselves develop the positive beliefs that allow us to feel committed to meeting those needs. Then we can go out and meet them.

THE SELF-ESTEEM MAP

The first step in understanding your own self-esteem is to draw what I call a self-esteem map (Figure 2.4). The self-esteem map is a simple diagnostic tool you can use to create a base line for understanding what the three parts of your current self-esteem look like.

In order to work with a self-esteem map, you need awareness. Being aware means paying attention moment by moment to what you are experiencing, then being able to articulate and report it. You must notice what is going on inside yourself so that you can check things out, determine what you are and are not feeling, and track the emergence of negative and positive beliefs. Without awareness, the self-esteem map is not helpful. You do not want to put things on your map that you are not feeling or speculate or use ideas you have read about. Your map should reflect *your actual daily experience.*

If you do not possess self-awareness skills—that is, if you don't know how to notice what is happening inside or how to use what is happening to help yourself—you need help raising your awareness level. You may be able to gain awareness on your own, but if you have trouble, a counselor or therapist can help you learn awareness skills. Books that can help you with awareness work include Shub (1994b), Stevens (1986), Feldenkrais (1992), Satir (1972), and Zinker (1978).

First you must use your awareness to assess your own self-esteem and to draw a self-esteem map with three parts.

Positive beliefs. What are your positive beliefs? Define them precisely. How strong are they? Put them down exactly as you feel them.

Negative beliefs. What are your negative beliefs? Define them precisely. How strong are they? How much do they interfere with your daily life?

Emotional needs. What are your emotional needs? Define them precisely. Do you have beliefs that help you feel committed to continuously meeting those needs?

Positive Beliefs

	How Strong?			
	Yarn	Plastic	Wood	Steel Rod
1.				
2.				
3.				
4.				
5.				

Negative Beliefs

	How Strong?			
	Yarn	Plastic	Wood	Steel Rod
1.				
2.				
3.				
4.				
5.				

Emotional Needs

	Are You Committed to Meeting These Needs?		
1.	Y ____	N ____	Unsure ____
2.	Y ____	N ____	Unsure ____
3.	Y ____	N ____	Unsure ____
4.	Y ____	N ____	Unsure ____
5.	Y ____	N ____	Unsure ____

Figure 2.4. The self-esteem map.

When you have drawn your self-esteem map and you begin to look at the way you function, you will gain a better sense of how you are coping with daily life. If you have many negative beliefs that are interfering in your life, you will begin to see why you have a problem moving forward. If you do not have any positive beliefs, you will begin to see why you keep collapsing when something goes wrong. If you do not have clearly defined emotional needs and the beliefs necessary to meet them, you will begin to see why you keep grinding to a halt, exhausted, and why you are not nurturing yourself so that you can move forward. These are just a few of the insights you might gain from studying your self-esteem map. The more you can sense what is going on with your map, the clearer you will be about where you are now and what lies at the heart of some of the difficulties you are experiencing.

> Sam has many negative *and* positive beliefs, so he is ambivalent and often experiences serious conflicts within himself. Sometimes he feels great; sometimes he feels terrible.
>
> Nancy has few negatives and some good positives. Her self-esteem is basically high, and she enjoys her life.
>
> Mary has strong negative and a few weak positive beliefs. She experiences many difficult times. Because she has little sense of her emotional needs and no management beliefs to support her, Mary does a poor job taking care of herself.

As you draw your own map, notice what is occurring in your daily life. As you add to the map, you will gain an increased understanding of your sense of self and how you function.

WORKING TO CHANGE YOUR OWN SELF-ESTEEM

So far, I have described self-esteem, including core positive and negative beliefs and emotional needs; discussed the self as a changing experience; and sketched the self-esteem map. Now I want to give you some ideas about working on your own self-esteem.

Filling in Your Map

After you have drawn your self-esteem map, you can use it as a prescription for how to proceed. In conjunction with your map, here are some general exercises for working on self-esteem.

Journaling. Many people recommend a journal for various purposes; I find journaling particularly helpful for self-esteem work. Your journal need not examine the events of your life. Rather, as you experience yourself living, using your self-esteem map as a lens, let your journal reflect your ability to track your processes, so that you can work more specifically on your self-esteem map.

For example, while fleshing out his self-esteem map, Perry decided to use a journal to learn more about what was going on inside his belief system. He wrote every night and produced pieces like this:

> My boss looked at me with a funny look today, and I felt a knot in my chest. Once again I felt anxious, and I began to understand that I feel inferior to the other employees.
>
> I felt really good on my date last night. I noticed after paying a lot of attention to myself that I really think that I am an okay guy. I don't like the way I communicate, I don't like much of the way I act, but I really think I'm okay-looking, and I like that about myself.
>
> I was aware today as I went to play softball that I got really nervous before we all met for the game. I felt my heart flutter and my throat get dry, and I started to hear that pounding in my head about not being athletic again. I've never noticed it so vividly. I've always wondered why I don't do more sports and why I don't enjoy going to those games more, and now I know.

Perry is paying attention to what is happening inside. He is beginning to notice his positive and negative beliefs. Perry wrote more entries:

> Well, I'm aware that I haven't thought much in the last four or five days about myself. I really don't know a whole lot about my emotional needs. I don't really think about what I need or what I want. I don't work on getting my needs met. Wow, I'm really shocked. I never realized that before.
>
> Now that I've been thinking about my emotional needs, I realize that today was a difficult one. I don't have any fun. I go to these sports things, and I'm nervous about them. I work really hard. I go on dates, but I'm not fun and I don't have fun. Why don't I have more fun? Why don't I *want* more fun? Today everybody was at the beach and they were chasing each other around with pails of water, and I was sitting there thinking it was stupid. But now that I am writing in my journal, I realize that it wasn't stupid. I just felt weird about it. I felt nervous. I judge them because I don't know how to have fun. I want to have fun. I think I might even need to have fun, but I'm not fun and I don't try to have any. What's wrong with me?

> Obviously I don't have any kind of belief that fun is important, and I don't know how to have fun. Wow, that's weird.

Journaling can help you tune in to what is happening inside you.

What are your negative beliefs? How do they manifest themselves? How strong are they?

What are your positive beliefs? How strong are they? Can you begin to notice them?

How much do you notice about your emotional needs, and how committed are you to meeting them?

Journaling can help you answer these questions, especially if you do it faithfully and in conjunction with your self-esteem map. Do not simply report the day's events. Write down more about your experiences, relating them to specific parts of your self-esteem map. Gradually, over the time that Perry journaled, he began to fill in his self-esteem map with more positive and negative beliefs and emotional needs. He began to get a better sense of himself.

Taping. Karen did not like to write, so every day she made tapes, which served the same purpose as a journal. She carried a small tape recorder with her and taped for four or five minutes whenever she had a chance. At the end of the week, she listened to her tapes. Here is an excerpt:

> Well, this ... I'm talking to my stupid tape recorder now, and I'm really mad. I'm *really* mad. There is no doubt about it, I am really mad. Why am I mad? I'm mad because once again, for the 400th time in my life, I don't think I'm as smart as everybody else. I'm really mad. Why don't I think I'm smart? I don't know why I don't think I'm smart. I went with everyone today out to a picnic in the woods, and we were sitting there having a wonderful time drinking wine and eating food that somebody prepared, it doesn't matter who, and Julie brought out a board game called *Wiz*. It's a combination of trivia and problem solving. It's a really neat game. I immediately felt bad, I didn't want to play, I was embarrassed, I was annoyed, I was upset, I was ashamed, I was worried, I was everything. This is ridiculous. I am a college graduate. I'm a smart woman. Why am I so unhappy when we have to do intellectual things? Nobody else thinks I'm not smart. I *am* smart.

Karen really got the hang of it and began expressing on both the emotional and experiential levels what happening inside. At the end of the week, she listened to her tapes and began filling in her self-esteem map. After a few months, she had completed it, at which point she began to think about working to change her self-esteem.

Other Methods. Some people like to paint or draw pictures, which can be just as effective as taping or journaling for understanding your inner process. These and other methods—such as listening to or writing music, choreographing a dance, or singing a song—can help you understand or become more aware of your inner process by making your feelings more palpable. You can use anything that helps you open the door to understanding what is happening inside your belief system. After you have drawn an accurate self-esteem map, you will want to begin taking steps to change yourself. How do you do that?

Working to Develop Positive Beliefs

Some of the experiments proposed here may sound simple, but they all require hard work, concentration, continued energy, and a commitment to stay with the process over time. Developing high self-esteem requires awareness, emotional investment, patience, a willingness to persevere, and attention to details, especially if you have many negative beliefs or few positive ones.

Ask Your Friends. Many people have trouble talking about themselves positively. If you are one of them, I suggest sending out a note like this:

> Dear Friends,
>
> This may sound a little different to you, but I'm in the process of trying to raise my self-esteem. In order to do this, I would like you to respond to the following questions.
>
> 1. What qualities do you notice about me that you think are really special?
> 2. What qualities do you notice about me that I seem to believe are special?
> 3. What do you see me do or hear me say about myself that is negative? For example, do I put myself down? If I do, what do I put myself down about? Do I tend to make negative comments about myself? Do you notice me hesitating to participate in activities because of what you perceive as my concerns about myself?
> 4. Do you think I'm good at taking care of myself? If so, in what ways do you think I'm good? If not, in what ways do you think I'm not good?
>
> Please write me back as soon as you can. I value your help with this questionnaire.

When you receive the responses, begin compiling the positive ones. If you send out enough requests, you will begin to notice patterns. Most people who know you well will make the same four or five points. These are the feelings they experience as they encounter you, your traits that are special, your aspects that touch them when they connect with you.

When you can hear the specific things people close to you are saying, you need to begin noticing them in your own behavior. The transition from hearing to noticing is difficult. It requires awareness. You must keep in mind the positive things the people close to you have said about you. You must work hard to pay attention to what you are doing day to day so you can observe these qualities in yourself.

Pay Attention to Feedback. Pay attention when people give you feedback. Notice what they say. Listen to the evaluations you receive at work. Listen to what your church committee tells you about a job you did. Listen to what the Cub Scout troop says about the last event held at your house. Listen to what your friends say about the party you threw. You will begin to hear the same responses.

After you hear these responses from others, start looking for the positives in your own behavior, which is more difficult. Can you see yourself being kind? Can you see people laughing when you try to cheer them up? Can you see that you brought a basket of apples from your tree when you had only a few and shared them with your neighbors? That is true generosity. Can you see in your own behavior the qualities you have been told about? As you begin to see these qualities, you will start to believe you really are the person people think you are.

Practice the "Notice Scenario." Because noticing traits in your own behavior is difficult, you might want to practice the "notice scenario." Think about yourself. Take each positive core belief on which you are trying to work and write out an event from the last month or so that embodied it. For example, if your positive core beliefs are strength, wisdom, and gentleness, think of times when you were strong, wise, and gentle. Write them all down. Use your narratives as scenario finders to sensitize yourself to really seeing positive aspects of your behavior. In your daily life, look for events similar to those you have written about. Note them. For many people, such noticing is difficult; but if you pay attention and struggle with the process, you will learn to see for yourself, through your own eyes and with your own heart, what you are doing well. You will learn to accept your positive attributes.

Become a "Martian Observer." Another way to help yourself develop positive beliefs is to become a "Martian observer." This is a way to get outside yourself in order to see yourself as objectively as possible. Imagine that you have come from Mars and landed next to your house. Perhaps your name is Penny. Well, for the next few weeks, you will remain Penny, but you will also be the invisible Deltaron from Mars. Deltaron is going to watch what Penny does and how she acts. In particular, Deltaron's job is to notice what people say about Penny. Then, at the end of every day, Deltaron will talk to Penny and give her objective feedback, which she will write down. If you have difficulty owning your own feelings or your own positive experiences, this playful fantasy can help you get outside yourself. It allows you to listen to what other people say about you, and to talk to yourself about it.

Examine Memorabilia. Examine memorabilia or objects from your past: certificates of achievement; letters of gratitude from people you helped; attendance awards; the pressed flower from Mrs. Berry, to whom you brought meals when she was sick; or the nice sweater your friend's mother knitted after you visited her in the hospital. Examining old objects and thinking about what they mean can give you more ideas about what the world is saying about your positive aspects.

Join a Group. Another way of working on your positive traits is to join a therapy or support group or any group that allows you to talk openly and honestly about yourself. Although a therapy group is probably the ideal setting, any group of people committed to growth provides a great setting to process information. You can try it with your family, although you may think they are biased, or with a group of friends if you are bold enough. If you join a group, ask the members to give you feedback as they get to know you. As these strangers learn about the you who really is there, they will tell you what you are like. You will begin to hear those things about yourself that are special. You will hear them, but you will not yet know them, feel them, or believe them.

If you are in a therapy group, you can discuss the reactions of others and how you do not feel or see them. After that, you can begin the hard work of asking for feedback, hearing the positive traits, listening for other people in your world to validate those traits, beginning to experiment with seeing the traits in your own behavior, and ultimately believing them and developing your core beliefs.

A group is a wonderful way to achieve insight. If you choose not to be in a therapy group, think about forming your own group of family or friends and using this book as a guide to help all of you develop high self-esteem.

Become Anonymous. The following case study demonstrates how you can use anonymity to learn about yourself:

> Sally wanted to work on self-esteem, but she was too shy and timid to begin the process at home with people she knew. Making herself

> vulnerable was just too scary, so she decided to take a shopping trip in a city about three hours away, where she did not know anyone. Once there, she began striking up conversations with strangers. She started talking to another woman in a store as they were trying on dresses. As they talked, Sally noticed comments the woman made about Sally and the woman's responses to what Sally said. She struck up a conversation with a woman in a mall restaurant. She talked to a man at the store where she bought film for her camera.
>
> All through that day and the next, Sally was brave enough to talk with people she did not know, which somehow was safer for her. Her anonymity allowed her to jump-start the process of exploring her self.

Many people have successfully used this experiment when they were too scared to share their feelings with people close to them. An anonymous activity may just work if you need a jump-start to begin hearing what is special about you, to see something in your own behavior, to firm up what you already know, or even to start at the very beginning of the process.

Working to Undo Negative Beliefs

Undoing negative beliefs is a complicated and difficult process that requires five distinct steps:

Step 1 is identifying the beliefs and returning to the past to discover where they came from.

Step 2 is holding the beliefs up to the light of day and seeing them for what they are.

Step 3 is confronting the emotions that give the beliefs life and allow them to float around inside you and surface on their own.

Step 4 is tracking the beliefs in daily life—noticing when they emerge, how strong they are, and if they decrease as you deal with the emotions.

Step 5 is moving beyond or transcending the negative beliefs as they weaken, so they no longer interfere with your daily life.

The work is difficult, but these suggestions can help you accomplish it.

Construct a Negative Timeline. After you have identified your negative beliefs, a negative timeline can help you isolate specific events from your life and relate them to negative emotions and beliefs. (A timeline also can be used for positive beliefs or to track both negative and positive beliefs.) Get a big piece of paper, lay it on the floor of a large room or hallway, and draw a long line—the longer the better. Begin with your birth and mark off all the significant emotional events of your life.

> Mary laid a long piece of butcher paper in her dog run, which was long and narrow. On a beautiful summer day, she began working on her timeline. She put in her birth; her father's departure for and return from the war, neither of which she remembered; being in her crib and crying for long periods of time when her mother did not care for her; her first fight with her father; going to kindergarten, which she hated because her parents both worked and never picked her up; the time her mother left her waiting at a friend's house for hours, having forgotten she was there; the first time she saw her father come home drunk and beat her mother. On and on through her life, she laid out the events that she felt had contributed to her negative beliefs.
>
> At the beginning of the timeline, she listed her negative beliefs about herself. Then she connected those beliefs to the events on her timeline.
>
> At first Mary's timeline was not extensive; she could only remember major events that stuck with her. But she left the paper in the dog run and, as she thought about it over time, she added new memories and events. Her picture of her negative beliefs solidified over the weeks as she filled in her timeline. She began to see more clearly what it was that had happened in her life that added to the beliefs, and where they had come from. She decided she wanted to work on them. Constructing her timeline brought forth feelings that Mary kept to herself or talked about with her friends as she began identifying her negative beliefs. The very act of constructing the timeline helped Mary discharge some of her pain and anger.

Create a Sculpture. Once you have identified a negative belief, and have monitored it so that you know it is there and you can hear its voice, one fruitful exercise is to make a sculpture of your family or of all the people who have influenced the development of that belief. You can do this by actually positioning people in relation to each other to form a human sculpture; you can mold clay to represent (abstractly or realistically) the people; you can make the sculpture with blocks, placing them so that they represent what you are thinking; you can make the sculpture with wire. Use your own creativity to make the sculpture in any way that works for you, so that you can look at the people involved and see where your belief originated.

Terri tried this exercise. At first she thought, "This is kind of dumb, but as long as you're suggesting it, I'm going to try."

First she used stuffed animals stuck together to represent her "I am irresponsible" negative thought. Terri was in the middle, and the animals all seemed to be sticking their tongues out at her, making fun of her because she did not follow through, she was not responsible, and she had a hard time living up to her mother's expectations. One animal represented her mother, whom Terri believed had contributed to her negative belief; one was Jody, her friend; some were the girls in her kindergarten class, who made fun of her because she did not turn in her homework all the time. (Terri did not turn in her homework because her mother constantly told her it was not good enough, and because she was scared of being judged.) She used animals to represent other people as well. These stuffed animals—fitted together in a pattern that somehow conveyed that they were not pleased with how Terri handled her life—created a powerful sculpture for her. It helped clarify for Terri where her negative belief had come from and how strong it was.

For each negative belief, Terri created another different sculpture. She used popsicle sticks, cut-up paper, and globs of something that looked like gelatin. Each was profoundly meaningful, and each helped Terri explore a negative belief and the events and people who had shaped it.

Write an Autobiography. Another way to track how your negative beliefs developed is to write an autobiography.

Joanne began an autobiography to help her understand how she felt about herself. She wrote what she had been told about her birth, and she continued with a comprehensive account of her life. As she wrote through the lens of understanding her negative beliefs, her story took on a life of its own. Words flowed from her pencil, and eventually into her computer, about what had happened to her and how it had happened. Writing her autobiography was a profound experience for Joanne. It helped her focus on what had happened to her as she grew up and where her negative beliefs originated.

Be Creative—Anything Can Work. You are not limited to using only the methods listed above. Anything that is meaningful to you can help in the process of understanding your negative beliefs.

Roger realized that he had learned some of his negative beliefs from his father, whom Roger had experienced as rejecting and cruel.

> Roger had already used a journal to identify his powerful negative beliefs, and he was working hard to undo them. He began to track in his daily life when his negative beliefs emerged. He felt a tightness in his head, experienced anxiety, and suddenly thought, "I can't do this, I can't do this, I can't do this."
>
> I suggested that Roger put his father's picture on a key chain and carry it with him everywhere. When the negative beliefs emerged, he was to find a private place, take out the key chain, and look at it. Then, in his mind (or out loud if he could), he was to talk to his father: "Why do you think I can't do it? Why did you tell me I was never good enough? Why did you always put me down and criticize me? I *can* do it. I'm sick of believing I can't. I don't want to feel this way. I'm angry. I'm hurt."
>
> As Roger talked to and worked with his key chain, he gradually moved from saying, "I hate living like this" to, "Dad, I'm angry with you. I am good enough. I am able to do these things, and I'm not going to listen to you anymore."
>
> Roger carried his key chain for a long time as he tracked the beliefs that emerged in his life. He worked with the three negative beliefs that came from his father, using the key chain as a focus, and they gradually weakened. The process took a long time and a lot of work. There were many tears and much anger and sorrow. But there was joy as well, as Roger remembered the positive aspects of his father.

This last aspect, the joy, is often a surprise. But very few parents represent the entire problem. What happened to you growing up and what is left inside are what you must deal with. You are not looking for people to blame. You are looking for ways to undo your negative beliefs.

Exploring Your Emotional Needs

Construct Your Emotional Dashboard. The clearest way to learn about your emotional needs (and have some fun doing so) is to construct your own emotional dashboard (see Figure 2.3). Draw the dashboard of a car, an airplane, or any other vehicle that captures your fancy. List on it the emotional needs you have identified. If you really want to be creative, get little Christmas lights with batteries and place a green (on), a yellow (caution), and a red (stop) light for each need. During the week, begin to consciously notice your needs. If you feel satisfied, keep your light green. If you notice you have not paid much attention to a need that week, put it on yellow. If you have gone a long time without meeting a need, put it on red. Your goal is to keep all your dashboard lights on green. Using your dashboard for several months will help you notice what you need. It also will help you develop clearer beliefs about meeting your needs. Practice helps you grow.

Take an Emotional Needs Inventory. An emotional needs inventory is another helpful and interesting exercise. Think about your daily life and what you would like it to be, then consider how you can achieve that goal. Gradually, you will become aware of what you need, such as "I don't like to be alone, so I need friends," or "I want to be able to really enjoy my weekends, so I need to learn to have fun," or "I would like to be in a relationship and have more intimacy, so I need to overcome my fear of closeness and start to date." An inventory is a great way to identify your emotional needs. When you have identified them, then you can begin working on them.

Work With an Emotional Shopping List. A fun way to learn more about your emotional needs is to ask your friends to fill out an emotional shopping list by mail or in person for you. A sample follows:

> This is a shopping list for me. Please fill it out, but instead of food items or household goods, list what you think or imagine I need more of in my life to make my life better for me. Here are some examples. Jennifer needs more love. Jennifer needs more attention. Jennifer needs more tenderness. Jennifer gets too much attention and needs to pay attention to other people more. Jennifer needs to be more responsible. Please fill out my list to help me understand more about what I need. I'm also going to fill out a shopping list for myself. I know you're not a professional or an expert, but you are my friend, and your contribution can help me. Please give it a try.

Now make your own shopping list. Think about it in terms of the ones your friends fill out. Consider the way you live your life. What do your friends, family, and people you know or work with see? What emotional needs did they list for you, and how successful are you at meeting them? How deep are your beliefs that you must meet these emotional needs? Continue working on your list until you develop one that works for you, with items that really matter, and use it each day to make sure you get the peaches, pears, plums, and nectarines you deserve so much. Enrich your life.

Talk to Your Friends About Their Emotional Needs. Another good method of discovering more about what you need is to ask your friends what they need. Often, by listening to what others need, we can learn more about ourselves. Just talking to people about their emotional needs, how committed they are to getting those needs met, and how hard they work to make those needs part of their lives will help you focus on your own. The more you talk with others about their need-meeting process, the more you will understand your own process.

WHERE TO TURN WHEN YOU ARE STUCK

We've looked at how you can work on your self-esteem on your own or with friends and family. But sometimes people get stuck and need outside help to move forward in the process. Many people can be helpful to you. Counselors, therapists, and therapy and support groups are potential sources of help. Good therapists and counselors are experts at helping people move toward high self-esteem.

I mentioned earlier the possibility—if you are bold enough—of assembling a number of friends, all of whom want to work on self-esteem in a group. Using this chapter and this book as guides in such a group, you can achieve wonderful results.

Clergy and other people with spiritual or mentoring roles in your life also can help you explore yourself and learn more about getting unstuck. Sharing this book with them and encouraging them to help you through the stages of self-esteem development can move you forward in your own process.

Finally, the exercises that follow can help you unstick yourself and move forward in your self-esteem development process.

CONCLUSION

As Bob and Mary Goulding (1979, p. 285) were fond of saying, "Redecision is a beginning. There is no free lunch." And, they might have added, there is no easy way. Working to develop high self-esteem is a struggle. And maintaining positive self-esteem over a lifetime continues to require great effort.

But as the Gouldings also noted, the rewards can be enormous: "There is no magic. The person discovers his ability to be autonomous and experiences his new free self free from the negative beliefs and with enthusiasm, excitement and energy." Developing high self-esteem can *be* a joy and can *bring* joy. The potential for experiencing your life in a new rich way is limitless, which is what encourages and motivates most people to attempt the process.

I hope this chapter has given you some ideas about developing and keeping high self-esteem. The experiments in it are designed to help you take your self-esteem map and work with it over time to change your belief system and develop the highest self-esteem possible. Your commitment to your own growth throughout your life is vital to the process, but the potential rewards are worth it.

Good luck and work hard on developing your self-esteem.

ACTIVITIES YOU CAN DO

ACTIVITY 2.1 PAINTING DIFFERENT FACES

Introduction: This exercise encourages you to explore your self-esteem by experimenting with your appearance.

Time required: 4 hours

Participants: You alone

Setting: Your house or apartment, with a good-sized mirror

Materials: Washable face paints; paper and pen or pencil

Procedure: Stand in front of a mirror. With washable face paints, paint your face to reflect how you feel about yourself right now. Let the paint dry and look in the mirror. Under the heading "Sense of Self in the Present," write down your thoughts and feelings about the image you see.

Wash your face and repeat the procedure. This time paint your face to represent what you would like to be in the future. Write down your thoughts and feelings under the heading "Who I Would Like to Become."

Repeat the procedure, this time painting your face to represent your most negative feeling about yourself. Write down your thoughts and feelings again.

Paint your face a fourth time to represent what you like most about yourself. Write down your thoughts and feelings.

Look at, read, talk about, and think about your collected perceptions of yourself.

Outcomes: This exercise allows you to get in touch with how you feel about yourself in the present.

ACTIVITY 2.2 CARTOONING

Introduction: This exercise encourages you to explore your self-esteem by imagining what your friends think of you.

Time required: Unlimited

Participants: You alone

Setting: Any quiet place where you can be by yourself

Materials: Paper and pen or pencil

Procedure: On a piece of blank paper, draw a cartoon of yourself encountering a friend. In the balloon over your head, write, "How do you feel about me?" In the balloon over your friend's head, write the answer.

Draw a second cartoon and write in your balloon, "What do you like best about me?" Write an answer in your friend's balloon.

Draw a third cartoon with a different friend and write in your balloon, "Do you enjoy spending time with me? If so, why?" Write an answer in your friend's balloon.

Draw cartoons using all of your close friends. Explore all aspects of the relationships: what they like about you, how they enjoy you, what they have difficulty with, and whether they feel you are a self-caring person.

Outcomes: The answers to the questions can help you learn more about your sense of self.

ACTIVITY 2.3A INVOLVING YOUR PARENTS

Introduction: This experiment can get sticky if your parents feel defensive or criticized because you have negative beliefs. People who are struggling seriously with their parents should not attempt it. But if your parents can handle the experience, this is a good exercise for working in a positive, respectful, and supportive manner with people interested in exploring self-esteem development with you and in helping you change your current self-esteem.

Time required: As much time as you need

Participants: You and your parents

Setting: A quiet place in your own or your parents' home

Materials: Paper and pens or pencils

Procedure: If your parents are willing, ask them if they will help you draw your self-esteem map. Ask them to read this chapter or the entire book, or explain to them the concept of a self-esteem map and the three major components of self-esteem.

Sit down with your parents and give each one a blank self-esteem map with your name on it. Ask them to fill in the self-esteem map so that it reflects what they know about you.

When they are done, pull out the self-esteem map you have already completed. In a gentle, loving way, compare notes. Discuss your map and their maps, and your perceptions of yourself and their perceptions of you. Talk about how you got the way you are, some of the things that were positive, and some of the things that might have been done better.

Compare perceptions until you have learned more about your own development and your parents have learned more about you. Then, together, draw a self-esteem map that reflects where you would like to be.

Outcomes: If done with great trust, vulnerability, and sensitivity, this exercise can develop a process you and your parents can participate in to help facilitate your growth.

ACTIVITY 2.3B INVOLVING YOUR PARENTS

Procedure: An interesting twist on Activity 2.3A is to ask each parent to draw his or her own self-esteem map. Then compare the maps. Through the process of comparing, family members can learn much about themselves. Many families who were not currently struggling with issues have tried this exercise. They have all found it to be helpful.

ACTIVITY 2.3C INVOLVING YOUR LOVED ONES

Procedure: A second variation on Activity 2.3A is to sit down with your spouse, children, partner, or lover. Do whatever variation makes sense on drawing a self-esteem map, and discuss the results. There are innumerable variations on this theme, but these three seem to be the most interesting and potent. Let me stress again the importance of *not* trying this exercise if you are involved in a serious conflict with your parents or with others you might ask to participate. Doing so without professional supervision can precipitate difficulties.

ACTIVITY 2.4 PEG POUNDING

Introduction: This exercise allows you to work on your negative beliefs in a concrete, physical way.

Time required: A few hours spread over a number of weeks or months

Participants: You alone

Setting: A small patch of ground in your yard

Materials: Wooden pegs and a mallet or hammer

Procedure: As you begin to identify your negative beliefs and to work on them with your self-esteem map or through other methods, place a peg in the ground in your backyard for each negative belief you identify.

As you are able to defuse a belief, pound its peg more deeply into the ground. Make sure that the pegs are in tight and are hard to pound.

If anger is part of the emotions surrounding one or more of your negative beliefs, let that anger out as you pound the pegs.

Outcomes: The closer the pegs get to the ground, the less likely you will be to trip as you walk over them. Metaphorically, you will living your life without tripping over your negative beliefs. If you are successful, eventually you will pound the pegs down parallel to the dirt's surface. Then you can walk over them any time you want without fear of tripping, a truly liberating experience.

ACTIVITY 2.5 THE THERMOMETER

Introduction: This exercise provides you with a physical representation of your efforts to defuse your negative beliefs.

Time required: A few hours spread over a number of weeks or months

Participants: You alone

Setting: Your home

Materials: A long piece of paper and a colored marker

Procedure: For each negative belief you have identified, draw a thermometer like those used for fundraisers. Instead of going from 0 to 100, go from 100 to 0. Place these thermometers on a wall.

As you work on each negative belief and feel its impact lessening, try to gauge how its impact weakens, then shade in its thermometer. At first, a negative belief will be 100% powerful. Gradually its thermometer should rise to 80, then 75, then 60, then 30, then 20. Eventually you should reach a point where the impact of the negative belief is negligible.

Outcomes: Each thermometer records your ability to defuse the feelings that charge a negative belief. It monitors your progress as you weaken a negative belief to the point where you can push it down yourself, so that it no longer interferes with your ability to live your life fully. A visual aid like the thermometer reminds you to track your negative beliefs and to work with them regularly to develop high self-esteem.

ACTIVITY 2.6 AN INTERFERENCE MAP

Introduction: An interference map lets you visualize, feel, and know how much a negative belief interferes with your daily life.

Time required: 3 or 4 hours

Participants: You alone

Setting: Your home

Materials: Paper and pencil

Procedure: On a large piece of paper, draw your map. Within it, place yourself, all your significant others, your job, your friends, your important social activities, your church or synagogue, and anything else you think is important.

Underneath the map, list one of your negative beliefs.

Draw a line from yourself to each object on the map. Be creative. The connections can look like a spider web, a cluster, an actual terrain map of your house or your life, or a geographical map.

Think about which of your relationships your negative belief is impeding. Indicate the intensity of the interference with a pencil line or a squiggle, or use some other indicator.

As you work on your negative belief and it becomes less potent, begin erasing the lines.

Outcomes: Tracking the weakening impact of a negative belief on your life helps intensify your feelings about it. It also helps you understand the importance of your self-esteem work.

ACTIVITY 2.7 THE GROCERY STORE

Introduction: This exercise helps you conceptualize your emotional needs more clearly while you learn how committed you are to meeting them.

Time required: Several hours spread over a few weeks

Participants: You alone

Setting: A grocery store and your home

Materials: A small amount of money, paper, and a pen or pencil

Procedure: On a day when you are feeling pretty good, go to a grocery store. You are going to purchase five items that remind you of yourself in a positive way and five that remind you of yourself in a negative way.

Take your time and walk up and down the aisles. Do you see Sunburst Cereal™? Does that remind you of something special about yourself? Do you see Ivory Snow™ Laundry Soap? Does that remind you of something special? Do you see a mousetrap? Does that remind you of a belief that gets in your way? Take all the time you need to choose the items, which need not be expensive.

Take the items home and write down what they remind you of.

Now think about what you need to do, and what you need from others in order to change those items. Do you need more support, attention, love, or validation? Do you need to be alone? What do you need?

Return to the grocery store and find items that represent what you need. Be spontaneous. Let whatever is inside you come out. Pick items that represent something you hunger for and need in order to feel good about yourself, but that you are not getting.

Take the items home and write them down. Think about them and struggle with the emotional needs they represent.

Outcomes: This exercise helps you clarify your emotional needs. These are the needs you must work on meeting and about which you must develop positive beliefs in order to create the energy you need to defuse your negative beliefs.

ACTIVITY 2.8 THE ANIMAL METAPHOR

Introduction: Choosing an animal that reflects your self-esteem will help you objectify how you see yourself.

Time required: A few hours spread over several days or weeks

Participants: You alone

Setting: Any quiet place

Materials: Paper and a pen or pencil

Part I

Procedure: Choose an animal that fits your current self-esteem map. Make sure the animal really reflects your current view of your self-esteem. Jot down notes about the animal. Draw it.

Jim picked a mouse with a loud squeak that was somewhat bold in chasing after cheese. Jim saw himself as having courage in his positive core beliefs. But he was also a "runt" (as his father called him) because he was short and easy to disregard. He sometimes hid because he did not want people to notice his height. Jim was, however, bold in chasing after cheese. He did know something about his emotional needs, and he aggressively pursued the things he needed.

The more complex your animal is, the more directly it will reflect who you currently are. Thus you will be able to see more clearly how you are functioning in the world.

Part II

Procedure: Now you will change your animal.

If you were going to redesign your animal, what would you do? Would you make it grow bigger and open its eyes so that it could see more clearly? Would you give it another set of claws or sharper teeth? Would you lengthen its tail? What would you do to enhance your animal's ability to function in the world?

Outcomes: The animal metaphor helps you conceptually understand how you move through the world by picturing how your animal moves through the world. Then, by changing your animal, you can picture changing yourself in the world.

REFERENCES

Buber, M. (1956). *Between man and man.* New York: Columbia University Press.

Clarkson, P., & McKewan, J. (1993). *Fritz Perls.* Thousand Oaks, CA: Sage.

Ehrensaft, D. (1995). *Parenting together: Men and women sharing the care of their children.* Champaign: University of Illinois Press.

Feldenkrais, M. (1992). *The potent self.* San Francisco: Harper.

Fuchs, V. R. (1995). Are Americans underinvesting in their children? *Society, 28*(6), 11-17.

Goulding, R., & Goulding, M. M. (1979). *Changing lives through redecision therapy*. New York: Grove.

Heidegger, M. (1961). *Being in time*. New York: Harper & Row.

Johnson, D. W. (1979). *Reaching out: Interpersonal effectiveness and self-actualization*. Englewood Cliffs, NJ: Prentice-Hall.

Kierkegaard, S. (1944). *Concluding scientific postscript*. Princeton, NJ: Princeton University Press.

Kierkegaard, S. (1945). *The point of view for my work as an author.* Princeton, NJ: Princeton University Press.

Kierkegaard, S. (1947). *The concept of dread*. Princeton, NJ: Princeton University Press.

Perls, F., Hefferline, R., & Goodman, P. (1951). *Gestalt therapy: Excitement and growth in the human personality*. New York: Dell.

Satir, V. (1972). *Peoplemaking*. Moab, UT: Real People Press.

Shub, N. (1994a). *The self and present-centered diagnosis*. Columbus, OH: Gestalt Associates.

Shub, N. (1994b). *Understanding awareness*. Columbus, OH: Gestalt Associates.

Stevens, J. L. (1986). *Awareness*. Moab, UT: Real People Press.

Szasz, T. (1994). Mental illness is still a myth. *Society*, *31*(4), 23-29.

Wilber, K. (1995). *How to fix everything*. Boston: Shambhala.

Zinker, J. (1978). *The creative process in Gestalt therapy*. New York: Vintage Books.

Chapter 3

INTERNAL DYNAMICS OF SELF

C. Jesse Carlock

Two competing forces are at work when it comes to the dynamics of self: a force toward greater self-enhancement and self-actualization, and a force toward self-consistency and stability. Both of these forces must be honored in order to change self-esteem.

The force toward self-enhancement represents the desire to improve ourselves, to be the best we can be. It is a drive toward wholeness and fulfilling our potentials. This book is based on the premise that people have an innate drive toward self-actualization. Most of us hold the value, desire, and ability to grow to our highest potential.

As we embark on this growth path, however, we are likely to encounter a second competing force: the striving for stability and self-consistency. While some may frame this force negatively as resistance to change, it also represents a healthy attempt to preserve the stability of the self and to protect the self from disorganization and identity confusion. However imperfect the self may be, it does organize our way of being in the world. Any threat to that identity, even attempts to shift the self-view in positive directions, likely will meet with a variety of defensive and compensatory mechanisms striving to bring the self back to a state of equilibrium. Therefore, an effective strategy for change must include a way to manage these natural conservative forces in the personality while moving toward the goal of greater wholeness. That is the focus of this chapter.

FORCES TOWARD SELF-CONSISTENCY

Forces toward self-consistency help to preserve a coherent sense of self, to make our worlds more predictable and manageable. A number of authors have suggested that people tend to lean toward what is familiar because it provides a sense of security (Josephs, 1991; McNulty & Swann, 1991). This pattern holds true even when the self-view is negative. Theories such as cognitive consistency theory (Festinger, 1957) and balance theories have been proposed to explain this drive toward self-consistency. However, as McNulty and Swann (1991) point out, these theories fall short of explaining why people care about consistency. McNulty and Swann contended that we strive for self-consistency so we can predict and control our social environments.

Josephs (1991) believed that we tend to duplicate our roots when we choose careers and interpersonal environments that recreate dimensions of our family of origin. We do this to ensure self-cohesion through changing times and contexts. In addition, Josephs (1991) proposed that we develop identity themes early in life which organize our perceptions. Anything that runs counter to these themes (for example, being obedient and self-controlled) must be disowned and projected since it represents a threat. We also develop themes for how we view the world (for example, the world is a hostile place) and how we view others (for example, people are generally good). Various internal mechanisms work to preserve these views. In the next section, I will outline some of these mechanisms of self-maintenance.

MAINTENANCE OF SELF-ESTEEM

Defense Mechanisms

Freud (1936) outlined a number of defense mechanisms used to protect the self-concept. These mechanisms, which he called *distortions*, are strategies we use to filter out unwanted information and temporarily cope with internal conflict. While defense mechanisms distort reality, they are, to some degree, adaptive measures. Without defenses we could not function. Some defense mechanisms and their relationship to self-esteem maintenance are shown in Table 3.1.

We resort to these defense mechanisms to protect our view of ourselves. We also employ them to adjust the demands of the external world to the de-

TABLE 3.1
Defense Mechanisms and Relationships to Self-Esteem Maintenance

Definition	Example of How the Defense Maintains Self
Repression: Knows only that something which should be present has disappeared. Operates at an unconscious level.	If a young man feels intense jealousy toward his older brother and wishes he would lose his job or fail, he may simply banish this intolerable thought from his conscious mind (it operates outside of his awareness). The hostility does not disappear, but his self-concept as a loving brother is preserved.
Projection: Symbolic means by which something actually inside the ego is perceived and represented as though it were outside.	A woman who is unable to accept her own tension and anxiety as a speaker may complain that the audience seemed very tense. In this way, she avoids dealing with her own anxiety.
Displacement: Transfer of emotion. The object of emotion is switched.	A man whose self-concept does not allow him to feel or express hostility to his boss, may come home and find some pretense to act out his anger with his wife or children.
Reaction Formation: Involves repressing a feeling inconsistent with the self-concept and then professing the exact opposite of that feeling.	A woman unaccepting of her own sexual desires may join a campaign against "immorality." In this way, she avoids coming to terms with the sexual part of self, which does not fit into her own image.
Intellectualization: Hides unacceptable feelings behind a smoke screen of fancy intellectual analysis, avoiding the pain of directly facing these feelings.	A man may talk about how difficult it is to make a relationship work, how many societal pressures put a strain on relationships. What he means is, "I feel like a failure. My wife chose to leave me." Through social analysis, he blocks out his emotional response.

Table 3.1. Continued.

Denial: A person simply denies whatever threatens his or her self-concept. Awareness is narrowed. Secrets are kept from the self.	A woman may refuse to believe that she has a drinking problem. Through denial, she presents herself as in control and adequately coping with life.
Sublimination: Impulses are rechanneled from forbidden outlets to more creative outlets that are acceptable to the self.	A man channels some of his high sexual appetite into productive work activities rather than into extramarital affairs. Beating someone on the tennis court may be his way to release anger toward a boss. In this way he can avoid directly confronting his own sexual and aggressive urges.
Regression: An inability to go on functioning at fully mature levels (i.e., thinking and judgment become impaired). Preserves the integrity of the psychodynamic system at some level short of complete dissolution.	When a woman is faced with a crisis she feels unable to handle, she dissolves into tears and retreats to bed. This enables her to avoid dealing with reality.
Dissociation: Snapping of the associating link between any of the elements of experience: behavior, affect, sensation, or knowledge.	During a traumatic sexual experience a woman experiences herself viewing the event from a point above. She describes the event devoid of emotion or physical sensation.

mands of our consciences. The defenses we employ, however, are only stop-gap adaptations. We can afford only a certain degree of distortion in our perception before our functioning is negatively affected. If our self-image continually must be protected from our actual feelings and character traits, the self-concept may be too rigid and unrealistic.

For example, if we believe we must *always* be nice, kind, and understanding, we are likely to resort to repression, denial, projection, or other defense mechanisms to maintain that image and to ward off repudiated aspects of our selves. Feelings such as anger or selfish behaviors are likely to be repressed or denied. People with low self-esteem–those who lack positive aspects to draw upon to affirm their overall image and counter threats–often must resort to rationalization or to downward social comparisons to restore feelings of adequacy (Spencer, Spencer, Josephs, & Steele, 1993).

To assess your adaptability of functioning, you might ask yourself these questions:

- To what degree am I functioning effectively in the world?

- To what degree is my behavior and thinking facilitating my movement toward my life goals?

- To what degree might my feelings be somaticized (that is, symptoms appearing in my body)?

- To what extent does my self-view match the feedback I receive from others?

If they are carried to an extreme, our defenses can block out or distort our awareness of important internal and external information and can impede growth and coping. On the other hand, if not carried to an extreme, these defenses are a part of how we cope.

When we are desperate, we tend to accept almost anything to satisfy our need. To a starving man, a piece of stale bread satisfies hunger as well as a steak. Likewise, a trace of a smile from an otherwise abusive, sadistic mother can be an oasis for a deprived child who yearns for some sign of acceptance and love. Needs can blind us to reality, and can alter the standards we normally expect. Like any intense emotion, fear also can blind us. This is exemplified by such expressions as, "I was blind with rage," "I was so angry I couldn't see straight," or "I was so afraid that I didn't hear anything you said after that." When the circuits get overloaded, the sensory and cognitive systems shut down.

After suppressing, denying, or projecting a need or feeling for some time, we may find ourselves suddenly flooded with the need or the feeling, and it finally breaks through the surface of its own accord, outside of our control.

Denial often keeps us in situations that, though harmful, are familiar. Many people adopt the position, "What I don't see can't hurt me." Often, one cannot escape being hurt by self-deception. Self-deception is the primary tool used to preserve the status quo. In a more positive vein, researchers tell us that early in the diagnosis and treatment stages of a life-threatening illness, denial is a way of modulating awareness so that the patient can focus on delegating responsibilities and undergoing medical tests, surgery, or whatever other immediate treatments are necessary. The full psychological impact of the disease must be held at bay or the patient might be overwhelmed and unable to function.

Facing "what is" often necessitates change. Although change is a natural part of human existence, most of us fear it. Some people avoid giving up outdated self-images, for with changes come endings, and with endings comes chaos. So resistance to change is natural. We have a strong need to preserve our sense of identity. Attempts to expand the self can be experienced as disorganizing and a threat to identity (Josephs, 1991). Learning to segment change into digestible units and to bear the chaos are skills we must master (see chapter 9).

COGNITIVE-PERCEPTUAL MECHANISMS

People with low self-esteem exhibit a number of common cognitive distortions. Several authors have stressed the role cognition plays in the development and perpetuation of psychopathology (Beck, 1967; Ellis & Harper, 1976; Meichenbaum, 1974). This view focuses on the roles played by our cognitive processes, beliefs, and perceptions. Different perceptual filters affect and are affected by self-esteem. As McNulty and Swann (1991) pointed out, our beliefs about ourselves lead us to expect treatment consistent with those beliefs. These expectations also influence behavior and perceptions. By heightening awareness and challenging our self-talk, self-labels and world view, we can effect change in our beliefs, perceptions, feelings, and ultimately our self-esteem.

Figure 3.1 stresses the cyclical, reinforcing nature of thoughts, images, emotions, and behavior on self-esteem. Each interacts with and influences the other (McNulty & Swann, 1991). So unrealistic and illogical thinking can seriously affect our mental health and perpetuate a negative self-image.

Beck (1967), Beck et al. (1979), Burns (1993), and McKay and Fanning (1987) described a number of thought distortions related to self-esteem. These (shown in Table 3.2) are applicable to children, adolescents, and adults alike.

Assumptions: Shoulds

Beck et al. (1979), Burns (1992), and McKay and Fanning (1987) described how assumptions and beliefs are related to self-esteem. Assumptions are part of the foundation of self-esteem and, while some may be innocuous or even enhancing of self-esteem, others may be harmful.

Our cognitions often are based on untested assumptions we learned early in life. These assumptions must be identified, and often revised, for high self-esteem to be established or maintained. For example, if I hold the assumption, "If I'm nice, bad things won't happen to me," then either it's my fault when bad things do happen or life is unfair (Beck et al., 1979; Burns, 1992). A number of automatic thoughts can stem from one primary assumption, and we must explore and modify the role these assumptions play in our feelings about ourselves (Burns, 1992; Gardner & Oien, 1981).

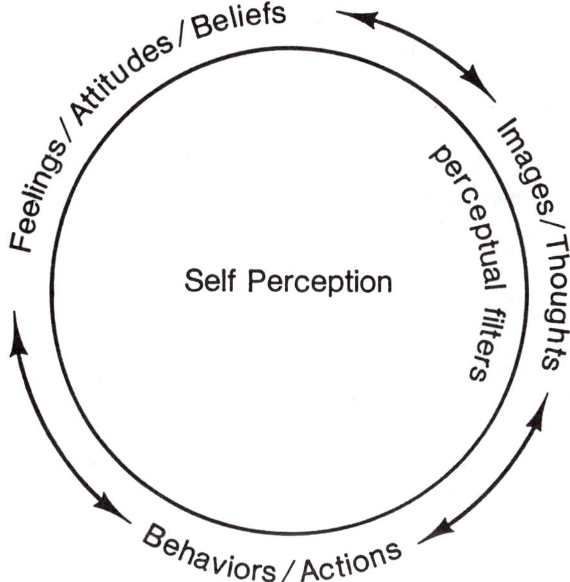

Figure 3.1. Bases of self-perception: Cycle of interaction and influence through perceptual filters.

Most negative emotions can be traced to self-defeating assumptions. Specific behavioral and cognitive techniques described by Beck et al. (1979) and Burns (1992) can be employed to modify such assumptions. One subtype of assumptions is "shoulds" or rules for living. We often hold an only partially conscious list of shoulds against which we measure our performance. These shoulds generally are adopted wholly (introjected) from significant others and cause us to judge ourselves as inadequate relative to impossibly idealistic standards. Some examples of these rules are, "Don't be angry," "Be perfect," and "Be responsible for everyone's feelings."

These standards, values, or rules for living usually are set in absolute terms (Beck et al., 1979; Burns, 1992) and, conveyed directly or indirectly, prevent us from identifying or enjoying our own successes, determining our priorities, deciding what we want, and expressing ourselves genuinely. Trying to meet other's expectations consumes our energy, and we seldom are successful in living up to such rigid rules. Shoulds create emotional jails (Satir, 1978).

As Aesop told us, "You can't please everyone. If you try, you lose yourself." Competing shoulds complicate the picture and create additional conflicts

(Text continues on page 96.)

TABLE 3.2
Cognitive Distortions Related to Self-Esteem

Distortion	Example
Engaging in negative free associations unconnected to an immediate external stimulus.	A high school student is given a surprise quiz by a teacher. The student begins to dwell on times in childhood when a parent labeled him inadequate, stupid, lazy.
Little attempt to direct thoughts; thoughts arise automatically and involuntarily.	A client tells a counselor that negative self-thoughs (such as "I'm worthless") enter her mind all the time; that she can do nothing about it, it just happens.
Magnifying failure or defect and minimizing or ignoring favorable characteristics.	A teacher is faced with a female student who says she knows she will flunk a science course because she flunked the last test. The student believes she is doomed to failure in science, even though she has had some good grades on quizzes.
Comparing oneself unfavorably with others.	A 10-year-old bay compares his skills with those of his older brother.
Blaming oneself with no logical basis.	A woman blames herself for all mistakes her children make, taking responsibility for people and matters over which she has no control.
Maintaining an enormous range of "shoulds" and "musts" with persistence, even when it is unfeasible to carry them out.	A man feels he should always be perfect on the job and never make a mistake.
Having an overall systematic bias against or for oneself.	A client almost always blames herself for unfavorable happenings. Clients of this sort frequently apologize. Others with high self--esteem may be overconfident and discredit evidence to the contrary.

Tending toward arbitrary inference, where conclusions are drawn from insufficient evidence and there is evidence to the contrary.	A boy is critical of himself because of his perceived inability to make friends, when actually he recently enrolled in a "cliquish" school.
Tending to focus on one detail of a situation, ignore other aspects, and conceptualize the situation based on this limited information.	A client has low self-esteem as a result of a recent argument with his parents. He blames himself for the argument, but his parents were upset that day because of an argument they had before he arrived.
Tending to magnify situations inappropriately.	A man tells himself he is a totally worthless person because he was laid off from work.
Perceiving a wide range of life experiences through the filter of low or high self-esteem.	A woman with low self-esteem develops a self-fulfilling prophecy that life generally provides a "raw deal" because she deserves it. On the other hand, a woman with high self-esteem, believing she is competent and worthy, notices opportunities and attends to peoples' positive reactions.
Engaging in polarized thinking.	A client sees everything as black or white, with no gray areas. She sees herself as either a raving success or a complete failure.
Mind reading.	A young girl projects her negative self-view onto others and assumes that others think she is boring or "stuck up."
Selective attention. Occurs when one attends to and interprets feedback that confirms one's self-view.	A man with low self-esteem is given a job review that contains several several high ratings and one lower rating. He focuses on the one low rating. A man with high self-esteem, on the other hand, focuses on the high ratings and emphasizes his strengths.

Note: Table is original. Idea initiated from Beck (1967); Beck, Rush, Shaw, and Emery (1979); and McKay and Fanning (1987).

and no-win situations. When these shoulds are examined thoroughly, we may decide we want to retain some, modify others, and discard a few. When we consciously evaluate and revise our own life rules, they are more manageable, more easily incorporated into our lives, and more easily acted upon.

When we attempt to meet all the competing expectations of significant others and institutions (for example, religious institutions), on the other hand, we are easily thrown into conflict and end up feeling torn, used, and inadequate. Beattie (1987) and Newman and Berkowitz (1977a, 1977b) pointed out several fears that arise when we contemplate giving up our need to please others, including these: "Who will I be without others telling me what to do and how to be? Who will tell me what to do then? Will it mean that no one will love me? Who will I blame if things go wrong?"

Comparing Self to Others

Comparing ourselves to others often results in diminished self-esteem, because we always will find some areas in which the others surpass us. These differences become more pronounced when we compare ourselves with a person who is in a "different league." For example, carpenter apprentices comparing their work to master carpenters are bound to come out on the short end. Comparing ourselves to other apprentices is a more logical point of comparison, while comparing our own performance over time or measuring our movement toward our goals is even better. If I have a picture of what my life will be like when I'm 30, and the reality of my life falls short of this image, it might be healthy to challenge myself: "What's keeping me stuck? What's happened to my dream? Am I taking enough risks?"

If we end up feeling negative about ourselves because of a comparison, the method of comparison needs to be modified, for it is self-damaging rather than growth-producing. *Healthy comparisons* result in our assessing our progress, highlighting the areas we might need to transform or strengthen. If we more fully identify our uniqueness, or we are encouraged to change, then the process of comparison can help us clarify or strengthen our sense of "I" and further define ourselves without judgment. An internal reference base is helpful and healthy; but an internal reference does not occur in a vacuum, it must relate to an external reference point.

Self-Blame

Individuals who take more responsibility than necessary (most commonly for flaws and failures) experience a high level of guilt and self-blame, which tends to erode self-esteem. Such affective symptoms typically arise from extremely high standards of behavior. In addition, people with low self-esteem tend to focus on their weaknesses, becoming preoccupied with these weaknesses in order to avoid failure, anxiety, humiliation, and rejection (Tice, 1993).

Individuals who suffer severe guilt tend to lay heavy blame on themselves. They often adhere to beliefs or values given them by important authorities with whom they interacted and upon whom their lives depended during childhood. These authorities typically were harsh in their punishment and tended to project their own self-hatred onto others.

Guilt is originally a response taught by parents in the service of control (Steiner, 1974). Steiner said that guilt prevents children from striving for the things that they want but that their parents don't want them to have. When we refuse to or are unable to meet the expectations of significant figures, we experience guilt.

We experience guilt, then, when our behavior (or even our thoughts) violates certain values, expectations, or shoulds. If we freely choose our shoulds, our guilt serves to alert us to a violation of our own integrity, so we can bring our behavior back in line with our values–which ultimately enhances our self-esteem. But if we adopt these values without critical appraisal, our guilt only signals that the values deserve evaluation, reevaluation, and perhaps revision.

Feelings and beliefs such as "I'm worthless," "I'm defective," "I'm bad," or "I'm flawed" are not "natural" to human beings. Children are not born with these beliefs or with low self-esteem. They are molded into their negative self-image. Figure 3.2 shows the experience of a child named Joan, who hears negative self-messages repeatedly from an entire network of people.

Messages such as these help us form a distorted "bad self" belief. This belief is not an accurate reflection of our self-worth, yet as children we swallow such beliefs about ourselves indiscriminately. Having introjected them, many of us go on to act out these images through self-effacing or destructive behaviors.

According to Whitfield (1987), family rules, family messages, and a lack of safety often prevent a child's true self from emerging (see Figure 3.3). Whitfield also maintained that many of us use compulsive behaviors to manage our internal conflict between competing beliefs (for example, "I am good" and "I am bad").

Self-Fulfilling Prophecy

Self-Consistency. People with high self-esteem tend to manifest success, while people with low self-esteem tend to manifest failure. Our picture of ourselves becomes a self-fulfilling prophecy that we often feel is inescapable. For example, if I believe I'm a lousy speaker, I will notice anyone in the audience who is fidgeting or looking away. In turn this selective attention and my

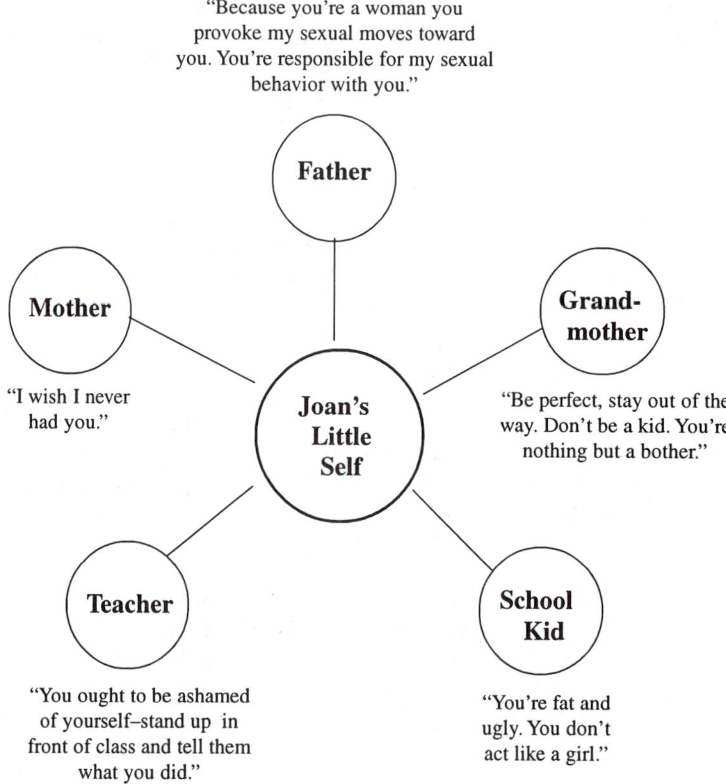

Figure 3.2. Formation of the "bad self."

projection of the meaning ("They are bored!") will increase my anxiety and my speech errors, and decrease my energy and enthusiasm, ultimately creating my original belief (I am a lousy speaker).

Through our attitudes and beliefs about ourselves, others and the world, we guarantee particular outcomes. Jourard and Landsman (1980, p. 187) explained this clearly:

> Thus, when persons form self-concept, thereby defining themselves, they are not so much describing nature as they are making a pledge that they will continue to be the kinds of people they believe they now are and have been. One's self-concept is not so much descriptive of experience and action as it is prescriptive. The self-concept is a commitment.

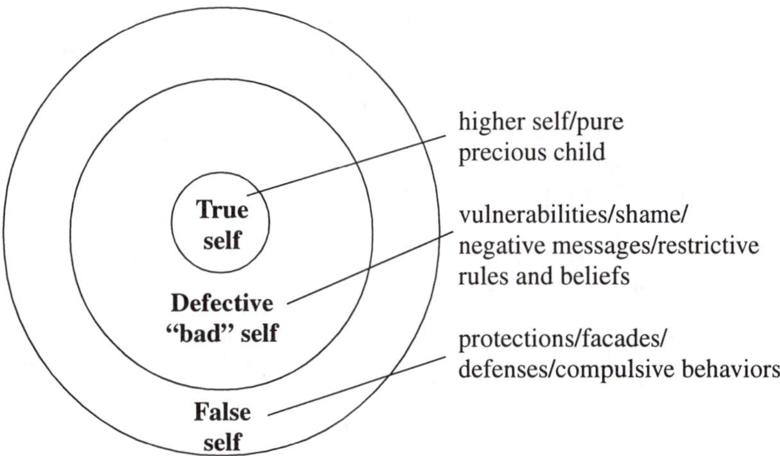

Figure 3.3. Layers of self.

Of course, such prophecies can work to advantage when predicting success or growth. Merely changing the language we use to describe ourselves can allow for the possibility of change (Satir, 1981). For example, we might change, "I'm terrible at giving speeches" to "Up till now, I've had a hard time giving speeches." Hope and hopelessness are revealed in our language.

We also validate our self-views by choosing people for our support network who verify these self-concepts, display identity cues (such as clothing, cars, or titles) that engender a particular self-view, and behave in ways that call forth feedback from others which confirms our self-perceptions (McNulty & Swann, 1991). By altering our support networks and identity cues to reflect the new self-view, we can facilitate a change in self-perception.

Goal Selection. In order to succeed we must be able to make an accurate assessment of ourselves, the situation, and our own ability to meet our commitments. If success is the desired outcome, then choosing goals slightly below our optimum capability is wise (Baumeister, Heatherton, & Rice, 1993). Individuals with both high and low self-esteem show patterns of goal selection that serve to keep their self-esteem consistent.

People with low self-esteem have a weakly developed knowledge of themselves (Baumeister, 1991). That is why it is crucial for parents, teachers, and other caregivers to help children come to know, believe, and articulate their core positive traits. Without such self-knowledge, they may be handicapped in judging their abilities and setting appropriate goals (Baumgardner, 1990;

Heatherton & Ambady, 1993). They may set goals so low that their achievements are relatively meaningless, or so high that they cannot succeed. They also are more likely to attribute failure to themselves than to externalize it (Heatherton & Ambady, 1993). In response to a threat or challenge, people with low self-esteem also tend to respond with self-protection (cautiousness, conservatism) rather than self-enhancement maneuvers. While adaptive, this response is not likely to increase self-esteem.

People with higher self-esteem tend to select higher goals, which leads to better performance (Levy & Baumgardner, 1991). Males in general tend to experience themselves as more competent and to choose more difficult goals, according to Levy and Baumgardner (1991). One study showed that ego threat appears to inhibit adequate self-regulation in males with high self-esteem. When their ego was threatened, males in this study (Levy & Baumgardner, 1991) tended to set goals that produced higher rates of failure. They tended to behave in irrational ways when their self-esteem was impugned.

Those with high self-esteem tend to take higher risks, which exposes them to increased numbers of failures, according to Heatherton and Ambady (1993). However, they use a variety of coping strategies to manage this: attributing failure to external causes, refocusing on positive qualities they possess, and discrediting others to enhance themselves. People with high self-esteem tend to respond to failure with increased persistence and predict optimistic performance even when increased persistence is unproductive, since it is attributable to external causes.

Illusions. Heatherton and Ambady (1993) explained that, in order to preserve self-esteem, we may ignore data and resist changing maladaptive behavior. We may ward off criticism, resulting in continued self-defeating behavior. The authors stressed that people who are more realistic about their good and bad points are less vulnerable to illusions of control, but also may be more likely to be depressed. According to Heatherton and Ambady (1993), extremely high and extremely low self-esteem may both, therefore, produce regulatory dysfunction.

Self-Serving Biases. Blaine and Crocker (1993) indicated that people with high self-esteem show biases in the meaning they place on positive and negative events, in what information they recall, in their judgments about the credibility of feedback, in changes in their self-view after feedback, and in their judgments of control. The authors noted that people with low self-esteem do not show these self-serving biases. Instead, they tend to show a negative self-basis. For example, they tend to avoid opportunities to perform publicly out of fear of embarrassment, and they avoid competition because failure would result in lowered self-esteem. Both individuals with high and low self-esteem prefer positive feedback.

Lacking adequate self-knowledge, people with low self-esteem tend to approach situations cautiously, with a goal of avoiding failure. Blaine and Crocker (1993) explained that people with low self-esteem will prepare excuses in advance; but, if failure ensues, they will not be surprised and will assume the failure resulted from their lack of ability. The authors also contended that people with low self-esteem often are unsure that they can maintain success in the future, and try to protect themselves by discounting positive feedback and by attributing success to external causes.

Self-Handicapping. According to Tice (1993), self-handicapping involves engaging in behaviors that are likely to have a negative effect on one's performance (for example, getting drunk the night before a big exam). "Self-handicapping both provides an excuse for failure and enhances credit for success" (p. 43).

Individuals with low self-esteem tend to structure situations so that self-handicapping provides protection for failure. On unimportant tasks, Tice indicated, they practice more if there is a *chance of failing*; on important tasks, they reduce their practice, which increases their chance of failure and adds ambiguity, thereby protecting self-esteem. In contrast, individuals with high self-esteem practice more on unimportant tasks if there is a chance to *look outstanding*, while on important tasks, they tend to self-handicap in order to enhance their self-esteem. In other words, individuals with high self-esteem self-handicap to *enhance* rather than to *protect* self-esteem. While the behaviors are similar, the goals are different.

People with low self-esteem also tend to avoid tasks on which they have performed exceptionally well in the past, and to persist at tasks on which they have had humiliating failures. Tice (1993) explained that they do this because they are determined to correct deficiencies in order to avoid failure and humiliation. People with high self-esteem, on the other hand, tend to avoid tasks at which they have failed, especially if the failure was humiliating. People with high self-esteem spend more time cultivating their successes, according to Tice (1993).

Safety-Risk Ratio. Thoughtful risk-taking helps to expand self-concept and strengthen self-esteem. Branden (1993, p. 56) stated, "confining yourself to the familiar and undemanding serves to weaken self-esteem." Opportunities for growth and revitalization are limited without appropriate risk-taking, and the self becomes stagnant. Spencer et al. (1993) indicated that people with high self-esteem tend to take more risks, whereas those with low self-esteem tend to avoid risks. Without risk-taking we cannot improve ourselves. Spencer et al. (1993) substantiated this belief, but only when individuals with low self-esteem expected to be informed of the outcomes. When individuals with low self-esteem did not expect to be informed of the outcomes, risk levels equaled those of high self-esteem individuals. Since people generally receive feedback on the risks they take, people with low self-esteem who take lower risks miss a lot of opportunities for self-development.

FORCES AND TECHNIQUES FOR SELF-ENHANCEMENT

Numerous authors throughout the years have claimed that humans have a drive toward self-enhancement and maximizing their perceptions of self-worth (Allport, 1955; Josephs, 1992; Kohut, 1977; McDougall, 1993). The Human Potential Movement of the 1960s, the current proliferation of pop psychology books and talk shows pursuing psychological and relational themes, the expansion of the self-help movement, and adult education all attest to the investment many people have in enhancing their self-worth. People of all ages seem to be willing to look at themselves and risk change. In this section we will review strategies that are useful in self-enhancement.

Awareness

Being aware of our sensations, feelings, thoughts, and fantasies puts us in touch with our needs and wants. Self-esteem increases when we are able to recognize our needs and take action to meet them.

As children mature in their language ability, they learn to read their internal signals and to communicate their feelings, thoughts, wants, and needs. A large part of this ability to accurately label experiences comes from the ability of parental figures to accurately label and meet the needs of infants and young children. For example, when a child is whiny and cranky in the middle of a stimulating and active day, the parent may accurately read these symptoms as fatigue and arrange for the child to have a nap. A parent who reacts to the whining with irritation and anger, instead of recognizing the underlining need and responding to it, impedes the child's learning the important skill of self-regulation–which includes self-awareness and need recognition and satisfaction.

Persons with low self-esteem often have difficulty recognizing and expressing feelings and emotions such as anger, fear, joy, and longing. When feelings habitually go unrecognized, psychological and physical symptoms frequently result. For example, backaches may be attributable to repressed anger (see chapter 5). If anger and resentments go unrecognized, the person is powerless to correct the situation and may dull the disturbing tensions and constrictions that accompany these feelings. Continued dulling or desensitization results in inadequate coping. The body, after all, does provide us with signals about our emotional life–if we will listen. When these cues are deadened, we become incapable of feeling and then meeting our needs. In order to experience ourselves fully, we have to achieve a certain level of body and feeling awareness–a friendly relationship with our bodies and our feelings.

While unconscious desensitization can impair self-esteem, choiceful desensitization can help preserve self-esteem. If you are bombarded with feedback and other stimuli, the ability to focus on one interaction and to desensitize yourself to other stimuli allows you to manage the situation more effectively–and effective coping enhances your self-esteem. Say, for example, that I need toothpaste. I go to a huge discount store to find it, but I have only a few minutes to make my purchase or I will be late for an appointment. I need the skill of desensitization to accomplish my task and avoid becoming distracted by all the other merchandise and tempting sales items. Otherwise, I might become overloaded and be unable to complete my task in the allotted time (Gestalt Institute of Cleveland, 1979).

Too much awareness also can prevent a person from being in an experience and enjoying it to the fullest: For example, too much self-consciousness in sex can inhibit pleasure and prevent orgasm. In our complex, modern world, the self also is a source of stress, and escape from awareness brings relief. High standards and worry over reaching goals can create enormous stress. Stress research shows that people need respite from unpleasant experiences–safe intervals to relax (Baumeister, 1991). It is the choiceful modulation of awareness that promotes and enhances self-esteem.

Parts of the Self

Awareness and ownership of everything about ourselves leads to high self-esteem (Satir, 1976, 1978). Satir (1978) stressed the importance of owning all our thoughts, images, feelings, words, body, voice, actions, gestures, fantasies, and triumphs. By owning all of our parts, we develop a healthy, productive relationship with ourselves. And by coming to know ourselves, we gain the knowledge we need to present ourselves in a positive, self-enhancing manner. According to Satir, we all have within us the resources we need to be effective and happy–all we need to do is own and tap these parts, work through conflicts arising among the parts, and encourage greater cooperation among parts.

Satir developed a vehicle called the *Parts Party* to identify and make manifest the various resources in a person's personality and to work toward the integration of these parts. To bring our internal processes to life, Satir created flesh-and-blood characters to represent our self-aspects. All the senses are involved, which enhances learning. Excitement builds as characters come alive, speak, move, and interact. Various characters portraying personality parts are invited to a party. What unfolds in the course of the party reflects what goes on internally. The Parts Party is a relatively untapped vehicle for expanding and changing self-concept (see Carlock, 1991).

The personality is shaped by a variety of genetic and environmental influences. Constitutional factors provide the foundation. The shape our personality takes is then influenced by our caretakers, who reinforce, limit, discourage, or punish particular behaviors through overt and covert rules (for example, "Be quiet," "Sit still," "Don't cry," "Don't talk back"). Punishment can take the form of verbal, physical, or emotional (rejection, abandonment) consequences. Critical interpersonal experiences at nodal developmental points also affect identity formation (Josephs, 1991). Such experiences affect a person's expressive functions and self-view.

According to Satir, distortions in self-concept can occur because of the parents' incompleteness: That is, caregivers may disown parts of themselves and project these qualities onto their children. Or, because of their own neurotic preoccupation or internal conflicts, they may neglect or abuse their children, seriously affecting their self-concept. Self-concept and self-esteem often are built on a "house of cards." Revision is necessary to clear distortions, reveal blind spots, and reconstruct a more realistic sense of self.

Habit patterns gradually cluster to form personality traits, until they finally crystallize into a particular pattern of behavior–a personality style (Millon & Everly, 1985). In Satir and Banmen (1983), Satir pointed out that the more particular behaviors are practiced, the more solid or entrenched they become, and the harder it is to entertain other behavior possibilities. We can entertain other possibilities, she claimed, only when there is trust (that you will be treated like you count, listened to, and heard), laughter, hope, and validation. The Parts Party, which incorporates each of these elements, can be a potent vehicle for changing self-image and self-esteem.

Parts we deny are like ropes around us, limiting our range of responsiveness. Often these limitations develop indirectly, because we lack models of particular behaviors, attitudes, and feelings. Or they develop directly, through prohibitions, beliefs, and rules aimed at governing our behavior. A cognitive map is formed through learned assumptions, which then limits our experience, behavior, and feelings. Many of these limits are outdated and ineffective. The Parts Party provides a "psychic hole" to highlight such limitations, to point out choice points; it allows us to look at what might happen if we were to activate these lost parts, thereby expanding and differentiating the self.

Through the Parts Party process, previously unknown personality parts and disowned qualities are better integrated into the personality, thereby reducing distortion and projection onto others. Disowned qualities include both positively and negatively valued aspects. Someone who experienced a childhood trauma, for example, may have introjected a "bad me" self-concept. In this case, room must be made to incorporate more positive traits, such as "intelligent," "loving," and "giving," which accurately characterize the person's strengths. Others must work to incorporate aspects valued negatively by or abused by caregivers, such as "powerful" or even "sexy."

One goal of the Parts Party is to help an individual honor whatever qualities are present and to affirm each part as a resource. Even within seemingly negative parts lie seeds of resources. However, typically people label parts as "good" and "bad," then deny or project those labeled bad. As a result, these parts become like neglected and hungry dogs, jumping and barking for recognition. Denied parts may result in symptoms of illness (physical, emotional, or spiritual) or some kind of interactional destructiveness (Satir & Banmen, 1983). The Parts Party provides a vehicle for reframing, modifying, and incorporating such negative parts.

Many of us behave as if we are not in charge of our parts. The Parts Party lets us practice directing parts in the service of self-selected goals. By assuming the "control tower" position and observing the interaction of our personality parts, we can assess which parts are in conflict, which could help in such conflicts, which are missing, which appear overdeveloped, and which might form alliances and effectively move the group toward our desired change. Since another goal is to move people toward greater wholeness, parts may be added to bring balance to the system (for example, balancing agentic and communal qualities or adding playfulness, spirituality, anger, neediness, creativity, or wisdom).

The Parts Party provides many possibilities for transformation. The entire experience is one of self-affirmation. A spiritual feeling develops when we openly reveal ourselves in a loving and appreciative context, for each part is valued and seen for its possibilities. The Parts Party is an exciting intrapersonal journey into inner awareness and self-healing. When we move toward wholeness, toward owning all parts of self, we move toward greater personal effectiveness and higher self-esteem. The greater the integration and harmony of these parts, the higher the satisfaction level. (For workshops on the Parts Party and other Satir methods, contact Carlock and Associates, 1105 Watervliet Ave., Dayton, OH 45420, 937/256-0500.)

DIFFERENTIATION

Bowen (1985, pp. 473-475) described a concept he called *differentiation of self*–the degree to which an individual has developed a "solid self" versus a "pseudo self" (see also Masterson, 1988). The concept is similar to emotional maturity. Differentiation is determined by how we differentiate our parts, our relationships with our parents, and the degree to which we have resolved those relationships (Bowen, 1985). Those with lower levels of differentiation are characterized by diffuse or rigid self-boundaries, while those with higher differentiation have firm but permeable self-boundaries. (See Figure 3.4 for the characteristics of each.) Bowen (1985) identified these common principles:

Differentiation is best assessed during stress.

When one family member makes a step toward differentiation, others in the family take corresponding steps. However, family members often disapprove of such steps, so the differentiating member needs support. Common responses from family members include, "You are wrong. Change back. If you don't, then ... (consequences)."

One who is attempting to differentiate must stay on course without defending self, counter-attacking, or seeking approval.

The *togetherness* or *fusion amalgam* is characterized by phrases such as, "We think," We feel," "It is wrong," "It is the thing to do." According to Bowen (1985), family members in this model are defined as alike in beliefs, feelings, principles, and values. In such families, a positive value is placed on thinking about others before self, sacrificing, and being responsible for others. Differentiation is treated as selfish and hostile (Bowen, 1985).

On the other hand, with self-differentiation, the "I" position defines principles and action. "This is what *I* think/believe/feel." Those with high differentiation do not force their own values on others, Bowen (1985) asserted, but assume responsibility for their own happiness and avoid blaming and making demands on others ("I deserve," "This is my right/privilege"). They also do not yield to others' demands and continue to do what they need to do for themselves. Those with high differentiation are capable of concern for others without expecting something in return.

If we have not worked through our emotional dependence on our parents or significant others, we fail to differentiate and develop personal autonomy. Then we unconsciously live out our parents' message about who we are and their rules for living, carrying their shame without awareness or consciously trying to meet their fantasy of the "ideal child."

The child's attitude toward self directly reflects attitudes of significant people in his or her life (Satir, 1981; Sinetar, 1990). Children who grow up hearing messages such as, "I don't know how you have any friends," "You're clumsy," and "You'll never be neat," are in danger of carrying these labels as lifelong imprints if these messages are not reevaluated. More harmful messages also can be carried, such as the toxic "You don't have the right to exist" (see chapter 2).

Figure 3.4. Differentiation of self.

Diffuse Personal Boundary

- Fuses emotionally with others; is emotionally dependent on others.
- Floods intellect with emotionality.
- Bases decisions on feelings in order to minimize risk of disapproval.
- Evaluates self based on interaction with others.
- Behaves dysfunctionally under stress.
- Creates a pseudo-self due to emotional pressure. This pseudo-self is composed of a vast assortment of principles and beliefs that are random and inconsistent with one another.
- Often is not aware of discrepancies.
- Becomes an actor, and can play many roles.
- Responds to a variety of pressures; the pseudo-self is unstable.
- Orients self totally toward relationships. So much energy goes into seeking love that none is available for life goals.
- Spends energy trying to keep relationships going and trying to achieve a level of comfort and freedom from anxiety.
- Conforms or rebels.
- Fuses emotionally with increased closeness, and then becomes distant and alienated.

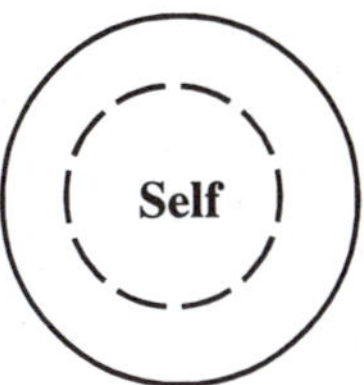

Rigid Boundary

- Resists change.
- Evaluates self unrealistically (far above or below reality) and, as a result, allows little input.

Figure 3.4. Continued.

- Is impervious to feedback.
- Resists emotional fusion through an exaggerated stance of rugged individualism.
- Finds it difficult to absorb stress.

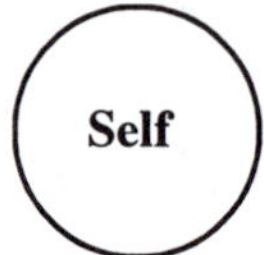

Firm but Permeable Boundary

- Maintains autonomy.
- Separates feeling and thinking. Is able to fully experience feelings and extricate self-worth with logical reasoning when needed.
- Can engage in goal-directed activity or lose self in intimacy.
- Reacts less to praise and criticism.
- Evaluates self realistically.
- Recovers rapidly from stress.
- Defines beliefs, convictions, and life principles carefully. Incorporates into self after careful, logical reasoning (assimilation).
- States own beliefs without the need to attack beliefs of others or to defend own.

Note: Material gleaned from Bowen (1985).

Negative messages often are firmly entrenched before they are revised or discarded. For many people, self-esteem is based on distortions that have no basis in reality. These learnings are rarely intentional and frequently are drawn from incomplete, inaccurate, and outdated information (Satir, 1981). Our parents learned exactly the same way. Satir (1981) indicated that children see the world through the eyes of their parents and the interpretations they make.

If we act out a self-image rooted in another, we are a prisoner of that person's construction of our self-concept. We have not taken the opportunity to evaluate the validity of such judgments and make our own decisions. A young boy who is living out his father's dream of being a football hero, not consciously deciding whether the dream is his own, is not likely to experience full joy in his accomplishments. The dream may be unrealistic, or it simply may not fit him. A boy determined to resist his father's dream, even if it is a perfect fit, is equally controlled.

As children grow, they must begin to make statements of protest and self-affirmation, to learn to say "nos" and clear "yesses." Sometimes this occurs spontaneously, as in the case of the average 2-year-old, who stiffens all over, shakes her heads, sticks out her jaw, and says "no" to everything. In order to establish and maintain our individuality, we must accept both the pain and the pleasure we experience in taking risks and leaving support (Keleman, 1975).

Those who have a problem saying "no" have difficulty affirming themselves and exercising their ability to form and maintain personal boundaries. A state of pathological confluence (or blurring of identity) may result, in which the individual has difficulty determining where he leaves off and others begin (Polster & Polster, 1973).

A crucial task in identity development is the ability to make clear "yesses" and "nos." When people exhibit a pattern of saying "yes" when they want to say no, self-esteem erodes. Such behavior conveys the attitude, "Your feelings and rights are more important than mine." This creates an energy block inside, which leads to a build up of resentment, anger, and hurt. Many times people say "yes" when they want to say "no" out of guilt, a misplaced sense of responsibility, or fear of conflict or reprisals. People experience "neurotic" guilt when they break confluence.

In confluence, the person acts as if no difference exists between self and other. If you want me to do something, I do it. If I believe something, you always agree. Many women, for instance, give up their personhood and fuse their identity with their spouse's or child's. There is a loss of self as center.

Others who succumb to pressure to think, behave, or feel a certain way do so for survival (emotional or even physical, in cases of abuse). Emotional fusion is a coping strategy in families where any attempts at individualization represent threats to the powers of authority.

As our self-determined identity forms, our values, beliefs, and guiding principles of behavior are revised until they are uniquely individual. Throughout life, then, these value, belief, and behavior boundaries are challenged through life experiences and, in healthy people, revised as necessary. These alterations are basic to growth and necessitate personal risk-taking in the expansion, contraction, or reshaping of these boundaries (Polster & Polster, 1973).

> For example, 16-year-old Jane was raised in a family in which an explicit rule prohibited expressing personal problems to anyone

> outside the family, and an implicit rule prohibited expressing personal problems inside the family: "Don't tell your mother that, she has a bad heart." Jane grew up stuffing her feelings, even manifesting psychosomatic symptoms. If she identifies, evaluates, and revises those original family rules, Jane might learn to express disturbing feelings to others, thereby expanding her expressive boundaries.

Family rules cover a variety of areas, are conveyed either explicitly or implicitly, and govern conduct that maintains the family system and its power structure. Breaking family rules can result in guilt, admonishment, punishment, or even abandonment or banishment by family members (Carlock, Hagerty, & Verdon, 1985). Family rules cover areas like play, privacy, trust, and expressiveness. Individuals who are growth-oriented reevaluate and refine such rules throughout life.

Taking a stand means making our own decisions, knowing and accepting that some will work and others will not. When we define our own values, needs, and beliefs, they are no longer a patchwork quilt of other people's. We become more than a watered-down version of ourselves whose main goal is to avoid others' displeasure. We become distinctly individual. In being honest, we risk rejection but, at the same time, reap the reward of knowing that when people like us, they like us for who we really are.

In order to change, we need to value and honor ourselves, and this means knowing ourselves. It means placing ourselves in the center of our lives and identifying the following:

- What I feel
- What I want
- What I need
- What I believe
- What I value

Honoring ourselves involves formulating a point of view and valuing that point of view as equal to others'. It involves making our boundaries more distinct and determining the direction of our lives. It involves exercising our inner barometer that registers events and tells us whether they bring happiness and satisfaction or tension and discomfort (Miller, 1976). If we live by others' "shoulds," we lose the use of this inner barometer; then we are like rudderless boats at sea.

AFFIRMATIONS

Many authors have stressed the positive effects of self-affirmation and paying careful attention to thoughts that generate feelings of joy, peacefulness, and abundance (Gawain, 1978; Moen, 1992; Ray, 1980; Roman, 1986). We have the power to create our own reality, but many of us are limited by our beliefs:

I can't ...

I don't deserve ...

I have to ...

I should ...

Negative beliefs and thought patterns produce blocks to positive action and put stress on our bodies. Notice what kind of feelings the following statements create in you:

I am happy with who I am.

I am bringing joy into my life.

I am perfect just as I am.

I am open to receiving love.

I am building my inner strength each day.

In order for such affirmations to be effective, they must be believable. They must resonate within. If there is no resonance, the affirmation needs to be revised, or objections to the affirmation must be satisfied first.

Affirmations state the desired outcome as already in the process of being realized. Negative thoughts produce negative results; positive thoughts improve the chances of producing positive results. According to Canfield and Self-Esteem Seminars (1986), the dissonance created by affirmations produces motivation to achieve desired outcomes. By associating the desired outcome with a visual image, affirmations can create even greater power.

Guidelines for Affirmations

The following guidelines for writing affirmations were adapted from Acker-Stone (1987), Canfield and Self-Esteem Seminars (1986), Gawain (1978), and Roman (1986).

1. Begin with the words, "I am ... "

2. Include your name in the affirmation.

3. Choose positive, expansive words.

4. Phrase your affirmations in the present tense.

5. Keep statements short, simple, and specific.

6. Choose affirmations that fit you and express something you want to do and believe you can do.

7. Incorporate your strengths within your affirmations.

8. Choose action words.

9. Include positive feelings words such as joy, serenity, peaceful, delightful, rejoicing, enthusiastic.

10. State affirmations that are in your control. (You cannot, for example, control whether someone else will marry you.)

11. Include a word ending in "ing," (I am serenely *accepting* compliments).

12. Include a feeling word to motivate action (I am *happy* when I receive compliments).

13. Create as many scenes as possible when writing or thinking about the affirmation.

14. Once you have constructed an affirmation, close your eyes, repeat the affirmation several times, and notice what inner images it evokes. If the images the affirmation evokes match your desired outcomes, your affirmation is a good one.

15. Use these images to deepen the effect of the affirmation. Draw a picture to represent each image or clip pictures from magazines to represent your images.

16. Tell your friends your affirmations and share your pictures with them in order to prepare them for your changes.

For best results, write your affirmations on 3" x 5" cards and carry them with you for 90 days. At least three times each day pull out the cards and read your affirmations. Follow this with booster doses one week per month for the next six months. Absorbing and retaining new self-attitudes requires considerable practice.

Another variation of affirmations suggested by Branden (1994) is a method he learned from his wife. Committed to being happy, Branden's wife makes a point each evening of reviewing everything good in her life. She also begins each day with two questions: "What is good in my life?" and "What needs to be done?" The first question focuses her on absorbing blessings big and small. The second question encourages corrective action. What a positive way to begin and end each day!

Framing

How we frame a situation also can affect our self-esteem. We can learn to change the frame we put around events and, thereby, alter the meaning of the event and the feelings around it. The situation remains unchanged, but the meaning associated with it is altered (Bandler & Grinder, 1982; Borysenko, 1987; Watzlawick, Beavin, & Jackson, 1974). To illustrate this concept, Watzlawick et al. (1974) wrote of a man with a severe stammer who was forced by circumstances to become a salesman. His new position heightened his concern about his speech problem. But he soon learned to view his stammer as an asset: Because people generally dislike salesmen for their smooth barrage of words, his stammer put them at ease. He also discovered that people often listen more carefully and patiently to those with handicaps. So he reframed his handicap as an asset. The handicap remained unchanged, but his way of looking at it changed.

Sometimes we must reframe our mistakes in order to increase our self-esteem (McKay & Fanning, 1992). No one is perfect; living means making mistakes. Mistakes often are signs that we are growing, taking risks, and trying new things. McKay and Fanning (1992) also emphasized that mistakes can be our best teachers; they help keep us from going too far astray. McKay and Fanning emphasized that everyone deserves a quota of mistakes. They suggested we allow ourselves an error quota of between one and three bad decisions for every ten decisions we make. The authors also stressed that mistakes are always easy to see after the fact. Can you love yourself, mistakes and all? Do you allow yourself an error quota?

Perspective

As Satir (1981) explained, there is a direct relationship between what people notice, what their attention is called to, and how they interpret the world. Actions are taken based on those interpretations. Satir noted that in Western culture, people tend to notice negatives. Most of the world has a highly developed attention to that which is wrong, bad, or destructive (Satir, 1981). How different our lives and the world would be if we noticed and commented upon what is positive.

Satir (1981) further explained that what we notice and attend to is determined greatly by our position in a system. She used the analogy of a globe.

> I will see what I am in a position to see. I behave as though what I see is all there is to see, and when you over there tell me what you see, I say, "No, it's not true." Then we can fight over who is right.

According to Satir, this fighting over who is right, when we actually are seeing things from different positions, occurs all the time. She noted that rigid people demand that we see the world through their filter and take the same actions they do.

Satir (1981) stressed the role of perception in self-esteem. These perceptions are influenced by the following:

1. the position of people–where they are located in the system;
2. feelings people have about themselves; and
3. the interpretation they place on the data they observe.

Satir contended that people's perceptions often are incomplete, inaccurate, and distorted.

Stilling the Mind

Many authors have pointed to a *lack of connection to our inner voice* as a major source of emotional problems. Mariechild (1987) connected this lack to feelings of despair, alienation, and loneliness. She outlined a familiar sequence of events:

loss of connection to self ⇒ loss of connection to others ⇒ fear and defense ⇒ physical tightening and perceptual narrowing

Our minds are cluttered with thoughts. Stilling the mind requires practice, but the mind can be trained through gradual disciplined cleaning. When our minds are "cleaned," we can hear our inner voice. According to Vaughn (1979), fear and desire are two of the main obstacles to this inner voice. You can choose from various meditative practices to guide you toward inner quiet (Chopra,

1992; Desai, 1990; Hahn, 1976, 1987; LeShan, 1974): Yoga, tai chi, transcendental meditation, healing music, imagery, and communion with nature are but a few.

In our culture we have become so attached to our minds that we have separated from other aspects of ourselves. Once the internal chatter is quieted, our inner voice, body feeling, vision, or dream can be experienced. According to Bennett (1987), our inner voice can help keep us on our path and prevent us from straying into physical, emotional, or spiritual discord. As Hahn noted (1987, p. xi), "If we are peaceful, if we are happy, we can blossom like a flower, and everyone in our family, our entire society, will benefit from our inner peace."

REPRESENTATIONAL SYSTEMS

Representational systems are the methods we use to gain access to our internal experiences. We use different representational systems to reinforce self-esteem. If we can come to understand how we maintain a negative self-image–by what processes, by what internal representational systems–we can more effectively short-circuit the effects. Additionally, we may develop newer, enhanced self-images through direct, purposeful use of these systems. According to Bandler and Grinder (1975) and Grinder, Delozier, and Bandler (1977), we use three main representational systems: visual, kinesthetic, and auditory. Any one of these may function as the lead or most highly valued system. Thus, any situation may be represented in at least three ways. Fire, for example, may be represented as such:

Visual: by seeing the flames

Kinesthetic: by feeling the heat

Auditory: by hearing the crackling flames

By identifying our lead system and the patterns of representational systems we employ, we can learn to reinforce or change our self-esteem. A number of books have addressed the application of Neurolinguistic Programming (NLP) to a variety of problem areas, including Cameron-Bandler (1985) and Cameron-Bandler, Gordon, and Lebeau (1985). Table 3.3 compares representational systems of students with high and low self-esteem who are about to deliver a speech.

Bandler and Grinder (1975) extended the idea of self-talk (Ellis & Harper, 1976), which involves the auditory representational system as the lead. Prior to the work of Bandler and Grinder (1975), the roles of negative and positive thoughts on self-esteem were considered primarily auditory. Now we know that each person uses a unique pattern of internal representational systems. Low

TABLE 3.3
Representational Systems: Comparison of Students with Low and High Self-Esteem About to Deliver a Speech

Representational Systems	Low Self-Esteem	High Self-Esteem
Visual	Pictures self forgetting the speech and imagines other students jeering	Sees self smoothly delivering the talk and pictures other students as attentive and interested
Kinesthetic	Feels a sinking feeling in his or her chest	Feels open, stands straight, breathes fully
Auditory	Imagines the other children laughing at him	Imagines the other children silent in their attentiveness; imagines remarks of encouragement and support; remembers reassurances of others

self-esteem may be maintained through automatic images, feelings, and self-talk, while positive self-esteem might be fostered by creating deliberate positive self-talk, kinesthetic responses, and images around particular experiences; encouraging practice with these can raise self-esteem and promote growth and change.

Other authors have noted the effectiveness of creative visualization in evoking positive change (Gawain, 1978; Lazarus, 1977; Moen, 1992; Singer, 1971). Visualization can help people achieve goals on physical, emotional, mental, and spiritual levels. According to Gawain (1978), visualization is effective in dissolving internal conflicts into a harmony of being. Assagioli (1965) developed a theory of behavior change using visualization as the primary approach in the dissolution of internal conflict.

CHANGING SELF-VIEW

In order to change our self-view, we must sidestep our tendency toward self-consistency. We must learn to tolerate gradual challenges to that view (McNulty & Swann, 1991). According to the authors, this use of disconfirming feedback slowly introduces uncertainty into the self-view.

Through practice of unfamiliar behaviors and attitudes, journaling, artwork, and movement, practice and integrate aspects of the emerging new self-view. We can grade these self-experiments so that they create enough anxiety to be challenging, yet not enough to be overwhelming. For example, a client, Jackie, was trying to develop a self-confident attitude toward herself. In the process of our work, she developed the following hierarchy of behaviors she could practice, numbered from least to worst anxiety-provoking.

1. Identify her beliefs about how to handle a problem among her work team and write these down.

2. Tell a supportive co-worker about her ideas.

3. Tell a co-worker who tends to be challenging about her ideas and while acknowledging the merits of the co-worker's ideas, support her own ideas.

In addition, McNulty and Swann (1991, pp. 213-237) offered the following suggestions to circumvent resistance to the enhancement of self-esteem:

1. Seek positive feedback in areas that do not threaten your self-view.

2. Continually assure yourself that you do know yourself and you are changing.

3. Exaggerate your self-view so that you can gain better perspective on how you actually are.

4. Assume that even though a side of you is underdeveloped, you probably still display that side at some times, in some places, and with some people.

5. Take the position that success on any task should not be taken seriously or alter one's view of self. This "no change" attitude will reduce resistance while having some effect on self-esteem. When success is separated from self-esteem, we are likely to continue to pursue activities that may foster increased success. As successes accumulate, dismissal of these experiences will be more difficult and will ultimately help to modify self-view.

6. Affirm your abilities and traits and point to evidence which substantiates the new self-view.

7. Introduce doubt into the negative self-view by underscoring specific behaviors that run counter to this view.

8. Understand that for a time you may have difficulty changing your view of yourself and will continue to react negatively even though you have changed.

9. Enlist the aid of family and friends in encouraging the new self-view. Otherwise, close associates are likely to reinforce the old, negative view. Ask them to positively reinforce changes in the direction of the desired behavior. Warn them not to criticize initial attempts at change, which may be clumsy.

10. Join groups or organizations likely to value the newly acquired traits or abilities.

The following suggestions also may assist you in changing your self-view:

1. Increase self-awareness to develop an accurate self-assessment and select effective goals.

2. Increase awareness of the pitfalls in your response to ego threats; learn more effective responses.

3. Work to recognize when increased persistence on tasks is effective, and when it is not. You may need feedback to make this distinction.

4. Increase your awareness of pervasive negative or positive self-bias. This will help you learn how and when to filter feedback.

5. Cultivate your strengths and successes so that they stand out more.

CONCLUSION

Self-esteem is a process. The groundwork for our self-esteem is laid in our genetics and in early childhood, although our self-concept is gradually shaped throughout our lifetime. Our attitudes and beliefs about ourselves influence how others view and treat us; our pictures of ourselves become self-fulfilling. But we can change those pictures at any time.

A large repertoire of internal mechanisms protect our views of self. We often prefer a negative self-view to a chaotic self-view. Disruption of the self-view creates confusion. our drive toward self-consistency can be managed, however, and the competing drive toward self-enhancement can be fostered through greater awareness. The increasing willingness to discover, own, and cherish all of our parts ensures the building of higher esteem. The willingness to let go of those beliefs, attitudes, and defenses that no longer fit also ensures a growing healthy self-esteem. A number of strategies have been cited here to help in the transformation of self-view.

We are always changing, continually evolving; but change is threatening. The fear of letting go of old ways is the fear of death. A myriad of emotions arise through the process of self-expansion and the shedding of outdated ways of being. By making room for this emotional journey and garnering support from others along the way, we can manage the disruptive aspects of change and feel the excitement of new beginnings.

ACTIVITIES YOU CAN DO

ACTIVITY 3.1 PARENT DIALOGUE

Introduction: In this activity participants are invited to have a fantasy dialogue with one of their parents in order to come to terms with the parent.

Time required: 45 minutes

Participants: Any number; adolescents and adults

Setting: Carpeted office or classroom

Materials: None

Procedure: Sit comfortably and close your eyes. Visualize one of your parents sitting before you. Take some time to really see your parent, and make contact with him or her. How is he or she sitting? What is he or she wearing. Notice all the details of your parent in front of you. How do you feel as you look at your parent?

Now begin by being completely honest with your parent. Express all the things you never told him or her. Say these things out loud, as if you were actually talking to your parent now. Express everything that comes to your mind: resentments you held back, anger you were afraid to show, love you didn't express, questions you never asked.

Be aware of how you feel as you do this, and notice if you begin to tense your body somewhere. Notice your breathing, your posture. Are you breaking any family rules? Be sure you stay in contact with your parent. Take about five minutes to do this.

Now become your parent, and respond to what you have just said. As your parent, how do you reply to what your child just said? Be aware of how you feel as you do this. How do you feel toward your child? Tell your child how you feel and what you think of him to her. Is this hard for you? Why? What kind of relationship do you have with your child?

Switch places again and become yourself. How do you respond to what your parent just said? What do you say now, and how do you feel as you say it? Tell your parent how you feel and what you think of him or her. How do you experience this relationship? Now tell your parent what you need and want from him or her. Take some time to say exactly and specifically what you want your parent to do for you, and be aware of how you feel as you do this.

Now, become your parent again. As your parent, how do you reply to this expression of needs and wants from your child? How do you feel as you do this? What understanding do you have of what your child is asking? Have you experienced anything similar in your life? Tell your child what you need and want from him or her.

Switch places again and become yourself. How do you respond to what your parent just said? Do you have any better understanding of him or her now? What do you gain by holding onto all these unfinished feelings toward your parent?

Become your parent again and respond. What do you say in reply? What is your relationship like now? Is any understanding developing, or is it still mostly fighting and conflict?

Switch places and become yourself again. How do you respond to what your parent just said? How do you experience your relationship, and what understanding do you have of your parent's situation? Tell your parent whatever understanding you have now.

Tell your parent what you appreciate in him or her. No matter how difficult your relationship is, there must be something you appreciate. Tell your parent about these things now, and be specific and detailed.

Now, become your parent again. How do you respond? Can you really accept your child's appreciation, or do you minimize or reject it? Now, express your appreciation for your child. Tell him or her in detail what you appreciate in him or her.

Become yourself again. How do you respond to the appreciation you just got from your parent? How do you feel toward each other now?

Continue this dialogue for some time, and switch back and forth between being yourself and your parent whenever you want to. Pay attention to what is going on in this interaction and make this explicit. For instance, if you realize that the parent is scolding and blaming, point this out and ask that he or she use "I" statements. Notice when you are tense and holding back, and express yourself more fully. See how much you can express and clarify about this relationship.

You may arrive at a place where both sides are stuck in an unyielding deadlock. As you become more aware of the details of this deadlock, it will gradually become more flexible; when you become fully aware of the conflict, it will begin to untangle. This may take many sessions of struggling, but each time some clarification and deepening of awareness is possible. Eventually, you will arrive at letting go of parents, giving up your demands that they be different, and forgiving them for their faults. You will recognize that they couldn't be other than they were, and that even "forgiving" is irrelevant.

Perhaps the hardest thing we can do in life is letting go of a lost relationship. When an important person in your life has died or left you, he or she continues to exist in your fantasies as if still alive. In a kind of self-hypnosis, you continue to be involved with a dead relationship. When you can complete this relationship and say goodbye, you wake up from your trance and become involved with the living people around you.

Outcomes: Gives a fuller appreciation of what a parent had to give and greater acceptance of the parent as a person with strengths and faults.

Note: Adapted from Stevens (1971, pp. 81-83). Reprinted by permission.

ACTIVITY 3.2 WEAKNESS-STRENGTH

Introduction: This activity helps participants to explore more fully what they perceive as their strong and weak sides, and what they gain and lose from each side.

Time required: 40 minutes

Participants: Any number; adolescents and adults

Setting: Carpeted classroom or office

Materials: None

Procedure: Close your eyes and turn your attention inward. Get in touch with your physical existence. Then have a silent conversation between weakness and strength. Start by being weakness, talking directly to strength. You might say something like, "I'm so weak, and you're so strong, you can do so many things," Talk to strength for a while, and be aware of how you feel, physically, as you do this. Go into specific details about how you are weak, and how strength is strong.

Now switch roles and be strength replying to weakness. What do you say as strength, and how do you say it? How do you feel in this role? How do you feel toward weakness? Tell weakness what it does for you to be strong. What do you gain by being strong?

Now switch roles and be weakness again. How do you reply to strength, and how do you feel as you do this? Tell strength what it does for you to be weak. What do you gain by being weak? Tell about the strength in your weakness. Tell all the advantages of being weak: how you can use your weakness to manipulate others and get them to help you. Go into specific details about the strength of your weakness.

Now become strength again and reply to weakness. What do you say as strength, and how do you feel now? Talk about the weakness in your strength. Tell about the disadvantages of being strong: how others lean on you and drain your energy. Go into specific details about the weakness of your strength.

Continue the dialogue for a while, switching roles whenever you want to, and see what you can discover.

Outcomes: Increases awareness of how you express your strength and weakness; helps you explore the relationship between your strength and weakness; shows the similarities that underlie opposites.

Note: Adapted from Stevens (1971). Reprinted by permission.

This kind of internal dialogue can be immensely useful for pointing out and clarifying relationships between any pair of complementary people, roles, qualities, or aspects, such as husband-wife, parent-child, planner-spontaneous person, strange-familiar, helper-helpless, honest-dishonest, boss-employee, neat-sloppy, male-female, responsible-irresponsible, mind-body, stupid-smart.

Notice what you have difficulty with in your life, then reduce the difficulty to a particular person, behavior, or quality. Think of the opposite of this person, behavior, or quality, and work with it in dialogue. If you invest yourself in this dialogue, you will discover the symmetry and similarity that lies beneath the apparent opposition. In the example above, there is the strength of weakness and the weakness of strength, and also that both sides, use different means to do the same thing: control each other.

ACTIVITY 3.3 TIME OF YOUR LIFE

Introduction: This activity encourages you to take charge of your life by adding more of what you find joyful and paring down those activities you find unrewarding. The activity can help you clarify values and set goals.

Time required: 20 minutes

Participants: Any number, adolescents, adults

Setting: Home, office, or classroom

Materials: Paper and pencil

Procedure: Think of a typical week. Section off the circle below like pieces of pie to indicate how you fill your time (A) and how you'd like to fill your time (B).

(A) How I spend my life

Example:

Your Life:

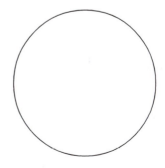

Evaluate how you are spending your time.

Is there a balance in your activities? For example:

- work and play
- active and receptive
- body, mind, emotions, and spiritual

How much time do you spend in activities you consider joyful?

(B) How I'd like to fill my life

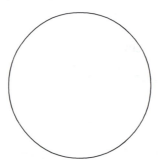

You have the power to change how you live. How could you make your life more joyful? What could you do right now? You can practice inner freedom now. What is your inner being calling you to do? What you love to do belongs in your life. What are your dreams for yourself?

Write your reactions to this activity. Do large discrepancies exist between circles A and B?

What keeps you stuck?

- obligations, shoulds
- needs to be needed
- fear
- feeling undeserving

Discuss your thoughts and feelings with a group of friends.

Outcomes: Heightens awareness of choices in how you spend time; encourages you to set goals to bring your behavior in line with your values.

ACTIVITY 3.4 INNER VOICE

Introduction: Hearing your inner voice requires time and practice in silent reflection. This activity directs you in that process by focusing your attention on your inner life.

Time required: 20 minutes

Participants: Any number; adolescent, adults

Setting: Classroom or office

Materials: None

Procedure: Think of a question that's been on your mind. Meditate on that question for a few moments until it is planted firmly in your mind.

Now imagine yourself in a beautiful, magical garden. The colors are splendid here. Look around at the sky, flowers, birds in the trees; take in everything. Listen to the sounds all around you. Take a deep breath and drink in the smells of the air. As you wander around, you come upon a small, clear pool of water. In the middle of the pool is a perfect lotus flower. Study the flower carefully. Notice the jewel in the heart of the flower. Allow yourself to be one with this jewel, and listen for the wise one inside. Guidance may come in many different forms: pictures, sounds, an inner sense, an object found. Allow yourself 5 to 15 minutes for this focused meditation.

Discuss the process with a friend. What new awareness surfaced?

Outcomes: Increases visceral awareness in order to strengthen trust of oneself.

ACTIVITY 3.5 RESOURCES

Introduction: This activity is aimed at helping you develop a quality that you consider valuable and would like to incorporate into your behavioral repertoire.

Time required: 30 minutes

Participants: Any number; adolescent, adults

Setting: Anywhere

Materials: Paper and pen

Procedure: Identify a quality, skill, or feeling you would like to develop. Once you have this in mind, allow an image of a person, animal form, or object to appear on your internal mental screen. Examine this representation. What qualities does it convey to you? Describe the image in detail.

Now become the symbol. What are you aware of as you identify with this representation? What qualities do you possess? What do you notice in your body as you identify with this resource? Give yourself time to be aware of differences in your body. Notice your posture, facial expression, internal sensations, and feelings.

Now imagine a situation in which you might need this resource. Allow your symbol to come to mind along with the memory of all your feelings and sensations as you imagine yourself displaying this resource.

Outcomes: Allows you to strengthen or develop a resource to help improve functioning.

ACTIVITY 3.6 LOVING EYES

Introduction: The activity uses the good feelings significant others have toward you to shift your own self-feelings in positive directions.

Time required: 45 minutes

Participants: Children, adolescents, adults

Setting: One-to-one work, group, classroom

Materials: Crayons, paper, pen

Procedure: Identify some significant person from your past or present whom you feel really loves (loved) you. If you have trouble identifying someone, you might think of God or a higher power or even an imaginary person. Write down the person's name and relationship to you. Next, describe this person in as much detail as possible. Include everything that makes this person special to you, how he or she looks, qualities of the person's voice, his or her ways of being.

How did this person help you feel special? Did he or she rock you and sing to you? Take you for walks in the woods? Express loving feelings toward you? Make you laugh or play with you?

Now draw a picture of this person with you. Don't worry about being "artistic." If worrying about your lack of artistic abilities gets in your way, try drawing the picture with your left hand. Use colors to express the person's voice, how you experience his or her hands, arms, and general way of being with you. Use colors to express how you feel being with this special person. Give your drawing a title.

Now, imagine you are this special person and, through loving eyes, describe how you see and feel about the other person in the drawing.

Finally, look at the picture of yourself again. Can you see yourself as lovable? Silently say to yourself, "I am lovable."

Outcomes: Develops an internally generated experience of being loved.

Note: Adapted from Childers (1989, pp. 204-209).

ACTIVITY 3.7 TEMPERATURE READING

Introduction: Take a reading of how you feel about yourself and examine changes you would like to make in your behavior.

Time required: 15 minutes

Participants: Any number, adolescents, adults

Setting: One-to-one work, group, classroom; the setting must be quiet

Materials: None; soft instrumental music can help set the mood

Procedure: Gently close your eyes and pay attention to your breathing. Notice the air as it moves in and out of your body. Be aware of what parts of your body move as you breathe in and out. Allow your breathing to become a little fuller, a little deeper now. Feel a sense of relaxation spread throughout your body as your mind begins to quiet. Follow your breath as it moves in and out, in and out, as you move deeper and deeper inside, becoming more and more relaxed.

Now go inside and create a visual picture of yourself. Take a minute and look at yourself. Be aware of what you see, your reactions, thoughts, and feelings. You have created that image. You have engineered it. Because you created it, you are the only one who can recreate it into a new picture. Did you know that you can engineer a new experience of yourself?

Look at yourself and notice what you appreciate about yourself. What do you appreciate about the kind of person you are? About how you treat others? About how you treat yourself? What specific things do you appreciate about your experiences in the last 24 hours? Perhaps you took a risk, gave someone support, allowed yourself to be open, cooked a sumptuous dinner.

Now take some time to appreciate yourself for just being alive, for surviving and coping, for all the small but important tasks you perform every day. Be aware of your feelings throughout this process. Appreciate yourself for being your unique self: You are one of a kind. Does the mirror image have anything to say to you? Listen for a moment.

Now, look at yourself again. What complaints do you have as you look at yourself? Are you gentle and loving with your complaints, or harsh and rough? How does the person in the mirror respond to your complaints? Does that person perceive the messages as friendly and loving, or as cruel and judging? Within these complaints lie seeds of recommendations for becoming more whole.

Check to see if each complaint contains an invitation to improve yourself. Perhaps there is a change you would like to make now. If so, acknowledge it. Picture yourself making the change–perhaps today, tomorrow, or over the next weeks or months. If there are changes you do not want to make, acknowledge that you are aware of the complaints but choose not to address them now.

Look at your image again. What puzzles you about yourself? Express your puzzles and questions. Does the mirror image have a response? Does he or she have any questions for you? Is there any new information you want to share with each other? Do so now. Update each other. Say whatever you need to say to each other. Are there any changes you've noticed in each other?

As you look at the mirror image of yourself, tell the image what your hopes, wishes, and dreams are. Listen to the mirror image of yourself as he or she tells you his or her hopes and dreams. Are they the same? Different? What kind of feeling is there between you and the mirror image? Allow yourselves to express that in a way that fits for you. Can you touch or in some way show your caring for each other? Take a minute to do that. Can you join together in common hopes and wishes? What are they? Take time to appreciate yourself for being open to this experience. Be aware of what you have learned, and find a way to bring it into the present.

Outcomes: Increases self-nurturance; helps update your self-view; and facilitates the forming of goals, hopes and dreams.

Note: Adapted from Zahnd (1990).

ACTIVITY 3.8 FAMOUS FIGURES

Introduction: This activity helps you identify and explore the positive qualities and negative aspects of yourself.

Time required: 30 to 45 minutes

Participants: Individual or group; children 8 and older or adults

Setting: Classroom or office

Materials: Paper and pen

Procedure: Make a list of five people–past or present, living or deceased, real or imaginary–whom you admire. Then describe the qualities each possesses that you admire.

Follow the same procedure for five people–past or present, living or deceased, real or imaginary–whom you greatly dislike. Make a list of characteristics each of these people possesses that causes you to dislike him or her.

The positive qualities we admire in others often represent the qualities we would like to have or already claim. The more positive qualities you are aware of possessing, the more likely you are to feel good about yourself.

The negative qualities you identified in people you dislike may represent your own disowned or hidden traits. See if you can identify at least one instance when a quality you label as negative could be an asset and used in your behalf. You may need to modify the trait. For example, hostility might be helpful to defend yourself from physical attack.

Outcomes: Helps you recognize both strengths and weaknesses based on your own value system; forecasts what you need to do to continue to feel good about yourself, and what you might avoid to enhance positive self-esteem.

ACTIVITY 3.9 SELF-LOVE

Introduction: This activity puts you in touch with the part of yourself that is capable of providing nurturance to themselves. The second half of the activity provides an opportunity for someone to join in and play the role of nurturer, saying and doing all the things you want.

Time required: 40 minutes

Participants: Any number; adults

Setting: Carpeted office, group room, or classroom

Materials: Crayons and paper

Procedure: Imagine yourself in a beautiful place. Use all of your senses as you visualize this beautiful environment. Notice sounds, smells, visual, and kinesthetic experiences. Once you are fully there, your nurturing friend (real or imaginary) visits; this forever-friend can be whomever you wish. What does your friend look like? Listen to the sound of his or her voice. Listen to the loving and supportive things your nurturing friend says to you. Say goodbye when you have completed this.

Take a crayon and, on one side of a large sheet of paper, write words or phrases that describe what you would like your *Nurturing Parent* to be like: for example, loves me, holds me, kind and gentle, always there, soft, warm.

On the other side of the paper, write what you would like your Nurturing Parent to say to you: "I love you, you're beautiful," and so forth.

Now locate a friend with whom you can practice. Give messages to each other while one holds the other on his or her lap or puts his or her arm around the other or cuddles him or her. The person being nurtured closes his or her eyes and lets the words soak in. Keep repeating.

After completing the practice, process the experience with your partner.

Outcomes: Increases the experience of self-love and deep love from another person.

Note. Activity is original. Idea initiated by Wycoff (1977).

ACTIVITY 3.10 SELF-FORGIVENESS

Introduction: Often it is hard for people to forgive themselves for real or imagined wrongs. This activity encourages you to examine events over which you feel guilt or shame and to move toward self-forgiveness.

Time required: 30 minutes

Participants: Any number; adolescents or adults

Setting: Classroom or office

Materials: Paper and pencil

Procedure: Think of an event in the past over which you feel guilt, shame, remorse, regret, embarrassment. Record the event:

- What was happening?
- Where were you? Who was there?
- Did you violate a precept that you truly value?
- How did you feel? What feeling was underneath?
- What were you needing?
- What were you thinking?
- What past pain might have influenced your behavior?

We all do the best we can with what resources we have at the moment. Can you accept yourself as you were then? *Accepting yourself is different from condoning your behavior.*

Imagine the nurturing part of you talking to the younger you about the event that troubles you. What would he or she say? Record the message.

What could you do to make amends and let go of your mistake? Record the amends.

If appropriate, complete the amends.

Outcomes: Achieves greater internal peace through self-acceptance.

ACTIVITY 3.11 THE WORTHY YOU

Introduction: At one time in all our lives, we were pure. At the very least, all of us were born innocent, devoid of low self-esteem. This activity allows you to get in touch with that younger, worthy you, and encourages you to nurture that part of yourself.

Time required: 30 minutes

Participants: Any number; children, adolescents, or adults

Setting: Classroom or office

Materials: Paper, crayons, soft music

Procedure: Draw a picture of yourself at whatever age you consider yourself to have been pure and worthy of love. Use crayons for this drawing. Place yourself in a safe, comfortable environment. Surround the entire area with a golden light of protection.

Send the child messages of his or her inherent goodness, spontaneity, and creativity. Tell the child anything he or she needs to hear. Be generous and anticipate any needs the child might have. Be sure to give the child such developmental affirmations as these (Clarke, 1983).

- "I'm glad you're here."
- "I'm glad you are a boy." or "I'm glad you are a girl."
- "Your needs are okay."
- "You don't have to hurry."

Record on your drawing all the messages you give to the child.

Share your drawing and messages with a group of four friends.

Pair up with someone in your foursome. Partner A identifies with the child in his or her drawing and partner B delivers the messages. Then reverse rolls. First with your partner and then in the group discuss your feelings and review which messages were hardest to absorb.

Contract with your group of friends to repeat the messages you most need to hear over the months ahead. Think of other people in your environment whom you could ask to remind you of these messages. Make a list of these people and ask them to help you. Choose people from family, school, church, work, and other organizations.

Outcomes: Helps assimilate basic messages of worth.

ACTIVITY 3.12 A MENU OF SELF-NURTURANCE

Introduction: Developing a menu of self-nurturing activities that play on different parts of the self can help strengthen and maintain self-esteem.

Time required: 45 minutes

Participants: Any number; adolescents or adults

Setting: Office, classroom, home

Materials: Paper and pencil

Procedure: Find a time when you will not be interrupted and list at least two or three enjoyable activities under the following categories:

- **Smells:** Sniff perfumes, scented candles, incense, and fresh flowers.
- **Tactile:** Touch soft clothing, stuffed animals, and warm comforters; bathe with bath beads; soak in a hot tub; get a massage.
- **Sounds**: Listen to music; listen to the sounds of birds; buy a wind chime for your yard; participate in chanting and drumming.
- **Visual:** Visit an art gallery or gardens; watch the sunset; look at the moon and stars.

- **Intellect:** Take a class; read a book on something you want to learn; interview an expert on a subject that interests you.
- **Emotions:** Go to a play or movie, or read a book that is emotionally evocative; plan experiences that evoke excitement, adventure, or joys; volunteer your time to worthy causes to generate feelings of warmth and compassion for others less fortunate.
- **Taste:** Practice savoring each bit of food; experiment with different herbs.
- **Spirit:** Meditate in a small chapel; pray silently; attend a worship service; commune with nature.
- **Nutrition:** Prepare a low-fat, low-sodium, nutritious meal plan.

Outcomes: Builds a repertoire of self-nurturing activities to aid in self-soothing and increase personal joy.

ACTIVITY 3.13 NURTURING THE INNER CHILD

Introduction: This exercise encourages your to nurture your inner self.

Time required: 30 minutes

Participants: Adolescents or adults

Setting: Homework assignment, classroom, group

Materials: Paper and pencil

Procedure: Imagine yourself as a child. What age are you? Describe your physical presence and demeanor. What are you wearing? Describe everything you notice about the child. Visit the child where he or she lives. Sit down next to him or her and talk together.

Allow the child to tell you all he or she wishes for but is not receiving. Allow the child to write these things to you with his or her left hand.

Whatever the child writes to you, you need to give to yourself. Prepare a daily plan for giving the child what he or she wants.

Outcomes: Helps to identify needs and create goals for self-nurturance.

ACTIVITY 3.14 STRENGTH EXPRESSION THROUGH ART

Introduction: This activity encourages you to focus on and experience your good parts–parts of yourself you fully appreciate.

Time required: 60 minutes

Participants: Any number; adults or adolescents

Setting: Group room, office, or classroom

Materials: Paper and art media

Procedure: Place a big sheet of paper in front of you. Get in touch with the feelings you would have throughout your whole being if you felt really good about yourself: Imagine yourself with this good feeling.

Now express that feeling inside of you on the paper using any media, sounds, and movements you wish. Be as abstract as you like. Use color, form, contrast, movement, and so on to capture the feeling.

Share and discuss your creation with a group of friends.

Outcomes: Lets you get closer in touch with kinesthetic, auditory, and visual expressions of self-respect and self-love.

ACTIVITIES FOR GROUPS

ACTIVITY 3.15 SELF-ESTEEM MAINTENANCE KIT

Introduction: The kit contains metaphorical tools children can learn to use when they encounter problems.

Time required: 2 hours (can be spread over time)

Participants: Children ages 6 to 11

Setting: Classroom, individual therapy, church groups, or other small groups

Materials: Art materials, such as colored paper, colored felt, markers, paste, scotch tape, glitter, and cardboard

Procedure: Explain the meaning and give examples of how to use the six symbols in the self-esteem maintenance kit.

1. **Detective Hat:** the ability to search out the facts

2. **Medallion:** the ability to say a clear "yes" and a clear "no"

3. **Golden Key:** the ability to take risks without being sure what is behind the door you are opening

4. **Courage Stick:** the ability to tap courage to take risks

5. **Wisdom Box:** the ability to look into yourself and trust that you know the right thing to do

6. **Heart:** the ability to be in touch with your feelings, your sensitivity to others' feelings, and your warmth and caring

Direct the children to make their own sets of "tools."

Find a place in the room where each child can each keep his or her tools.

When problems come up, direct the children to their tools and encourage them to pick one or more that will help them.

Outcomes: Teaches children to look inside for resources to solve problems.

Note: This activity, based on the work of Virginia Satir, was developed by Doris Purdom (1997).

ACTIVITY 3.16 HEART BEAR

Introduction: This activity encourages children to look inside to find their own direction, which fosters self-confidence, inner-directedness, trust in self, and taking action based on their experience.

Time required: 15 minutes

Participants: Children ages 5 to 10

Setting: Any quiet setting

Materials: Heart Bear (a stuffed bear with a big heart showing)

Procedure: Find a soft bear and attach a large heart to its chest, or make a bear with a heart in advance or with the child.

Ask the child to hug the heart bear, saying, "This special bear helps you to speak your feelings. Listen to the bear's heart and tell me what the heart says. What does the heart say you want?"

The child might respond with, "I want Mommy and Daddy to love me" or "I want to be good."

Say to the child, "Now listen to heart again. What does the bear's heart say you need to do to get what you want?"

The child might say something like, "I need to listen to Mommy," "I need to say thank-you," or "I need to be kind to my friends."

Now take heart bear and hug it, saying, "I'm listening to my heart now." Use the bear to teach the child a lesson. For example, "My heart says you are very lovable to me." Then tell the child about a time when you experienced him or her as lovable.

Now hand the bear back to the child and ask him or her to hug it again, saying, "Listen closely to what the heart bear has to say. Can you remember a time when you felt Mommy or Daddy (or some other person) really, really loved you? Maybe when you were sick and the person was caring for you, or maybe one time the person was holding you or putting you to bed or reading your favorite story? Picture a time now." Allow a moment of silence. "Do you remember a time?" Wait for a moment. "Tell me about that time." Wait for child to tell you a specific time.

If the child is having trouble finding a moment, ask him or her to make one up, to create a moment he or she would like. Ask the child to get inside the picture. For example, if the child remembered a time when his or her grandmother read a bedtime story, you might say, "Can you imagine yourself in the bed now? Feel the pillow under your head, the soft covers over you. Look around the room at some of your favorite things. Can you see Grandma sitting on your bed?"

"Listen to her voice as she reads your favorite story. Look into her eyes. Be aware of the warmth you feel inside. Can you feel grandma's love right now?" Wait for affirmative reply.

"Where do you feel that love in your body?" Wait until the child responds. "Place your hand on your body where you feel it most." Wait until child places his or her hand. "What does it feel like? Is it warm? Tingly? Soft?" Wait for child to respond.

"Can you let that feeling travel from that spot up to the top of your head and down to the tips of your toes? Tell me when that feeling has traveled all the way through your body." Wait for affirmation. Then, ask the child to do this with other individual memories.

Say to the child, "Now, when Mommy or Daddy is angry and you get scared that you are not lovable, do you think you can remember that picture of your memory and those feelings of love traveling from that special spot where love touches your body, and imagine it traveling all the way to the top of your head and down to the tips of your toes?" Wait for affirmation.

"Let's practice that. Remember a time when Mommy or Daddy was really, really angry with you. Remember how Mommy looked and sounded. Maybe she was shouting at you, or her face was red, or she was shaking her finger at you." Model how an angry person might look. "Do you remember now how she looked and sounded?" Wait for affirmative response.

"Now remember how you felt inside. Can you step into the picture with the angry Mommy?" Wait for affirmative response. "What do you feel inside? Do you feel a tightness in your chest or belly, tears in your eyes. or your chin shaking? What do you feel?" Wait for a response.

"Now practice remembering that picture of your loving memory and those happy feelings inside when you feel that love. Feel those feelings inside you now. Can you feel them?" Wait for an affirmation.

"Remember that even when Mommy or Daddy is really, really mad at you, you still are lovable.

"Now listen to your heart bear again. I bet your bear loves you, too."

Outcomes: Helps children begin to use prior positive experiences and inner resource to cope with stressful times.

Note: Adapted from a resource provided by Connie Lundgren, 25235 134th Court SE, Kent, WA 98042.

REFERENCES

Acker-Stone, T. (1987). *What I say is what I am*. Hyannis, MA: Wonder Works Studio.

Allport, G. (1955). *Becoming*. New Haven, CT: Yale University Press.

Assagioli, R. (1965). *Psychosynthesis: A manual of principles and techniques*. New York: Viking.

Bandler, R., & Grinder, J. (1975). *The structure of magic: Vols. 1 & 2*. Palo Alto, CA: Science and Behavior Books.

Bandler, R., & Grinder, J. (1982). *Reframing*. Moab, UT: Real People Press.

Baumeister, R., (1991). The self against itself: Escape or defeat. In B. Curtis (Ed.), *The relational self* (pp. 238-256). New York: Guilford.

Baumeister, R., Heatherton, T. F., & Rice, D. M. (1993). When ego threats lead to self-regulation failure: Negative consequences of high self-esteem. *Journal of Abnormal and Social Psychology, 61*, 141-156.

Baumgardner, A. H. (1990). To know oneself is to like oneself: Self-certainty and self-affect. *Journal of Personality and Social Psychology, 58*, 1062-1072.

Beattie, M. (1987). *Codependent no more*. Center City, MN: Hazeldon Foundation.

Beck, A. (1967). *Clinical, experiential, and theoretical aspects*. New York: Harper & Row.

Beck, A., Rush, A. J., Shaw, B. F., & Emery, G. (1979). *Cognitive therapy of depression*. New York: Guilford.

Bennett, H. Z. (1987). *The lens of perception*. Berkeley, CA: Celestial Arts.

Blaine, B., & Crocker, J. (1993). Self-esteem and self-serving biases in reactions to positive and negative events. In R. Baumeister (Ed.), *Self-esteem: The puzzle of low self-regard* (pp. 55-85). New York: Plenum Press.

Borysenko, J. (1987). *Minding the body, mending the mind*. New York: Bantam Books.

Bowen, M. (1985). *Family therapy in clinical practice*. New York: Jason Aronson.

Branden, N. (1993, January). A woman's self-esteem. *New Woman, 23*(1), 56-58.

Branden, N. (1994, January). Choosing happiness. In *Self-esteem today, 8*(1). New York: National Council of Self-Esteem.

Burns, D. (1992). *Feeling good: The new mood therapy*. New York: NAL-Dutton.

Burns, D. (1993). *Ten days to self-esteem*. New York: Morrow.

Cameron-Bandler, L., Gordon, D., & Lebeau, M. (1985). *Know how*. San Rafael, CA: Future Pace.

Cameron-Bandler, L. (1985). *Solutions*. San Rafael, CA: Future Pace.

Canfield, J., and Self-Esteem Seminars. (1986). *Self-esteem in the classroom*. Self-Esteem Seminars, 17156 Palisades Circle, Pacific Palisades, CA 90272.

Carlock, C. J. (1991). *The parts party for self-concept: Differentiation and integration*. Unpublished manuscript, Peoplemaking Midwest, Carlock & Associates, 1105 Watervliet Avenue, Dayton, Ohio, 45420.

Carlock, C. J., Hagerty, P. T., & Verdon, T. R. (1985). *Satir family instruments*. Dayton, OH: Peoplemaking Midwest, Carlock & Associates, 1105 Watervliet Avenue, Dayton, OH 45420.

Childers, J. (1989, February). Looking at yourself through loving eyes. *Elementary School Guidance and Counseling, 23*, 204-209.

Chopra, D. (1992). *Unconditional life*. New York: Bantam Books.

Clarke, J. I. (1983). *Ouch, that hurts!* Plymouth, MN: Daisy Press.

Desai, A. (1990). *Working miracles of love*. Lenox, MA: Kipalu.

Ellis, A., & Harper, R. (1976). *A new guide to rational living*. North Hollywood, CA: Wilshire.

Festinger, L. (1957). *A theory of cognitive dissonance*. Palo Alto, CA: Stanford University Press.

Freud, S. (1936). *The problem of anxiety*. New York: Norton.

Gardner, P., & Oien, T. P. (1981). Depression and self-esteem: An investigation that used behavioral and cognitive approaches to the treatment of clinically depressed clients. *Journal of Clinical Psychology, 37*(1), 128-135.

Gawain, S. (1978). *Creative visualization*. Berkeley, CA: Whatever Publishing.

Gestalt Institute of Cleveland, Post Graduate Training Program. (1979). *Lecture: Cycle of experience*. Cleveland, OH: Author.

Grinder, J., Delozier, J., & Bandler, R. (1977). *Patterns of hypnotic technique of Milton H. Erickson, M.D.: Vol. 2*. Cupertino, CA: Meta Publications.

Hahn, T. N. (1976). *The miracle of mindfulness*. Boston: Beacon.

Hahn, T. N. (1987). *Being peace*. Berkeley, CA: Parallax.

Heatherton, T., & Ambady, N. (1993). Self-esteem, self-prediction, and living up to commitments. In R. Baumeister (Ed.), *Self-esteem: The puzzle of low self-regard* (pp. 131-145). New York: Plenum Press.

Josephs, L. (1991). Character structure, self-esteem regulation, and the principle of identity maintenance. In R. Curtis (Ed.), *The relational self* (pp. 3-16). New York: Guilford.

Josephs, L. (1992). *Character structure and the organization of the self*. New York: Columbia University Press.

Jourard, S., & Landsman, T. (1980). *Healthy personality* (4th ed.). New York: Macmillan.

Keleman, S. (1975). *The human ground*. Palo Alto, CA: Science and Behavior Books.

Kohut, H. (1977). *The restoration of the self*. New York: International Universities Press.

Lazarus, A. (1977). *In the mind's eye*. New York: Rawson Associates.

LeShan, L. (1974). *How to meditate*. New York: Bantam Books.

Levy, P., & Baumgardner, A. H. (1991). Effects of self-esteem and gender on goal choice. *Journal of Organizational Behavior, 12,* 529-541.

Lundgren, C. (1997, April 23). Personal communication.

Mariechild, D. (1987). *The innerdance*. Freedom, CA: Crossing Press.

Masterson, J. (1988). *The search for the real self.* New York: Free Press.

McDougall, W. (1993). *The energies of men: A study of the fundamentals of dynamic psychology.* New York: Scribner's.

McKay, M., & Fanning, P. (1987). *Self-esteem.* Oakland, CA: New Heritage Publications.

McKay, M., & Fanning, P. (1992). *Self-esteem* (2nd ed.). Oakland, CA: New Harbinger Publications.

McNulty, S., & Swann, W. (1991). Psychotherapy, self-concept change, and self-verification. In R. Curtis (Ed.), *The relational self* (pp. 213-237). New York: Guilford.

Meichenbaum, D. (1974). *Cognitive behavior modification.* Morristown, NJ: General Learning Press.

Miller, J. (1976). *Toward a new psychology of women.* Boston: Beacon.

Millon, T., & Everly, G. (1985). *Personality and its disorders.* New York: Wiley.

Moen, L. (1992). *Guided imagery: Vol. 1.* Naples, FL: United States Publishing.

Newman, M., & Berkowitz, B. (1977a). *How to be your own best friend.* New York: Random House.

Newman, M., & Berkowitz, B. (1977b). *How to take charge of your life.* New York: Bantam Books.

Polster, E., & Polster, M. (1973). *Gestalt therapy integrated: Contours of theory and practice.* New York: Brunner/Mazel.

Purdom, D. (1997, April 11). Personal communication.

Ray, S. (1980). *Loving relationships*. Berkeley, CA: Celestial Arts.

Roman, S. (1986). *Living with joy*. Triburon, CA: H. J. Kramer.

Satir, V. (1976). *Making contact*. Berkeley, CA: Celestial Arts.

Satir, V. (1978). *Your many faces*. Berkeley, CA: Celestial Arts.

Satir, V. (1981, August). AVANTA Process Community conference, Park City, Utah.

Satir, V., & Banmen, J. (1983). *Virginia Satir-Verbatim, 1984*. Delta, BC: Delta Associates.

Sinetar, M. (1990). *Self-esteem is just an idea we have about ourselves*. Mahwah, NJ: Paulist Press.

Singer, J. (1971, Spring). The vicissitudes of imagery in research and clinical use. *Contemporary Psychoanalyst, 7*(2), 442.

Spencer, J., Spencer, R., Josephs, A., & Steele, C. (1993). Low self-esteem: The uphill struggle for self-integrity. In R. Baumeister (Ed.), *Self-esteem: The puzzle of low self-regard*. New York: Plenum Press.

Steiner, C. (1974). *Scripts people live*. New York: Grove.

Stevens, J. O. (1971). *Awareness: Exploring, experimenting, experiencing*. New York: Bantam Books.

Tice, D., (1993). The social motivations of people with low self-esteem. In R. Baumeister (Ed.), *Self-esteem: The puzzle of low self-regard*. New York: Plenum Press.

Vaughn, F. (1979). *Awakening intuition*. New York: Anchor.

Watzlawick, P., Beavin, J. H., & Jackson, D. (1974). *Change*. New York: Norton.

Whitfield, C. (1987). *Healing the child within*. Deerfield Beach, FL: Health Communications.

Wycoff, H. (1977). *Solving women's problems.* New York: Grove Press.

Zahnd, W. (1990). *Temperature reading*. Unpublished manuscript, Department of Sociology and Social Work, California State University, Chico.

Zinker, J. (1977). *Creative process in Gestalt therapy*. New York: Vintage Books.

Chapter 4

SOCIAL SYSTEM AND SELF-ESTEEM

C. Jesse Carlock

The people who surround you, the groups and organizations to which you belong, the subcultures with which you identify, and world events all affect self-esteem. Self-esteem is influenced not only by the play of internal forces within people but also by their social environments, relationships, and interactions, and by sociocultural factors. This chapter explores the role of the social system on self-esteem.

THE IMPACT OF THE FAMILY

Every one of us is born into a family, whether a two-parent or a single-parent family, a blended family, a family with 10 children, or any of a myriad of different constellations. The family is our primary and most powerful teacher. Every interaction teaches us something about ourselves. The teachings might be about the reactions we generate in others, how others react to us, or how others treat us. Through family interactions (through words, voice, tone, touch, eyes, body language, and spatial dynamics), we develop an early picture of ourselves.

The Context of Birth

From the very beginning, we receive messages about ourselves, either directly through verbal messages or indirectly through behavior, context, and actions. Think back for a moment about your birth. Describe the context in which you were conceived. That is, where were you conceived? What was the relationship between your biological mother and biological father at that time? Was your conception the result of a one-time fling, a rape, or a loving, committed relationship? Were you a first child? A last child? The first boy? Were you conceived as a replacement for a child who died? Were you welcomed into the world? Were your parents glad you were the sex you were? What was happening in the world at the time of your birth? What was happening in your parents' relationship? Your nuclear family? Your extended family? (To explore family influences in greater detail, see Carlock, Hagerty, & Verdon, 1985.)

Next, write a fantasy of your birth. Imagine you are in your mother's womb. Describe how each member of your family feels about your birth. Imagine the actual birthing experience—what is it like? Describe how you enter this world. If you cannot find the actual details of your birth, use your imagination.

The context of your birth influences your early life. Your perceptions of this event are just as important as the actual facts. Be in touch with both. Were you welcomed into the world? A child who is born out of wedlock and whose adolescent parents are forced to marry has a very different beginning than someone born to parents who are more mature and settled in a marriage or otherwise committed relationship. Being born in the midst of an economic depression is different from being born in a time of prosperity. Being born to a mother who has experienced several miscarriages may influence the expectations others have of you or the feeling around your birth. A child born to a mother who is grieving a significant death (for example, of her own parent) might not be cared for in an optimum way. The fourth girl born to a parents who are longing for a boy might be a repository of feelings of disappointment.

From the beginning, we draw conclusions about ourselves based on our observations of and interactions with our parental figures. We form beliefs in childhood about our own power, others' power, our worth (judged by responses of others), and our freedom to be both separate and connected. These beliefs are based as much on touch and tone of voice as on words. This is especially true of younger children and infants who have not developed their language capacity. Reflect on the following:

If you are a girl,

- How did your mother treat herself?
- How did your mother allow others (male and female) to treat her?

- How were you treated by your mother? By your father?
- How does your mother treat your father?
- How does your father treat your mother?

If you are a boy,

- How did your father treat himself?
- How did your father allow others (male and female) to treat him?
- How were you treated by your father? By your mother?
- How does your father treat your mother?
- How does your mother treat your father?

Through such direct and indirect means, we begin to put a picture together about our worth. This picture often is incomplete and distorted. Based on your answers to these questions, what conclusions do you think you drew about your worth?

Your Family Role

In looking at the family system as a whole, children have a tendency to try to relieve the pain, fill in the holes, and hide the shame in a malfunctioning family. They also adopt styles aimed at gaining the attention they need. They do this by adopting a variety of roles in the family, including hero, scapegoat, mascot, and lost child (Black, 1982; Blevins, 1993; Wegscheider, 1981).

Each role attempts to pick up functions or express parts that are not being performed or permitted by the chief architects of the family—the parents. Because they are young, dependent, and lacking in adult skills and resources, children can never adequately make up for or repair the "family machine." This "failure" can become a major root source of not feeling good enough. Children can never adequately compensate for such deficiencies—though, miraculously, as young as they are, they do help maintain the family equilibrium.

- What was your role in your family of origin?

Sculpt your family using small dolls, clay, or friends to play different family members; or draw your family. Use space, gestures, postures, facial expressions, and directions to convey relationships and attitudes. How would your mother be in relation to your father? Where would the first-born be in relation to them? Second-born? Third-born? Make a moving sculpture if you like. How does each feel? What is the posture of each? What is your role in this sculpture? What functions do you serve? What do you need? What patterns do you notice as you look at the sculpture? Are there any changes you want to make?

You can find clues about your role in your given names and nicknames, in how you were labeled as a kid, and in what predictions were made about you.

For example:

"You'll never have any friends."

"You're just like your father. You'll never amount to anything."

"You've got the gift of good luck."

"She's the brains of the family."

"She's our little pet."

"He's the little man of the family."

Part of our motivation for adopting these roles is compassion and love; another part is a survival need. Each of these roles results in both deficiencies and strengths (see Table 4.1).

A number of family climate dimensions can influence the development of self-esteem (from Carlock & Hagerty, 1988; Curran, 1983; Karpel, 1986; Satir, 1983, 1988b; and Whitaker & Napier, 1978):

1. How positive or negative, critical or encouraging is the family?

2. How well does the family allow connection and disconnection?

3. Are individual differences acknowledged and appreciated?

4. Is the family flexible enough to allow other people to enter the system now and then? Can members leave the family when they are ready?

5. Is the family overprotective or underprotective? Are members given responsibilities, independence, and guidance in accordance with their abilities?

6. Are generational boundaries respected? That is, are mother and father clearly at the top of the hierarchy? Are parental functions in

TABLE 4.1
Family Norms/Family Roles

Role	Deficiencies	Strengths
Hero	builds worth on doing rather than being emotional self underdeveloped seeks approval doesn't know how to relax and play lacks spontaneity has trouble admitting when wrong	posses leadership abilities and sense of responsibility high achiever restores pride to family independent helpful
Mascot	fears (s)he doesn't belong fragile insecure fears breaking down	knows how to get dependency needs met fun to be with reduces tension and anxiety in the family system
Scapegoat	defiant acts out distances others draws anger and attack	knows how to get attention able to express anger and tolerate other people able to break rules, break confluence with the system
Lost Child	timid, shy isolated withdrawn doesn't get needs met low energy afraid to take risks has difficulty making decisions	excellent observer avoids becoming a target of criticism, abuse self sufficient

Note: Adapted from Wegscheider (1981)

their hands only? Are alliances between one parent and the children discouraged? Are there clear rules defining the relationships between parents and children?

7. Is there variety and resilience in interpreting events?

8. Does the family stress accountability, commitment, admission, repair of wrongs, and forgiveness without attack of members' worth?

9. Are vulnerability, dependency, and neediness permitted without judgment?

10. Is each person separate while a part of the family?

11. Do dialogues occur in relationship, and are relationships reliable and constant over time? Are mistakes and differences expected, acknowledged, and accepted?

12. Is there a relatively stable level of emotional contact and accessibility?

13. Does the family support maturation and change of values through life experience? Are learning and growth expected and encouraged?

14. Are family members able to interact with an unfamiliar world?

15. Does give and take occur among members?

16. Do members show respect for each other, communicating that all are valued and their feelings and contributions are important?

17. Are humor and playfulness used to reduce shame and to reframe highly charged emotional material?

18. Is communication direct, clear, specific, and honest, as opposed to indirect, vague, and dishonest?

19. Are members willing and able to protect others in the family?

20. Can people depend on each other?

21. Do hope and belief exist that effort and involvement in the family will pay off?

22. Is scapegoating distributed so that one person is not blamed and dumped on?

23. Are family rules flexible, humane, appropriate, and subject to change, as opposed to rigid, inhumane, and nonnegotiable?

Reflect on your family of origin as well as your current family as you consider these questions. What are the strengths and weaknesses of your family? Set two to three goals to improve the weak areas, and appreciate the good parts of your family. Check your views against the views of other family members. By sharing you can learn more about others' perspectives and move closer. You also can strengthen the positive influence of the family on all its members.

CULTURE-SUBCULTURE

Each culture accents different values, norms, and role patterns. Some cultures are more reflective; some are more anxious, others more depressed; some are more expressive, others more reserved; some, like ours, value the accumulation of wealth and power and prestige; others value spiritual enlightenment.

American culture places strong emphasis on the accumulation of wealth, power, and prestige, and stresses productivity and upward mobility. As the economy and unemployment rates rise and fall, the stability of our self-esteem is affected. The rapid and drastic transitions Americans face in career, family forms, and technology all influence self-esteem.

The subcultures with which people identify also influence their self-esteem. Some subcultures are valued, others are oppressed. Whether a person belongs to the American Medical Association, the gay liberation movement, the Black Caucus, Hispanic organizations, a Chinese church, the National Organization of Women, Alcoholics Anonymous, Overeaters Anonymous, or some other organization or institution, that membership influences his or her identity, values, and feelings about self.

If one is a member of the American Medical Association or the Junior League, the association likely enhances one's esteem, since power, prestige, education, and status are valued by our culture. If one is African-American, gay, overweight, or in some other minority subculture, participation in organizations can help protect one's self-esteem by providing support for behaviors and attitudes not held by the majority culture, which does not readily accept and appreciate differences. For people in such subcultures, joining an organization can engender a sense of pride in their differences. Such groups provide vehicles for support, affirmation, and political action.

Breaking or not fitting with societal norms results in explicit or insidious disapproval and discrimination, which can erode self-esteem. Persons labeled *deviant* may tend to exaggerate their deviance as a defense against, an attack upon, or a fulfillment of society's label. As Schur (1971) explained, when a person's behavior is labeled deviant and his or her life becomes organized with a self-concept of deviance, he or she then is set apart and often becomes deviant. The positions people hold in the culture—their social status, deviancy or normalcy, attractiveness or unattractiveness—affect their self-esteem, unless they do what they can to affirm their worth.

YOUR SUPPORT NETWORK

The healthy individual has a support network of dozens of people upon whom to draw. We need people available to support the different aspects of our lives. Herek, Levy, Maddi, Taylor, and Wertlieb (1990) cited literature that strongly supported the direct and positive relationship between a person's number of friends and memberships in organizations and his or her health. Greater social support increases the rate of recovery from illness, reduces mortality, aids adjustment to chronic illness, and increases compliance to medical regimens (Herek et al., 1990). A study by Richter, Brown, and Mott (1991) also showed that social resources and self-esteem are related to recovery from addiction. Greater numbers of nonabusing friends helps ensure sobriety. The greater the satisfaction with their social resources, the fewer problems people report in major life areas. Support helps counterbalance peer pressure and provides models of coping skills.

According to Gambrill and Richey (1988), the average number of friends people report is 15; the average number of intimate or close friends is 6. However, some people are quite happy with just a few friends and infrequent social contact (Brammer, 1991). Gilles (1976) and Schlossberg (1989) provided a framework for viewing one's circle of support (see Activity 4.5 at the end of this chapter).

Social relationships also provide a sense of belonging and validation for our beliefs, feelings, and self-worth (Brammer, 1991; Gambrill & Richey, 1988). Networking with others helps people enlarge their skill and knowledge bases; offers the enjoyment of shared activities; and provides emotional support in times of need, a cheering gallery to celebrate our transitions and successes, and a community to give us a sense of belonging. McNulty and Swann (1991) cautioned that some individuals actually tend to run away from relationships with people who are overly favorable to them. Awareness of this tendency can help these people instead learn to lean into positive support.

Children should be encouraged to pursue their interests through community classes, extracurricular activities, and organizations. Such early and ongoing involvement provides support for identity development and arenas to practice social and leadership skills. If we are not steered in these directions early on, we need to learn how to channel our interests and find avenues for meeting like-minded others later in life.

Joining groups or organizations that value traits or abilities we are trying to expand also can support our growth (McNulty & Swann, 1991). Opportunities to expand social contacts present themselves every day: at work, clubs, classes, and organizations; in bookstores, buses, trains, and airplanes; at parties, grocery stores, restaurants, and health clubs; anywhere we frequently find ourselves. Taking advantage of such everyday settings to initiate even brief contacts with people can result in a much richer social life. Joining an interest group, such as a club or a study group, provides a mutual focus that makes conversations easier to initiate and maintain.

Being aware of your own interest areas can help you decide where to go to meet people with similar interests and values. Check which of the following you would enjoy:

___ volunteer work

___ exhibit/shows (e.g., antiques, automobiles, horses, computers)

___ sports

___ hiking and camping

___ cultural events (e.g., music, drama, poetry, opera, dance)

___ church events

___ classes

___ parties

___ community organizations (e.g., Junior League, Chamber of Commerce, local boards)

___ sports

___ hobbies (e.g., photography, investment, reading, chess, gardening)

___ card-playing

___ informal get-togethers

___ music groups (e.g., choirs, bands, orchestra)

___ dancing

___ bars/lounges

___ politics

___ formal networks (e.g., Alcoholics Anonymous, singles groups, Parents Without Partners, senior citizens' organizations)

Isolation is one of the most painful aspects of human existence. With the mobility of our culture, families often are dispersed; and with urbanization, even greater isolation has resulted. Valuing and developing a sense of community are imperative. People need each other. When pretenses are dropped, when people are real with each other, and when conflicts are faced, love abounds (Peck, 1987).

BLOCKS TO RELATIONSHIPS

Look at the kinds of issues people use to impede the development of new relationships (Gambrill & Richey, 1988; Lerner, 1990).

Fear of rejection. One of the most common blocks is the fear that people won't like us. It's true, not everyone will like us. But, so what? Others will.

Fear of criticism. Many people are perfectionists and fear looking foolish. But only by risking can we grow.

Fear of intimacy. Some people are afraid of intimacy because they have been in relationships in which they felt swallowed up. Others have never had the experience of emotional closeness and simply lack the skills and self-awareness (Lerner, 1990; Malone & Malone, 1987).

Feeling awkward. Initial encounters are awkward for many people. Even though they appear confident and relaxed, most people experience anxiety in some social situations. You're not unique in this. Learning definable skills (discussed later in this chapter) can help alleviate some of this anxiety and awkwardness.

Faulty beliefs. Beliefs such as those listed below can get in the way of forming relationships (see chapters 2 and 3):

- I'm unlovable and not worth knowing.
- People will disappoint me.
- Relationships take too much work.
- People can't be trusted.

By identifying beliefs that prevent us from expanding our social support network, working on the painful events associated with these beliefs, and replacing them with more realistic beliefs, we can clear a path to a happier existence.

Interpersonal Skills

Therapist: "What are you wanting from your partner?"

Client: "I just want her to hear me ... "

Being heard reduces the stress of isolation. But here, as with anything, there are two sides of the coin: On one side are the responsibilities of the listener who is trying to understand the message and convey that understanding; on the other side are the responsibilities of the communicator, who must learn how to communicate so that others can hear. Learning a few skills can improve all your relationships, from brief encounters to long-term commitments. Well-learned skills can help us feel better about ourselves and improve people's reaction to us.

In chapter 7, Cordell discusses the importance of teaching children and adolescents communication skills to build and maintain peer relationships. Learning prosocial behaviors is as important to their success and happiness as is academic competency. Cordell describes a skill-streaming program that teaches eight behaviors to children with Attention Deficit and Hyperactivity Disorder (ADHD), skills that all children can use. The skills she teaches are these:

Controlling oneself
- listening
- expressing one's feelings

Getting along with friends
- understanding the feelings of others
- responding to teasing

Getting along with adults
- making a complaint
- dealing with another's anger

Getting one's duties done
- arranging problems by importance
- getting ready for a difficult conversation

Dr. Cordell has included a number of communication exercises for children at the end of chapter 7 as well.

Communication: Verbal and Nonverbal

Knowing just a few simple skills can take the edge off the anxiety of initial encounters. Three important skills in initiating conversations are greeting or making opening remarks, exchanging basic information, and making small talk (Gambrill & Richey, 1988).

Greetings. Greetings include remarks such as "Hi," "How are you?" "Good to meet you," and "Welcome." Such greetings are best delivered with a smile, full eye contact, and a clear, audible voice. When you know the person's name, adding that is helpful as well. Most people like to hear their names used.

Exchanging Basic Information. After the greeting, generally you engage in an exchange of basic information, including your names, where you work or live, and what you do for a living. Depending on the setting, other openers are also effective (Gambrill & Richey, 1988):

Requesting directions or help: "Can you show me how to work this machine?"

Asking simple questions: "What's your role in this company?"

Complimenting the person: "That's a beautiful sweater."

Making a casual observation: "That salad looks delicious."

Asking to join the person: "May I sit here?"

Offering something: "Would you like to read this newspaper?" "Can I help you load that? It looks heavy."

Sharing an opinion or feeling: "This year's presidential race should be exciting." "This play is fantastic! I love how the director has interwoven several scenes on the stage simultaneously. How are you liking it?

Small Talk. While repugnant to many people, small talk serves an important function in initial contacts. It gives people a chance to feel each other out for future topics of conversation. Having several topics handy can help alleviate anxiety, freeing up your energy for responding. Topics can be drawn from literature, talk shows, films, personal interests or interests of the other, and the like. By deliberately scanning literature and reflecting on current interests, you can easily identify a number of possible topics. Some people do this without preparation, since it comes easily to them. Others find it helpful to plan conversation leads in advance.

In general, the more positive you can be the better. Focusing on assets, yours and others, increases your listener's comfort and receptivity. According to Gambrill and Richey (1988), a spark of humor is useful if it is natural to you. As a general strategy, approach people as if they were treasure chests: Your job is to identify the gifts they have to offer. Your curiosity and interest will pay off. People generally like to talk about themselves, especially if you lead the way.

As a relationship develops, you need other skills to deepen the interaction. People enjoy being listened to. Several skills can help with this, including reflections of feelings and paraphrasing the content of a message. You might make encouraging comments like these: "That's great!" "Yeah, I see what you mean." "Tell me more about it." Open-ended questions are good beginners, especially when followed by more specific questions.

You should work to achieve a good balance between listening and expressing your own opinions and feelings. People with low self-esteem tend to favor listening rather than expressing themselves. They need to learn to initiate conversations and stretch themselves to talk for longer periods. Others with low self-esteem may be too dominant and must learn to be less assertive and controlling in order to improve their communication skills and enhance their self-esteem (Rancer, Kosberg, & Silvestri, 1992). Dominating the conversation will alienate others as quickly as being too passive will. The more congruent you are—that is, the closer your insides match your outsides (Satir, 1988b)—the closer you'll feel to others.

Skills such as self-disclosure, assertion, setting boundaries, filtering, metatalk, and nonverbal activity also enhance communication (Carkhuff, 1993).

Self-Disclosure. In order for us to be known to others and feel closer to others, we must use the skill of disclosure. Self-disclosure involves sharing information about yourself, your views, your feelings, and your perceptions or intentions. Here are some examples of self-disclosure statements:

"I really like the feel of this room."

"I don't think we can afford to wait on that repair."

"I'm feeling anxious right now."

"I really enjoyed being with you."

"I'm going on vacation next week to Belize. The diving there is great!"

In addition to making yourself known to others, disclosing your feelings invites others to deepen the exchange (Ornish, 1992). "High disclosers" generally are seen as friendlier people, though the context for disclosure must be appropriate. People who tell too much about themselves too soon can put others off. The level of disclosure must match the type of relationship as well as the context.

Although self-disclosure can improve contact, many people hide their true feelings and thoughts. People typically put up a front to gain acceptance and recognition, or simply to survive. We all recognize some of the images people adopt, including the good little girl, the tough guy, and Don Juan. Such masks or roles keep us safe from the pain of rejection, since we hide our true selves behind them. But hiding also keeps us from experiencing intimacy, warmth, and love. What is intended as a means of protection ultimately deprives us of needed contact. Self-disclosure breaks down facades, allows for personal contact, and can enhance self-esteem.

Likewise, if we play an exclusively nurturing role in order to please others, we betray ourselves and often resent those others. Everyone, of course, plays certain roles at various times, but role-playing reaches a destructive level when we become alienated from ourselves as well as others. We lose touch with our feelings, wants, and needs. *Role-playing*, defined here as *facade*, is different from legitimate *role-taking*. When we hide ourselves behind role-playing, we may not be harmed directly but we do not receive any nourishment to grow. The more we risk, the more nourishment is possible.

Through the skill of self-disclosure, we can reveal our feelings and open ourselves to response (comfort, confrontation, encouragement). The self longs to express itself. Self-expression is a need of the organism, although the favored form of expression (dialogue, music, writing, and art, for example) varies from person to person.

Self-disclosure connects people to one another and enhances mental health (Jourard, 1971). Other skills that bond people are reflection of others' feelings, stating observations, and identifying mutually shared and uniquely experienced themes.

Through self-disclosure, we discover how we are alike and different from others. These perceptions bond us together, increasing the strength of our support and helping us feel good.

Assertion. Assertion skills enable us to express and meet our needs. Individuals who lack these skills are unable to meet their needs effectively. Assertion involves standing up for your rights and expressing your feelings, thoughts, and wants in direct and appropriate ways (Alberti & Emmons, 1990; Jakubowski & Lange, 1978). Table 4.2 lists some examples of assertive skills for personal relationships.

TABLE 4.2
Examples of Assertive Skills

Receiving compliments	Refusing requests
Stating your needs, wants, or preferences	Not allowing yourself to be interrupted without good reason
Returning an item to a store	Giving a compliment
Telling others when they do something that bothers you	Making positive statements about yourself
Changing the topic of conversation	Attempting interruptions
Openly discussing someone's criticism of you	Reporting good news about yourself
Expressing a divergent opinion	Adding facts to facts
Expressing positive feelings	Expressing feelings of anger

Not surprisingly, men and women often show significant differences on assertion skills. Blier and Blier-Wilson (1989) found that females are significantly more confident than males in expressing vulnerable feelings of fear and sadness, regardless of the gender of the target person. They also found that males are less confident in expressing anger toward women than they are toward other men, and that women are more comfortable expressing positive feelings to males than are males.

While some people habitually err on the side of nonassertion, others lead their lives in almost continuous self-assertion. Fighting over every issue results in heavy energy depletion. Tubesing (1979) offered these three questions as a way of evaluating whether or not to fight:

Is the threat real?

Is the value or principle at stake important enough to expend the energy to fight?

If I choose to fight, am I likely to make an impact, or is the energy likely to be wasted?

If the answer is "no" to any of these questions, Tubesing recommended letting the issue go. He warned against spending ten dollars worth of stress on a ten cent problem, or spending ten cents worth of psychic energy on a ten dollar problem. Appropriate allocation of energy results in more efficient, positive functioning and, consequently, higher self-esteem.

Once we make a decision to assert ourselves, we must develop the skills, the beliefs about our personal rights, and the tenacity to stand firm on the issue despite initial resistance. In doing so, we further define ourselves and enhance our self-esteem.

Setting Boundaries. Related to self-assertion is the skill of setting boundaries (Cloud & Townsend, 1992; Katherine, 1991). When parents are able to provide adequate caring and nurturance, a child internalizes the caring, and the "me" becomes separate and distinct from the "not me." In other words, ego boundaries are developed to guard inner space. According to Fossum and Mason (1986), ego boundaries are the means by which one screens, interprets, and regulates interaction with the world. Adequate ego boundaries are essential to the formation of identity. Fossum and Mason (1986) used the metaphor of internal and external zippers to explain the differences between people who have healthy ego boundaries (i.e., an internal zipper) and those who have faulty ego boundaries (i.e., an external zipper). These are illustrated in Table 4.3.

For further description of healthy and unhealthy boundaries, see Table 4.4, which describes boundaries that are too permeable (unhealthy), semi-permeable (healthy), and impermeable (unhealthy).

Feedback. Feedback is an important source of information about the self. Self-esteem develops out of a relatively stable perception of ourselves. In part, our perceptions are formed by feedback we receive. Sometimes this feedback is colored by the projections of others, and we may develop a faulty self-view if the information is not filtered. Young children have not yet developed these filtering abilities, and so may introject the flawed feedback of others. Changing that self-view requires introducing new data about the self; and the new data must be repeatedly reinforced or presented in a powerful or novel way to increase its impact. It is usually not until adulthood that people become aware of and sort through the feedback they internalized as children. Part of the individuation process involves becoming aware of introjects and evaluating these messages.

We are continually given feedback, both verbal and nonverbal. Therefore, it is important that we learn to *filter feedback*. This involves sifting what is received, sorting through and owning what seems to fit, and discarding what does not. In this process, it helps to ask yourself two questions:

What grain of truth can I identify with in this?

What doesn't fit?

For example, if Leon gives Jake feedback regarding Jake's behavior, the feedback may be truer for Leon than for Jake. In other words, Leon may be *projecting* onto Jake feelings, attitudes, behaviors, or thoughts he considers unacceptable and so avoids recognizing in himself. Jake may display at least a piece of the behavior/attitude/feeling Leon is projecting, and so might ask himself, "What grain of truth can I identify with in this?"

This kind of question facilitates the sorting Jake needs to do so that he does not take in what more aptly belongs to Leon (or to some significant person in Leon's history).

TABLE 4.3
Healthy and Faulty Ego Boundaries

Internal Zippers (Healthy)	External Zippers (Faulty)
Can say "No"	Believe they are regulated by others and the outside world
Can walk away	Feel invaded and victimized
Can monitor closeness	Allow others to mind-read: "You feel ... " "You don't think that way"
Express opinions assertively	Have incomplete interpreting screens
Can wonder aloud	Denial and repression prevent assessment of what is safe and what is harmful
Can ask questions freely	Display highly stereotypic sex role behavior: for example, helpless female or macho man
Can keep things private and secret without feeling guilt	Allow intellectual blurring, created through criticizing, blaming, mind-reading, prying, mind-raping (attempting to turn your thoughts into another's thoughts), comparing, belittling
Can stand up for themselves even when in the minority	
Can choose what feelings to express to others and has some control over feelings	
Able to maintain nonblaming stance	

Table 4.3. Continued.

Know their failings are not dependent on other's actions or the cause of others' behaviors and feelings	Allow physical blurring through abuse, teasing about the body, bathing, enemas
Can sit with another person in pain without taking on feelings	Allow emotional blurring. Created when parents share with child secrets that should be for spouse only; when lonely, angry parents share intimate feelings with children; through emotional deprivation or psychological abandonment
Respect others' distance boundaries	
Have good esteem about physical self	
Able to touch and be touched with discrimination	
Able to nurture and receive	
Engage in regular exercise; eat a balanced diet	
Able to be vulnerable when safe	
Know there is a shadow side as well as light side to each of us	

Note: Based on work by Fossum and Mason, (1986).

Feedback is laden with values. In sifting feedback, therefore, we might ask ourselves, "What value underlies this feedback? Do I agree with this value?" In so doing, we protect our esteem.

Sometimes we need to learn from feedback that is difficult to own but has some truth; at other times, we need to hold our ground and resist feedback that does not resonate. People generally experience two common problems with filtering:

1. **The personal boundary is almost impenetrable.** In this case, we allow little feedback to enter, whether negative, positive, or neutral. But feedback can help increase our awareness. The more aware we are, the more effective we can be. Feedback can help us discover behaviors or attitudes that are not effective in meeting our needs.

TABLE 4.4
Boundaries—Too Permeable, Healthy, and Impermeable

UNHEALTHY (too permeable)	HEALTHY (semi-permeable)	UNHEALTHY (impermeable)
Telling all.	I consider the other person's level of interest and caring before opening up to them. I also consider my own readiness to talk about particular subjects.	Not talking; not opening up at all.
Falling in love with anyone who shows interest.	When someone reaches out to me, I ask myself whether the person has the qualities I need. I selectively allow myself to love and be loved.	Not allowing anyone's love in, and not allowing myself to love anyone.
Acting on first sexual impulse.	My feelings and my self-esteem decide whether I act on sexual impulses. "Will I feel good about myself?" is my first question.	Not allowing myself to be sexually excited or aroused, even when I feel good about the person. Not allowing myself to act on these feelings, even when I believe the timing is right.
Letting anyone close who wants to get close.	I am wary of someone who wants to get too close too soon. I evaluate how close I want to be, with whom, and how soon.	Never letting anyone get close to me.
Touching a person without asking.	I don't touch others without thinking about whether they have given me signals, direct or indirect, that it is okay. I ask for feedback about touching.	Not touching others

Table 4.4. Continued.

Letting others describe my reality.	I assume that my perception of what is going on is just as accurate as another's perception. I refuse to allow others to tell me, "You don't feel that way." I trust my own feelings and perceptions and filter feedback according to what fits for me.	Not being willing to listen as others describe their reality.
Expecting others to anticipate my needs.	I do not expect others to read my mind about what is going on with me. I tell them what I want/need.	Not allowing others to take care of my needs.

Note: Adapted from *Overeaters Anonymous* handout.

Without awareness, our ability to change is inhibited. We may block even positive feedback, as illustrated by this case study:

> Joe couldn't allow love in. He couldn't even accept or feel his wife's love. At the heart of this block was his core belief that he was unlovable, which stemmed from the way his mother had treated him and his perception that his mother did not love him as she did his brothers. Indeed, Joe's mother did feel differently about him: While she was pregnant with Joe, she learned that her husband was involved in an affair. She had felt defeated and depressed during Joe's early years, so she had not bonded with Joe as she had with her other children.

2. **The personal boundary is overly penetrable.** In this case, we allow too much feedback to enter, without discriminating between useful and toxic. If we accept feedback indiscriminately, we are likely to ingest others' "garbage" as well as their "gifts."

Either problem can inhibit the stability and enhancement of self-esteem unless we develop the skills to gain more flexibility and choice with regard to our boundaries.

Hoyle, Insko, and Moniz (1992) demonstrated the impact of self-consistency on feedback, finding that people with low self-esteem tend to evaluate most favorably those who give them average feedback rather than success or failure feedback. Average feedback is more comfortable for them. This resistance to more positive feedback may be due to a fear of being unable to maintain success feedback. The authors also found that individuals with high self-esteem who are evaluated favorably tend to view their evaluators unfavorably, perhaps because they see themselves at risk of hearing at disconfirming evidence. Being aware of the distortion tendencies that are at work to help preserve the consistency of our self-esteem may help us to more choicefully absorb feedback from others. Ultimately, we can develop a more accurate view of ourselves when our boundaries are semi-permeable.

Another skill we must learn is controlling the flow of feedback. If feedback is too voluminous or fast, we can learn to say, "I need to slow down. Let's take this a piece at a time"; or "I don't think I can absorb any more feedback right now. Let's pick up next time after I've had a chance to think about this"; or "I've had a bad day. I don't think I can listen well now. Can we discuss your feedback later?"

Positive feedback is effective in raising performance expectancies in men and women. McCarty (1986) found that men and women also tend to lower their performance expectancies in response to negative feedback or no feedback. However, McCarty maintained, men who receive no feedback have confidence levels as high as women who have received strong positive signals, since women's confidence levels tend to be lower than men's. This indicates that if supervisors, trainers, and educators have limited time, their focus might be better spent giving women feedback in order to bolster their confidence and increase their chances of advancing in school, training, and work situations.

Meta-Talk. The skill of meta-talk (or commenting on the process) allows us, at least temporarily, to avoid reacting and, instead, to step out of the interchange to examine more objectively what is happening. A new direction may then emerge.

> Rose, who usually is quite kind, suddenly becomes irritable and finds fault with everything Sophie does. Sophie can either respond with defensiveness or say, "I'm feeling irritated that you seem to be picking at me. Is something going on with you?" In this way, Sophie reacts to the process rather than to the content.

In allowing us to step out of the interaction, meta-talk gives us the emotional distance necessary for greater objectivity, which may help protect our self-esteem. By stepping out, Sophie could observe that Rose was behaving in a peculiar way and could ask what was going on with her rather than internalizing the criticisms, feeling hurt by the attack, defending, or counterattacking.

Nonverbal Behavior. Flexibility in nonverbal behavior is associated with higher self-esteem. Our behavioral repertoire needs to include a balance of communal and agentic qualities, as shown in Table 4.5.

When we are able to operate in both a receptive mode (for example, in silence, our lips parted, with small body movements) and an active mode (for example, with more talking and larger body movements), we can meet more of our needs. When our nonverbal behavior is congruent with our verbal message, our communication is most powerful (Mehrabian, 1972). The more flexible we are, the more needs we are able to meet, and the higher our self-esteem.

The more we are able to tune in to the nonverbal aspects of communication, the deeper our exchanges are likely to be. When we notice the nonverbal behaviors of others we have more data to assess how best to proceed.

> Joe, the manager of a store, saw one of his employees dealing aggressively with a customer. When he pointed out to Larry his aggressive behavior, Joe noticed Larry's mouth and jaw tighten, as he replied in a sharp tone, "Okay."
>
> Joe decided to report his here-and-now observations to Larry, noted his tone and the tension he observed around Larry's mouth, and asked what he was feeling. Larry replied, "I guess I'm angry. That customer is abusive to the sales personnel every time he comes in this store!"
>
> This was new information to Joe. Joe suggested that he and Larry discuss more effective ways of handling difficult customers.

TABLE 4.5
Receptive and Active Modes

Receptive	Active
speaking softly	speaking loudly
respecting another's territory	challenging another's boundaries
softening the eyes	hardening the eyes
standing still	moving forward
not touching	touching

This example illustrates how a person can use nonverbal observations to help draw someone out and communicate more effectively. Similar data can be used to gauge how a person responds. Words can hide feelings, but nonverbal responses are not easily masked. Nonverbal cues hold a great deal of informational power. However, it should be noted that the same nonverbal cue can have different meanings for different people, so it is important to check out how the cue relates to the person you're dealing with. For example, a flushed face can mean the person is physically hot, angry, embarrassed, or ill.

According to Gambrill and Richey (1988), people who are receptive to nonverbal cues can decode affect, interpersonal orientation (e.g., dominance and submissiveness), and intentions (e.g., when a person is ready to leave). Nonverbal skills also can help us differentiate literal and metaphorical communication and identify sarcasm and joking. Attention to dress, mannerisms, and the like can cue us to roles or social scripts (e.g., professional, priest, mechanic) that can help guide the interaction. An enormous amount of valuable information is given by physical appearance, touch, gestures, proximity, posture, gaze, and facial expression (Knapp, 1980).

For example, confidence is expressed in nonverbal presentation; and nonverbal presentation can influence our confidence. Confidence is displayed nonverbally by such cues as few self-touches or self-adapters, few speech disturbances, a lower pitched voice, faster speech rate, steady eye contact, little blinking, louder speech, easy smiling, and faster responses to questions about facts (Kimble & Seidel, 1991).

Ingredients of an Interaction. You'll find several common ingredients in every interpersonal interaction. These are key concepts to improve our communication (Satir, Banmen, Gerber, & Gamori, 1991). When we deliver a message, we do so with both words and affect (see Figure 4.1).

"Where's the newspaper!?"

The content of this message is a simple question on the whereabouts of a newspaper. However, in addition to the content (words), we deliver the message with particular vocal qualities, a specific facial expression, gestures, gaze quality, and body posture, all of which convey our attitudes and feelings.

Perhaps this particular message was delivered with a slight bite in the voice, a glare of the eyes, a wrinkled forehead, and a questioning intonation. Other nonverbal expressions may have been present as well, but *we select what we attend to based on our feelings about ourselves and our past experiences*. What we see and hear represents Area 1 of Figure 4.1. This is our lens.

For example, if self-esteem is low, we are likely to attend to negative cues. In essence, we attend to that which is familiar. In the newspaper question ex-

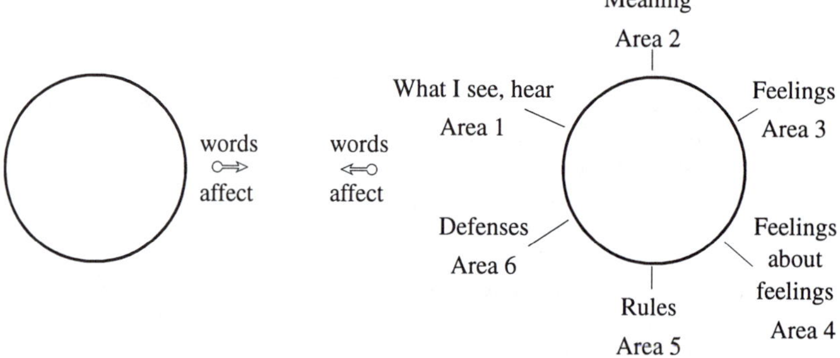

Figure 4.1. Ingredients of an interaction.

Note: From Satir and Banmen (1984) and Satir, Banmen, Gamori, and Gerber (1987).

ample, perhaps the receiver had a father who regularly delivered his messages with a bite in his voice. Problems in communication develop when we react to behaviors and attitudes we associate with important figures in early life (parents, other authority figures, siblings). Sullivan (1968) referred to these inaccuracies in perception as *paratoxic distortion*. Our selection of what we attend to is an inside job. What we select out of the totality of someone's communication, we run through past experience.

Based on what we attend to in the communication, we assign *meaning* to it based on our past experiences (Area 2 in Figure 4.1). In our example, the receiver might assume that the speaker is blaming him or her for the newspaper not being on the table where it usually is kept. Sometimes the meaning we attach is based on *projection*. In this case, the receiver might blame others but is unable to own this attitude and, instead, attributes blaming to others.

Or, perhaps the receiver was blamed a lot as a child and so reacts with *feelings* such as fear or defensiveness (Area 3, Figure 4.1). To complicate matters further, the receiver will then have *feelings about* fear and defensiveness (Area 4, Figure 4.1). Let's presume in this case the receiver feels ashamed about being afraid and unlovable. These feelings usually are connected with survival rules associated with that feeling. "If I'm afraid and defensive, does that mean I'm no good? Or that I shouldn't exist? Shouldn't live?" These are survival fears.

How the receiver actually responds to the message, "Where's the newspaper?!" depends on the *rules* he or she learned about commenting (Area 5, Figure 4.1). We all learn rules in our families about whether it's okay to talk about our thoughts, experiences, and feelings. In some families, commenting on internal reactions is encouraged and safe. In others, rules such as the following inhibit commenting:

"I shouldn't be afraid."

"I should be perfect."

"I should take care of my own problems."

"I should protect others from my feelings."

Rules like these affect how we take care of our feelings and, ultimately, ourselves.

When we experience survival fears, we typically resort to one of three *defenses* (Area 6, Figure 4.1):

Ignoring: "I don't see it."

Denying: Saying to ourselves, "It isn't so."

Projecting: Thinking, "You think I'm no good," rather than owning, "I think I'm no good."

On the other hand, if we have high self-esteem we can acknowledge our feelings and our survival fears, and we do not need to habitually defend. The more freedom we feel to experience and talk about our beliefs and feelings, the higher our self-esteem will be.

Our past experiences, the rules we learn about commenting, and our survival fears all affect our perceptual filters, the meaning we attribute to events, and our ability to communicate effectively. All these elements, according to Satir et al. (1991), are the ingredients of an interaction.

As an antidote for constricting rules, Satir (1976) proposed five freedoms:

1. The freedom to see and hear what is
2. The freedom to express thoughts and feelings
3. The freedom to accept feelings as they are
4. The freedom to freely ask for wants and needs without permission
5. The freedom to take risks

These freedoms represent direct challenges to the shoulds and oughts with which many of us were raised and encourage breaking from the familiar to achieve even greater freedom.

NEGATIVE FEEDBACK

In a variety of settings (both personal and work-related) we often are faced with negative feedback that is directed at us. Gottman (1994) differentiated criticism from negative feedback, stating that *criticism* attacks someone's personality or character whereas a *complaint* refers to a specific behavior. If we learn to handle complaints well, we can avoid unfair blame while accepting responsibility for our behavior and maintaining our self-respect. Three frequent problem responses to negative feedback are *defending*, *counterattacking*, and *distancing*. With practice, however, we can learn more effective ways of handling criticisms and complaints. Here are some guidelines:

1. **Relax and try to just hear the person.** Support yourself by breathing deeply and keeping your feet planted on the floor. Hearing the person out does not mean you should allow yourself to be abused. If the person yells at you, calls you names, and so on, ask him or her to change the behavior. If the person does not alter the behavior, you can end the exchange.

2. **Clarify the complaint.** Often criticisms are not specific and people use labels that have various meanings or that incite an emotional reaction (Satir, 1988a). Talk until you get a clear picture of a specific complaint.

   Example: "You're lazy!"

   Response: "Tell me more about that. What's your picture of how I'm lazy?"

3. **Agree with the part of the criticism you can claim, and give back the rest.** Parts of criticism often hold some truth. Avoid arguing over parts with which you disagree (Satir, 1988a).

   Example: "You are so irresponsible! You're never on time, you don't pay the bills when you say you will, and I can never depend on you."

   Response: "You're right, I was late. I'm sorry. I should have called" (McKay & Fanning, 1987; Satir, 1988b).

4. **Own the behavior or attitude.** Agreement with a critic generally stops the criticism quickly. *It should only be used, however, when you actually can take responsibility for the criticism.*

   Example: "I'm really having a problem with your controlling behavior in this group."

   Response: "Yeah, I have a problem with that part of me, too. You're right, and I'll pay attention to that."

5. **Tell the person how you're feeling.** For example, "I feel embarrassed about this mistake," or "I'm trying to listen but I have a hard time taking criticism."

6. **Consider asking for help in changing the behavior.** For example, "Let me know if I start to lecture you again. I'm not always aware of it."

At times we will receive criticism about a third party. This happens because many of us have as much trouble expressing our criticism directly to others as we do hearing criticisms. If we avoid expressing ourselves directly, when tensions run high enough we will look for another outlet. It is best to stay out of the middle in such situations and to encourage the person to express the criticism to the appropriate receiver. Since people often find such exchanges risky, they may need support to express their feelings directly to the person.

Children are especially likely to be targets of criticism about a third party, especially when a parent is in the midst of a divorce. This is especially harmful to children. In the absence of good judgment on the part of parents, children might be encouraged to cautiously set limits with their parents: "Mom, I know you're angry, but it hurts me when you talk about Daddy that way," or "Dad, would you talk to Mommy about that? This stuff is hard to hear."

Children are very vulnerable to criticism. The younger they are, the less capable they are of detaching from it. They lack the cognitive ability that allows them to realize that Dad or Mom might be having a bad day, or that underneath Mom's criticism is sometimes fear.

> Virginia Satir once directed a group activity in which participants walked around a room holding pieces of paper labeled "self-esteem" in front of them. As they walked, people criticized each other; each time they leveled a criticism, they tore off a small piece of the other person's paper. By the end, they had very little of the paper representing self-esteem left.

Adults, adolescents, and children alike are affected by such a critical climate, but children have much less power and little freedom to remove themselves from toxic environments or to protect themselves in other ways.

We need to have as much skill to give negative feedback as we do to receive it. Following are some guidelines for giving negative feedback to others (Clarke, 1983; Gambrill & Richey, 1988; Gottman, 1994; Notarius & Markman, 1993).

1. **Decide if it is an important issue.** Sometimes it's important to let things go. Choose your fights carefully, and ask yourself these questions: Is it important to you? Will it be helpful to the other? Does the behavior happen frequently Will revealing your feelings improve your relationship?

2. **Pick an appropriate context.** Timing is crucial to a successful exchange. Pick a mutually acceptable time and place, and be sure you've answered these questions: Is there enough time and energy to thoroughly work through the problem? Is there privacy? Is the person in a receptive place? Has the person consented to hearing your negative feedback?

3. **Be as specific as you can.** Describe the behavior or attitude and provide specific examples.

4. **Own your complaint.** "I feel annoyed that you interrupted me when I was talking about my problem at work. This was hard for me to tell you."

5. **Avoid judgmental or emotion-laden words.** These are likely to close down communication. Present your complaint evenhandedly, and use descriptive words referring to specific observable data.

6. **Offer recommendations for change.** Ask yourself what you would like. This keeps the exchange more positive and shows you are willing to share some responsibility for making things different.

7. **Keep your feedback to one issue, and be brief.**

8. **Be alert and stay on the subject.**

9. **Assure the person that you care about him or her and the relationship** and want to work through the problem. Some people are so sensitive to criticism that they think it is the end of the relationship, or that this negative feedback means you think they are "bad."

10. **Keep in mind that the optimal praise-to-criticism ratio is 4:1.** You must balance negative feedback with respect, empowerment, and recognition of desired performance (Indermill, 1992).

Most people are not experienced in giving negative feedback effectively or in receiving it. Women, especially, are uncomfortable giving negative feedback. In a study by McCarrey, Piccinin, Welburn, and Chislett (1989), women reported being more upset than men when they give negative feedback and reported feeling less effective than men in receiving negative feedback. While men and women reported giving and receiving negative feedback in about equal amounts, women feel more vulnerable than men and reported higher risks associated in receiving negative feedback (McCarrey et al., 1989).

McCarrey et al. (1989) also found that, compared to men, women report greater benefits from receiving negative feedback from friends and less benefits from receiving it from business transactions. While women reported feeling less proficient in giving negative feedback, the observers rated men and women equally proficient in both giving and receiving negative feedback. This finding may be related to women's general tendency to rate themselves more harshly, which appears over and over in the literature, or it may be due to the fact that giving negative feedback runs counter to the "female role," which demands that women interact harmoniously with others. In other words, giving negative feedback may be seen as incongruent with sex-role.

Lower proficiency in giving and receiving negative feedback may be related to a fear of negative self-evaluation, to irrational beliefs, and to self-esteem (Lemelin, Piccinin, Chislett, & McCarrey, 1986). However, Lemelin et al. found that people with greater proficiency reported slightly higher social anxiety and slightly more irrational beliefs. Perhaps this is because they are taking more risks and breaking rules or norms.

COMMUNICATION STANCES

Self-esteem affects how we communicate with others. People adopt defensive stances that grow out of low self-worth (Satir, 1988b; Satir et al., 1991). Satir outlined four communication stances found in people all over the world: placator, blamer, irrelevant, and super-reasonable.

Placator. The placator apologizes for everything, tries to please everyone, promises anything, asks for nothing, and hides his or her own needs. The person is in a one-down position, conveying the feeling, "excuse me for my existence." According to Satir (1988b), placators evoke guilt, using this power to be spared. Nothing touches them. The placator position originates as a survival technique when a person is completely dependent upon another for survival. Nonverbally, the placator might display a caved-in posture, with shoulders rounded, eyes averted and looking down, backing away, whiny voice. Underneath is the fear that comes with complete dependence.

Blamer. Blamers find fault with everything, take credit for everything (regardless of whether they had a part in it), and use phrases such as "never," "always," and "Why don't you ever?" Satir (1988b) noted that, by evoking fear, the blamer gains power. The more fear and terror blamers feel, the more they need to lay blame. As a result, the distance between the blamer and others grows, and painful loneliness develops. In relation to body posture, blamers put their entire selves on the line. Jaws, chest, and temples may tighten. The image blamers convey is that of an accusing pointed finger. This is their distorted way of saying, "Please love me," "Value me," or "I am frightened."

Irrelevant. This person is constantly moving both verbally and physically. People who favor this stance are powerful in their irrelevance. One of their powers, explained Satir (1988b), is to evoke fun. All survival needs are wrapped up in continual movement. Through distraction, the person's needs, feelings, and relationships are ignored. Distractors avoid responding to the verbal point. They have a tremendous ability to deflect and disrupt; and they will go to extremes to get attention because, underneath, they feel unlovable. Physically, such persons are generally unbalanced.

Super-Reasonable. These people are extremely erudite. According to Satir (1988b) and Satir et al. (1991), they evoke envy, give long explanations, and express little or no feeling. Their manner conveys the attitude that only ideas and things are important. They hide their feelings and needs. The super-reasonable person is likely to have a monotone voice and be motionless. Underneath, he or she often feels alienated and withdrawn, hiding behind intelligence and a wide vocabulary.

According to Satir (1980), an individual becomes more congruent when he or she can allow feelings to come to the surface. Satir (1976, 1988b) explained that, through the use of these communication stances, people try to prevent what is on the inside from showing. This creates great internal stress and hopelessness. Each stance represents a creative solution to allay fears and cover a lack of wholeness. Each needs something added to it for the person to become whole:

Placator: Add, "What do you want to do for yourself?"

Blamer: Add love.

Irrelevant: Add grounding through touch.

Super-Reasonable: Add, "How are you feeling?" Connect with touch, laughter, feelings. Sidle up to the person, hold the person's hand, make the person laugh, generate sensation.

Satir (1988b) noted that people need to learn how to apologize rather than placate, be reasonable without being a robot, change the subject without distracting, and state disagreements in a nonblaming way. Satir (1980, 1988) also maintained that, by learning these skills, we can become more congruent and improve our chances of meeting our needs. This congruency is reflected in nonverbal demeanor: Congruent people stand upright, have a relaxed stance, make relaxed eye contact, hold their shoulders straight and their knees slightly flexed, and keep their breathing full.

People with high self-esteem are likely to display a balance in activity and reactivity, counterdependence and dependence, self and other responsibility, clear boundaries, and nonverbal behavior that is congruent with what is communicated verbally and experienced internally.

HANDLING CONFLICT

The key to successful relationships is the ability to handle differences. Disagreement is normal. People come from different backgrounds and have different needs. Research by Gottman (1994) and Notarius and Markman (1993) identified conflict patterns that lead to relationship trouble and patterns that can help contain conflict. Self-esteem can be maintained if we possess skills for mastering conflict and building healthy communication patterns.

Both Gottman (1994) and Notarius and Markman (1993) emphasized the importance of positive communication. According to Notarius and Markman, a single negative exchange will wipe out 20 acts of kindness. They encouraged bolstering our "bank accounts" with small acts of kindness to balance the stress of turbulent times. Likewise, Gottman (1994) encouraged freely expressing validation and admiration of others, keeping the ratio of positive to negative high on the positive side.

Gottman (1994) and Notarius and Markman (1993) outlined a number of patterns (listed below) that tend to block communication. If we are aware of these patterns, we can learn to alter our styles of interaction so that we can resolve our differences without creating serious threats to our relationships:

1. **Mind-reading:** This involves making statements about what another thinks, feels, wants, needs.

2. **Excuses and explanations:** Rather than listening to another's gripe, we defend ourselves with rationalizations for our behavior.

3. **Criticism:** We attack someone's character, often with blaming. If we feel criticized, we find it difficult to hear anything else others may say.

4. **Negative problem talk:** This is conveying problems in a negative manner (e.g., using a nasty tone of voice, muttering under your breath, blurting out, yelling, whining, or being sarcastic).

5. **Negative solution talk:** We generate solutions that are unrealistic, unreasonable, unfair, or impractical.

6. **Hopeless talk:** We make pessimistic statements about the relationship, the topic, or our partner.

7. **Invalidation:** This involves put downs, attacking another's character or personality, and criticizing the person rather than the behavior.

8. **Hot thoughts:** These are negative thoughts that serve to keep a person fired up inside, including these:

   - **Character assassination:** We use vague, general, negative labels such as wimp, passive-aggressive, or senile.

   - **Always-never talk:** We use the words "always" or "never" when talking about someone, which intensifies character assassination: for example, "He's so selfish. He never pays attention to what I want."

   - **Hopeless self-talk:** This conveys hopelessness about a relationship: for example, "We're never going to be able to resolve this."

   - **Should self-talk:** We tell ourselves our partner should or should not do something: for example, "She should do things I want to do."

9. **Kitchen-sinking:** We drag everything and anything into an argument (past and present gripes) and mix them with sarcasm and criticism.

10. **"Experting":** We use what therapists and authorities say, "throwing" this expert advice at our partner in destructive and critical ways.

11. **Distracting:** We might leave the TV on or continue reading or listening to music while we're talking about something important.

12. **Distancing:** This involves walking away from a conversation, looking away, ignoring your partner, changing the topic, or hurrying closure.

13. **Deflecting:** We focus on our partner's behavior and not our own.

14. **Contempt:** This involves insulting and psychologically abusing your partner through words and body language. Contempt includes insults, name-calling, hostile humor, sarcasm, mockery, body language, and facial expressions that dismiss or disparage the other.

15. **Defensiveness:** We deny responsibility, cross-complain, counter-attack, yes-but, and repeat our position over and over. Defensiveness is characterized by nonverbal signs such as a false smile, shifting the body from side to side, and folding the arms across the chest.

16. **Stonewalling:** This involves closing another out by not reacting at all, shrugging, or simply leaving the room. The attitude conveyed is disapproval, disinterest, coldness, and smugness.

In addition to pointing out problematic patterns of communication in conflict, Gottman (1994) and Notarius and Markman (1993) outlined a number of skills that can facilitate conflict resolution, including these:

- **Replace hot thoughts**, which fuel conflict, **with more positive thoughts.**

- **Use positive problem talk**. Give information about the problem, ask questions in a level way, use I-statements, and use listening talk that shows you hear the speaker's message. Be there emotionally, nod to acknowledge what is being said, sit facing your partner, and be sure you communicate your understanding to him or her. *Showing that you understand what your partner is saying is not the same as agreeing or disagreeing.* Try to see the problem from your partner's point of view and, if you can, acknowledge that your partner's point holds some validity. If you have trouble with this, at least tell your partner you are trying to understand and will consider another point of view.

- When you can, **acknowledge that your actions may have provoked your partner's response**. Owning mistakes and apologizing can have powerfully positive results.

- **Take control of your own arousal** by editing out destructive talk; calming yourself, using relaxation techniques and planned stop-action or time-out agreements; being aware of hot thoughts and replacing them with soothing, positive thoughts about your partner; and interpreting your partner's attacks as representing the strength of his or her feelings and the desire that you pay attention to them. Pause before you attack your partner, and ask yourself what you hope to accomplish.

- **Keep your statements short and to the point**, being specific about your gripes and giving clear indications that the behavior can change. Use declarative statements rather than questions designed to bait and hook. State your complaints in a way that your partner is not likely to take as a personal attack.

- **Listen and speak nondefensively**. Try to have a positive view of your partner. Remember specific and happy memories about him or her and try to think empathetically. You might even make a list of your partner's positive traits to use when interrupting your habitual negative line of thought in order to change your inner script.

- **Avoid belligerence**, patronizing, bullying, veiled or direct threats, and other manners of speaking that tend to trigger people's defensive responses.

With practice, we can learn to resolve conflicts in healthy, effective ways. While we may feel instant gratification when we clobber another person with criticism and contempt, it is short-lived. Each such destructive interaction poisons the relationship. We rarely feel good about ourselves in the end. Using the tools described above, we can learn to manage our differences, achieve deeper intimacy, and improve the longevity of our relationships.

A "STROKE ECONOMY"

A stroke is any positive, affirming verbal or nonverbal message. Healthy rules around strokes are crucial to satisfying relationships and high self-esteem. While complaints are commonplace, people often are stingy about expressing positive feelings. Wycoff (1977) explained the "stroke economy" to which many people adhere (see Figure 4.2).

✘ Don't ask for stroke you want.

✘ Don't take in strokes you get.

✘ Don't reject strokes you don't want.

✘ Don't give strokes to others.

✘ Don't give yourself strokes.

Figure 4.2. Stroke economy.

Note: Adapted from Wycoff, (1977).

According to Wycoff (1977), such a stroke economy breeds a shortage of love. There's an old story about a town whose people began hoarding "warm fuzzies" for fear they would run out if they gave too many away. The townspeople soon withered away and died. People in our culture seem to operate from a similar limitation mentality rather than from a premise of abundance.

Don't Ask for Strokes

Many people believe if we have to ask for a stroke it does not mean as much—that the stroke is not genuine or meaningful if we must ask for it. If we are to get beyond this rule, we need to abide by a corollary rule: *that we give only strokes we genuinely feel and want to give*. Remember that asking for the strokes we want increases our chances of getting what we want. Wishing and hoping does not accomplish the same end, since most people cannot read our minds.

Don't Take in Strokes

Many of us have difficulty fully receiving the positive feedback we receive. We often deflect positives verbally ("Oh, this was just something I threw together. Yours is much better.") or nonverbally (by holding one's breath or looking away). For many people, it is easier to accept strokes based on facts than those based on judgment. ("I appreciate your being on time," versus "You look beautiful today.") But we can and should learn to accept positive feedback. With practice, we can master the skill of accepting strokes.

> When receiving a stroke, breathe in deeply and allow yourself at least 30 seconds to drink it in. Focus on absorbing the stroke.

Some of us feel so badly about ourselves that we feel we don't deserve strokes. Some of us are afraid people will find out we are frauds; that underneath we are incompetent or worthless (see chapters 2 and 3). Still others fear we will never be allowed to make a mistake if we receive the stroke; that, eventually, we have to pay a price for praise. Despite all of these obstacles, strokes are essential to self-esteem. Only continued repetition of strokes can make a dent in our automatic defenses against the nurturance desire.

Don't Reject Strokes

Sometimes we feel we cannot reject unwanted strokes. But there are times when it is in out best interests to refuse strokes. For example, an attractive female lawyer may need to learn how to reject strokes around her appearance in circumstances when strokes for her competence are more appropriate.

Don't Give Strokes

While there are innumerable times we *could* give strokes every day, many of us withhold them. What would the world be like if we all went around looking for ways to compliment people? We are all hungry for strokes. The ideal praise-to-criticism ratio is 4:1. Stroke deficits create all kinds of emotional and physical problems. Remember that people who are not used to getting strokes are not likely to reward you for your efforts at first. With persistence, however, change is possible. Do not despair. Giving strokes is an act of kindness. The world needs more acts of kindness to overshadow all the acts of negativity and violence (McCarty & McCarty, 1994).

Don't Stroke Yourself

Our society has all kinds of prohibitions against stroking ourselves. You wouldn't want to get too big an ego—a "big head" some call it. Bragging is not permitted. But putting ourselves down or minimizing our accomplishments is acceptable. If we do give ourselves strokes, chances are someone (particularly someone with low self-esteem) will try to tear us down. Miller, Cooke, Tsang, and Morgan (1992) differentiated between making positive self-statements and boasting, which emphasizes power, status, and wealth and exaggerates strengths and competencies. Boasting implies being better than others. If we make positive self-disclosures, avoid gloating, and recognize the role of others in our success, we are likely to be better received. We need to learn to encourage positive self-disclosure. With permission and support, we can break the "stroke economy" and start a more positive cycle.

COMMUNICATION SKILLS IN THE WORKPLACE

The majority of personal and relational problems in the workplace are related to self-esteem (Indermill, 1992). By learning a variety of communication skills, managers can foster self-esteem in their employees, create a positive work climate, and increase productivity and general health.

By developing a supportive climate, managers can help individuals respond more positively to suggestions from others on how to improve performance and alter self-perceptions in a positive direction (Arnold & Rezak, 1991).

Many people in the workplace suffer from low self-esteem and their performance is affected as a result. According to Arnold and Rezak (1991), many people with low self-esteem display learned helplessness, which results from repeated failures or from experiences they interpreted as failures. People who operate from a helpless position drain supervisors and coworkers with their constant need for reassurance. Those with low self-esteem also tend to be cautious and passive rather than take initiative and risks (Arnold & Rezak, 1991). These are barriers to productivity. Table 4.6 lists several problematic behaviors that reflect low self-esteem and responses that can help to improve self-esteem.

Arnold and Rezak warned that managers should be aware of the "change back" phenomenon, since the larger system has an investment in maintaining the status quo. Also, because learned helplessness often is part of a person's identity, a new self-image must be formed before the person can give up the old view. Moving from the familiar to the unfamiliar involves risk and requires lots of support. Employees also need help forgiving themselves for their prior helpless orientation. The manager must reinforce the strength and courage it takes to change.

Employees with low self-esteem require extra time and effort. If managers resent this, they may subtly undermine the employees' efforts at change. But if we are aware of potential obstacles, we can minimize the negative effects.

CONCLUSION

A variety of forces, both inside us and in our environment, serve to anchor, enhance, or diminish our self-esteem. People in our support satellites can help ground and strengthen our self-esteem and establish stability. When our social

TABLE 4.6
Problematic Behaviors

Characteristics of Low Self-Esteem	Supervisor Response
Habitual and unthinking self-derogation	Ignore self-deprecation
	Question basis for remark
	Use self-disclosure to help worker consider possibility for change ("I used to feel that way.")
Define competence as perfect, unassisted performance	Place employee on team
	Reward with praise for work on team
	Praise for going ahead with job under imperfect conditions
Focus on failures and ignore successes	Reassure that perfection is impossible
	Reward for effort as well as for finished products
Shrink from action and work and endlessly plan	Redirect attention to strengths and seemingly trivial accomplishments
	Divide task into component parts
	Work with employee to get task started
	Watch for and reward initiative and action

Note: Adapted from Arnold and Rezak (1991, pp. 102-103).

system is weak, our self-esteem is more susceptible to erosion. The quality of our relationships both reflects our self-esteem and can maintain, strengthen, or diminish it.

Individuals with low self-esteem often display self-defeating behavioral patterns. For instance, our skill in self-criticism may be overdeveloped while our skills at stroking and asserting ourselves may be underdeveloped. Another way of looking at it is that certain parts of our personalities are not as easily accessed—our muscles in those areas are not used much, and so are weak.

Of course, exercising those muscles requires commitment and daily practice. We often are in search of an easier solution that requires less work and commitment. We want a magical cure, a pill that will make us "better" instantly. Such easy fixes are not possible.

Opting to develop new skills involves venturing into new territory, facing the fears and awkwardness of learning something new, and taking risks. The more stable and supportive our external environment, the more we are likely to take prudent risks. Initially, our goals must be focused on strengthening our internal and external support systems. Once these are strengthened, we will be in a better position to take risks, expand, and stretch our self-esteem to ever-higher levels.

With each goal we set and accomplish, we take another step to enhanced self-esteem. At the same time, we learn we are in charge of our lives and can paint whatever picture we want. To do this, we must identify our goals, categorize them into long-term and short-term goals, and identify the smaller steps we must take to meet them. Too often we avoid the task of choosing a direction and we don't notice or give ourselves credit for the small, daily steps toward our major goals.

The more we opt for safety, the more we uphold the status quo, which lowers our self-esteem. In extreme cases, this dependence on safety results in boredom, complacency, and even death (spiritual as well as physical). Through self-chosen risk-taking we can stretch ourselves to achieve our maximum potential. Without risk-taking, no new edges are developed; we become stagnant.

Self-esteem also can suffer when the opposite occurs: Excessive, reckless risk-taking creates too much stress. If we do not permit ourselves enough time to integrate changes or we do not give enough attention to the consequences of a particular action, our self-esteem may be jeopardized. Thus, the healthy individual strikes a balance in this safety-risk dimension and is able to manage effectively.

If we have low esteem, we may have difficulty moving onward after pushing for what we want. We may not see ourselves as able to transform or to effect changes in our lives. Instead, we tend to collapse when we encounter resistance. Consequently, our needs go unmet. Seligman (1975) called this phenomenon "learned helplessness." The individual gives up, feeling impotent to affect change. Each time we yield, our self-esteem shrinks a bit more; each time we choicefully press against the environment, our self-esteem expands. Enhancing our self-esteem involves learning how to develop an optimistic perspective and move beyond our boundaries effectively and to yield when appropriate.

ACTIVITIES YOU CAN DO

ACTIVITY 4.1 NEW EXPERIENCE

Introduction: This activity asks you to venture into the unfamiliar, trying something you have always wanted to do but never took the time or had the courage to do.

Time required: Varied time for homework parts; 30 minutes for discussion

Participants: Any number; adolescents and adults

Setting: Office or classroom

Materials: None

Procedure: Have three new experiences in the next week. For example:

- Try skiing
- Call someone you met recently and ask him or her to lunch
- Buy a piece of clothing that is different from what you normally wear
- Arrange to get a massage
- Get a "reading" from an astrologer
- Organize an adventure (e.g., rafting, skydiving, gliding)
- Try something you've thought of doing but never took the initiative to try

Record your feelings and thoughts before, during, and after this activity.

Share your experiences with a small group of supportive people.

Outcomes: Expands your familiarity boundary and stretches your ability to nurture yourself.

ACTIVITY 4.2 NOURISHING

Introduction: This activity encourages you to share their appreciation with other people rather than to hoard it.

Time required: 20 minutes

Participants: Any number; all ages

Setting: Group or classroom

Materials: None

Procedure: Think of one or two people in the class or group who has made you feel good. How did this person make you feel good? What did he or she do? How did you feel? What did you like about it?

Go to the person you have these feelings toward and share your feelings and appreciation. What impact did sharing these feelings have on your relationship?

Outcomes: Frees up expression of positive feelings and appreciation.

ACTIVITY 4.3 WITH WHOM DO I HAVE THE PLEASURE?

Introduction: This activity helps clear away blocks to fully experiencing a person for who he or she is, thereby heightening contact.

Time required: 40 minutes

Participants: Any number; adolescents and adults

Setting: Classroom or office

Materials: None

Procedure: Form pairs and sit directly across from your partner.

Put your feet flat on the floor and be aware of the chair supporting you. Now tune into your breathing. Imagine breathing in and out of an area around two inches below your navel. Breathe slowly and deeply as you count your breaths from 1 to 10.

Close your eyes and think of yourself as a camera and your eyes as lenses.

Open your eyes, take a picture of your partner, then close your eyes.

With your eyes closed, look at your picture of your partner. Is it clear? How do you feel about the picture? How do you feel about the person in the picture? File that picture away for later.

Open your eyes and look at your partner for any ways in which he or she reminds you of anyone you have known, seen, or heard about (e.g., eyes, coloring, haircut, facial expression, body shape).

Close your eyes. If your partner did remind you of someone, let yourself know how you feel about the person you remembered.

Visualize this remembered person. Now bring back to your memory the picture of your partner. Compare the two.

Open your eyes once again and let yourself pay attention to what you notice first about your partner.

Close your eyes. What meaning do you put with what you noticed?

Open your eyes. Make up a story about what you think your partner is seeing, hearing, and thinking in relation to you. Be aware of what you told yourself and how you are feeling about it.

Close your eyes again and remember all the information you can about your partner that came from a third party (another person, a newspaper, gossip). Be aware of what you feel and think as you gather this information.

With your eyes still closed, remember any previous contacts you've had with your partner. Recall how you feel about those contacts now.

Share the information that came up with your partner; be in touch with your feelings as you do so.

Check to see if you feel any differently about your partner now. Take another picture. Check how you feel inside. Be aware of the differences.

Outcomes: Helps you to recognize projections and other communication blocks and to increase contact with others.

Note: From Satir (1984).

ACTIVITY 4.4 CHILDHOOD LABELS

Introduction: Through this activity, you will identify and evaluate labels that were applied to you when you were growing up and recognize the effect of these labels on your self-esteem.

Time required: 20 minutes

Participants: Any number; adolescent or adult

Setting: Classroom or office

Materials: Paper and pen

Procedure: Think of four labels that were used to describe you as a child. Pick two you think are positive and two you find negative. Then answer these questions:

- What memories do you associate with each label?
- What other labels describe you?
- How did you get each label? (Describe the where, when, how, and with whom.)
- Which of your labels refer to physical aspects? Personality traits? Behavioral characteristics? Cultural background?
- What do the labels say about the norms of the group, rules of behavior, or parental wishes and expectations? For example, if your father labeled you stubborn and said it in a disparaging way, did he mean that he couldn't altogether control you and force you to conform? Maybe being stubborn was a way you held onto yourself.
- Did you swallow theses labels without evaluating their "fit?"
- Do you still apply these labels to yourself today? Do they need updating? How? For example, say you were labeled clumsy in adolescence; maybe this clumsiness was related to your rapid physical development at that time. Are you still clumsy, or are you wearing an outdated label?

Now evaluate each label: Is a piece of the label still true for you? Under what conditions or in what context does the label fit? For example, maybe you behave clumsily when you are anxious or rushed. Was the label applied to you a disowned part of the person who assigned it?

Outcomes: Enables you to reevaluate old labels and update your self-perception.

Note: Adapted from Carlock and Shaw (1988). Idea initiated by Duhl (1983).

ACTIVITY 4.5 ASSESSING YOUR NETWORK

Introduction: An adequate support network is essential for our physical and emotional health.

Time required: 60 minutes

Participants: Adolescents, adults

Setting: Homework, group, classroom

Materials: Paper and pen

Procedure: Identify the key people in your interpersonal support system by referring to the following categories:

- Family (including extended family)
- Acquaintances and potential friends
- Close friends
- Close colleagues
- Limited friendships
- Other colleagues
- Interest groups (hobby, political, cultural, social, or sports groups)
- Life task/maintenance supporters (doctors, lawyers, accountants, home repair workers, mechanics, etc.)
- Religious or spiritual support

Place these key people at appropriate distances from you to indicate how close you feel to them. Use the symbols in Figure 4.3 to indicate the nature of the relationship.

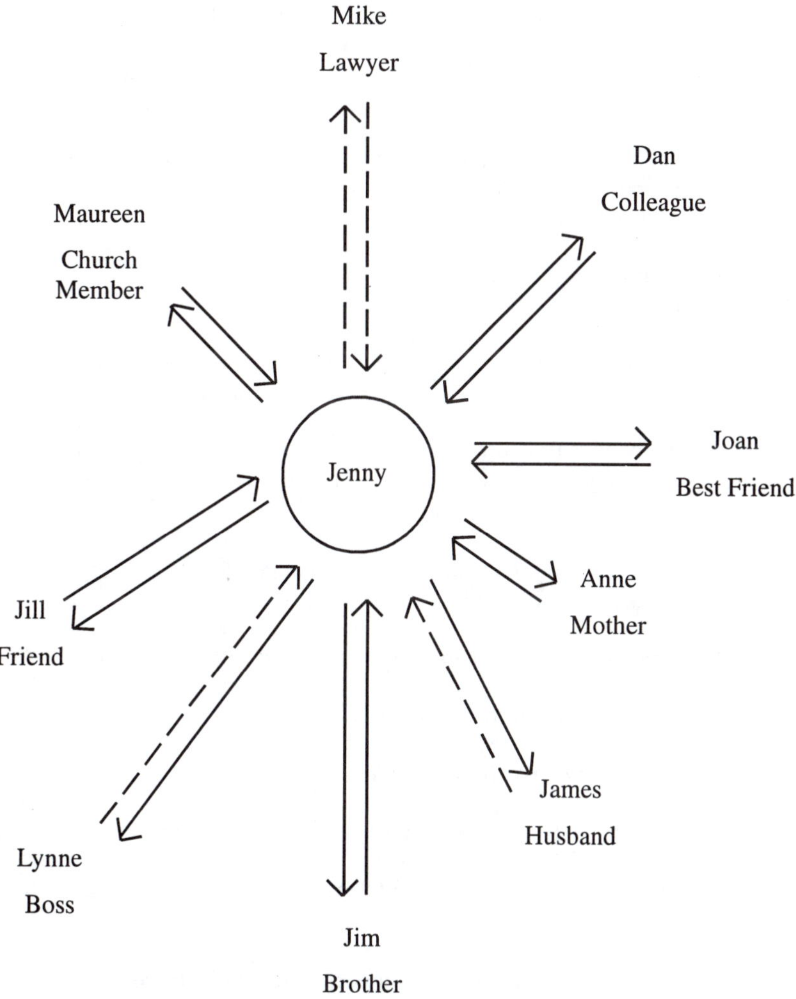

Figure 4.3. Illustration of distance others can be placed from an individual.

Use Brammer's (1991) list of functions to indicate the form of support you receive from each person:

- respect
- satisfaction from contributing to others
- love, caring, warmth
- emotional sharing
- physical intimacy
- companionship (sharing, belonging, friendship)
- encouragement (emotional support, appreciation, affirmation)
- acceptance (trust, empathy, understanding
- comfort (forgiveness, reassurance)
- example (model, mentor)
- direction (advice, assistance)
- help (material and physical assistance)
- knowledge (cognitive exchange, expertise, information, instruction)
- feedback (honest opinions, perspectives)

Look over your network. Are there changes you'd like to make? What are they? For example:

- Strengthen support between my husband and me
- Ask my boss for more feedback
- Increase reciprocity with my friend Jill
- Identify a couple of people who could serve as mentors for my work

List the changes you'd like to make, and establish some goals for yourself.

What are the strengths of your support system? List these.

Outcomes: Helps to create a solid support system that can strengthen your coping ability. Also helps you recognize and use your support system to the fullest.

ACTIVITY 4.6 THE MEDICINE BAG

Introduction: In this activity you will collect healing stones and other sacred items to remind yourself of resources that can be used for inner healing.

Time required: Several hours, spread over several weeks

Participants: All ages

Setting: Classroom, group, one-on-one; involves homework

Materials: Medicine bag, tape recorder, blank audio tape, paper, and pen

Procedure: Make or find something to serve as your medicine bag. List friends and family who know you and with whom you feel close. Ask each person on your list to identify a resource he or she sees in you and to find a symbol to represent this resource. The symbol should be small enough to fit in your medicine bag. Meet with each person and ask him or her to present this symbol to you and to place it in your medicine bag. As each person places a symbol in the bag, he or she is to reveal the resources this symbol represents and tell you a memory of a time you displayed this resource. Record each of these presentations on audio tape. Next, make a transcript of the audio tape.

Draw on the symbols, the audio tape, or the transcript whenever you feel discouraged or self-critical, or you want a booster for your self confidence.

Outcomes: Focuses on your strengths; lets you receive positive feedback from significant others.

ACTIVITY 4.7 CRITICISM CLUES

Introduction: If we are to filter feedback, we must understand the difference between constructive and destructive feedback.

Time required: 20 minutes

Participants: Individual or group, children or adults

Setting: One-on-one, classroom, group, homework

Materials: Paper and pen

Procedure: Think about times you have sent or felt like sending destructive feedback. What were the circumstances? List as many as you can. The following are examples:

- When I am tired
- When I am ill
- When someone is not listening to me
- When I am scared
- When I think you won't agree with me
- When someone recently put me down
- When I'm angry about something else
- When I'm frustrated
- When I'm jealous

At times people give us destructive feedback. Think about what might be behind the destructive criticism others give you. Try to become less impulsive in accepting it. Imagine a screen in front of you. Practice absorbing the feedback that is true of you. Learn to filter feedback that might be coming from an uncentered place.

Outcomes: Increases awareness of others' motives for giving feedback; helps you to determine what information you need to filter.

ACTIVITY 4.8 NURTURING PARTNER EXCHANGE

Introduction: This exchange creates the possibility for greater closeness and nurturance between two people in an existing relationship.

Time required: 15 to 30 minutes for homework; 20 to 30 minutes for discussion

Participants: Any number; adolescents and adults

Setting: Group room or classroom

Materials: None

Procedure: Complete this exercise with a person you have known for some time; review the impact each of you has had upon the other.

Exchange feelings and thoughts on the following statements:

- What I give to you; what you give to me
- What you mean to me; what I think I mean to you
- What I teach you; what you teach me
- How I am special to you; how you are special to me
- Perceptions of your most special moments together
- The positive changes you have made in your relationship

Outcomes: Increases your ability to nurture another person.

ACTIVITY 4.9 WISHING WELL

Introduction: Many people cut off their wishes even before they are completely aware of them. "I can't have that" is the familiar internal response that kills a wish before it is expressed. This activity will help you formulate and express your wishes.

Time required: 1 to 2 hours

Participants: Group of 6 to 12; all ages

Setting: Carpeted group room or classroom

Materials: None

Procedure: State three wishes you want fulfilled during a 15-minute span of time. Be as specific as you can so you get exactly what you want.

Describe your process of determining your wishes.

How difficult was it for you to ask for and receive your wishes? How can you apply this in your life?

Outcomes: Increases your willingness to ask for what you want.

ACTIVITY 4.10 FUN DECK

Introduction: Many people could use a little more play in life to balance their serious workday selves. Play helps people to feel more relaxed.

Time required: 60 minutes

Participants: Children, adolescents, and adults

Setting: One-on-one, group, class, homework

Materials: Index cards, paper, and pen

Procedure: Gather a group of your most playful friends and family and brainstorm a list of as many fun things to do as you can think of. If you have trouble coming up with ideas, think back to different ages and recall what you did for fun. Often these same activities (roller skating, using a hula hoop, playing leapfrog, building sand castles, going on treasure or scavenger hunts, building a snowman, rolling in the fall leaves, Trick or Treating) can be fun for adults, if you can break free of your inhibitions. Come up with activities you can do alone, with a partner, or in a group. Record your activities on index cards—one per card.

Carry out at least one fun activity each week.

Outcomes: Develops your ability to be playful and decreases stress.

ACTIVITY 4.11 STROKE SHEET

Introduction: This group activity helps you identify your strengths.

Time required: 30 minutes

Participants: Any number; adolescents or adults

Setting: Classroom

Materials: One sheet of paper, two pins, and one pen per person

Procedure: Pin sheets of paper to each other's backs.

Move around the room writing strokes or positive affirmations you have for people on their sheets.

Take off sheets and fold them. Don't look at them.

When everyone is together, look at the sheets and share the wording with each other.

Hang all the sheets where they can be seen.

Outcomes: Self-esteem is enhanced by receiving feedback on strengths. The written stroke sheet can remind you of your strengths when you need a boost.

Note: Activity is original; idea initiated by Wycoff (1977).

ACTIVITIES FOR GROUPS

ACTIVITY 4.12 OBJECT IDENTIFICATION

Introduction: In this fun activity, children find objects to represent the different parts of themselves. These objects can be used to expand or shift self-concept and to encourage the conscious use of resources to deal with problems.

Time required: 30 to 45 minutes

Participants: Children ages 6 to 10

Setting: Classroom, group, individual therapy, church group

Materials: Small objects around the house that parents will allow children to use at school

Procedure: Ask the children to find several small objects around their house that represent different positive qualities they believe they possess. Be sure they get their parents' permission. Show the children several common objects you have collected to represent how you see yourself.

Have the children bring their items to the classroom, along with a written list of what each object represents. Turn this list over so that the children cannot see. Have them write their names in the middle of small circles and place their objects around their names, with a piece of paper by each object.

Ask the children to walk around looking at the names and the objects, guess what quality each object represents and, write the quality on the piece of paper.

Now have the children sit in a circle with their objects and tell the others what their objects really represent.

Ask the children to think about all the people with whom they are close: mother, father, grandparents, siblings, aunts, uncles, neighbors, priest, rabbi, minister, teacher, and so on. Now ask them to think about the qualities they came up with for themselves; ask which of these people possess each of these qualities. For example, "I'm warm, and my Mom is warm, too."

Now talk about the influence of others on how we see ourselves.

You might also ask, "Who really appreciates your positive qualities? How do they show this appreciation? How do they react when you show your "problem" qualities? Do they help you with those?

Have the children read aloud the others' guesses about each object, and state whether they think that quality fits them. Have them identify which qualities are surprises and which they might add to each other's lists.

Creative application: A creative application of this activity is to have the children make a basket for their parts. Then, when a child has a problem to solve, ask him or her to go to the basket and pick out one or more resources that might help solve the problem. Direct the child to bring this resource to bear on the problem and guide the child in doing this. When the child's behavior is problematic, you can go with the child to the basket and come up with a resource that could help, or find a resource in another child's basket that could help and that the child might want to develop and add to his or her resource basket. The child who owns that particular resource could be asked to help teach the child about this resource.

Outcomes: Makes qualities concrete and helps with self-differentiation and self-expansion; helps children begin to understand the influence of others on self-esteem.

ACTIVITY 4.13 FUZZY GIFTS

Introduction: This activity shows children the importance of giving and receiving fuzzies (positive feedback).

Time required: 20 minutes

Participants: Children ages 6 to 10

Setting: Classroom, church group, group or individual therapy

Materials: Paper and crayons (optional), 50 small pompons

Procedure: Review material in this chapter on giving and receiving feedback.

Explain what fuzzies are and the different ways you can give them: by talking, touching, writing, singing, or drawing. Few people get enough warm fuzzies. Some people do not know how to take them in.

Ask the children to imagine themselves as plants in need of watering. A plant may be leaning over, looking very sick, but once you water it, the plant drinks in the water all the way down to its roots. That is what people need to do, too—soak up that fuzzy.

Explain that it helps if the fuzzy they give tells the person exactly what they liked. That makes the fuzzy stronger. Sometimes when people are feeling like very droopy plants, they have a hard time soaking in fuzzies. But if the fuzzy tells them exactly what you like about them, it's harder for them to stay droopy. For example, if your Dad looks droopy, you might tell him, "You really helped me a lot with my homework tonight, Dad. I understand it all now."

Tell the children that it helps to tell people exactly what they like—even people who don't seem droopy. We all need these "super-chargers."

Ask the children to spend the next few days thinking about the people around them and what they like about those people. They can be classmates, children in their church or synagogue groups, teachers, family, friends, kids on their soccer team, whoever. Remind the children each day and ask them for a couple of examples of what they are noticing. Help them to say exactly what they like, and what they saw or heard in the other that reminds them of what they like.

At the next meeting ask the children to think about one person and exactly what they like about this person, with an example.

Next, direct the children to either voice this to the person, make a drawing that represents what they like about this person, write a poem or song about the person's quality and how he or she shows it, or write a note to the person about the quality, using specific examples.

When they deliver their fuzzies, ask the children to notice how the person responds and how they feel inside as they deliver their fuzzy message.

Ask the children to report back on their experiences.

Outcomes: Teaches children how to deliver effective positive feedback and how to receive positive feedback.

REFERENCES

Alberti, R., & Emmons, M. (1990). *Your perfect right*. San Luis Obispo, CA: Impact.

Arnold, R. M., & Rezak, W. N. (1991, Sept. 28). Overcoming learned helplessness: Managerial styles for the 1990s. *Journal of Employment Counseling*, 99-106.

Black, C. (1982). *It will never happen to me!* Denver: MAC Printing & Publishing.

Blevins, W. (1993). *Your family, yourself.* Oakland, CA: New Harbinger.

Blier, M., & Blier-Wilson, L. (1989). Gender differences in self-rated emotional expressiveness. *Sex Roles, 21*(3/4), 287-295.

Brammer, L. W. (1991). *How to cope with life transitions: The challenge of personal change*. New York: Hemisphere.

Carkhuff, R. (1993). *The art of helping*. Amherst, MA: Human Resource Development Press.

Carlock, C. J., & Hagerty, P. T. (1988). *Bridges to intimacy: Couples workbook.* Dayton, OH: Peoplemaking Midwest.

Carlock, C. J., & Shaw, C. A., (1988). *Self-esteem for adult children of alcoholics* [audio cassette]. Muncie, IN: Accelerated Development.

Carlock, C. J., Hagerty, P. T., & Verdon, T. R. (1985). *Satir family instruments.* Dayton, OH: Peoplemaking Midwest.

Clarke, J. I. (1983). *Ouch, that hurts!* Plymouth, MN: Daisy Press.

Cloud, H., & Townsend, J. (1992). *Boundaries.* Grand Rapids, MI: Zondervan.

Curran, D. (1983). *Traits of a healthy family.* New York: Random House.

Duhl, B. (1983). *From the inside out and other metaphors.* New York: Brunner/Mazel.

Fossum, M. A., & Mason, M. (1986). *Facing shame.* New York: North.

Gambrill, E., & Richey, C. (1988). *Taking charge of your social life.* Belmont, CA: Wadsworth.

Gilles, J. (1976). *Friends.* New York: Coward, McCann, & Geoghegan.

Gottman, J. (1994). *Why marriages succeed or fail.* New York: Simon & Schuster.

Herek, G. M., Levy, S., Maddi, S., Taylor, S., & Wertlieb, D. (1990). *Psychological aspects of serious illness: Chronic conditions, fatal diseases and clinical care.* Washington, DC: American Psychological Associates.

Hoyle, R., Insko, C., & Moniz, A. (1992). Self-esteem, evaluative feedback, and preacquaintance attraction: Indirect reactives to success and failure. *Motivation and Emotion, 16*(2), 79-101.

Indermill, K. (1992). Managing self-esteem in the workplace. *National Council on Self Esteem, 6*(3), 14.

Jakubowski, P., & Lange, A. (1978). *The assertive option: Your rights and responsibilities.* Champaign, IL: Research Press.

Jourard, S. M. (1971). *The transparent self.* Princeton, NJ: Van Nostrand.

Karpel, M. (1986). Testing, promoting, and preserving family resources: Beyond pathology and power. In M. Karpel & W. R. Beevers (Eds.), *Family resources* (PP. 175-232). New York: Guilford.

Katherine, A. (1991). *Boundaries*. New York: Friends/Parkside Recovery.

Kimble, C., & Seidel, S. (1991). Vocal signs of confidence. *Journal of Nonverbal Behavior, 15*(2), 99-105.

Knapp, M. L. (1980). *Essentials of nonverbal communication.* New York: Holt, Rinehart & Winston.

Lemelin, M., Piccinin, S., Chislett, L., & McCarrey, M. (1986). Consistency between self-report and actual proficiency in giving and taking criticism. *Psychological Reports, 59,* 387-390.

Lerner, H. (1990). *The dance of intimacy*. New York: Harper & Row.

Malone, T. P., & Malone, P. T. (1987). *The art of intimacy.* New York: Fireside.

McCarrey, M., Piccinin, S., Welburn, K., & Chislett, S. (1989). Declaration of women of self-reported criticism skills. *Journal of Social Psychology, 130*(3), 317-323.

McCarty, M., & McCarty, P. (1994). *Acts of kindness*. Deerfield Beach, FL: Health Communications.

McCarty, P. (1986). Effects of feedback on the self-confidence of men and women. *Academy of Management Journal, 29*(4), 840-846.

McKay, M., & Fanning, P. (1987). *Self-esteem*. Oakland, CA: New Harbinger.

McNulty, S., & Swann, W. (1991). Psychotherapy, self-concept change, and self-verification. In R. Curtis (Ed.), *The relational self* (pp. 213-237). New York: Guilford.

Mehrabian, A. (1972). *Nonverbal communication*. Chicago: Aldine-Atherton.

Miller, L. C., Cooke, L., Tsang, J., & Morgan, F. (1992). Should I brag? *Human Communication Research, 18*(3), 364-399.

Notarius, C., & Markman, H. (1993). *We can work it out.* New York: Putnam.

Ornish, D. (1992). *Reversing heart disease without drugs or surgery.* New York: Ballentine.

Peck, M. S. (1987). *The different drum*. New York: Simon & Schuster.

Rancer, A., Kosberg, R., & Silvestri, V. (1992, June). The relationship between self-esteem and aggressive communication predispositions. *Communication Research Reports, 9,* 23-32.

Richter, S., Brown, S., & Mott, M. (1991). The impact of social support and self-esteem on adolescent substance abuse treatment outcome. *Journal of Substance Abuse, 3,* 371-385.

Satir, V. (1976). *Making contact*. Berkeley, CA: Celestial Arts.

Satir, V. (1980). *Communications*. A workshop sponsored by the Family Institute, South Bend, Indiana.

Satir, V. (1983). *Conjoint family therapy*, *3rd Ed.* Palo Alto, CA: Science and Behavior Books.

Satir, V. (1984). *Tiyospaye*. A workshop in the Black Hills, South Dakota.

Satir, V. (1988a, May). *The Phil Donahue Show*, New York: Columbia Broadcasting System.

Satir, V. (1988b). *Peoplemaking*. Palo Alto, CA: Science and Behavior Books.

Satir, V., & Banmen, J. (1984). *Virginia Satir—Verbatim*. N. Delta, BC: Delta Psychological.

Satir, V., Banmen, J., Gamori, M., & Gerber, J. (1987). *Satir model and ingredients of interaction*. AVANTA annual meeting, Crested Butte, Colorado.

Satir, V., Banmen, J., Gerber, J., & Gamori, M. (1991). *The Satir model*. Palo Alto, CA: Science and Behavior Books.

Schlossberg, N. (1989). *Overwhelmed: Coping with life's ups and downs*. Lexington, MA: Lexington Books.

Schur, E. M. (1971). *Labeling deviant behavior*. New York: Harper & Row.

Seligman, M. (1975). *Helplessness*. San Francisco: Freeman.

Sullivan, H. S. (1968). *Interpersonal theory of psychiatry*. New York: Norton.

Tubesing, D. (1979). *Stress skills*. Duluth, MN: Whole Person Associates.

Wegscheider, S. (1981). *Another change: Hope and health for the alcoholic family.* Deerfield Beach, FL: Health Communications.

Whitaker, C., & Napier, A. (1978). *The family crucible*. New York: Harper & Row.

Wycoff, H. (1977). *Solving women's problems*. New York: Grove.

Chapter 5

BODY AND SELF-ESTEEM

C. Jesse Carlock

Our level of body satisfaction relates strongly to our self-esteem. *Body image* is the picture we have of our bodies at rest or in motion at any moment. It is derived from internal sensations, postural changes, contact with outside objects and people, and our emotional experiences and fantasies (Freedman, 1988; Salkin, 1973). According to Hutchinson (1985), body image includes feelings, attitudes, and beliefs about our bodies.

We begin developing our sense of body image during the second six months of life, although our image becomes more defined as we develop a sense of self-identity. Some theorists have contended that early body image has a critical influence on developing self-concept (Sears, Rau, & Alport, 1965). However, our body image continues to develop over a period of time and is subject to later modification.

DEVELOPMENT OF BODY IMAGE

Infancy and Childhood

Through the process of feeling, handling, and tasting, infants gradually distinguish between what is self and what is not, where they physically end and the world begins. This process of identity exploration begins at birth (Sullivan, 1953). Babies make full use of their bodies and are completely absorbed by them. Each newly found ability–to grasp with the hand, to kick, to crawl, to bounce on a bed–totally captures the child's attention (Nelson, 1975).

Infants' early attitudes toward their bodies are influenced not only by kinesthetic pleasures but also by attitudes their primary caretakers hold about sex and bodily processes. These attitudes are first conveyed through touch and tone of voice and later by words. Life begins as an extension of mother, and mother is the first teacher of body image (Freedman, 1988). All the other caretakers and people with whom the infant comes into contact provide further information about body image.

The origins of guilt, shame, and unhealthy sexual attitudes lie in this initial period of bodily exploration. A number of circumstances may block the child's total body absorption at this point: physical illness, a parent's inability to determine and respond to the child's needs, criticism of the child's early spills and falls, disapproval of the child's natural exploration and enjoyment of his or her body, or physical or sexual abuse or neglect. According to Lebe (1986) body image for girls is more complex than for boys, since their sexual organs are partially internal and, therefore, not easy to see and touch.

In response to messages prohibiting expression of feelings, thoughts, or needs, children learn to constrict the muscles associated with such expressive functions. In attempting to protect their newly developing bodies, children also tend to constrict their musculature. Unless deliberate attempts are made to help them regain this connection–through revising beliefs or through activities such as sports, body awareness, and movement games–they begin steadily disconnecting from their bodies (Barlin & Greenbert, 1980; Benson & Stuart, 1992; Freedman, 1988; Nelson, 1975).

Another important element in the evolution of selfhood is our increasing control over our bodies. Our pictures of ourselves grow as our motor control increases and we can do more and more. The way people respond to our growth also influences our attitudes toward our bodies. Later, in middle childhood, changes in our size and rate of growth and our increasing ability to coordinate affect our success both in school and in our peer culture, ultimately affecting our self-esteem.

Children seem to be influenced early by cultural stereotypes and to incorporate others' opinions about their weights (Lerner & Gellert, 1969). Even young children are conscious of the weight of adults and children. They tend to favor normal-weight children over obese children. Children who are overweight have lower opinions of their bodies and appearance than do normal-weight children (Johnson, 1984; Mendelson & White, 1982). Although some studies have found the overall self-esteem of overweight children to be lower, the findings are inconsistent. Mendelson and White (1982) identified the ages of 7 through 12 as a time when being overweight affects body esteem; but, they contended, lowered body-esteem often has not generalized to self-esteem at this age. If this is accurate, then early intervention is important.

Adolescence

According to Jersild (1952), our greatest concern with our bodies comes after elementary school. The body seems to take on intense meaning during adolescence, when we experience so many overt bodily changes, inner hormonal fluctuations, and dramatic morphological changes (Hoover, 1984; Peterson & Taylor, 1980). Even minor deviations are viewed with alarm at this time. In a study by Huenemann, Shapiro, Hampton, and Mitchell (1966), an increasing number of girls from 9th to 12th grade described themselves as fat and as dissatisfied with their physical appearance, even though objective classification of the number of obese girls did not increase. In a more recent study of adolescent girls, Debold, Wilson, and Malave (1993) also found critical views toward physical characteristics, with 64% of the girls reporting a negative body image.

According to Lebe (1986), at puberty girls often feel rejected by their fathers, who tend to withdraw from the relationship because of their own anxieties about their sexual feelings in response to their daughters' developing sexuality (see also Rasmussen & Heriza, 1984). This abandonment at a time of such significant body changes may cause the girls to have conflicted feelings about their developing bodies and their sexuality. On the other hand, inappropriate attention to the adolescent's developing sexuality is likely to be even more harmful.

Female adolescents tend to be more critical of their bodies than male adolescents (Clifford, 1971; Debold et al., 1993). Self-concept is tied more closely to females' ratings of their body parts than to their ratings of self-effectiveness; for males, the reverse has been true, until recently (Lerner, Orlos, & Knapp, 1976; Lerner, Iwawaki, Chihara, & Sorrell, 1980). Some studies have shown both men and women preoccupied with body weight and appearance (McCaulay, Mintz, & Glenn, 1988). Yet Worsley (1981) presented evidence that body image is more important to girls than to boys in adolescence. A study by Offer, Ostrov, and Howard (1981) also showed that normal adolescent girls are more negatively affected than boys by normal bodily changes. The girls in their study reported feeling ugly and ashamed of their bodies.

According to Debold et al. (1993), girls at this age begin internalizing the scrutiny of their bodies that they experience from boys and men, judging themselves the way boys and men judge them. In order to defend herself, the researchers explained, the adolescent girl shifts from experiencing her body to observing it. Overweight teenage girls often are predisposed to feelings of anxiety, inferiority, and inadequacy at this difficult time (Hoover, 1984).

According to Huenemann et al. (1966) and Robinson (1994), during adolescence boys also report increasing concern with becoming more muscular. Boys' self-esteem during this period is influenced by their body build, height, weight, physical appearance, physical adequacy, rate of maturity, and the appearance of secondary sex characteristics (Biller & Liebman, 1971; Jones & Mussen, 1958; Mussen & Jones, 1957; Strang, 1957; Yeatts, 1968). Several studies have demonstrated that men who are underweight express greater body dissatisfaction (McCaulay et al. 1988; Silberstein, Striegel-Moore, Timko, & Rodin, 1988), and may get involved in body building because they are short or skinny (Klein, 1993).

By late adolescence, the body reestablishes an equilibrium. If adolescents can accept their physical uniqueness from others and the disparity between their real physical selves and their ideal physical selves, they will be satisfied with themselves. Several recent studies have shown, however, that while overall body esteem is correlated with self-esteem for both men and women, weight dissatisfaction is not associated with self-esteem for women (Silberstein et al. 1988; Tiggemann, 1992). Researchers have postulated that, because body dissatisfaction in women is so universal, its effects on self-esteem may be buffered.

Adulthood

An early study by Calden, Lundy, and Schlafer (1959) showed that college students were no more completely happy with their physical characteristics than with their psychological attributes. Men wanted larger chests, women wanted larger busts, both sexes wanted smaller noses, and female students wanted to weigh less.

More recently, Debold et al. (1993) and Mintz and Betz (1986) reported that women tend to have greater dissatisfaction with their bodies than men do. Women tend to perceive themselves as overweight while men tend to perceive themselves as underweight (Mintz & Betz 1986). McCaulay et al. (1988) reported that women tend to see themselves as one weight category larger than their actual size. For both sexes, less positive attitudes toward body were related to lower levels of self-esteem (Mintz & Betz, 1986), although the relationship for women was stronger than for men.

Generally by middle age, people begin experiencing traumatic losses and various degrees of breakdown of their bodies. These losses continue and accelerate through later life. Beginning in midlife, for example, visual and auditory acuity diminishes; a general slowing of the nervous system occurs after age 50; and chronic disorders such as arthritis, cancer, cardiovascular problems, and diabetes occur more frequently (Hayflick, 1994; Solomon, Salend, Rahman, Liston, & Reuben, 1992). Some physical deterioration, however, may be related to our beliefs about aging and the cumulative effects of abuse and neglect of our bodies. Luce (1979) wrote an inspiring book that dispelled self-limiting beliefs about aging, longevity, and sexuality in later life.

The body speaks clearly, revealing the character of the life a person has lived. Body and mind are reflections of each other. Emotions and experiences that form the personality directly affect the formation and structure of muscles and tissue. As such, the body offers the person trained in body awareness a wealth of data and an avenue for helping. As a result of expanding knowledge about the body, counseling has grown from a purely verbal approach to approaches that directly comment on body processes (alterations in breathing, muscular tensions, postural changes, or eye movement, for example). As Keleman (1975), Kepner (1987), and Kurtz and Prestera (1984) emphasized, the body not only reveals the person, *the body is the person*. By examining a number of dimensions of the body (such as muscle tone, skin color, posture, proportions, tensions, and movements), we can develop a sense of the life and history of the person within.

CULTURAL EFFECTS ON SELF-ESTEEM AND BODY IMAGE

How we feel about our bodies is closely related to how we feel about ourselves (Rosen & Ross, 1968; Secord & Jourard, 1953). In a culture that places so much emphasis on rigid and idealized standards of beauty and acceptability, it's no wonder that few of us escape self-esteem problems related to body image. Increasingly, researchers have emphasized the effects of such rigid standards in weight, physical attractiveness, and even height (Brownell & Rodin, 1994; Freedman, 1988; Gillis, 1982).

Standards of Attractiveness

Not many of us measure up to the images the media establishes as standards of beauty. These standards leave little room for differences, though they vary widely from society to society. Our perception and evaluation of our bodies are strongly influenced by cultural and societal standards.

Physical attractiveness is highly valued in this culture. People whose body images are not congruent with their physiological images often find themselves in emotional difficulty. As mentioned in chapter 1, the more congruent our real and ideal selves are (including physical selves), the higher our self-esteem. As a result of socialization, women especially equate physical attractiveness with self-worth (Greenspan, 1983).

While we are programmed to adopt rigid physical criteria for attractiveness, most people cannot meet those criteria. As aging continues, even those few who manage to meet such standards inevitably suffer losses. Those who place primary emphasis on their bodies as the main source of self-esteem (for example, body builders and models) risk increasing damage to their self-worth as they age.

In a culture that places such a premium on measuring up to an unrealistic ideal, we can see the damage that can occur to self-esteem when women age and their skin loses some of its elasticity, men begin balding, physical endurance diminishes, hair starts graying, and people look in the mirror and notice deep wrinkles in their faces or bags under their eyes. Rigid and perfectionist body ideals leave no room for the appreciation of differences or respect for the natural transformation one's body undergoes through the life cycle (see Boston Women's Health Collective, 1984).

Obsession with Weight

Brownell and Rodin (1994), Bruch (1973), Chernin (1981) and many others have commented on the detrimental effects of the American preoccupation with weight. Demands that we conform to an unrealistic image of a "good body" have a distorting effect. Women's magazines, diet clubs, diet foods, and diet drinks all attest to *the big issue* on the American woman's mind: fear of fat. Our culture is obsessed with thinness (Chernin, 1981; Debold et al., 1993; Fallon, Katzman, & Wooley, 1994; McCoy, 1982).

The "fat industry" is a $30 billion a year enterprise (Brownell & Rodin, 1994). Even slim people experience nagging terror over every bite they eat, worrying that they will become fat if they "let themselves go." People either fear getting fat or are ashamed of being fat.

Women, in particular, are persecuted for their weight; TV and movie images and fashion advertisements convey the message that only slim women are worthy of love. Ironically, even in clothes catalogs for larger women the models typically are slimmer than the catalog's target audience. Women are in a double-bind: They are given the message, "lose weight," and are faced with the fact that most attempts to lose weight and maintain weight loss over time end in failure. Numerous studies have shown that even when weight loss occurs, most people soon return to their baseline weights (Garner & Wooley, 1991). (Of course, not all people fail; some studies of nonclinical samples show promising results; see Brownell & Rodin, 1994.)

Brownell and Rodin (1994) have stressed the negative effects of dieting; they emphasized the goal of accepting one's body type rather than pursuing an unrealistic ideal. Fat people are in a double-bind: If they lose weight and try to maintain a goal weight that is considered normal on weight charts, they must accept some degree of hunger and unsatisfied appetite as a way of life (Asher, 1974).

Research has shown that certain body processes impede efforts at weight loss. A study by Keesey (as discussed in Stunkard, 1980) showed that each of us has a set point around which body weight is regulated; this point defends the body against weight loss. Natural body processes therefore impede our ability to shed excess weight.

Another hypothesis on why it is so difficult to maintain weight loss posits that, while the number of fat cells in our bodies can increase at any age, it cannot be reduced by weight loss. Bjorntorp and Brodoff (1992) outlined physiological changes that shift with weight loss and serve to inhibit further loss and promote regaining of weight.

Given all of this information, the prevention of weight gain rather than weight loss probably is a better goal. Evidence shows that repeated weight loss and gain can lead to arteriosclerosis, heart attacks, and strokes (Stunkard, 1980). But if overweight people choose not to lose weight, they are likely to be subjected to ridicule, continued persecution, and resultant self-hatred. Many people in this country are on a dangerous roller-coaster of binging and starving (Brownell & Rodin, 1994; Rosen, 1982). Public education and interventions aimed at increasing self-acceptance and self-assertiveness and promoting exercise and good nutrition can help buffer self-esteem (Johnson, 1993; Schroeder, 1992).

One of the few programs to help compulsive overeaters maintain longstanding positive results is Overeaters Anonymous. This 12-step program, which is free to participants, is modeled after Alcoholics Anonymous and addresses all dimensions of a person–physical, emotional, intellectual, and spiritual–in an effort to relieve the compulsion to overeat.[1] Overeaters Anonymous provides a positive model for living in a world with ups and downs and numerous stresses without escaping into harmful dependencies. The program can help satisfy the spiritual hunger that gives rise to compulsive behavior.

While many studies have shown poor long-term results of dieting, Brownell and Rodin (1994) reported good long-term results from programs combining low-calorie diets with behavior modification and education. For some, these

1. For more information, write to Overeaters Anonymous at 4025 Spencer St., #203, Torrance, CA 90503. Some beginning materials that may be helpful are *Overeaters Anonymous* by Bill B. (1981), *Listen to the Hunger* (Anonymous, 1987), and *Twelve Steps for Overeaters* by Elizabeth L. (1988).

programs may be a viable alternative to Overeaters Anonymous or may be useful in conjunction with such a program.

If you decide to forgo dieting and seek a more well-rounded approach to food, several good books are available to help. Orbach (1979, 1982), for example, contended that compulsive overeaters are out of touch with themselves and that preoccupation with food masks other problems. She also stressed the relationship between compulsive eating and women's overgiving role in society and the complicated social meanings of food, femininity, and body size. She was one of the first to view compulsive eating and dieting as a compulsion.

Roth (1982, 1989) continued to correlate the relationship between a person's physical self and emotional well-being. If people hate their bodies, they will have low self-esteem. Roth emphasized that eating is not the real issue–that the core of the problem is an "inside job" (see also Hillman, 1996). Compulsive eating serves a function and, until the needs it fulfills are addressed, the person will continue to regain weight. Weight problems may signal an underlying anxiety or depressive disorder, for example, or serve as a blanket to hide one's womanliness in the absence of adequate sexual assertiveness skills.

Hollis (1994) examined the role of anger toward mothers in compulsive overeating. She also examined the role of family in the dysfunctional process. Hollis maintained that compulsive overeaters develop "as if" personalities as they try to please others. This is directly related to the encultured female role in our society. According to Hollis (1986), food is used to drown out the true person inside, and recovery involves a journey to the real self. Hollis stressed that family members help overeaters to live the lie, and that recovery depends on increasing awareness of their role as well. She emphasized the issues of control and vulnerability in the recovery process.

According to Boskind-White and White (1991), Chernin (1981), Fallon et al. (1994), and Neuman and Halvorson (1983), eating disorders have become more widespread in the last 20 years: Doctors have seen a drastic increase in anorexia, a disorder that causes people (mostly women) to starve themselves in order to become very thin, and bulimia, a condition that causes people (again mostly women) to eat and then fast, or eat and then purge (through vomiting, laxatives, or diuretics). Bulimia is now epidemic on college campuses (Boskind-White & White, 1983; Chernin, 1981). Because of their intense fear of being fat, anorexic subjects experience a significant distortion in their body image: Most grossly overestimate their body size (Bell, Kirkpatrick, and Rinn, 1986; Hsu & George, 1990).

Obese subjects also tend to distort their body size (Bell et al., 1986; Hsu & George, 1990). Researchers have found that the further subjects are from the weight norm, the greater they tend to over- or underestimate their appearance (these results have been replicated by Birtchnell, Dolan, & Lacy, 1987). According to Mable, Balance, and Galgan, (1986), women tend to estimate their weight at 15% above their actual weight. Mable et al. (1986) and Thompson and Thompson (1986) also related lowered self-esteem and depression to overestimation of body weight in normal-weight subjects.

Much of the research on preoccupation with body weight has focused exclusively on females (Mable et al., 1986; Mintz & Betz, 1986; Pliner, Chaiken, & Flett, 1990). While a few studies have compared overweight males and females, researchers are only beginning to identify the effects being underweight on males (Harmatz, Gronendyke, & Thomas, 1985; McCauley et al., 1988; Silberstein et al., 1988). Harmatz et al. (1985) found that underweight males have extremely negative self-images and show poor social adjustment that matches or exceeds that of overweight females. Tucker's (1982) research supported the idea that the muscular male body is the most socially desirable. Muscular males receive much more positive feedback and tend to feel better about themselves (Klein, 1993; Robinson, 1994). According to Robinson (1994) and Tucker (1982), to the degree that men's bodies deviate from the mesomorphic type, their self-concepts tend to decline rapidly.

Accepting our body types and resisting unrealistic weight ideals are two positive directions suggested by the literature. But what about the increasing number of obese people in our society?

The more obese one is, the more health risks one incurs. Brownell and Rodin (1994) argued that the obese are a legitimate target of treatment efforts, whereas others who are closer to normal weight might better be educated to accept their body shapes. We would go a long way in decreasing obesity if we emphasized teaching people how to follow two fundamental guidelines: Eat when you're hungry and stop when you're satisfied. Both of these guidelines emphasize eating to meet basic needs and having the requisite interoceptive awareness to discriminate satiety and the self-respect to stop at that point. They are simple guidelines, but they are not easily attained in our culture of body detachment.

Body Detachment

Both men and women in our culture tend to experience a detachment from their bodies. This split develops in a variety of ways.

Women have a greater need to camouflage their "deficiencies." They do this with cosmetics or, more radically, through plastic surgery. Increasingly, men are seeking to change their appearance as well, through hair transplants and other cosmetic corrections.

While women have been pressured into a preoccupation with weight, until recently they have been discouraged from pursuing physical activity unless it was defined as gender-appropriate. Consequently, women have been conditioned both to comply with external appearance standards in order to please others and to avoid physical activity that might benefit their bodily attachment, sense of self-sufficiency, and independence. Debold et al. (1993) stressed the importance of girls and women learning to act forcefully in their bodies and to find joy and pleasure in them.

Most of us have difficulty evaluating our bodies realistically. We avoid looking at ourselves in mirrors and wear clothes meant to conceal or deceive. We often feel strong emotions, such as guilt and shame, when we do look at ourselves, which produces an avoidance reaction. Looking at our bodies becomes unpleasant, causing us to look away as a defense.

According to Fisher (1973), the average person "keeps a distance" when viewing him- or herself. People even have difficulty accurately visualizing the size of certain body parts. We have a hard time recognizing what we look like, even though we have more contact with our bodies than with anything else in the environment. As a result, for many people body image is distorted (Cash & Pruzinsky, 1990). Programs developed by Cash (1991), Freedman (1988), and Hutchinson (1985) can be used to facilitate enhancement of body image.

Hooker and Convisser (1983) claimed that many women separate their bodies from their persons. This perpetuates the problem of body distortion. Some body parts are simply difficult to examine visually: the anus, genitals, and back, for example. Most of us have only a vague notion of our internal organs and body systems. While practical limitations restrict our ability to examine some parts of our bodies visually, we can use other sensations–sensations such as pain, temperature, and touch, for example–to increase our body awareness.

Many people also learn negative attitudes about their bodies from religious and moralistic sources. Montague (1971) suggested that many body taboos probably grew out of a fear closely related to the Christian traditions: the fear of bodily pleasure. Most people are body phobic: that is, they do not attend to their bodily sensations except when they are sick or experiencing an intense physical symptom, either positive or negative. Body awareness soon becomes associated only with matters of health or illness. At the other extreme are those who experience somatization disorders; they are preoccupied with body symptoms and sensations and amplify even normal signals. People with somatization disorders generally do not have an adequate language for feelings.

According to Baker and Kepner (1981) and Satir (1981), we detach from our bodies to avoid uncomfortable sensations. Uncomfortable feelings arise when our experience does not fit with the rules we believe we must follow in order to be loved. For example:

Experience: I am angry.

Rule: Anger is not okay.

Result: I tighten my jaw. I squeeze in.

According to Kepner (1987), under normal conditions, emotion is expressed through movement out to the environment, where needs can be completed. For example:

Longing: reaching out with arms and hands

Sadness: vocal sobs, facial expressions, contraction of the muscles involving breathing

When family or cultural rules prohibit expression, physical tensions develop to block such expressions, which would otherwise be punished or criticized. For example:

Rule	Prevents Expression of
Boys don't cry	crying
Be nice	anger
Be strong	fear

Parts that are denied because of such rules gradually become inaccessible, cause unaware acting-out, or are projected onto others. In fact, many relationships are based on projective identification, in which each partner reflects disowned parts of the other (Scarf, 1987).

Chronic tension eventually causes a lack of sensation. Muscular contractions were first employed as a creative method of survival when we were powerless, unable to change our environment. At that time they protected us from a flood of "dangerous" sensations (Baker & Kepner, 1981; Satir, 1981). Unfortunately, these tensions can become chronic and habitual, gradually developing into structure (for example, a caved-in chest). More appropriate responses to a changed environment often are not developed.

Most people seem to have an inner drive to regain body sensitization that has been blocked. According to Baker and Kepner (1981) and Debold et al. (1993), increased awareness of body sensation improves contact with reality, enhances self-knowing, and increases self-assurance. Baker and Kepner (1981) described two main sources of sensation: internal stimuli, which ground people in themselves, and external stimuli, which ground people in the world. Internal stimuli include kinesthetic stimuli (the sense of movement), proprioception (one's sense of location of body parts), and visceral receptors (sensations of pressure, pain, internal images, and thoughts). External stimuli are those experienced through vision, hearing, smell, taste, and touch (Baker & Kepner, 1981). In recovering sensation, Baker and Kepner (1981) suggested that we discipline ourselves to concentrate on sensations and stay with those sensations, avoiding premature labeling. Our senses require reawakening and education.

Smith (1985) reviewed the meaning of several sensory experiences (see Table 5.1), explaining how each reveals particular energy dynamics. Such a body scan can pinpoint areas in need of body work and help identify which are in need of exploration to locate the presence of toxic introjects (see chapter 4).

Most of us do not live in our bodies; we live in our heads. This is understandable, given the negative messages we often receive about our bodies and our cultural prohibitions against bodily pleasure. If we could become better friends with our bodies, get to know and give our bodies what they need, our bodies could become finely tuned barometers, invaluable in need satisfaction and coping (Borysenko, 1993; Chopra, 1991; Jencks, 1977).

Body awareness is inhibited not only by our early experiences but also by the body depersonalization encouraged in Western culture (Fisher, 1973). We see a dualism in this culture between mind and body. This split is evidenced

TABLE 5.1
Types of Sensation

Hot Spots*	When energy charge exceeds discharge; charged and held energy
Cold Spots*	Deadened or deenergized areas; areas where energy has been withdrawn to prevent aliveness
Tension*	The experience of chronic muscle contraction
Pain*	The result of strong, prolonged tension
Numbness*	The result of nerve pressure due to prolonged tension or pain; sensation of coldness may coexist if tension interferes with blood flow
Tingling, Prickly Feelings	Appear when deadened areas (cold and/or numb) become enlivened
Energy Streamings	Deep vibrations that run up and down the body; free-flowing excitement

*Words used by Smith (1985, p. 106).

TABLE 5.2
Examples of Attempts at Resensitization

Potentially Destructive	Constructive
Extremely spicy foods	Body awareness work (Trager, massage, Aston Patterning, etc.)
Fast Driving	Saunas
Smoking	Yoga
Drugs	Sports or other forms of movement (dance, marital arts, Tai Chi Chuan)
Thrill-seeking dangerous activities	Touch (light stroking, rubbing, vibrating, tapping, rocking)
Films packed with violence, suspense	Breathing work, body scanning, relaxation exercises

linguistically when people say "I like my body," "My body is tired today." We do not *have* bodies, *we are our bodies*. In the process of "civilizing ourselves," we have shown increasing disregard for our bodies.

Even the fashion industry encourages detachment from body sensations. We are pushed to conform to current styles, regardless of their comfort, compatibility with our own feelings, or even practical considerations. This is one way we ignore our physical preferences.

But we do resist body depersonalization. We attempt to regain connections with our feelings and sensations in both constructive and in potentially self-destructive ways (see Table 5.2).

Direct body manipulation through massage, Trager psychophysical work, Reichian therapy, and other body-focused approaches can enhance our awareness of sensation and feeling (Jourard & Landsman, 1980; Rubenfeld, 1992). According to Lowen (1967), identity stems from adequate body contact. Most of us have considerable difficulty developing a clear, meaningful picture of our bodies. Body work has been successful in increasing levels of self-awareness and body satisfaction.

Sensation

The opposite of body detachment is being sensorially aware. Sensation is the raw data of our experience (Baker & Kepner, 1981). Developing our sensory apparatus is crucial to healthy functioning and high self-esteem. Explore your senses by considering the following questions:

1. When you look, what do you see? Is there a difference between looking and seeing?

2. How much do you take in with your hearing? Can you close off your hearing?

3. How do different things feel? Texture, warmth, pressure, form? How much do you give and receive through touch?

4. Really taste your food today. What do you notice when you focus on savoring your food? What kinds of tastes appeal to you most? Least?

5. Can you identify different smells? How keen is your sense of smell?

6. How tuned in are you to your internal world? Of what internal sensations are you aware (for example, cold spots, numbness, tensions, warm areas)?

7. How much do you take in through each sense? Which are your favored senses? How can you resensitize the underdeveloped ones?

Another aspect of resensitizing our bodies is revitalizing deadened areas (Baker & Kepner, 1981). To determine which areas of your body are deadened, look for areas that lack arousal, feel numb, are hardened (muscular armor, for example, in a man's overdeveloped chest), or are flaccid. According to Baker and Kepner (1981) and Kepner (1987), you can resensitize these deadened areas by rubbing, moving, touching, and exercising them.

The Mind-Body Connection

Fisher (1973) associated various physical problems with specific psychological issues. In this way, we can become more closely attuned to our emotional state and, therefore, cope more adequately. Feelings usually have a somatic base. By attending to sensation, we may be guided to reconnect with lost feelings. For example, feeling your jaw tense may tell you about anger or anxiety you are feeling. Increased body awareness can help us find our way back to our feelings. If we consider our bodies as metaphors for what is happening emotionally, we can hypothesize several relationships (see Table 5.3).

Borysenko (1987) cited studies showing that 75% of visits to doctors are for illnesses that will improve without care or that are related to stress and anxiety. Many sources classify such illnesses as arthritis, migraines, bronchial

TABLE 5.3
Body Metaphors

Body Condition	Emotional Condition
Sprained ankle	Emotionally ungrounded
Hemorrhoids	Holding onto feelings too tightly
Stomach problems	Up-down issues; self-esteem issues
Headache	Perfectionism; anger and frustration; sadness
Astigmatism	Feeling unbalanced
Pimples	Irritation
Asthmatic	Dependent on a person or situation, afraid to break away, wants to control or dominate; full of ideas to get ahead but fearful of pushing against opposition; have not learned free expression; rage trapped in chest
Cold	Combination of helplessness and suppressed anger; an inner "crying" over something they feel they can't do anything about and are angry because they can't
Ulcers and stomach	Great need to be loved and secure; great need to be successful in business to justify being loved; rooted in the feeling of guilt; great need to be loved but they may not feel worthy of love; introverted types have "inside" ailments
Mononucleosis	"Victims" were pressured, consciously or not, by higher-ups beyond what they could or wanted to do; young people out of school and on their own for the first time and finding a career or romance hard to handle are susceptible
Gallstones, kidney stones	People hold in things that bother them and bury them deep in their system rather than letting them go
High blood pressure	Suppression of inner hostility and rage for fear of hurting someone they love
Diabetes	The sweets of life have been taken away from them; may have been caused by a loss of loved one

Table 5.3. Continued.

Lower backache, other back pain	Thrown out of balance; feelings about the injustice of balance of power; not feeling fully supported or feeling the burden of supporting another; not being able to ask for help in carrying the load; people who can give but have a hard time accepting; perfectionistic
Foot problems	Relates to one's foundation; one's footing; feeling stepped on and feeling sorry for oneself
Heart	Symbol of the love of one's life and the people in one's life; relates to loneliness, loss of love and connection to others
Sore throat	Restrained anger

asthma, hypertension, and certain types of colitis as psychosomatic. Achterberg, Dossey, and Kolkmeier (1994) and Borysenko (1993) offered a number of suggestions to help bridge the body-mind split and decrease symptomatology. Achterberg et al. (1994) described ways to use imagination and ritual to treat such disorders as irritable bowel, hypertension, back pain, and hypercholesterolemia as a compliment to medical intervention. They believe a person's mind and beliefs are major components in healing and describe a variety of healing rituals aimed at tuning into what's going on inside the body, sending healing messages to the body, teaching health education, and controlling habits. Achterberg et al. (1994) believed that imagery can be a potent body-mind bridge.

Hay (1985) and Steadman (1979) encouraged people to look at pain in the body as an indicator that they are "off the path." Kepner (1987) also believed in a correlation between body estrangement and illness.

Siegel (1986) stressed that a fundamental vulnerability to illness comes from our inability to love ourselves–the result, he said, of not having been loved in childhood. Siegel attempted to teach us how to behave lovingly toward ourselves and to develop a greater spiritual awareness. Meditation and visualization are two of the tools he recommended to promote inner peace and harmony of mind, body, and spirit.

Borysenko (1987; 1993), Ornish (1990), and Siegel (1986) also emphasized the importance of faith, hope, and prayer in unlocking healing energies. Borysenko (1993) explored the "idea of using a crisis" as signal to quest for meaning. She examined some of the beliefs that tend to limit growth through crisis. Anxiety, tension, and stress release increased adrenaline and cortisone, which inhibit the immune system (Borysenko, 1987; Kabat-Zinn, 1994). According to Borysenko, daily meditation along with a practiced flexible attitude toward adversities of daily life can yield physiological as well as psychological rewards. Learning to let go, to stay open and patient, and to accept ourselves, imperfections and all, can help reduce stress and improve our physical health (Borysenko, 1987). Levine (1992) emphasized that our bodies react to how we talk to them. Levine also suggested monitoring and redirecting our inner talk to more positive veins.

Body as Friend

Most of us treat our bodies as our enemies rather than experiencing a unity of mind and body. For example, I might say, "Oh, I have a headache. I wish it would go away. I'll take two aspirins. I can't get anything done like this."

We treat our pain as an inconvenience or annoyance that needs anesthetizing. Another way of treating the symptom is to see the headache pain as a signal: The body is trying to give its owner a message about something (e.g., stress, the need to cry, a sinus problem, hunger). We can use our pain as a signal to tune inside and identify the need expressed by the symptom. Without this perspective, our response is to try to silence the symptom without listening to its message. In reowning our bodies for higher self-esteem, we will learn to listen to ourselves, to use physical signals as resources for awareness and fulfillment of needs.

The importance of developing a loving relationship with our bodies cannot be stressed enough. Satir (1980) told a story about a woman who hated her legs. Satir asked her, "Tell me, have your legs ever done you any good?" The woman thought a few moments and then replied, "Well, one time when someone tried to attack me, they helped me escape. I ran so fast he couldn't keep up." Satir replied, "Now your legs are receiving love, before they only got hate."

If we are to be healthy and whole, we must learn to be in touch with and appreciate all parts of ourselves, including our bodies, and to work in coordination with all parts. Exercises combining visual and kinesthetic approaches aimed at restoring body awareness and a more positive body image can help heal the body relationship (Hutchinson, 1985; Kabat-Zinn, 1990).

In recent years a number of researchers have studied the effects of various forms of physical activity on body satisfaction and self-esteem. Clance, Mitchell, and Engleman (1980) demonstrated an improvement in children's satisfaction with their bodies and body processes through awareness training and yoga exercises. Engelman, Clance, and Imes (1982) also demonstrated significantly improved body and self-cathexis for adult yoga subjects as compared with controls. Ornish (1990) suggested the use of yoga (including breathing, meditation, visualization, relaxation, centering, and stretching) to help redirect the person inward. Yoga includes powerful techniques that help in the achievement of union (Ornish, 1990).

Overall fitness is believed to contribute to overall physical and mental health (Cooper, 1989). One study by Ben-Shlomo and Short (1986) suggested psychological benefits of aerobic conditioning for sedentary females. Brown, Morrow, and Livingston (1982) suggested that a variety of conditioning programs may affect selected aspects of self-concept in women, if participants engage in a program long enough to effect change. Trujillo (1983) showed that women assigned to a weight-training program evidenced significantly larger gains in self-esteem than those assigned to a mixed activity program or a running group. Gains in strength, tonality, and success in a male-dominated sport are possible explanations of these results. Ornish (1990) and Claire (1995) also supported including aerobic exercise (such as golf, bowling, and baseball) and aerobic activity (such as swimming, walking, and cross-country skiing) in one's schedule to enhance health and longevity. Freedman (1988) stressed the importance of healthy exercise for fitness, fun, and as a way to nurture ourselves rather than focusing exercise solely on losing weight or competition.

Awareness of our sexuality also can be developed through physicality. Heightening awareness of the pleasure of movement and dancing can increase feelings of peace and freedom, according to Achterberg et al. (1994). The authors urge readers to nurture their bodies through sensory reinforcement. By paying close attention to what our bodies enjoy (foods we like, rocking, relaxation, water-play, massage, feather pillows, the smell of candles, our favorite perfumes, a warm tub, a soft rug on bare feet) and giving our bodies these pleasures, we can enhance our inner peace (Freedman, 1988).

BREATHING, GROUNDING, AND CENTERING

People with high self-esteem have a sense of having their feet firmly planted on the ground. Our personhood, our feeling of solidarity is reflected in our bodies. We can learn to feel contact with the ground, to feel a sense of being anchored and connected to the earth beneath our feet. But this feeling needs tempering with flexibility to be able to withstand the turbulence of life.

An individual who is ungrounded–one who exhibits a chronic lack of contact with the ground–is literally a pushover. The footing of people who are ungrounded is tenuous and their breathing lacks fullness. Such people deal with high-energy drives by containing them and live with a terror of becoming completely disorganized. Fear immobilizes their self-assertion, stress overwhelms them, and their self-esteem suffers. They are cut off from feeling and unable to adequately support themselves.

Breathing, of course, is an essential element in the centering or grounding process. Centering involves taking a deep breath, letting go of tensions, and quieting the mind (Achterberg et al., 1994). It is how we regain the balance of our physical, mental, and emotional parts when they get out of whack. Relaxation, visualization, and other behavioral techniques have been shown to alter death rates in both cancer and heart disease patients (Benson & Stuart, 1992; Simonton & Henson, 1992).

According to Speads (1978), the quality of our breathing is directly related to the quality of our life. Our bodily organs and our emotional and intellectual life depend on sufficient oxygen supplies. Yet, the majority of Americans go through life nearly breathless. Ornish (1990) pointed out that changes in our bodies, thinking, and feeling affect our breathing. By becoming aware of our breathing, and by using its full support, we can increase our quality of life and heighten our self-esteem. According to Lowry (1980), our breathing patterns influence our outlook on life and our feelings about ourselves. He speculated that a relationship exists between chronic underbreathing, depression, low energy, and low self-esteem.

More effective breathing results in clearer thinking and in positive changes in mood. Speads (1978) emphasized that we are influenced by any variation in our breathing. We are influenced positively when our breathing supports us adequately, and negatively when our breathing is blocked in any way. Our breathing is affected by all our life experiences. But, instead of allowing our breathing to fluctuate naturally, we often cling to a disturbed pattern until it becomes habitual. Kabat-Zinn (1990), Ornish (1990), and Speads (1978) offered a series of well-sequenced exercises that aim at increasing awareness of breathing, allowing it to change, and decreasing the time of recovery from poor breathing states.

Human beings tend to display a pattern of compressing excitement until it builds up to a certain point, then expressing it with focused satisfaction. This is true, for example, of verbal expression ("I couldn't hold it in any longer, I had to tell him!") and in the orgasmic phenomenon, with its building to a climax. Habitual blockage of this cycle, even at the bodily level, results in impairment of our capacity to take in and discharge energy, thereby affecting our self-esteem. Interference with the rhythm of expansion and contraction of energy, according to Keleman (1975), is debilitating. These holding patterns can be released through breathing exercises.

Quieting the Mind

Quieting the mind is another critical part of centering. The mind is our primary source of peace and stress. By learning to quiet the mind, one can drift into a state of peacefulness. Ornish (1990) described a number of secular and religious ways to bring about a calming of the mind. Calming the mind has been shown to lower blood pressure, improve performance, and diminish heart disease as well as increase a sense of oneness and inner peace, according to Ornish (1990).

There are all kinds of meditation forms, from sitting meditation to Sufi dancing, from Tai Chi to prayer. What is common to all is a focusing of awareness and attending to ourselves until we are in a state of absorption in the present moment, free from distractions. We can practice in every day life by learning how to become fully absorbed in daily activities such as eating, washing dishes, walking, or cleaning (Enomiya-Lassalle, 1987).

By quieting the mind we open ourselves to our higher selves. Beyond the din of inner chatter, self-scolding, and constant analysis sits the wise part of ourselves. Some people call this the Higher Self, others call it God. The more we reach this still point, the greater the benefit to our psychological, physical, and spiritual selves. The work of Hanh (1976) and Kabat-Zinn (1994) can be helpful in learning this mindfulness.

BODY AS COMMUNICATOR

Nonverbal communication conveys four times the information power as verbal communication (Knapp, 1972). Yet, even though this dimension holds such impact, we rarely are in touch with what our nonverbal behavior conveys or how we could express ourselves more effectively.

The nonverbal dimension of human behavior involves several different categories, including kinesics (physical characteristics, such as touching), paralinguistics, and proxemics.

Kinesics

Kinetic behavior includes gestures; movements of the body, limbs, hands, head, feet, and legs; facial expressions; eye behavior; and posture. According to Knapp (1972), kinesics include a furrow of the brow, slump of shoulder, and tilt of head. Body shapes, height, weight, skin tone, general attractiveness, and body odors also are included in the study of kinesics.

Touching behavior encompasses stroking, hitting, greeting, and holding. Even though the therapeutic use of the hands can be traced throughout ancient history, American culture places strict limitations on tactile interaction with others. Yet, Krieger (1979) reported that therapeutic touch affects patients' blood components and brain waves and elicits a generalized relaxation response. The importance of touch in nurturing others is generally underestimated (Wilson, 1982).

Physical contact (in addition to tone of voice) is the earliest and most primitive means of communication (Frank, 1957). Stroking, verbal and nonverbal, is necessary for maintaining positive human functioning. Yet, most American adults will tell you that touching should be confined to personal and intimate relationships, which makes most touching "sensual" in nature and, thereby, a scarce commodity.

Montague (1971) stated that early tactile experiences seem crucial to later mental and emotional adjustment. Likewise, it's probable that ongoing tactile experiences are crucial to continued emotional adjustment. Touch serves a primary role in nurturing and consoling another person. Touch also has been shown to increase self-disclosure (Lomranz & Shapiro, 1974) and to stimulate self-exploration (Pattison, 1973). Generally, we do not touch people we do not like (unless we are fighting with them). The very act of touching says, "I accept you," "I care about you," "I want to give to you." Touch, therefore, is a critical skill in nurturing self and others and in helping people relate to the outside world.

Paralinguistics

Paralanguage is *how* something is said and includes voice qualities such as pitch range, pitch control, rhythm control, tempo, articulation, and resonance (Knapp, 1972). This is a basic and early mode of preverbal communication.

Proxemics

Proxemics is the study of the individual's use and perception of social and personal space (Knapp, 1972). Individuals with low self-esteem often spatially distance themselves from others to a greater degree than average. Individuals with high self-esteem take charge of space around them and use it to enhance their lives. They manage their space in such a way to encourage social interaction and develop their potential.

TOTAL BODY IMAGE

Certain nonverbal behaviors can be clues to self-esteem problems. Feelings of insecurity, for example, might, be manifested in an individual's slouched shoulders, head tilted to the side, persistent self-touching, and a high pitched voice with many verbal segregates (for example, speech errors and latency).

We cannot refrain from communicating. We communicate our feelings through tone of voice, body posture, facial expressions, and gestures, as well as with words. We continually give clues about how much we value ourselves (see Table 5.4). In turn, these clues influence how others value us (Carkhuff, 1993; Miller, Nunnally, & Wackman, 1975).

TABLE 5.4
Physical Manifestations of Low and High Self-Esteem

Bodily Cues	High Self-Esteem	Low Self-Esteem
chest	soft but firm	sunken, constricted
eyes	bright, alert	dull
skin tone	smooth, firm	erupted
breathing	full	shallow
muscle tone	elastic	tight or flaccid
proportion of body	segments coordinated	top-bottom split, uncoordinated
gait	light, balanced	burdened
neck	pliable	rigid
head	moves easily	does not move freely; immobile; movements jerky
pelvis	swings freely	frozen
alignment of body	aligned	off-center
hands	well cared for, smooth, nails clean and trimmed, expressive	rough, nails bitten or dirty; hidden out of sight
movements	coordinated	awkward
shoulders	relaxed	slumped/raised
actions	supported by total body, moving from the "center," flowing	incomplete, chaotic
posture	relaxed, spine straight	slumped or rigid
arms	animated	hang lifelessly
jaw	relaxed, loose	juts out, tight
total body energy	vibrant	dull

As Kurtz (1971) and Kurtz and Prestera (1984) pointed out, the way we walk often gives clues to our attitude. With regard to self-esteem, we might notice the following differences:

Confidence: head erect, shoulders straight and loose, chest breathing fully and easily, gait light, movement generated from the person's "center" (about two inches below the navel)

Defeat: drooping head, slumped shoulders, caved-in chest, slow, burdened gait, unbalanced movement

Discouragement of bodily contact produces intense longing for contact and feelings of helplessness, shame, and self-hatred ("I hate myself for wanting"). According to Keleman (1975), this undermines the bodily self, which is the basis of self-esteem. When we are in contact with our bodies we, are in contact with our feelings, desires, sensations, and pleasures.

CONCLUSION

Our bodies are the oldest expressions of ourselves. The body is a catalog of our life experiences. In a unified way, we physically express ourselves to the world, making statements about ourselves and our relationship to the world. Attention to our physical sensations can provide a path to our inner barometer. Through a close and friendly relationship with our bodies, we create possibilities of higher functioning and enhanced self-esteem. The body is a powerful avenue for human change and human nurturance.

ACTIVITIES YOU CAN DO

ACTIVITY 5.1 THE LONG BODY

Introduction: Your body broadcasts what you have experienced. It is an image in the world that is meant to evoke responses. It is the result of the impact of the environment on self. Your body will tell you the story of all your experiences–and how you survived.

Time required: 30 minutes

Participants: Any number; adolescents or adults

Setting: Office or classroom

Materials: Large sheets of paper and crayons

Procedure: Draw the current image you have of yourself. What does your body say to you? Notice especially:

- How your head sits on your neck (forward, back, or balanced)
- Hypertonics (forced rigidity) versus collapsed posture (self-worth not developed)
- Attitude (defiant, defeated, or relaxed)
- Locations of tensions, numbness, liveliness, rigidities, or softness

Now derive a few propositions:

- What are you saying to yourself about the world? About sexuality? About what it means to be a woman? A man?
- What does your body say about who you want us to believe you are? (For example, "I can handle things, I don't need you.")
- How do you soften yourself? Walk that way.
- What is it that your body inhibits you from doing?
- What is it that you want to communicate?

The long body is the whole process of your body from infancy onward. The memory of the childhood body still exists now, though you are mostly in contact with your present form. Within each person are the following forms:

- Child
- Adolescent
- Adult
- Older adult

What is it that you do to hide your previous body images? People often practice someone else's image of what they should be: good little girl, stoic man, and so on. What images are you practicing? What image is trying to be without all things that interfere with it?

Get in touch with images you had of yourself at different ages. For example:

- At 6 months: racing around in a walker, energy, motion
- At 10 years: athletic, hand on hip, motion

Come up with at least five images from various life stages.

What do those forms say about you? Was the world bigger or smaller than you? Were you angry or disappointed? What is the feeling conveyed?

Physically imitate each image from the inside out. Go back and forth from 1 to 2 several times. Then 3, 2, 1, 2, 3, and on up. Feel the changes in your body as you go from one to another.

1, 2, 3, 4, 5

5, 4, 3, 2, 1

relax

Are 1, 2, 3, and 4 still alive in you now? How did you know how to get from 1 to 4?

Run through each state–up and down. Stay with your own confusion, your own disorganization.

What did each image tell you about yourself in relation to sensation? Record your awarenesses.

Outcomes: Increases body awareness and awareness of the messages one's body image conveys to the world.

Note: Written from memory of exercise conducted at workshop by Keleman (1976).

ACTIVITY 5.2 BODY APPRECIATION

Introduction: This activity helps you focus on what you appreciate about your body and encourages you to develop a friendlier relationship.

Time required: 30 minutes

Participants: Any number; adolescents or adults

Setting: Office or classroom

Materials: Paper and pen

Procedure: Look at yourself in a full-length mirror. Make a list of what you appreciate about your body. Pay attention to your skin, hair, fingers, eyes, arms, everything about your physical self. Concentrate on what you like. Try to skip over areas you often criticize. Make affirming statements about what you appreciate.

Now, go back to those areas you tend to criticize. Is there anything you can find to appreciate about these parts? For example, "I don't like my hair because it's hard to manage since it's very fine. However, my hair is very much like my deceased father's hair, so it reminds me of him. I like remembering him." Write whatever aspect you can find to appreciate.

For those areas you criticize and cannot find something to appreciate, go back and see if you can accept each. Write a statement of acceptance. For example, "I don't like the fact that my upper torso is large in comparison to my lower body, but this is something God gave to me and I accept it."

Outcomes: Focuses on the positive aspects of your physical self and encourages self-acceptance.

ACTIVITY 5.3 RELAXATION IMAGERY

Introduction: Performing this activity helps you learn how to relax.

Time required: 45 minutes

Participants: Any number; adolescents and adults

Setting: Office, group room, or classroom

Materials: Paper and pencil

Procedure: Rate your degree of tension and relaxation using the following scale.

100	=	the most tense you could ever be; tension is unbearable
75	=	a good deal of tension and anxiety

50	=	a moderate amount of tension
25	=	calm, a little tension
0	=	the calmest and most relaxed you could ever be

List some things you do that are very relaxing to you.

List some things you do well.

Choose your favorite item from the relaxing list and your favorite of things you do well. Picture each, one at a time, with as much detail as possible. Use those scenes that make you feel relaxed and happy. To design each scene effectively, follow these guidelines:

- Describe all the sights, sounds, and smells in the scene.
- Describe exactly what you are doing.
- Describe how you look and how you feel.
- Write each scene and read into a tape recorder at a slow, even pace.
- Relax, using the deep muscle relaxation method.

Picture the relaxation scene in your mind for 15 to 20 seconds. Picture the competency scene in your mind for 15 to 20 seconds. Picture the relaxation scene again, then repeat the competency scene, the relaxation scene, and so forth. Switch back and forth 5 to 10 times.

Now rate your level of tension and relaxation again.

Notice how your images can affect your mood and level of tension and relaxation.

Outcomes: Increases your sense of relaxation and provides a strategy to reduce or manage tension and anxiety.

ACTIVITY 5.4 BREATH OF LIFE

Introduction: Breathing can have an important effect on your feelings about yourself. The body literally has less energy to work with when you breathe shallowly.

When people are young, they learn to hold their breath when they are afraid or tense; for, in cutting off their breathing, they cut off some of the painful feelings. This shallow breathing then becomes solidified into a pattern of holding which describes an uptight person. Lots of energy is invested in defending the person. People with low self-esteem often feel low in energy and power, both emotionally and physically.

Time required: 30 minutes

Participants: Any number; adolescents and adults

Setting: Carpeted office or group room

Materials: None

Procedure: Find a comfortable place to lie down. Relax and take in a deep breath. Fill your chest, lungs, and stomach with air. Find your physical center and relax. With each breath you will feel lighter and lighter. Stay focused on your breathing as you exhale and blow all other thoughts away. Do this several times. Stay in the here and now. Notice how your body feels.

When you've had the time to thoroughly rest yourself, slowly come back to the room and open your eyes.

How did that feel? What were you aware of?

How hard was it to let go? Did your feelings about yourself shift?

Repeat this exercise frequently throughout the day

Outcomes: Increases your awareness of your breathing and the supportive nature of breath.

ACTIVITY 5.5 BODY COMPLIMENTS

Introduction: Most people are taught to be critical of their bodies. Many are hard-pressed to say even one thing they appreciate about some aspect of their physical being. They don't look at themselves that way. They look through a different lens. This touch exercise asks you to change your lens and look at yourself admiringly.

Time required: One hour

Participants: Any number; adolescents and adults

Setting: Class, group, one-on-one, homework

Materials: Paper and pen

Procedure: Write down 15 to 20 meaningful compliments you could make about your body or your general appearance. Write about the feelings and thoughts you had as you compiled the list. How long did you take to finish the list? Find a partner and share these self-compliments. How do you feel as you do this? What sensations are you aware of? What are your thoughts? Process these questions with your partner.

Outcomes: Shifts lenses and helps you view your body with loving eyes.

ACTIVITY 5.6 YOUR BODY SPEAKS

Introduction: Many people are detached from their bodies. If we learn to listen to our bodies we can be more emotionally in touch with ourselves and be healthier physically as well.

Time required: 30 minutes

Participants: Any number; adolescents and adults

Setting: Classroom, group, one-on-one work

Materials: None

Procedure: Turn inward and notice a sensation in your body that is calling for your attention. Locate this area by putting the palm of your hand over it. Allow that area to experience the warmth and gentleness of your palm. Thank that part of you for sending you the message. Allow the palm of your hand to express that.

While at this point you may not understand the message that sensation is trying to send, state if you are willing to listen and change the pattern that is creating this feeling. If you are ready to listen, imagine a hidden screen appearing before you in the theater of your mind. Soon images will appear on that screen. I don't know what those pictures will be; they could be memories, wishes, fears, or something else. Just watch the screen and see what comes. Pay attention to each image. As you watch you may not understand the message. Don't worry. Just record it. If you don't get a response right away keep trying from time to time. Pay attention to the sensation and repeat this procedure at various times until you establish communication.

Once you begin to see images, freeze-frame each image. Do not go on to the next frame until you can answer all of the following questions:

- Can you accept that you were doing the best you could at the time and under those circumstances?
- Based on your knowledge and life experience, what other ways might you respond to this situation now? Imagine in detail responding in different ways. Take your time and slowly walk through these different ways of responding.
- Do you need to let go of a feeling that belongs to the past or to someone else? If the feeling belongs to the past or to someone else, can you let it go?
- Can you give up that old way of responding, or at least add to it some other options?

Finally, thank that sensation for being the messenger and helping you be in better contact with yourself. Make a promise to this symptom to work on being more and more in contact so that it will not have to work so hard.

Outcomes: Increases body awareness and fosters a better relationship with your body.

ACTIVITY 5.7 TOUCHSTONE EXPERIENCES

Introduction: This activity helps you remember physically pleasurable experiences and feel more joy in your body.

Time required: 30 minutes

Participants: Children, adolescents, adults

Setting: Class, group, one-on-one, homework

Materials: Paper and pen

Procedure: Divide your life into categories: childhood, early adolescence, late adolescence, early adulthood, middle adulthood, older adulthood.

Reflect on each period and record times you experienced pleasure in your body: sensual pleasures, pleasures of movement, touch that felt good, things that turned you on, experiences of arousal. Some specific examples might be spinning, rolling in leaves, rolling down a grassy hill, playing in mud, swimming, massages, putting oils or lotions on your body, soaking in a hot tub, having someone stroke your head, brushing your hair, dancing, sitting in a sauna, having your back scratched, lifting weights, riding a horse. Once you've exhausted your memory, find a partner and share your lists. Perhaps your partner's list will trigger more of your own memories. Add these new memories to your list. Your partner's list might also contain items you would like to experience. Add these to a separate wish list.

Look over the earlier periods in your life. Are there body experiences you had in childhood that you could reincorporate into your life now? What can you add to your life to experience your body more fully?

Discuss how you feel remembering all these pleasurable bodily experiences.

Outcomes: Decreases body detachment and helps you live more fully in your body; increases comfort with physical pleasure; establishes a lifeline with your desire.

ACTIVITY 5.8 BODY TIME

Introduction: Body awareness is an important skill in developing and nurturing self-esteem. A positive relationship with your body requires attention and work.

Time required: 20 minutes

Participants: Any number; adolescents and adults

Setting: Classroom, group, one-on-one

Materials: Paper and pen

Procedure: Notice your posture. Describe on paper what you notice: for example, "I notice my shoulders are rounded, I'm hunched over some, and my neck is bent."

Reflect on how you feel about your body at this moment. Write down words that come to mind as you reflect on your body: for example, "strong, fat, sore, soft." Next record these adjectives using the following format: "I am ... " As you reflect on the tone of these words, how would you characterize your relationship with your body? Record this.

How would you like your relationship with your body to be different? How would you like to feel about your body? What words would you like to use to describe your body? Record these words in the same format: "I am ... "

Now, repeat this list of words out loud three times. For example:

- I am strong.
- I am hearty.
- I am soft and I am firm.
- I am round.

How do you feel as you say these words? Describe your feelings. How difficult is it to absorb these qualities?

Each night before you go to sleep recite this new list of "I ams" until they feel more comfortable to you.

Find a partner and repeat your list while he or she listens and provides witness. Record your experience.

Outcomes: Increases your body awareness and awareness of your attitude toward your body.

ACTIVITY 5.9 BODY ACCEPTANCE

Introduction: This exercise helps you create a friendlier relationship with your body parts through dialogues.

Time required: 20 minutes

Participants: Any number; adolescents and adults

Setting: One-on-one, group

Materials: Paper and pen

Procedure: Shut your eyes and imagine yourself nude and looking in a mirror. What part of your body would you least like to have anybody look at? Put your hand over that part. Now open your eyes and record your body part and the feelings you have about that part.

Now shut your eyes again, and place your hand gently on that body part. Now carry on a conversation with that body part. First be you and tell the body part how you feel about it. Next be the body part and respond with how you feel and what you need. Keep switching back and forth until you reach a point of greater acceptance.

Record your feelings, other awarenesses, and learnings from this experience.

Outcomes: Increases your body esteem.

ACTIVITIES FOR GROUPS

ACTIVITY 5.10 A LIFT

Introduction: This activity teaches a group how to physically nurture one person. Being held, rocked, and hummed to by a group of loving individuals can provide warm comfort for a person.

Time required: 30 minutes

Participants: Adults, 8 to 20 participants

Setting: Carpeted group room or office

Materials: None

Procedure: One person lies in the center of the circle, flat on his or her back. Group members hold hands in a circle, close eyes, and move to deep, slow, peaceful breathing.

As members exhale, they should let some natural nurturing sounds come out. When they are ready, they break contact with the circle and make some physical contact with the focus person, blowing those nurturing feelings onto the focus person as they breathe out.

When the last person makes contact, members slowly place their hands underneath the focus person and lift him or her slowly and gently waist high into the air, rocking and humming as they move.

After a few minutes, the group raises the person slowly higher, then gently and slowly lowers the participant, all the while making natural, nurturant sounds.

Again, each person in the circle makes some kind of physical contact with the focus person to say goodbye. They resume holding hands and finish with a meditation on their positive, relaxing feelings.

Outcomes: Provides a person with an intense feeling of nurturance and support.

ACTIVITY 5.11 MAGIC CARPET RIDE

Introduction: Learning to relax is a skill even children need. Relaxation is an important tool children can use when they are tense or agitated.

Time required: 10 minutes

Participants: Children of any age

Setting: Quiet setting that is carpeted

Materials: Soothing music

Procedure: Play soothing music and ask the children to lie on the carpet. (They can sit in chairs if lying on the floor is not possible or practical.) Introduce how important relaxation is as a coping strategy and self-care skill. Next, ask the children to pay attention to their bodies. Take the children on a trip through their bodies, noticing areas that are tense or relaxed. Then, ask the children to rate their bodies as a whole from 1 to 5 according to how tense or relaxed they feel (5 = very tight and jumpy; 1 = as relaxed and loose as Raggedy Ann doll).

Say to the children, *"Now we're all going to go on a magic carpet ride. Close your eyes and imagine what your magic carpet looks like.*

What color is it? Is it all one color or is it many colors? Is it plain or does it have pictures or designs on it?

"How does the carpet feel? Is it soft? How thick is it? How big is your magic carpet?

"Soon, you will be able to feel your magic carpet begin to move and carry you out the window and off into the beautiful blue sky. Notice how well the carpet supports your whole body. You don't have to do any work at all. It's like you're floating on a raft in a calm lake.

"Up, up you go, over tree tops, safely on your own magic carpet. Can you see all kinds of wonderful things as you float in the sky? I'll bet you can even see a rainbow if you look hard enough. See all those pretty pastel colors shaped in an arch over there? The yellows, blues, pinks, and greens? Maybe you can even float right through one of those fluffy white clouds. Clouds feel so soft and cuddly.

"It's like floating on a great big pillow as you continue on your magic carpet ride. It's even nice to close your eyes. Feel the soft carpet underneath you and smell the fresh air. Feeling the gentle rocking of the carpet, your body feels kind of like Raggedy Ann, all loose and relaxed.

"Now it's time to travel back. You pass through those fluffy clouds again and that pretty rainbow, over tree tops and back through the open window, gently setting down on your own private landing pad here with me. When you've safely arrived, you will find yourself here with me. Slowly and gently open up your eyes. You're here. Welcome back!"

Before asking the children to sit up, ask them to rate their tension-relaxation level again from 1 to 5. Did their scores change?

Ask the children to report on their experiences, saying, "Tell me about your trip. What did you see? Did you have fun? Was it relaxing? How does your body feel? What do you notice about your body that is different from before? Is your belly looser? Are your shoulders more relaxed?"

Remind the children that they can take a ride on their magic carpet any time they want. If possible, take them on a magic carpet ride at every session so they practice this skill and begin to integrate it. If there are times that you sense one or more of the children could use a magic carpet ride, you might direct the children to take a ride after having the children rate themselves on the tension-relaxation continuum.

Outcomes: Teaches children how to relax through imagery and to use all of their senses to achieve a state of peacefulness. Also teaches beginning body awareness.

Note: You'll have to alter the experience using different images if you have children who are afraid of heights or water.

ACTIVITY 5.12 BODY GAMES FOR KIDS

Introduction: Here are a series of activities that can help children learn to relax while having fun.

Time required: 15 minutes

Participants: Children of any age

Setting: Any setting where there is plenty of room to move

Materials: None

Procedure: Ask the children to stand in a circle with the front of their bodies facing the back of the person beside them (they're making a "massage circle"). Ask the children to put their hands on the shoulders of the children in front of them. By moving their hands and fingers in a variety of ways, the children are to convey the following:

- the warmth of the sun
- pouring rain
- galloping horses
- sprinkling rain
- hail

Keep altering the sequence of the sensations. Feel free to add others as they occur to you (e.g., rabbits hopping). You might also ask the children to change directions.

Ask the children to pretend they are blocks of ice–solid, straight, and stiff as boards. Then, ask them to allow their bodies to follow as they pretend that the block of ice is left out in the sun on a warm, sunny, summer day. "Feel your body melting until you are a puddle on the floor."

Now ask them to pretend they are Raggedy Ann and Andy dolls and to walk around the room like that.

Outcomes: Helps children learn how to relax their bodies in a playful way.

REFERENCES

Achterberg, J., Dossey, B., & Kolkmeier, L. (1994). *Rituals of healing*. New York: Bantam Books.

Anonymous. (1987). *Listen to the hunger*. Minneapolis, MN: Hazelden.

Asher, W. L. (1974). Appetite suppressants as an aid in obesity control. In L. Lasagna (Ed.), *Obesity: Causes, consequences, and treatment* (pp. 53-57). New York: Kreiger.

B., Bill (1981). *Overeaters Anonymous. The basic text for compulsive overeaters*. Minneapolis, MN: CompCare Publications.

Baker, F., & Kepner, J. (1981, February). *Retroflection and desensitization*. Cleveland, OH: Gestalt Institute of Cleveland.

Barlin, A. L., & Greenbert, R. (1980). *Move and be moved*. Van Nuys, CA: Learning Through Movement.

Bell, C., Kirkpatrick, S., & Rinn, R. (1986). Body image of anorexic, obese, and normal females. *Journal of Clinical Psychology, 42*(3), 431-439.

Ben-Shlomo, L., & Short, M. (1986, Winter). The effects of physical conditioning on selected dimensions of self-concept in sedentary females. *Occupational Therapy in Mental Health, 5*(46), 27-46.

Benson, H., & Stuart, E. (1992). *The wellness book*. New York: Simon & Schuster.

Biller, H., & Liebman, D. (1971). Body build and sex role preference and sex role adoption in junior high school boys. *Journal of Genetic Psychology, 118*, 81-86.

Birtchnell, S. A., Dolan, B. M., & Lacy, J. H. (1987). Body image distortion in non-eating disordered women. *International Journal of Eating Disorders,* 6, 385-391.

Bjorntorp, P., & Brodoff, B. N. (Editors). (1992). *Obesity*. Philadelphia: Lippincott.

Borysenko, J. (1987). *Mending the body, mending the mind*. New York: Bantam Books.

Borysenko, J. (1993). *Fire in the soul.* New York: Warner.

Boskind-White, M., & White, W. C. (1983). *Bulimarexia*. New York: Norton.

Boskind-White, M., & White, W. C. (1991). *Bulimarexia: The binge/purge cycle* (2nd ed.). New York: Norton.

Boston Women's Health Collective. (1984). *The new our bodies, ourselves.* New York: Simon & Schuster.

Brown, E., Morrow, J., & Livingston, S. (1982). Self-concept changes in women as a result of training. *Journal of Sport Psychology, 4*, 354-363.

Brownell, K., & Rodin, J. (1994). The dieting maelstrom. *American Psychologist, 49*(9), 781-791.

Bruch, H. (1973). *Eating disorders: Obesity, anorexia nervosa, and the person within*. New York: Basic Books.

Calden, G., Lundy, R. M., & Schlafer, R. J. (1959). Sex differences in body concepts. *Journal of Consulting Psychology, 23,* 276.

Carkhuff, R. (1993). *The art of helping*. Amherst, MA: Human Resource Development Press.

Cash, T. T. (1991). *Body image therapy*. New York: Guilford.

Cash, T. F., & Pruzinsky, T. (1990). *Body images*. New York: Guilford.

Chernin, K. (1981). *The obsession: Reflections on the tyranny of slenderness.* New York: Harper & Row.

Chopra, D. (1991). *Perfect health: The complete mind-body guide.* New York: Harmony Books.

Claire, T. (1995). *Body work.* New York: Morrow.

Clance, P. R., Mitchell, M., & Engleman, S. (1980, Spring). Body cathexis in children as a function of awareness training and yoga. *Journal of Clinical Child Psychology, 9*(1), 82-85.

Clifford, E. (1971). Body satisfaction in adolescence. *Perceptual and Motor Skills, 33*, 119-225.

Cooper, R. K. (1989). *Health and fitness excellence.* Boston: Houghton Mifflin.

Debold, E., Wilson, M., & Malave, I. (1993). *Mother daughter revolution.* Reading, MA: Addison Wesley.

Engelman, S., Clance, P. R., & Imes, S. (1982). Self and body: Cathexis change in therapy and yoga groups. *Journal of American Society of Psychosomatic Dentistry & Medicine, 29,* 77-88.

Enomiya-Lassalle, H. (1987). *The practice of Zen meditation.* San Francisco: Aquarian.

Fallon, P., Katzman, M., & Wooley, S. (1994). *Feminist perspectives on eating disorders.* New York: Guilford.

Fisher, S. (1973). *Body consciousness: You are what you feel.* Englewood Cliffs, NJ: Prentice-Hall.

Frank, L. (1957). Tactile communication. *Genetic Psychology Monographs, 56,* 209-255.

Freedman, R. (1988). *Body love.* New York: Harper Perennial.

Garner, D. M., & Wooley, S. C. (1991). Confronting the failure of behavioral and dietary treatments for obesity. *Clinical Psychology Review, 11*, 729-780.

Gillis, J. S. (1982). *Too tall, too small.* Champaign, IL: Institute for Personality and Ability Testing.

Greenspan, M. (1983). *A new approach to women and therapy.* New York: McGraw-Hill.

Hanh, T. H. (1976). *The miracle of mindfulness*. Boston: Beacon.

Harmatz, M., Gronendyke, J., & Thomas, T. (1985). The underweight male: The unrecognized problem group of body image research. *Journal of Obesity and Weight Regulation, 4,* 258-267.

Hay, L. (1985). *You can heal your life*. Farmingdale, NY: Coleman.

Hayflick, L. (1994). *How and why we age*. New York: Ballentine.

Hillman, C. (1996). *Love your looks*. New York: Simon & Schuster.

Hollis, J. (1986). *Fat is a family affair*. San Francisco: Harper/Hazelden.

Hollis, J. (1994). *Fat and furious*. New York: Ballentine.

Hooker, D., & Convisser, E. (1983, December). Women's eating problems: An analysis of a coping mechanism. *Personnel and Guidance Journal, 62*(4), 236-239.

Hoover, M. (1984). The self-image of overweight adolescent females: A review of literature. *Maternal-Child Nursing Journal, 13*(2), 125-137.

Hsu, L., & George, K. (1990). *Eating disorders*. New York: Guilford.

Huenemann, R. L., Shapiro, L. R., Hampton, M. C., & Mitchell, B. W. (1966). A longitudinal study of gross body composition and body conformation and their association with food and activity in a teenage population. *American Journal of Clinical Nutrition, 18*, 325-338.

Hutchinson, M. (1985). *Transforming body image*. New York: Crossing Press.

Jencks, B. (1977). *Your body: Biofeedback at its best*. Chicago: Nelson-Hall.

Jersild, A. T. (1952). *In search of self: An exploration of the role of the school in promoting self-understanding*. New York: Columbia University Teachers' College.

Johnson, C. (1993). *Self-esteem comes in all sizes*. New York: Doubleday.

Johnson, E. (Producer). (1984). *On being obese* [video]. Dayton, OH: Grandview Hospital.

Jones, M. D., & Mussen, P. H. (1958). Self-conceptions, motivations, and interpersonal attitudes of early and late maturing girls. *Child Development, 29,* 491-501.

Jourard, S., & Landsman, T. (1980). *Healthy personality*. New York: Macmillan.

Kabat-Zinn, J. (1990). *Full catastrophe living: Using the wisdom of your body and mind to face stress, pain, and illness.* New York: Delacorte.

Kabat-Zinn, J. (1994). *Wherever you go, there you are*. New York: Hyperion.

Keleman, S. (1975). *The human ground.* Palo Alto, CA: Science and Behavior Books.

Keleman, S. (1976, December). *Concepts and images of the body.* A workshop with Joseph Campbell. Redwood, CA.

Keleman, S. (1979). *Somatic reality.* Berkeley, CA: Center.

Kepner, J. (1987). *Body process.* Cleveland, OH: Gestalt Institute of Cleveland.

Klein, A. M. (1993). *Little big man: Body-building subculture and gender construction.* Albany: New York Press.

Knapp, M. L. (1972). *Nonverbal communication in human interaction.* New York: Holt, Rinehart & Winston.

Krieger, D. (1979). *The therapeutic touch.* New York: Harper & Row.

Kurtz, R. M. (1971). Body attitude and self esteem. *Proceedings of the 79th Annual Convention of APA, 6,* 467-468.

Kurtz, R., & Prestera, H. (1984). *The body reveals.* New York: Harper & Row.

L., Elizabeth, (1988). *Twelve steps for overeaters.* New York: Harper & Row.

Lebe, D. (1986). Female ego ideal conflicts in adulthood. *American Journal of Psychoanalysts, 46*, 22-32.

Lerner, R. M., & Gellert, E. (1969). Body-build, identification, preference, and aversion in children. *Developmental Psychology, 1,* 456-462.

Lerner, R. M., Iwawaki, S., Chihara, T., & Sorrell, G. T. (1980). Self-concept, self-esteem, and body attitudes among Japanese male and female adolescents. *Child Development, 51*, 847-855.

Lerner, R. M., Orlos, J. B., & Knapp, J. R. (1976). Physical attractiveness, physical effectiveness, and self-concept in late adolescents. *Adolescence, 11*, 313-326.

Levine, B. (1992). *Your body believes every word you say*. Boulder Creek, CA: Aslan.

Lomranz, J., & Shapiro, A. (1974). Communication patterns of self-disclosure and touching behavior. *Journal of Psychology, 88*(2), 223-227.

Lowen, A. (1967). *Betrayal of the body*. New York: Collier.

Luce, G. (1979). *Your second life*. New York: Dell.

Mable, H., Balance, W., & Galgan, R. (1986). Body-image, distortion and dissatisfaction in university students. *Perceptual and Motor Skills, 63*, 907-911.

McCaulay, M., Mintz, L., & Glenn, A. (1988). Body image, self-esteem, and depression-proneness: Closing the gender gap. *Sex Roles, 18*(7/8), 381-391.

McCoy, K. (1982, July). Are you obsessed with your weight? *Seventeen, 41*, 80-81.

Mendelson, B., & White, D. (1982). Relation between body-esteem and self-esteem of obese and normal children. *Perceptual and Motor Skills, 54*, 499-905.

Miller, S., Nunnally, E., & Wackman, D. (1975). *Alive and aware*. Minneapolis: Interpersonal Communication Programs.

Mintz, L., & Betz, N. (1986). Sex differences in the nature, realism, and correlates of body image. *Sex Roles, 15*(3/4), 185-195.

Montague, M. F. A. (1971). *Touching: The human significance of the skin*. New York: Columbia University Press.

Mussen, P. H., & Jones, M. C. (1957). Self-conceptions, motivations, and interpersonal attitudes of late and early maturing boys. *Child Development, 28*, 243-256.

Nelson, E. (1975). *Movement games for children of all ages.* New York: Sterling.

Neuman, R., & Halvorson, P. (1983). *Anorexia nervosa and bulimia.* New York: Van Nostrand Reinhold.

Offer, D., Ostrov, E., & Howard, K. (1981). *The adolescent: A psychological self-portrait.* New York: Basic Books.

Orbach, S. (1979). *Fat is a feminist issue.* New York: Berkley Books.

Orbach, S. (1982). *Fat is a feminist issue: Vol. 2.* New York: Berkley Books.

Ornish, D. (1990). *Reversing heart disease.* New York: Ballentine.

Pattison, J. (1973). Effects of touch on self-exploration and the therapeutic relationship. *Journal of Consulting and Clinical Psychology, 40,* 170-175.

Peterson, A. C., & Taylor, B. (1980). The biological approach to adolescence: Biological change and psychological adaptation. In J. Adelson (Ed.), *Handbook of adolescent psychology* (pp. 117-155). New York: Wiley.

Pliner, P., Chaiken, S., & Flett, G. L. (1990). Gender differences in concern with body weight and physical appearance over the life span. *Personality and Social Psychology Bulletin, 16,* 263-273.

Rasmussen, L., & Heriza, T. (Producers & Directors). (1984). *Heroes and strangers* [video]. Wayne, NJ: New Day Films.

Robinson, K. (1994, March 28). Males build self-image on ripple theory. *Dayton Daily News,* 3B.

Rosen, B. (1982, December). Love-hate affair with my body: The story of a food addict. *Mademoiselle, 88,* 141-143.

Rosen, E. M., & Ross, A. O. (1968). Relationship of body-image to self-concept. *Journal of Consulting and Clinical Psychology, 32,* 100.

Roth, G. (1982). *Feeding the hungry heart.* New York: New American Library.

Roth, G. (1989). *Why weight?* New York: Penguin.

Rubenfeld, I. (1992). Gestalt therapy and the bodymind: An overview of the Rubenfeld Synergy Method. In E. C. Nevis (Ed.), *Gestalt therapy: Perspectives and applications* (pp. 147-177). Cleveland, OH: Gestalt Institute of Cleveland.

Salkin, J. (1973). *Body ego technique*. Springfield, IL: Thomas.

Satir, V. (1980). *Communication and the family*. Workshop presented by Family Therapy Institute, South Bend, IN.

Satir, V. (1981, August). Presentation at AVANTA Process Community conference, Park City, Utah.

Scarf, M. (1987). *Intimate partners*. New York: Random House.

Schroeder, C. R. (1992). *Fat is not a four-letter word*. Minneapolis: Chronimed.

Sears, R., Rau, L., & Alport, R. (1965). *Identification and child-rearing*. Palo Alto, CA: Stanford University Press.

Secord, R., & Jourard, S. (1953). The appraisal of body-cathexis and the self. *Journal of Consulting Psychology, 17*, 343-347.

Siegel, B. (1986). *Love, medicine, and miracles*. New York: Harper & Row.

Silberstein, L., Striegel-Moore, R., Timko, C., & Rodin, J. (1988). Behavioral and psychological implications of body dissatisfaction: Do men and women differ? *Sex Roles, 19*(3/4), 219-232.

Simonton, O. C., & Henson, R. (1992). *The healing journey.* New York: Bantam Books.

Smith, E., (1985). *The body in psychotherapy*. Jefferson, NC: McFarland.

Solomon, D. H., Salend, E., Rahman, A. N., Liston, M. B., & Reuben, D. B. (1992). *A consumer's guide to aging*. Baltimore: Johns Hopkins University Press.

Speads, C. (1978). *Breathing: The ABCs*. New York: Harper Colophon.

Steadman, A. (1979). *Who's the matter with me*? Marina del Rey, CA: DeVorss.

Strang, R. (1957). *The adolescent views himself.* New York: McGraw-Hill.

Stunkard, A. (1980). *Obesity*. Philadelphia: Saunders.

Sullivan, H. S. (1953). *The interpersonal theory of psychiatry*. New York: Norton.

Thompson, J. K., & Thompson, C. M. (1986). Body size distortion and self-esteem in asymptomatic, normal weight males and females. *International Journal of Eating Disorders, 5,* 1061-1068.

Tiggemann, M. (1992). Body size dissatisfaction: Individual differences in age and gender, and relationship with self-esteem. *Personality and Individual Differences 13*(1), 39-43.

Trujillo, C. (1983). The effects of weight training and running exercise. *International Journal of Sports Psychology, 14,* 162-173.

Tucker, L. (1982). Relationship between perceived somatotype and body cathexis of college males. *Psychological Reports, 50,* 983-989.

Wilson, J. M. (1982)., The value of touch in psychotherapy. *American Journal of Orthopsychiatry, 52*(1), 65-72.

Worsley, A. (1981). In the eye of the beholder: Social and personal characteristics of teenagers and their impressions of themselves as fat and slim people. *British Journal of Modern Medical Psychology, 54,* 231-242.

Yeatts, P. (1968). Analysis of developmental changes in the self-report of Negro & White children, grades 3-12. *Dissertation Abstracts, 29*(3-A), 823.

PART II

EXPLORING SPECIAL SELF-ESTEEM ISSUES AND INTERVENTIONS

Chapter 6

GENDER AND SELF ESTEEM

C. Jesse Carlock

Research on gender differences in self-esteem has mushroomed in the past 20 years. Overall, this research has found no reliable evidence of differences in the self-esteem of males and females (Alpert-Gillis & Connell, 1989; Josephs, Tafarodi, & Markus, 1992; McRae, 1991; O'Brien, 1991). However, research has shown that self-esteem may be related to what we consider central or most salient. Josephs et al. (1992) contended that self-esteem seems to be related to the degree to which we fulfill the goals ascribed to our gender. The authors also emphasized that the odds seem stacked against women in this regard: What it takes to be "a good woman" is at odds with what it takes to be "a good person" in our culture, but there is consistency between what it takes to be "a good man" and "a good person." Yet even the male role has its binds.

Differences in the self-esteem of males and females point toward problematic cultural patterns that handicap each gender. Since most self-esteem problems reflect an inability to achieve an integration of self that balances agentic and communal aspects, we need interventions that help persons of both genders affirm their strengths and fill in their shadow sides. We need to make each more well-rounded, rather than "half-wits," in Satir's (1981) words. These kinds of changes require a *paradigm shift*: Men and women must change the organizing principles that determine how they evaluate themselves.

WOMEN AND SELF-ESTEEM

People experience themselves first as human beings and then as male or female. The gender role assigned to women prescribes that they be more concerned with relationships and maintaining positive connections with others. It also may predispose women to have a collectivist schema for themselves—one that includes representations of valued others as part of or within the self (Gilligan, 1982; Josephs et al., 1992; Markus & Kitayama, 1991; O'Brien, 1991). These authors also reported several studies showing that women tend to display greater interpersonal competency at a younger age and greater social responsibility. Their self-esteem is built less on doing a job well and more on fostering and sustaining positive relationships. However, in our culture, a healthy person is expected to become autonomous, goal-oriented, and resist being overly influenced by others. This underdeveloped side presents a growing edge for women.

Gender Training

Gender training begins early and permeates our experience in direct and subtle ways throughout our development. Families are the most powerful teachers, followed by the individuals associated with the major institutions (school and church, for example) with which we interact. Our everyday interpersonal transactions and experiences give clues to gender expectations.

By the age of 2, children can distinguish between males and females (Golombok & Fivush, 1994). Most researchers believe that gender identity has become the core of self-concept by age 3 (Osherson, 1986; Sanford & Donovan, 1985). As noted before, girls are trained to be relationally oriented. As such, they tend to be externally directed, learning to keep a keen eye on what others think, want, and need (Bepko & Krestan, 1991; Steinem, 1992). This has been found to be true of other oppressed groups whose survival depends on this "other" orientation. As a result, *women lose the sense that they are at the center of their lives.* Through their training, girls learn to feel anxiety, guilt, and shame when they act from their own center and follow their own needs and wants. Bepko and Krestan (1991, p. 9) described several injunctions that form the foundation of how to be feminine; they labeled these the *code of goodness.* This "code" instructs women on what to do and how to be in order to be considered feminine (see Figure 6.1).

Brown and Gilligan (1992) found that younger girls are much more outspoken, strong, and clear. However, as they begin to experience how little they are valued and how much women are exploited—as they begin to accommodate to the code of goodness—they lose much of their native strength and trust in themselves. Debold, Wilson, and Maleve (1993) further explained that girls are discouraged from "authorizing" themselves and come to view their thoughts,

✘ Be attractive

✘ Be a lady (stay in control)

✘ Live to give

✘ Make relationships work

✘ Be competent without complaint

Figure 6.1. Code of goodness.

Note: From Bepko and Krestan (1990, p. 9). Reprinted by permission of HarperCollins Publishers, Inc.

desires, feelings, and needs as "selfish" and "bad." Steinem (1992) contended that when girls' innermost feelings and preferences are ignored or repressed, they come to believe there is something wrong with them.

Gender training starts in the home and expands as girls interact with various social institutions. Norms of the system—the "rules" for who gets attention for what kinds of behavior, who holds the power in what domains, and the nature of that power—shape the female sex-role. The family is the ultimate source of patriarchal power. Carter and McGoldrick (1988) found that most people still view the one-up position of men in marriage as ideal. Yet, according to Debold et al. (1993), girls begin to express anger and disappointment as they witness their mothers deferring to men in their lives, allowing themselves to be subjected to emotional or physical violence, favoring men over daughters, and encouraging abandonment of feelings, thoughts, and behaviors when faced with anger or disagreement. Girls feel betrayed and silenced.

Perhaps the next most powerful social system children encounter is our educational system. In an article by Hundley (1988), McMahon-Klosterman pointed out that children in our educational system still are taught the ABCs of sexism. According to McMahon-Klosterman, girls' achievements tend to be ignored; moreover, girls are not challenged as much boys are in their performance. Boys are prompted, praised, and challenged more often (Hundley, 1988; Steinem, 1992).

Steinem (1992) also cited research showing sex bias in reading and language arts texts. She summarized the results of a 1991 study, commissioned by the American Association of University Women, which documented a significantly greater decline in girls' discontentment with themselves as compared with boys' between age 9 and high school. According to Steinem (1992), studies of college classrooms found that women are called upon less in class, are responded to less often, are interrupted more often, and generally receive less attention and informal coaching from professors than do men.

Girls continue to receive messages about their secondary status from religious institutions as well, where, for the most part, women are relegated to low-status roles. An article in the *Dayton Daily News* (Kepple, 1994) documented this ongoing struggle of the church with women: It has been only 20 years since women were admitted into the priesthood in the Episcopal Church, and they continue to struggle to gain admittance to leadership positions. As the Episcopal Church is more liberal than many other denominations, one can see that women continue to have difficult work ahead in their attempts to be recognized as worthy of leadership positions. Many churches also further women's socialization into the code of goodness.

As women enter the labor market, they are again faced with devaluation. They find that, while their earning power has inched up during the past decade, most often it does not measure up to that of men; and that occupational segregation persists, largely limiting women to lower-paying jobs (Kleiman, 1994). Current evidence of this can be seen in what has been called the *feminization of psychology and medicine*. As a result of changes in the health care industry, incomes of physicians and psychologists are declining. As this occurs, men are beginning to migrate out of these fields, shifting the male-female ratios.

While the gender gap has narrowed some in the last century, women continue to be trained by their families, social institutions, and political institutions into a role that diminishes their power. Girls hit a "wall" in our patriarchal culture, which values women less then men (Debold et al. 1993). Being a "good woman" still means giving up their trust in themselves, their thoughts, feelings, and needs. That cost is too great.

Identity Development

Erickson (1968) proposed a formulation of female identity development that showed identical tasks for males and females until adolescence, whereupon the developmental tasks diverged. According to this model, males confront identity issues before intimacy issues whereas females confront identity and intimacy tasks simultaneously. In the 1960s a female's primary identity task was to locate a male partner to fill her inner void, thereby completing herself. The female's identity, therefore, was tied to attaching herself to a partner. At that time, the primary avenue to identity achievement and self-worth for a woman was finding a man with acceptable assets. This fusion of a woman's identity with her partner's sense of self created dependency, which led to patterns of compliance, manipulation, lack of self-responsibility, and low self-worth. In such a relationship, the woman fails to develop her own sense of potency and efficacy and instead relies on her partner to provide a vicarious experience.

Marcia and Friedman (1970) noted the potential cost to women who achieve identity through intimacy, skipping the stage of identity moratorium and prematurely foreclosing their development. During the identity moratorium, the task is to evaluate and define one's talents, skills, and values; to experiment with and "try on" various lifestyles, philosophies, career options, and other sources of identity before arriving at what fits (Marcia & Friedman, 1970; Prager, 1982). Premature intimacy aborts this process (Bardwick, 1979; Bepko & Krestan, 1991; Debold et al., 1993; Gilligan, 1982; Morgan & Farber, 1982; Steinem, 1992).

Brown and Gilligan (1992) also noted the negative effects of this identity moratorium. Their research shows that the self-esteem of adolescent girls plummets as they encounter their increasing devaluation and begin to accommodate to the code of goodness, which trains them to put others at the center of their lives and to abandon their own needs. Of course, the ultimate blow to self-esteem comes from the inevitable failure to live up to the code, regardless of how hard they try. This can lead to feelings of unworthiness and shame.

Debold et al. (1993) pointed out that adolescent girls display more symptoms of psychological distress than do boys (including depression, eating disorders, body distortion, and anxiety). When girls exhibit distress, they tend to "act in"—internalizing, blaming themselves, and engaging in self-destructive behaviors—whereas boys tend to "act out" on the environment (Debold et al., 1993; Zuckerman, 1989).

Acting in, which harms no one but herself, is perhaps the girl's ultimate manifestation of the code of goodness, which emphasizes taking care of others at the expense of self. Debold et al. (1993) pointed out that suicide attempts for girls are four times higher than for boys. Girls' overall mental health declines in adolescence (Schonert-Reichl & Offer, 1992), as does their academic performance (Debold et al., 1993).

Debold et al. (1993) also reported results of a nationwide survey by the American Association of University Women which indicated that girls' feelings about themselves dropped precipitously between grade school and junior high school, whereas boys tended to hold themselves in high self-esteem. Rubenstein (1992) also has shown that girls' satisfaction with their bodies and their looks tends to drop significantly between grade school and high school, whereas boys' estimates of their looks do not change significantly.

Examining sources of self-esteem, the survey by the American Association of University Women (Debold et al., 1993) also found that boys tend to base their positive self-feelings on their talents, whereas twice as many girls base theirs on appearance. Here, again, is evidence that the code of goodness is in force. Debold et al. (1993) did find, however, that African-American girls apparently are able to maintain their self-esteem in adolescence more than Latina or Caucasian girls, due to strong family support and the strong role women play in African-American families.

There is little information on how Asian girls, Native American girls, lesbian girls, and girls with disabilities manage the oppression they face. For most girls, entry into adolescence is marked by the devaluation of female relationships and the idealization of romantic relationships with men. According to Debold et al. (1993) and Steinem (1992), girls begin to look to men for their deepest satisfactions rather than looking inside themselves.

Revamping Women's Development

Noting the effects of the traditional enculturation process on women, many have called for the insertion of what amounts to a missed stage in women's development. The new choices open to contemporary women in career and leadership roles, as well as changes in marital and family patterns, only serve to emphasize the need for women to develop individual identities and personal autonomy.

If women are to expand their self-views and incorporate the skills of autonomous behavior, they need considerable support from their families, friends, and progressive leaders in our social institutions. Women tend to experience anxiety, guilt, and intense conflict as they attempt to break from the traditional feminine role and defy the code of goodness. Without this support, women may slide into old behaviors or run toward other compulsive behaviors in the face of these distressing feelings and the backlash they face as they attempt to shift their roles (Bepko & Krestan, 1991). If women can find the support they need to give voice to what they feel ashamed of and guilty about, they will disempower these feelings and challenge the underlying beliefs (Bepko & Krestan, 1991; Satir, 1981).

Clearly, women need encouragement to rewrite the code of goodness and to focus more on *feeling good* rather than *being good*. This means reorienting themselves from external indicators to their internal barometer of satisfaction. In following the code of goodness, women limit their goals based on distorted perceptions and unrealistically high standards of appearance (Bepko & Krestan, 1991). They harm their bodies trying to meet these standards, distance themselves from other women, and feel unlovable because they are not attractive enough.

Meeting the code also requires women to "be ladies," to control their natural responses. In effect, they are told:

Don't be angry. Don't be competitive.

Don't be loud. Don't be aggressive.

Don't seek power. Don't challenge.

Don't show strong emotion.

Satir (1981) labeled these "rules about how *not to be*" and used a powerful image to describe them: a person with ropes and gags binding another to prevent spontaneous responses. If a woman complies with the code of goodness, she agrees to remain bound. Her key experiences, then, are loss of control, fear, and anger. But girls can learn to use their anger as information and energy to resist the code of goodness.

Girls and women often find surfacing conflict difficult, since it requires facing fears of rejection and abandonment. They fear that relationships will not tolerate their assertion of differing wants, options, interests, and needs (Lerner, 1985). But, as Debold et al. (1993) stressed, whatever is driven underground in pursuit of acceptance ultimately is magnified, whether in anger, playfulness, spontaneity, or some other expression. Eventually, the submerged bursts forward. If it remains suppressed, women risk becoming numb and dissociated, threatening their wholeness and integrity (Debold et al., 1993). An effective support system can help girls learn to use their anger to forge a new, more congruent way of being in the world, based on Satir's (1976) five freedoms:

- to use your eyes and ears to see and hear without distortion
- to say what you feel and think
- to honor what you feel
- to ask for what you want
- to have courage to take risks and challenge

When women first begin practicing conflict, they go through a counter-dependent phase, trying to behave independently but feeling dependent underneath. In time, however, they can learn to nurture themselves and build strength internally, until they are truly able to stand on their own two feet and make decisions for themselves without permission or approval. True independence begins as women shift their emphasis from others to self. Once they have more awareness of themselves and are secure in knowing what they want, they can choose to relate to others from a stronger, more equal position. During this interdependent phase, they can own their strength while reconnecting with their more sensitive, vulnerable, needy side.

A New Model

The new model for women calls for a humane set of guidelines (rather than a rigid code) that emphasizes balance in attention to self and other and supports the voices of girls and women. Such new guidelines might include these (Bepko & Krestan, 1991):

Focus on feeling good rather than looking good. This reorientation will help women learn to accept their bodies, express themselves through their own tastes and style, value their inner lives as well as their appearance, and enjoy their sensuality and sexuality.

Be direct and honest about what you feel, and voice what you think and know. Women can learn to focus on their own values and to express and assert themselves. Most women need practice being their own authorities. Some helpful paths include yoga, self-hypnosis, meditation, and dream work.

Be honest and empathic with others. Women can learn to be responsive to others' feelings without taking responsibility for them. They can give to others without abandoning themselves. Women must learn to make the essential difference between *caring for* and *being responsible for* others.

Nurture and empower yourself and others. Women and men must learn that mutual respect and responsibility in a relationship can support the growth and welfare of both parties.

Be firm and set limits. Women need to master the skills of setting priorities, saying "no" to unrealistic demands, and asking for help. They need skills in assertiveness (Jakubowski & Lange, 1978) and in conflict initiation and management. We might also include cognitive techniques in the new armament to challenge and restructure old beliefs, reframe perceptions, teach detachment, and strengthen women through positive self-talk. Body work and movement therapy can help women learn to reverse their habitual patterns of collapsing and withdrawing. Through guided experiments, women can learn to push back rather than folding and retreating.

All of these guidelines demand that women be centered in themselves, that they learn to be in touch with their feelings rather than be reactive. *Body awareness* is helpful in this regard, helping women reconnect with their physical selves, experience and monitor what feels good and what does not, and increase their sense of integration. Body awareness facilitates an intuitive or inside-looking-out approach (Barlin & Greenberg, 1980; Jencks, 1977; Kepner, 1987).

As I noted before, support from family and other adults is crucial in helping girls and women challenge the training that pervades our culture. Debold et al. (1993) and Steinem (1992) offered a number of excellent suggestions on how parents, teachers, family members, friends, and others can support the voices of girls (and of women):

Listen to girls. When you can, validate the way they experience the world.

Challenge perfectionism. Perfectionism is an attempt to avoid loss, and girls need to learn that they are worthy of love without being perfect.

Be fair to girls. Support their attempts to demand fair treatment from others, and add your authority to theirs.

Allow space when asked. Acknowledge the desire for privacy.

Respect girls' boundaries and the limits they set.

Respond to the feelings and thoughts girls express, and validate their experience whenever you can.

Give girls permission to be angry (even at you).

Support girls in expressing themselves, even when they hold a different point of view. Acknowledge and respect differences. Give the message that they can be different without losing your love.

Help girls to think things through rather than conform to your point of view.

Encourage girls to stand up for themselves, fight when necessary, and work through conflicts without belittling or humiliating.

Teach girls that they can voice their rage, frustration, and grief, and not be abandoned. By allowing such expression, girls also can learn that they can regain composure.

Reveal your own struggles. Model truth-telling that is selective and bounded.

Teach girls that they can be choiceful about when to voice and when to be silent.

Try to enter and understand the girl's culture.

Encourage individual interests, values, styles, and tastes.

Encourage girls to participate in sports. Sports help break stereotypes about women and give them a taste of power, competency, and mastery.

Encourage girls to build the competencies necessary to move into positions of authority.

Provide room for girls to express experiences of desire, pleasure, and passion. In this way, the experience of desire is not limited to the sexual arena.

Encourage girls to learn self-defense, so they can learn how to live forcefully in their bodies.

While the challenges to women's self-esteem are great, opportunities for change are abundant. Families, teachers, religious leaders, and other significant adults can all play important roles in empowering females and challenging the tenets of the code of goodness.

MEN AND SELF-ESTEEM

The women's movement seems to have stimulated men to begin critically examining the definition of what it means to be a man. Men have begun to look at the impact this definition has on their self-esteem, their emotional and physical well-being, and their ability to form and maintain healthy intimate relationships.

Several authors have noted that men tend to have a more individualist or autonomous schema for self, where others are distinct from self (Gilligan, 1982; Josephs et al., 1992; Markus & Kitayama, 1991). Men's self-esteem seems to be tied to the degree to which they fulfill the central goals ascribed to their gender. Dominance, for example, is central to the self-concepts of men. Men also are more concerned with individuating achievements and in seeing themselves as unique. Some believe that the requirements of the male sex-role give men an advantage over women in self-reported self-esteem scales, since men are more comfortable indicating that they are above or surpass others (McRae, 1991; Rubenstein, 1992). But regardless of what might show on such scales, there are high costs attached to being a man in our society.

Men's propensity toward autonomous, individualistic, and goal-oriented behavior fits with the independence that Americans value; as such, it is an asset. However, any strength can become a weakness when taken to an extreme. For men, this often has resulted in the neglect of other dimensions, such as attention to emotional life, an ability to be vulnerable, a value of interdependence, connectedness with others, and spiritual satisfaction.

Gender Training

Some researchers have claimed that the very basis of our society's definition of "manhood" is obsolete and maladaptive in today's world (Gaylin, 1992; Goldberg, 1979; Kupers, 1993). Others have noted that, because of the erosion of relationships between sons and fathers, many men base their ideas about masculinity on stereotypical, overblown myths of manhood (e.g., Pittman, 1993). According to Osherson (1986), beginning at age 3, boys search desperately for a masculine model upon which to build their sense of self. By age 3, the child knows whether he has been assigned to the category of boy or girl; this knowledge directs the attitude and behavior he takes (Malquist, 1985). By age 5 or 6, the sex-role identity is stabilized. The 3- to 5-year-old boy begins to withdraw from mother and to adopt stereotyped images of what it means to be like daddy.

Briggs (1975) noted that between ages 8 and 10, boys and girls need same-sex adult models. Without an available and confident model of manhood, boys are left vulnerable; they must distance themselves from mother without a clear and understandable model of the male gender upon which to base their emerging identity (Malquist, 1985; Osherson, 1986; Pittman, 1993).

Gaylin (1992) contended that, since the time of the caveman, manhood has been defined by three roles; protector or warrior, procreator, and provider. All three of these props for men's self-esteem are being challenged today. Gaylin (1992) pointed out, for example, that taking a warrior stance with a mugger may get a man killed, when all the thug really wants is a watch or wallet; taking a warrior stance with his boss may get him fired. Gaylin also contended that, except in a limited number of professions and only in rare times in history (for example, during war), the warrior role is passé. In regard to procreation, with the availability of sperm banks, men are not even essential for making babies. And work, or the role of provider, is no longer singularly the domain of men, Gaylin asserted (1992). While Gaylin may have overstated his case, his point that men's role is sorely in need of updating seems legitimate. As civilization progresses, as women empower themselves, men no longer need to assume total control and dominance.

Could it be that men are being trained into archaic, outdated roles? Are we raising our sons by exaggerated cultural stereotypes, instead of providing appropriate role models in their personal lives? Perhaps, as Pittman (1993) suggested, the result has been the emergence of hypermasculine behavior. Lacking role models, men may feel inadequate and so more prone to masculopathic displays emphasizing aggression, excessive competition, and physical strength.

They also may be more phobic about embracing anything they consider remotely feminine. According to Bly (1990), a boy must feel his mother's love and blessing and leave her; feel his father's love and blessing and leave him; then go out into the world and find his manhood. All too often, boys are fatherless, either literally or through psychological distance, leaving them lost in their attempts to establish their identity as men.

Gaylin (1992) and Goldberg (1976) pointed out that boys are taught early to avoid any feminine behavior or risk being labeled a "sissy," "fag," or "Mamma's boy." Young boys relate masculinity to physical strength; as they grow older, they relate it to emotional control and strength of character (Pittman, 1993). Any show of emotions is viewed as loss of control; so not only must men shut down emotionally, they also must stop others from stimulating their emotions.

In order to keep their ego inflated, men believe they must *know*, must be *right*, and that *others* must think they *know*. These beliefs fuel men's need to dominate others with their ideas and to control the world and everyone and everything in it. This is a mammoth undertaking. In the process, men lose their centers. Their masculinity is at stake, so vulnerabilities, mistakes, and admissions of ignorance aren't allowed.

In order to secure their masculinity, *men must control others*, particularly women. According to Malquist (1985), most parents expect their sons to be aggressive; during adolescence, independence, dominance, power, and sexual conquests become sex-typed. These emphases then are carried into adulthood.

Men's pride and self-respect come to rest almost solely upon their degree of power, status, and position in the world (Gaylin, 1992). Gaylin reported statistics showing that men commit suicide at a rate seven to eight times higher than women; most often, these suicides are connected with business failures. Depression and suicide in men are highly associated with loss of status, whereas women tend to get depressed and suicidal over the loss of a loved one. Gaylin (1992) and Weiss (1990) pointed out that the very nurturing a man needs during a time of such social humiliation further threatens his sense of manhood.

Men often believe they must establish their sexual credentials in order to prove their manhood. They typically do this by fathering children or by sexual conquest. They believe they must demonstrate physical power, dominance, and courage and provide for the more vulnerable (women, children, the elderly) as part of their prescribed sex-role. Increasingly, men have to find symbolic ways of fulfilling these primary roles of manhood. As Gaylin (1992) reported, they learn to make a "killing" in the market and find outlets in power games and power symbols. These become emblems of their worth (Weiss, 1990). Gaylin (1992) insisted that men must stop sacrificing true pleasure for the pleasure of status. He emphasized that men need to learn how to love and play without worrying about proving manhood.

Ornish (1990) contended that such competitive, hard-driving, and isolated personalities and lifestyles create chronic stress and ultimately can lead to illness. Aggression mixed with hostility constitutes one of the most lethal elements in Type A personalities. While underlying the success of the driver personality, Type A behavior also predisposes men to heart attacks (Keen, 1991; Ornish, 1990). Ornish (1990) believed that the resulting isolation produces a sense of lack, which then drives the man in a compulsive need to acquire (more money, sexual conquests, accomplishments, or muscles) in a desperate attempt to fill the void within. This results in a feeling of never being good enough.

Men often feel defeated if they acknowledge emotional pain or need. Pretending or intensifying activity in order to stifle feelings and cope with stress tends to deepen their isolation and loneliness (Zuckerman, 1989). Pittman (1993) also believed that men who are highly competitive often are trying to catch the attention of fathers who did not help them feel like men and who turned away from them. Repeated contests are fruitless attempts at capturing a sense of worth. Men's worth then becomes rooted in their earning power (Rubenstein, 1992).

After working with large samples of men, Ornish (1990) determined that one of the solutions to reducing isolation and filling the void is greater intimacy within self, between self and others, and between self and a higher power. His treatment program for heart disease includes work on body awareness, awareness and expression of feelings, principles of good communication, forgiveness, developing trust, practicing altruism, prayer, and meditation.

In reviewing the literature, it appears that men have been trained into a code of behavior comparable to women's code of goodness, which might be termed the *code of strength* (Keen, 1991). *This code*, comprising a number of tenants, *is no less crippling* in its one-sidedness than the code of goodness (see Figure 6.2).

Following this code leaves men out of touch with their feelings, alienated from themselves and others. A vast shadow side threatens their psychological and physical health. Manly silence strangles the expression of pain. All men fall short of meeting the impossible standards embodied in the code, so self-esteem suffers. This suffering, too, is done in silence.

The code of strength also causes men to neglect their health (Kipnis, 1991). Men are less likely to seek medical help at early stages and less likely to ask for help with emotional problems. They become deaf to their physical and emotional signals (Goldberg, 1976; Ornish, 1990). Many men even think it unmanly to be selective about their diets. After all, heroes can eat all kinds of junk

- ✗ Be strong
- ✗ Be in control
- ✗ Be powerful, brave, bold, and aggressive
- ✗ Suffer without complaint
- ✗ Protect others
- ✗ Be reasonable

Figure 6.2. Code of strength.

Note: Drawn from Bly (1990), Gaylin (1992), Keen (1991), Kipnis (1991), and Pittman (1993).

and fat-laden food (Kipnis, 1991). Men also tend to encourage each other to drink excessively. Many believe it unmanly to be sensitive to their bodily or emotional needs. Kipnis (1991) went on to note that men are not taught to do self-exams for testicular cancer as women are taught and encouraged to perform breast exams, nor are men educated with regard to prostate cancer, even though 1 in 11 men develop prostate cancer at some time in their lives.

Most men relate any "failure in their penis to perform" as reflective of inadequacy in their manhood. Even this wording conveys the detachment men feel with regard to their bodies. They have greater fear about prostate surgery than women do about genital surgery, and they have more fear about voluntary vasectomy than women do about tubal ligation (Kipnis, 1991). Kipnis also noted that men often feel that the main reason they are loved is connected with their penis's ability to perform sexually through intercourse.

Paradoxically, the code of strength leaves men fragile and terrified of tenderness and mortality. They are controlled by their fear of impotence—Kipnis (1991) renamed this sexist term *diminished erotic response*—and by their unconscious dependency needs (Keen, 1991). Anything that threatens men's efforts at control must be repressed or evaded. Human feelings such as fear and hurt run counter to the male role, as do dependency needs. According to Keen (1991), having been alienated from their feelings for so long while focusing on achieving goals and developing a hard-driving, strong-willed stance in the world, men are often afraid to look inside for fear they will find nothing. Indeed, as Keen (1991) pointed out, years of frozen emotions do not thaw easily.

Beyond the numbness lie pools of grief and sorrow. Keen (1991, p. 135) noted, "The path to a manly heart runs through the valley of tears." The grief, Keen explained is for passing life, aging, death, lost innocence, and the void of the absent father. Aging and illness force men into dependent roles and reduce their perceived power and status, often precipitating a crisis in self-esteem. Zuckerman (1989) noted that stress related to health is more associated with lower self-esteem in men. Yet it is on the path of vulnerability that men can find a more grounded and rounded sense of who they are.

Identity Development

One of the psychological tasks of the 3- to 5-year-old is attachment to the opposite-sex parent (Briggs, 1975). Once this has been established (by age 6), boys begin to shift their preference to their fathers and other boys. A prolonged identification with members of his own sex gives the boy a feel of masculinity and helps to establish his sexual identity. In boys, this identification intensifies until the middle teens (Briggs, 1975).

During the period of identification with males, boys let go of what they consider feminine by devaluing and ridiculing it (Osherson, 1986). They learn not to cry, show tenderness, or be demonstrative in an attempt to break away from their mothers (Gaylin, 1992). Osherson (1986) pointed out that young boys begin to repress and hide their wishes to be taken care of and remain close to mother. They learn that feelings of dependency and vulnerability are unacceptable and, therefore, have difficulty coming to grips with these feelings. When these needy parts are not attended to, grown men may experience anger and sadness, and this child-like residue shapes their adult relationships. This extreme rejection and denial of anything "feminine" leaves men with only half of the resources they need for healthy living.

A further dilemma boys face as they separate from their mothers and look to their fathers is that fathers are often distant or unavailable. Without role models who are close enough to provide guidance in male identity formation, boys are vulnerable to loneliness and shame and struggle for self-affirmation. Many boys also become more fearful of coming under female control (Pittman, 1993). Pittman believed that boys without adequate models may become slaves to their penises. He asserted that continually proving their heterosexuality makes it safer for men to be closer with each other.

Without close relationships with their fathers, boys must find some way to compensate through even small bits of contact with other adult males, peers, brothers, media heroes, or even fictional characters. Thus, stereotyped role models may produce hypermasculine behavior. Pittman (1993) explained that the less fathering a boy has, the more he needs to be with other boys in the same boat, yet the less likely he is to be able to let his guard down. Pittman also noted that men who do not feel anointed by their fathers often run from brotherhood, since they envy other men, and try to feel man enough by winning victories over others. Pittman believed that these men also run from intimacy in marriage as they try to dominate women in order to prove their masculinity.

There are men whose personalities, temperament, and interests do not lend themselves to meeting the demands of the traditional male role. In these cases, even those who have a strong role model may experience internal tension and lower self-esteem since they repeatedly fail to live up to their fathers' images of masculinity. For example, boys who are not inclined toward sports or who are less aggressive interpersonally may feel rejected if their fathers are disappointed with them or invalidate and disparage their natural inclinations.

No man can live up to the code of strength. Every man comes up short in one way or another. Conforming to the code reduces a man's ability to be intimate and creates a deadly isolation. The "heroic" man who is able to follow the code offers resources of strength, courage, and capability, but these are earned at the expense of interdependence. Such a man probably never learned to live within a circle of close friends. Those who lack the natural proclivities necessary to come close to meeting the code often possess a connection with their feelings, humility, sensitivity, and gentleness; but this comes at the expense of self-respect and a sense of their personal power and efficacy.

Revamping Men's Development

Two major changes must take place in the developmental paths of boys if they are to be able to own their shadow "feminine" side.

First, instead of encouraging separation from mother in an attempt to achieve a sense of manhood and autonomy, *the connection between mother and son should be redefined.* As Keen (1991) stressed, men must stop looking at themselves through the eyes of women. But severing ties with mother and rejecting anything "feminine" is a costly strategy for achieving autonomy. Valuing the connection with mother while redefining the relationship is a necessary step toward integrating more communal qualities into men's self-concepts and experience.

Second, *men must develop closer relationships with their sons,* with other young boys in need of role modeling, and with each other. Often children learn about and come to know their fathers primarily through the eyes of their mothers. This can endanger the relationship between

> mother and son and father and son, and negatively affect the son's feelings about himself as a man. Mentors and heroes can inspire boys to go beyond the models provided by fathers. It also is essential that adult men in the family value women. Modeling an appreciation of women's contributions and qualities encourages the internalization of these traits in a boy's identity.

The very foundation upon which "being a man" is based needs to be altered. Carried to an extreme, the male role that emphasizes competitiveness, toughness, and aggressiveness can be dangerous, even leading men to violence, in addition to being costly to their own emotional lives. The answer does not lie in a role reversal, with men assuming feminine identities, but in a gradual diminution of the sharp differences between the two sexes. We must identify the attributes underlying the traditional roles men have assumed and redirect them into appropriate areas. These attributes represent strengths when used in the right context. Underdeveloped qualities must also be incorporated into the new role in order to create a better balance.

A New Model

Our society sorely needs a new model for what it means to be a man. This new model must rest on men's being able to admit that they need their fathers' love and intimacy with others as well. Men must recontact their hunger for real intimacy with their fathers, and eventually their need for others. If boys are to be able to tell their fathers their deepest yearnings, fathers must develop the emotional strength to handle hearing them rather than being threatened and responding with rage. Fathers also must come to encourage the continued connection of boys to their mothers as well as demonstrate a respect for the women in their lives.

If this is not possible, then sons must come to recognize their fathers' wounds and limitations, delve deeply into their fathers' histories, and come to know their fathers as human beings with their own limitations who may hold values different from their own (Osherson, 1986). This awareness can help with separation-individuation. Sons need not be chained to their fathers' scripts. By coming to see their fathers more clearly, men can learn to accept their fathers' flaws, accept their own imperfections, and experience and work through their grief at the loss of the fantasized all-powerful father of their childhood dreams.

The process of healing may lie partially in reconciling with one's father, but healing is possible without such reconciliation *because what needs to be changed is the internal image of father and the sense of masculinity that the son carries in his heart* (Osherson, 1986; Satir; 1981). By identifying the family dynamics that led to the disconnection, men can learn how to correct that as they cocreate their own families.

In order for the new model to take hold, men must band together and turn competition into brotherhood. They must invest their time and energy in influencing other men and boys to expand their view of what it means to be a man. Through relationships with other men, men and boys can explore and test out more satisfying male identities and expand their view of what it means to be a man (including the role of nurturer). They need not live up to any narrow, societal image of manhood.

The process of healing involves living out the new image they forge. Becoming a nurturing father/husband/person can help heal the wound (Osherson, 1986). Men's groups have popped up here and there to help men forge this new view of manhood. Even the religious right is organizing men into a group called Promise Keepers, which aims at training men to be more responsible to God, their church, their wives, and other men (Woodward & Keene-Osborne, 1994). Through such male-bonding groups, men are developing skills in patience, listening, and understanding.

According to Reid and Fine (1992), if men are to achieve greater intimacy with other men, they must overcome four obstacles: competition, homophobia, aversion to vulnerability and openness, and lack of role models. Cohen (1992) added the need to be in control as a barrier.

Reid and Fine (1992) explained that competition in male friendships inhibits the disclosure of feelings or discussion of personal or emotional subjects. When questioned, most men in their studies did not cite competition as a inhibitor but, rather, expressed concern that such disclosures would not be reciprocated and that they would not be accepted by other men. Reid and Fine (1992) found that when men do disclose personally, they most often do so with women friends. But even with female friends men often do not disclose equally and, when they do disclose, they often ask for perspectives on love relationships.

When pressed, men usually can identify at least one male in their social network with whom they could risk self-disclosure. Starting with a disclosure of factual information may be a manageable first step. If the friend is willing to respond with a reciprocal disclosure, the man might be willing to step up his risk to a more personal self-disclosure. Men who cannot identify a safe prospect can be encouraged to expand their social contacts to groups or organizations that are more likely to attract men who are more open. Twelve-step groups or other support groups, church discussion groups, therapy groups, or educational classes in communication are some possibilities.

In order to quell fears of homosexuality, becoming involved in a community of other men is helpful. In such men's groups and networks, homosexual fears can be discussed openly and distinctions made between emotional intimacy and sexual intimacy. Men can learn that when they are intimate, they are bound to feel warmth in their bodies, but that this warmth can be differentiated from sexual arousal (Farmer, 1991). In an environment where closeness between men is normative, men can learn that they can achieve emotional closeness and keep charge of the sexual boundary. They can explore sharing emotions at increasingly deeper levels while encountering their fears in doing so.

Reid and Fine (1992) also found that men who are married often limit their disclosures to women friends in order to meet the cultural norm of reserving intimacy for the marital relationship. Marriage often diminishes men's involvement in friendships (Cohen, 1992). This funneling of intimacy results in increased dependence on wives for emotional support. Many men report that their wives or intimate partners are their only and best friends. Parenthood also tends to increase men's social withdrawal because of time constraints. However, Cohen (1992) pointed out that working men may be more protective of ties with buddies, since these friends them tolerate their jobs and provide missed gratification.

Seidler (1992) believed that men learn to deny their need for friendships as they focus themselves on their achievements. Any acknowledgment of a need for friends could be interpreted as a sign of weakness. Competition and jealousy also interfere with men's friendships, as does men's need to be seen as independent and self-sufficient (Seidler, 1992; Goldberg, 1979). Where friendships do flourish, vulnerability typically is limited to prevent the creation of dependency.

Men also tend to conceal their difficulties, according to Seidler (1992), since they fear damage to their image and do not wish to place demands on friends to hear about conflicts. Weiss (1990) added that men fear that asking colleagues for support will reduce their self-confidence and threaten their image in the eyes of others as competent, thus creating a burden to reestablish their credibility.

If role patterns are to change and men are to develop the depth of support they need from other men, they must come to change their views of vulnerability. Vulnerability goes against everything men have been taught about how to be a man (Farmer, 1991). Vulnerability is the polarity of toughness, yet it takes a great deal of strength to reveal one's vulnerability. There are times when everyone needs to be tough. Toughness can be an asset. Toughness adds vitality and, as Bly (1990) asserted, "wild man" energy is essential. Yet, opening up, revealing feelings of fear, unmasking, and showing one's human vulnerabilities requires great courage--perhaps more than it takes to climb a mountain or tackle a tough opponent in the workplace.

Attributes men acquire in their quest to be *real men*—attributes such as self-control, physical strength, aggression, and power—are invaluable. When men do not limit themselves to these qualities, they add a refreshing expression of "maleness." However these traits must be balanced with sensitivity, emotionality, vulnerability, receptivity, and other communal aspects, creating a new vision of masculinity. That takes courage. These men are our current "heroes."

ACTIVITIES YOU CAN DO

ACTIVITY 6.1 PERSONAL RIGHTS

Introduction: Asserting yourself helps you to grow. This activity helps girls and women enhance assertiveness and is appropriate for both children and adults.

Time required: 45 minutes

Participants: Females, age 9 and older

Setting: Office or classroom

Materials: None

Procedure: Describe at least three situations in which you felt you wanted to act assertively but held back. Now brainstorm your personal rights in each of these situations.

Imagine giving yourself this collective group of rights. Really take each one in deeply and hear these rights called out one at a time as you picture yourself growing stronger and stronger, as you feel yourself expand and grow.

Imagine how your life would be different. See yourself moving through a typical day while deeply feeling all your personal rights.

Did you have difficulty accepting any of the rights? Did you feel guilty when you asserted your needs? How far did you let the rights in? How did you feel or act differently when you imagined having all those rights?

Outcomes: This activity helps you bestow these rights upon yourself each day. When you find yourself in situations where you want to act assertively, take in all your rights and breathe deeply the strength they impart.

ACTIVITY 6.2 RECEIVING

Introduction: This activity gives women and men an experience in receiving support and nurturance.

Time required: 30 to 45 minutes

Participants: Any number; adults

Setting: Group, workshop, couples

Materials: None

Procedure: Find a partner. Complete the following activity once with a same-sex partner and once with an opposite-sex partner.

Allow your partner to fully support one of your hands. Notice how you feel as you allow this support. Notice any resistance inside.

Allow your partner to explore and stroke your hand in various ways. Pay attention to fully receiving this stroking. Notice any ways you block this receiving. Give your partner specific feedback on how to touch you in a way that is more pleasing to you. Do this nonverbally. Ask for exactly what you want.

Process your feelings with your partner. How do you feel about receiving without giving in return? Were you able to fully receive? Were you aware of and could you ask for the kind of touching you wanted? How did you feel about doing this?

Reverse roles and repeat the procedure.

Outcomes: Increases your ability to receive.

ACTIVITY 6.3 MAKING REQUESTS

Introduction: This exercise helps women practice the skill of making simple requests to counterbalance the tendency to "overgive."

Time required: 5 to 30 minutes

Participants: Adult females

Setting: Classroom or office

Materials: None

Procedure: Practice making small daily requests of those around you. Make the requests simple and able to be completed within 15 minutes.

Some examples:

- Would you give me a 15-minute back rub?
- Will you make me a cup of coffee?
- Will you listen to a problem I'm having for a few minutes?
- Notice any resistance you have to completing this task. Make note of this. How do you feel asking and allowing others to give to you? How did people respond to you?

Outcomes: Increases your ability to ask for what you want and allow others to give to you.

Note: If you get stuck trying to think of requests, notice small things you do for others. Often we do for others what we would like others to do for us.

ACTIVITY 6.4 INNER GUIDE

Introduction: This activity invites you to listen inwardly to the still small voice inside.

Time required: 5 to 30 minutes, and repeated at other times

Participants: Any number; adolescents or adults

Setting: Classroom or office

Materials: Soft music

Procedure: Allow your eyes to close. Pay attention to breathing. Breathe into that spot you call the center of your body. For some, it is two inches below the navel. Allow yourself to breathe in and out of this center part of your being. With each exhalation, expel all of the air from your lungs. Allow your mouth to drop open slightly, exhaling completely through your mouth and nose.

As you breathe in imagine filling your lungs and our whole body with a cleansing, pure, white light. With each exhalation, expel any tensions you are holding anywhere. Continue this for a few moments.

Gradually, make your way to that safe, quiet spot deep inside you—that place in your body where you're beginning to feel the deepest sense of relaxation, calm, and peacefulness. It is here you may find a door to that secret room where you can relax in the comfort of your inner being. Find this place of comfort. Make yourself a place where you are peaceful, undisturbed, and open to yourself. Pay attention to your breathing as you make your way along the path to your inner quiet place. Notice everything about the place--colors, textures, smells--use all of your senses to experience your safe place.

Find a comfortable position in the place where you are and ready yourself to receive any messages that might be forthcoming from your wise one. Focus on a specific question on your mind or a problem in your life. When you have this in focus, ask your wise one for guidance. Do not search but merely wait to receive. Messages may come to you in many forms: colors, songs, images, memories, thought forms--perhaps you find yourself moving in some way that will be a symbol to you. Expect anything. Even the most seemingly insignificant experience you have in the next few moments may be a message to you. Open yourself to whatever comes and discover its meaning for you. Take a few moments now to rest in yourself as you open to your inner world. Be aware of your breathing as you do this.

Take a moment to thank yourself for any messages that were delivered to you. As you open more and more to your inner experience, many more gifts will be offered. If you had difficulty opening to yourself, repeat this activity intermittently over time. Be patient with yourself. Gradually, your breathing into relaxation will lead you to a deeper place inside yourself. Patiently practice and await what is to come.

Once again, breathe deeply into the center of your being. Then slowly, as you are ready, begin to leave this place, carrying with you the messages you received.

Outcomes: Increases inner-directedness.

ACTIVITY 6.5 ENSLAVING CARETAKER

Introduction: This activity heightens your awarenesses of care-taking roles and the impact of self-esteem.

Time required: 15 to 30 minutes to record, plus 15 minutes to discuss with a partner

Participants: Any number; adults

Setting: Classroom or office

Materials: Pen and paper

Procedure: In the middle of a piece of paper draw a circle and put your name in the center of it. From this circle draw lines outward. Allow space for many lines. At the end of each line draw another circle. In each outer circle write the role you fulfill daily or infrequently, such as mother, wife, daughter, friend, sister-in-law, chef, church member. Include all the different roles you play.

For each role write a brief job description (one or two sentences). Ask yourself how often care-taking duties are part of each role. Is this helpful to your self-esteem? Do you feel you must be nurturing, caring, supporting, and care-taking to all persons all the time? Have you confused care-taking with loving? How do you define yourself? How do you want others to define you?

For each role you indicated, write beside the circle ways in which you could ask the person involved for nurturing and support in return. Think of ways these relationships could be more reciprocal. Choose one role on which to work as a goal. Try to ask that person for what you are needing. If you want to receive, you have to ask.

Outcomes: Helps you create more reciprocal relationships.

ACTIVITY 6.6 GRIEVING YOUR LOSSES

Introduction: Men, especially, need to learn how to grieve the losses in their lives rather than burying their feelings. This exercise allows you to practice grieving.

Time required: 60 minutes

Participants: Any number; adults

Setting: Classroom, group, office

Materials: Pen and paper

Procedure: Identify several important losses or disappointments you experienced from each phase of your life: childhood, adolescence, young adulthood, adulthood. For each loss record your age, a description of the event, the place, and the characters involved. Describe what you felt and tell what you did with your feelings.

Now share the events with a partner. Were you able to share your feelings with anyone back then? How would you like to have handled the event? What do you feel as you reflect on the experience now?

Homework: Share one of your losses with a trusted friend in your life.

Outcomes: Increases awareness of painful feelings and facilitates expressing those feelings. The activity also gives you an opportunity to increase your level of intimacy with a chosen partner.

ACTIVITY 6.7 FACING YOUR FEARS

Introduction: Many men won't allow themselves to be in touch with their fears and vulnerabilities. By opening up to those feelings, you can achieve greater intimacy with others.

Time required: 20 minutes

Participants: Adult males, any number

Setting: Group, classroom

Materials: None

Procedure: Find a partner and alternate completing the following sentence stems:

"I feel afraid of ... " Complete 10 times.

"I feel vulnerable when ... " Complete 10 times.

As you spoke, what were you aware of in your body? (tensions, tremors, heat changes, eye contact, voice changes, breathing patterns, etc.). Share your observations with your partner. Share the feelings you experienced during this exercise. Tell your partner how you ordinarily deal with your fears and vulnerabilities.

Outcomes: Allows you to increase your awareness of fear and vulnerability and provides an opportunity for owning such taboo feelings in a safe environment. The activity also provides an opportunity for increased body awareness.

ACTIVITY 6.8 EXPRESSING AFFECTION

Introduction: Men slightly are often emotionally constricted and unfamiliar with expressing love and affection. This exercise gives you an opportunity to experiment with expressiveness.

Time required: 45 minutes to 3 months

Participants: Adult males; any number

Setting: Homework assignment, classroom or group

Materials: Paper and pencil

Procedure: Tell at least five people what your appreciate about them. Be as specific as you can. (If you are in a class or group, do this now. Otherwise, complete within one week.) Notice and record how you feel as you do this and the responses of your recipients.

Then, over the next three months, keep a journal of the times you express appreciation to others. Set a goal of expressing appreciation at least once each day. Log your reactions at the end of each day: What do you notice in your body, in your mood when you do this? What do you observe in the recipient? What impact did these expressions have on your relationships? Share some of your entries with someone.

Outcomes: Helps you express affection and increases awareness of the impact of those expressions on others.

ACTIVITY 6.9 COMING OF AGE

Introduction: This exercise is aimed at helping women reclaim who they are, the incidents of ordinary courage in their lives that help define themselves.

Time required: 90 minutes

Participants: Adult females; any number

Setting: Homework, classroom or group

Materials: Paper and pencil

Procedure: Begin at age 8 or 9 and record anything you remember from that time through early adolescence (your room, friends, teachers, favorite clothes, games, books, family gatherings, family stories). Think of your favorite and least-liked things, people, and places. Use photographs to jar your memory and talk to childhood friends and family.

Tell the story of your coming of age. Use critical incidents to tell your story. Free-associate and add as much detail as you can. What incidents helped you to become the person you are today? Who you are is reflected in how you are, who you choose to have in your life, the contexts you create, and how you spend your time. Revisit and write what you discover.

Outcomes: Increases your awareness of key maturation points and ways they helped define who you are.

ACTIVITY 6.10 MOMENTS OF AUTHENTICITY

Introduction: Many women learn to sacrifice authenticity to get the security they want. By working toward greater authenticity, women can reclaim parts of themselves that have been driven underground.

Time required: 60 minutes

Participants: Adult females; any number

Setting: Homework, classroom, or group

Materials: Paper and pencil

Procedure: Separate your life into two periods: before age 12 and after age 12. Revisit moments when you recall having compromised yourself. Record these (includes ages). Did you try to be perfect? Did you put up a front? Now recall times you engaged in conflict, resistance, and rebellion. These are moments of authenticity—times you opposed or withstood pressures to conform. Record ages as well.

Review your notes and record any patterns you notice. How can you be more courageous in your life and relationships? Has your courage increased or decreased as you've aged? If you had periods of more courage, what might have been responsible for these periods?

Finally, record several stories that demonstrate your mother's courage.

Outcomes: By remembering self-defining moments in your life, you can begin to be more deliberate in the choices you make in withstanding or yielding to pressures.

ACTIVITIES FOR GROUPS

ACTIVITY 6.11 ROLE BELIEFS

Introduction: Sex-role beliefs are formed early. Challenging such beliefs early can help children widen their awareness and open opportunities to broaden their role boundaries.

Time required: 45 minutes

Participants: Girls and boys, ages 9 to 13

Setting: Any group or classroom setting

Materials: Xeroxed copies of open-ended statements

Procedure: Distribute lists of the following open-ended statements and ask participants to complete them:

- When girls get angry they usually ...
- When boys get angry they usually ...
- Boys like girls who ...
- Girls like boys who ...
- When an opportunity comes along for someone to take the lead, I usually ...

- When I disagree with something, I tend to ...
- When someone is angry with me, I usually ...
- When I am afraid, I ...
- Boys who cry are ...
- If I say what I think and others do not listen, I ...
- When I don't want to be touched and someone touches me, I ...
- One of the people I admire is ...
- I find it hard to say what I want when ...
- If someone hurts me I ...
- Five adjectives that describe me are ...
- Some of the jobs I think I'd like to have when I grow up are ...
- Girls shouldn't ...
- Boys shouldn't ...
- When I need help I ...

Now separate the group by gender, girls on one side and boys on the other.

Post the children's responses to each question and look for gender patterns in responses.

Highlight these patterns and gently challenge the beliefs. Explore the origins of these beliefs.

Now separate the children into mixed-gender groups of four or five. Ask the children to talk about these beliefs. Be aware of any tendency for the boys to dominate the discussion. Encourage the girls to take equal air time and the boys to share time. Work with boys to listen, as needed. Process feelings if conflicts emerge.

Use information from chapter 6 to introduce new ways of seeing.

Outcomes: Helps boys and girls become aware of gender stereotypes and the limits of these stereotypes. Also helps identify patterns of behavior associated with gender and provides openings to challenge assumptions underlying these patterns.

ACTIVITY 6.12 NO MORE "HALF-WITS"

Introduction: From an early age children are socialized into gender-specific role behaviors. This activity challenges arbitrary role assignments and encourages the children to experiment with a wider variety of activities, so that they do not grow up "half-wits" but learn skills, attitudes, and behaviors of both genders that can help them be more whole.

Time required: 45 minutes

Participants: Children, ages 10 to 13

Setting: Classroom

Materials: Slides showing boys playing games or engaging in activities traditionally considered girls' fare, and girls playing games or engaging in activities traditionally considered boys' fare. For example, you might show girls playing with action figures, boys playing with dolls, a boy doing the dishes, a girl helping her father in his woodworking shop, a boy taking ballet, a girl who is president of her class. If you can, find pictures of adults engaging in nontraditional activities: for example, a man cooking, a woman repairing a sink, men in a gardening club, women in an investment club, or a man taking his children Christmas shopping.

Procedure: Introduce the slide show by discussing how gender-specific roles are changing. Give examples to show changes across time that the children can relate to. Now show the slides.

After the slide show, lead a discussion, asking these questions:

- Have you played any games or engaged in any activities traditionally assigned to the opposite sex?
- If yes, what did you experience or learn through these activities? If not, why not?
- What different skills can you learn by playing games or doing activities typically assigned to the opposite sex? (for example, leadership,

nurturing and caring, competitiveness, cooperation, aggressiveness, mechanical skills, small motor skills).

- Can you still be a boy or a girl and enjoy both sets of experiences?

Outcomes: Helps to get children expand their view of the kinds of activities boys and girls can do.

ACTIVITY 6.13 WHAT'S OKAY NOW?

Introduction: Over the recent past, many beliefs about what activities and occupations are acceptable for males and females have changed dramatically. The gender gap is closing. This activity attempts to continue that challenge of old beliefs.

Time required: 45 minutes

Participants: Any number of boys and girls, ages 7 to 18

Setting: Group, classroom

Materials: Slides and slide projector or videotapes and VCR

Procedure: Prepare a collection of slides or video clips that challenge sex-role stereotypes. Select images of boys and girls and women and men engaging in activities and occupations that traditionally have been performed by members of the opposite gender. For example:

MEN/BOYS	WOMEN/GIRLS
Nurse	Physician
Administrative secretary	Chief executive officer
Ballet dancer	Construction worker
Floral arranger	Professional baseball player
Chef	Police officer
Kindergarten teacher	Senator
Clothing designer	Race car driver
Hairdresser	Bank president

Present the slide show or video tape to the group.

Process the reactions of the group. Challenge any stereotypical beliefs and attitudes. Discuss how workers of both genders can enrich the professions and widen participants' range of skills. Address income disparities in male-dominated and female-dominated professions and any other issues that come up.

Outcomes: Encourages members of both genders to widen their views of what is acceptable, thereby expanding their options.

REFERENCES

Alpert-Gillis, L. J., & Connell, J. P. (1989). Gender and sex-role influences on children's self-esteem. *Journal of Personality, 57*(1), 97-114.

Bardwick, J. (1979). *In transition.* New York: Holt, Rinehart & Winston.

Barlin, A. L., & Greenberg, T. R. (1980). *Move and be moved.* Van Nuys, CA: Learning Through Movement.

Bepko, C., & Krestan, J. (1991). *Too good for her own good.* New York: Harper Perennial.

Bly, R. (1990). *Iron John.* Reading, MA: Addison Wesley.

Briggs, D. C. (1975). *Your child's self-esteem.* New York: Doubleday.

Brown, L., & Gilligan, C. (1992). *Meeting at the crossroads: Women's psychology and girls' development.* Cambridge, MA: Harvard University Press.

Carter, B., & McGoldrick, M. (1988). *The changing family life cycle.* New York: Gardner.

Cohen, T. F. (1992). Men's families, men's friends. In Peter Nardi (Ed.), *Men's friendships* (pp. 115-131). Thousand Oaks, CA: Sage.

Debold, E., Wilson, M., & Maleve, I. (1993). *Mother daughter revolution.* Reading, MA: Addison Wesley.

Erickson, E. (1968). *Identity: Youth and crisis.* New York: Norton.

Farmer, S. (1991). *The wounded male*. New York: Ballantine.

Gaylin, W. (1992). *The male ego*. New York: Penguin.

Gilligan, C. (1982). *In a different voice*. Cambridge, MA: Harvard University Press.

Goldberg, H. (1976). *The hazards of being male*. New York: New American Library.

Goldberg, H. (1979). *The new male*. New York: New American Library.

Golombok, S., & Fivush, R. (1994). *Gender development*. Cambridge, England: Cambridge University Press.

Hundley, W. J. (1988, March 1). The ABCs of sexism. *Dayton Daily News*, p. 13.

Jakubowski, P., & Lange, A. (1978). *The assertive option: Your rights and responsibilities*. Champaign, IL: Research Press.

Jencks, B. (1977). *Your body*. Chicago: Nelson-Hall.

Josephs, R., Tafarodi, R., & Markus, H. R. (1992). Gender and self-esteem. *Journal of Personality and Social Psychology, 63*(3) 397-402.

Keen, S. (1991). *Fire in the belly*. New York: Bantam Books.

Kepner, J. (1987). *Body process*. Cleveland, OH: Gestalt Institute of Cleveland Press.

Kepple, D. (1994, June 27). Woman might be bishop. *Dayton Daily News*, B1.

Kipnis, A. (1991). *Knights without armor*. Los Angeles: Tarcher.

Kleiman, C. (1994, June 27). Women more likely to have low earnings. *Dayton Daily News*, Smart Money, p. 11.

Kupers, T. (1993). *Revisioning men's lives*. New York: Guilford.

Lerner, H. (1985). *The dance of anger*. New York: Harper & Row.

Malquist, C. (1985). *Handbook of adolescence*. New York: Jason Aronson.

Marcia, J. E., & Friedman, M. L. (1970). Ego identity status in college women. *Journal of Personality, 7,* 84-104.

Markus, H., & Kitayama, S. (1991). Culture and the self: Implications for cognition, emotion, and motivation. *Psychological Review, 98,* 224-253.

McRae, J. A. (1991). Rasch measurement and differences between women and men in self-esteem. *Social Science Research, 20,* 421-436.

Morgan, E., & Farber, B. A. (1982). Toward a reformulation of the Ericksonian model of female identity development. *Adolescence, 11,* 199-211.

O'Brien, E. (1991). Sex differences in components of self-esteem. *Psychological Reports, 68,* 241-242.

Ornish, D. (1990). *Reversing heart disease*. New York: Ballantine.

Osherson, S. (1986). *Wrestling with love: How men struggle with intimacy*. New York: Fawcett.

Pittman, F., (1993). *Man enough*. New York: Putnam.

Prager, K. (1982). Identity development and self-esteem in young women. *Journal of Genetic Psychology, 141,* 177-182.

Reid, H. M., & Fine, G. A. (1992). Self-disclosure in men's friendships. In Peter Nardi (Ed.), *Men's friendships* (pp. 132-152). Thousand Oaks, CA: Sage.

Rubenstein, C. (1992, October). New Woman's report on self-esteem. *New Woman, 22*(#10), 58-66.

Sanford, L., & Donovan, M. E. (1985). *Women and self-esteem*. New York: Penguin.

Satir, V. (1976). *Making contact*. Berkeley, CA: Celestial Arts.

Satir, V. (1981, August). *Presentation at Avanta Process Community*, Park City, UT.

Schonert-Reichl, K., & Offer, D. (1992). Gender differences in adolescent symptoms. In B. Lahey & A. Kazdin (Eds.), *Advances in clinical child psychology: Vol. 14*. New York: Plenum.

Seidler, V. J. (1992). Rejection, vulnerability, and friendships. In P. Nardi (Ed.), *Men's friendships* (pp. 15-45). Thousand Oaks, CA: Sage.

Steinem, G. (1992). *Revolution from within: A book of self-esteem.* Boston: Little, Brown.

Weiss, R. (1990). *Staying the course: The emotional and social lives of men who do well at work.* New York: Fawcett Columbine.

Woodward, K., & Keene-Osborne, S. (1994, August 29). The gospel of guyhood. *Newsweek*, 60-61.

Zuckerman, D. M. (1989). Stress, self-esteem, and mental health: How does gender make a difference? *Sex Roles, 20*(7/8), 429-444.

Chapter 7

SELF-ESTEEM IN CHILDREN

A. S. Cordell

Antoinette S. Cordell holds a Ph.D. in human development from the University of Chicago, specializing in clinical psychology. She completed her residency in clinical psychology at the University of Illinois Neuropsychiatric Institute. She is a consultant in Newborn Medicine at Children's Medical Center in Dayton, Ohio, as well as in the child welfare system. Dr. Cordell is on the clinical faculty of the School of Professional Psychology and School of Medicine at Wright State University.

What is self-esteem in children? We all have known individuals who are able to persevere in the face of great obstacles. They have persistence and determination as well as a generally robust nature. They seem focused within themselves and to value their own ideas and sense of direction. They are generally hearty souls, and others respond to them well. We could say that they have confidence and a sense of competence as well as high self-esteem.

We also all have known individuals who seem to have difficulty even in the best of circumstances. They may avoid other people and thereby limit themselves. They may be needy and demanding, alienating others in their attempts to fulfill themselves. They seem to set up situations that "turn back" on them. Their lives show evidence of the "boomerang effect." In addition to being unsure and experiencing undue failure, they show low self-esteem.

Self-esteem is important because it enables people to tackle problems directly and to succeed. It allows children to enjoy life and to feel pleased with their own achievements as well as the accomplishments of others. Self-esteem is an inner quality that relates to how children process and understand their life experiences. How can we nurture this gift in all children?

Most parents desperately want to see their children happy. Parents often say they want their children to "have" self-esteem. As parents, we seem to be trying hard to "give" our children self-esteem. But self-esteem is an inner quality that cannot be handed off in this way. What we do not seem to realize is that self-esteem comes from struggle, hard work, and adversity. We have been far too busy "giving" our children what we want them to have instead of providing opportunities for them to develop their own skills for dealing with problems.

As children grow and develop, they compare their actions and decisions with their developing inner sense of self. If there is a good match between what they observe about themselves and their ideal sense of self, they develop high self-esteem. Coopersmith (1967, p. 5) defined self-esteem as the "extent to which the individual believes himself to be capable, significant, successful, and worthy." This measure of self-esteem includes such items as "I'm doing the best work that I can," "I'm pretty sure of myself," "I wish I were someone else," and "I often get discouraged in school." Self-esteem involves a personal assessment of worthiness and capability that can be seen in the beliefs and attitudes children maintain toward themselves.

Self-esteem enables children to have positive, gratifying experiences. Even experiences that others might interpret as failure, those with high self-esteem see as learning opportunities. Self-esteem seems to contribute to a resilience that allows people to handle adversity and to solve problems. It makes possible a future orientation, so that we can set goals and accomplish them. Thus, people with high self-esteem are active contributors to the world around them. High self-esteem is an important quality for parents to have in building their families and raising their children.

Individuals with low self-esteem often have histories of failure and emotional disappointment, often including low academic achievement, delinquency, substance abuse, and depression. Such people can be destructive in their actions to others as well as damaging to themselves. These problems drain the resources of our society.

SELF-ESTEEM AND NARCISSISM

Our modern concept of self-esteem does not seem to recognize the importance of being realistic. It is important for children to recognize their own limitations. They need to be aware that the world does not revolve around them. We have a high degree of narcissism in our culture these days; individuals of all ages do what they choose to do simply because they want to, believing that their own needs come before all else. This is the problem of our times–the "underside" of self-esteem. Instead of "too little," we may be in danger of having "too much" without a realistic base. Parents, seeking to protect their children from the harsh realities of failure, seem to equate love with giving everything they have. Children learn that they are entitled, and that everything should be easy. Consequently, when they do not experience immediate success, our children simply quit.

A correlate of this is "excessive dependency on the opinions of others" (Gardner, 1992, p. 103). If we are criticized, we immediately believe the other person is right. We feel bad. We live in a limited way to please others. This can adversely affect academic performance as we hesitate to take risks. We may be friendly and flexible but passive and unassertive.

But learning how to master tasks and adapt to the environment also leads to the approval of others as well as to our own self-satisfaction. These experiences "substitute for the narcissistic illusion of omnipotence and become the basis for good self-esteem" (Huizenga, 1983, p. 161). It seems that many children today want to win or be first in their endeavors with a minimum of effort. They equate success with ease of performance. They actually believe in Superman, and that superstars like Michael Jordan take it easy. In actuality, hard work and sacrifice are prerequisites for success.

Self-esteem involves a realistic appraisal of our own abilities, a calm acceptance of our weaknesses and faults, and an understanding of others and of how we fit into the social world.

DEVELOPING SELF-ESTEEM

What do theorists teach us about the development of self-esteem? Several terms have been used to describe the interaction between the developing child and the environment, including "competence motivation," "industry versus inferiority," and "personal agency."

Competence Motivation

White (1959) proposed the term *competence motivation* for the inborn trait of striving toward mastery. This trait leads children to be curious about the world around them and persistent in learning new tasks that initially seem insurmountable, such as riding a bicycle. The level of competence motivation varies in children as they grow, develop, and receive feedback from the environment on the results of their efforts.

Following a social learning analysis of this process (Harter, 1978, 1983), competence motivation leads children toward independent attempts at mastery. They may receive positive or negative feedback from several different sources, including their own assessments of the outcome as well as the reactions of others. Positive feedback leads to feelings of success and renewed efforts. It also contributes to the child's inner sense of capability and worthiness. Overly negative feedback leads to a sense of failure and to lower competence motivation. It also contributes to a child's tendency to avoid challenges, to depend on others for solutions, and, ultimately, to fail more often. However, this model does not incorporate the opportunity for learning offered by "constructive criticism."

Industry Versus Inferiority

Erikson's (1968) fourth stage of psychosocial development, *the crisis of industry versus inferiority*, finds children ready to interact with others as they learn to be competent and productive. This stage of development requires that children recognize their weaknesses and perceive realistically when their skills are inadequate. They can choose then to achieve in their areas of strength, which further enhances their sense of accomplishment. When children feel worthwhile, they believe they can set goals and achieve them. Their success in turn bolsters their sense of competence and self-esteem.

Personal Agency

"Personal agency" is another term that refers to this inner sense of capability (McGraw, 1987). There are indications that infants as young as 4 months have an understanding of their impact on the physical world, such as in playing with a mobile. Young infants also are aware of the effect of their behavior on other people.

To what degree does parental sensitivity contribute to a child's inner sense of personal agency? The early stages of self-awareness begin with body awareness, which develops from self-directed actions and sequences of behaviors in interacting with the environment or other people. Parents differ in how well they respond to their children's signals. Sensitive parents respond with loving concern and specific actions, such as feeding or changing diapers, when their baby cries. They try to figure out what they should do in response to the baby's behavior. Sensitivity in parents is related to an improved sense of personal agency in infants (Lamb & Easterbrooks, 1981). These typical parent-child interactions contribute to the development of personal agency. Babies learn that they have an effect on the environment when their parents respond appropriately to their signals. On the other hand, the lack of congruence between behavior and response can generalize into a sense of learned helplessness–a belief that one cannot control events in one's life (Seligman, 1975).

So it is important for young children not just to learn specific skills and behaviors but to acquire an overall belief in their ability to affect their world. *Developmentalists* maintain this belief grows from interactions between babies and caretakers. When there is no consistent or congruent response, babies learn they cannot have an effect on the world around them. They give up. *They have learned helplessness.* In addition, babies who have learned helplessness on one task will behave similarly on other learning tasks (Finkelstein & Ramey, 1977). In contrast, when infants receive nurturance in response to their expressions of need, they develop a general belief about their ability to control people and events around them. This is illustrated even by simple play interactions, such as when father and baby imitate each other by sticking out their tongues.

Play and Imagination

I cannot overstate the importance of play and imagination in early development. Using fantasy helps children delay gratification and deal with frustration (Singer, 1973). This has implications for success in the classroom and in life. Parten (1932) identified five ways preschool children play:

In solitary play, children are unaware of others and play alone.

In onlooker play, children watch others play.

In parallel play, children play side by side with no interaction.

In associative play, children interact and share.

In cooperative play, children play together, helping and taking turns. In this way, they learn that relationships involve reciprocal interaction patterns. They are able to practice listening, sharing, and responding to others appropriately.

Personal Space

Another way of viewing self-esteem development is to look at how children handle personal space, as DiLeo (1983) did in an analysis of children's drawings. Typically, children keep distance between themselves and people they do not know. They need space in their social relationships for self-protection. The more they trust a person, the less distance they need, as seen in their physical proximity to parents versus strangers. Greater space between figures in drawings and smaller figures can indicate lower self-esteem.

Self- and Other Awareness

Young children learn about themselves and others in terms of age and gender. Preschool children use height and facial features to discern age. They use hair, clothes, and behavior to decide upon gender. In addition, there is a developmental trend from physical to psychological statements about self and others. School-age children describe their friends using inner qualities and characteristics that are stable, not just reflective of temporary appearance. From the preschool to the school-age years, children move toward defining themselves in comparison to others rather than by using absolute terms. Older children then develop the ability to recognize that people can be both good and bad simultaneously.

So there are three changes that occur in the development of self- and other awareness during childhood, which parallel the development of thought: Children shift from describing people in terms of changeable physical attributes to defining them by stable inner traits; they begin to use descriptions that are comparative rather than absolute; and they develop the ability to see several traits in the same person at once.

Becoming aware of differences between the self and others is an integral part of developing self-esteem (Selman, 1980). As described by McGraw (1987) and Hetherington and Parke (1993), Selman's work showed the development of perspective-taking (see Tables 7.1, 7.2, and 7.3). *Egocentrism*–the lack of understanding about how others feel and think–is part of the human condition. As we grow, we must learn that others have valid but different perspectives from our own. We must develop the skills to understand the perspectives of others. Piecing together another person's viewpoint in our own mind is hard for children especially. Our ability to see another's perspective improves in adolescence, but our learning may continue throughout our lives.

As children enter adolescence, they experience changes in how they view themselves; these changes reflect their ability to think at an abstract level. In early adolescence, the child realizes there is an inner part of the self that directs thought. Later, he or she concludes that this part of the self is not in total control. There is some developing awareness of the unconscious mind. The self becomes an integrated whole of physical attributes, thought, and unconscious process.

Morality

Self-esteem has an important role in the development of morality. Children with positive self-concepts seem more likely to make good behavioral choices and to refrain from immoral behavior so as not to feel guilty (Lefrancois, 1986). Those who work with children can enhance their ability to make good choices, and thereby their self-esteem, by teaching problem-solving skills and how to converse with peers in making decisions.

(Continued on page 296.)

TABLE 7.1
Selman's Levels of Self-Awareness

Level O: The Undifferentiated Self

- I am an undifferentiated physical entity. I make no distinctions between mind and body.

Level 1: The Superficial, Apparent Self

- My mind and body are separate entities; thus, I have both an inner reality and an outer appearance. But to know my inner reality, all you have to do is look at me. I am what I say and do.

Level 2: The Thinking, Psychological Self

- The real me lies behind the scenes. Sometimes what I say and do corresponds to the real me, but sometimes not. My mind is in control of my body.

Level 3: The Self as Observing Ego

- My thoughts and intentions are an important part of me, just as my behavior is, but the real me is the part of me that directs both thoughts and behavior. This is my observing ego. With it, I can deceive people through my behavior, and I can even deceive myself. That is, I can make myself think or believe something just by willing it.

Level 4: The Conscious and Unconscious Self

- Just as before, I believe that the observing ego monitors my inner reality and outer appearance. But I no longer believe that the conscious ego is totally in charge. In addition to the ego, which provides conscious control, there is an unconscious part to me that even the conscious ego cannot always fathom. Thus, it is possible that I will direct myself to behave in certain ways and to think certain thoughts and yet not truly be aware of how I have chosen to behave and think in this way.

Note: From Selman (1976).

TABLE 7.2
Selman's Five Stages in the Development of Perspective Taking

Stage	Age Range[1]	Child's Understanding
Stage 0 Egocentric Viewpoint	3 to 6 years	Child has a sense of differentiation of self and other but fails to distinguish between the social perspective (thoughts, feelings) of other and self. Child can label other's overt feelings but does not see the cause and effect relation of reasons to social actions.
Stage 1 Social-Informational Role Taking	6 to 8 years	Child is aware that other has a social perspective based on other's own reasoning, which may or may not be similar to child's. But child tends to focus on one perspective rather than coordinating viewpoints.
Stage 2 Self-Reflective Role Taking	8 to 10 years	Child is conscious that each individual is aware of the other's perspective and that this awareness influences views of each other. Putting self in other's place is a way of judging his intentions, purposes, and actions. Child can form a coordinated chain of perspectives but cannot abstract from this process to the level of simultaneous mutuality.
Stage 3 Mutual Role Taking	10 to 12 years	Child realizes that self and other can view each other mutually and simultaneously as subjects. Can step outside the two-person dyad and view interaction from a third-person perspective.
Stage 4 Social- and Conventional-System Role Taking	12 to 15+ years	Person realizes mutual perspective taking does not always lead to complete understanding. Social conventions are seen as necessary because they are understood by all members of the group (the generalized other) regardless of their position, role, or experience.

[1]Age ranges for all stages represent only average approximations.
Note: Based on Selman (1976, p. 309). Reprinted with permission.

Table 7.3
How Do I See You? How Do You See Me?

Is there a systematic developmental progression in role-taking skills? The results of this study by Selman and Byrne (1974) suggest that there is.

Groups of 4-, 6-, 8-, and 10-year-old children were presented with filmed stories and questioned about the perspectives and thoughts of the characteristics in the story. A sample story is as follows:

> Holly is an 8-year-old girl who likes to climb trees. She is the best tree climber in the neighborhood. One day while climbing down from a tall tree she falls off the bottom branch but does not hurt herself. Her father sees her fall. He is upset and asks her to promise not to climb trees anymore. Holly promises.
>
> Later that day, Holly and her friends meet Sean. Sean's kitten is caught up in a tree and cannot get down. Something has to be done right away or the kitten may fall. Holly is the only one who climbs trees well enough to reach the kitten and get it down, but she remembers her promise to her father (Selman & Byrne, 1974, p. 805).

The questions were structured to assess the levels of role taking attained by the child. The questions are as follows.

Level 1–Subjective Role Taking

(a) Does Holly know how Sean feels about the kitten? Why?

(b) Does Sean know why Holly cannot decide whether or not to climb the tree? Why or why not?

Stage	Age 4	Age 6	Age 8	Age 10
0	80	10	0	0
1	20	90	40	20
2	0	0	50	60
3	0	0	10	20
Total	100	100	100	100

Source: Percentage of children in different ages reaching a given role-taking level by Selman and Byrne (1974) as seen in Hetherington and Parke (1986, p. 377).

Table 7.3. Continued.

(c) Why might Sean think Holly will not climb the tree if Holly does not tell him about her promise?

Level 2–Self-Reflective Role Taking

(a) What does Holly think her father will think of her if he finds out?

(b) Does Holly think her father will understand why she climbed the tree? Why is that?

Level 3–Mutual Role Taking

(a) What does Holly think most people would do in this situation?

(b) If Holly and her father discussed this situation, what might they decide together? Why is that?

(c) Do you know what the Golden Rule is (explain if the child says no)? What would the Golden Rule say to do in this situation? Why? (Selman & Byrne, 1974, p. 805).

A steady progression can be seen through these role-taking stages. No 4- or 6-year-old children have attained stage 2 or 3 role taking, whereas most age 8- and 10-year-old children have reached at least stage 2 and some have attained level 3.

Note: From Selman and Byrne (1974) as seen in Hetherington and Parke (1986, p. 377).

Theorists such as Kohlberg (1985) and Piaget (1932) have emphasized the importance of peer interaction in learning how others feel and in developing a sense of morality. However, parents also have a role in moral judgment development. Research by Hetherington and Parke (1975) indicated that consistent discipline using reasoning, explanation, and concern for the feelings of others leads to self-restraint and a higher level of moral thinking in children. Parents who simply spank their children with no explanation of wrongdoing do not provide a prosocial learning environment. Explanations allow children to learn that there are social rules underlying behavior that benefit all of us. They learn that other people have comparable feelings and experiences, so they care more about others and their reactions. This more humanistic approach to child-rearing promotes a greater degree of concern about the welfare of others. Parents teach their children how to "read" and understand others as they ascribe motives to other people and model responses. Parents also model prosocial behaviors and provide opportunities for practice.

GUIDELINES FOR PARENTS

We are not "trained" for our jobs as parents. There is no training manual for all the difficult tasks of parenting. But there are resources parents can draw upon. Briggs (1975) outlined some guidelines for parents on building self-esteem in their children and families.

According to Briggs, self-value is based on the belief that one is lovable as well as worthwhile and competent. The sense of self is learned from interactions with others; it is a social accomplishment. Through sensory input and language, infants come to know their social surroundings and to develop self-awareness. "What counts is the total number of loving or disinterested messages, together with their intensity" (Briggs, 1975, p. 12). Parents, relatives, neighbors, teachers, and peers are "mirrors" for the child. Briggs also emphasized that "words are less important than the judgments that accompany them" (1975, p. 19). The experience of mastery in this social context provides the building blocks of self-esteem. However, the child's own assessment of what matters is pivotal in the process.

According to Briggs (1975), children's self-image is a reflection of how others treat them as they build their own self-views not only from the words but from the actions, attitudes, and judgments of others. Children observe themselves and compare what they see to how others react. Their behavior then is brought into line with their self-views.

It is important to realize that children may feel confident in one area but not in another. In this case, you may hear both positive and negative self-statements. Feelings of inadequacy lead to the expectation of failure. Expecting to win leads to a greater likelihood of success. If a little boy has a "warped mirror," he views himself as inadequate and tends to build defenses to protect himself and his belief that he is unlovable and unworthy. This view of himself changes and grows, expands or contracts throughout the course of his development. A major area of concern, however, is when a negative self-view becomes entrenched. Such rigidity results from many negative experiences over a long period of time. In order to help the child turn this around, others must provide a nurturing environment that allows for corrective emotional experiences and specific successes for a comparable length of time or impact.

Specific Parenting Skills

Briggs (1975) also maintained that children need genuine human relationships with their parents. It is important for parents to keep working to develop trust in their relationships with their children. Parents can be open with their children in appropriate ways. Using I-messages, for example, conveys a nonjudgmental attitude. A parent might say, for example, "I feel angry when you do not do your chores, because you are dumping your responsibility on me" as opposed to, "You are lazy and worthless." Most parents understand this skill, and many think it sounds easy. But it can be hard in the heat of the moment!

Being able to cherish our children's special qualities and to distinguish them from their behavior is important, too. However, we may subconsciously view our children's behavior as a measure of our own effectiveness as parents; if so, we may pressure our children unrealistically when our egos feel bruised. We must allow our children to have their own feelings and respect their right to respectfully disagree. This helps children learn how to think for themselves. Empathy grows from respect and appreciation of differences. Children have their own temperaments and capabilities and develop according to an overall plan that we, as parents, can nurture but not dictate.

As parents, we often are quick to judge, deny, or problem-solve. We need to learn to recognize the feelings behind our children's expressions. Our children need us to be active listeners who can understand negative feelings and help channel them into acceptable outlets. We must realize that anger is part of normal child development and, while we want to help our children learn to handle their anger, we cannot expect that anger to disappear completely. It is not a measure of ourselves as parents or an indictment of us as individuals if our children have times of anger and frustration.

Cherry (1985) offers a useful list of specific parenting skills and I-statements, like "I feel angry" instead of "You make me angry." He also includes examples of how parents can offer their children choices, such as this:

> "You can pick up your junk and have a big hug, or you can have a time out and then pick up your junk."

Instead of threatening like this:

> "You either pick up that junk or you'll get a paddling."

The Hurried Child

Children in our society are "growing up too fast, too soon," according to Elkind (1981). We used to spoil children by allowing them to do whatever they wanted, and our spoiled children feared their own power. Today, however, children appear to be stressed by being hurried. Hurried children fear failure and not achieving fast enough or high enough. Such hurrying harms children. They become afraid to take risks, even though much of learning is based on jumping in and taking risks. Further, young children perceive hurrying as rejection. Elkind (1981) maintained that we are pressuring our children for early intellectual attainment and ignoring the concept of readiness because we are insecure as parents; we need our children as symbols of our own attainment. Growth into personhood takes time and cannot be hurried. Pressure means skipping essential achievements in one or more stages.

Parents' Self-Esteem

Our culture today accords less status to the role of parent than ever before. "It is unfortunate that our culture no longer encourages people to feel self-esteem for the work involved in raising a family" (Covitz, 1986, p. 7). Parents experience relatively limited self-esteem and gratification from assuming the parental role. This adds to our vulnerability to feeling overwhelmed, inept, or dependent on our children to support us or meet our needs. It is harder for parents in this situation to provide affirming environments for their children.

As parents, we view our children through many of our own life experiences, successes, and failures. We may have standards for our children or expectations that do not fit them. When they do not meet these standards, we may feel disappointed. And when we convey that disappointment, our children's self-esteem is impaired.

It is easy for parental expectations to be off the mark. Sometimes we expect way too much or believe that children should be smaller versions of adults. If children misbehave, we may view it as a slap in our face, a reflection of our failure as parents. In reality, children misbehave when they are hungry, tired, bored, or upset. Our expectations of our children are more likely to be positive if they are based on what is known about child development, as well as sensitivity to the situation the child is in. When you have met many of your own needs successfully, you are less likely to put unrealistic pressures on your children. Thus, it is important for us as parents to be able to increase our own self-esteem and self-acceptance.

Family Interaction Styles

Two dimensions of parental behavior can be used to analyze family interaction patterns: *affection* (warmth versus hostility) and *control* (permissiveness versus restrictiveness). Children's behavior and sense of self-esteem varies depending on the combination of these two dimensions. "In general, responsive parents who are consistent, are moderately restrictive, and use appropriate explanations and attributions in their discipline practices have children who are socially and cognitively confident" (Hetherington & Parke, 1975, p. 529).

Coopersmith (1967) found several family factors to be related to high self-esteem.

First, if parents show high self-esteem, their school-age children are more likely to have this quality as well. *Thus, it is important for us as parents to work on ourselves.*

Second, parents who accept their children as people, know their children's friends, and enforce clear limits of acceptable behavior tend to have children with higher self-esteem.

Finally, allowing individual expression within acceptable limits, such as letting children set their own bedtimes, relates to high self-esteem.

Baumrind (1971) found similar results in her study of youngsters with high versus low self-esteem. She identified three types of family interaction patterns described as *permissive*, *authoritarian*, and *authoritative*. Permissive families have low control and moderate warmth, leading to low warmth when the children's behavior is undercontrolled. Authoritarian families have high control and low warmth. Authoritative families have moderate control and moderate to high warmth.

We know from earlier studies that permissiveness (allowing children to do whatever they want) backfires and is a misguided way to approach self-esteem. The child who does whatever he or she wants becomes obnoxious after awhile and has a difficult time gaining acceptance and feeling loved. Permissiveness also means that children gain no experience at delaying gratification. Social life is based on the ability to delay gratification in an effort to relate successfully to others. So children from permissive families tend to have a harder time socially.

Authoritarian discipline means that the parents have the power to make the rules and enforce them. Children in authoritarian families tend to perform better in the outside world than children from permissive families. However, there is more frustration for children of authoritarian families and less opportunity for them to spread their wings and learn problem-solving skills and approaches.

Many parents object to the idea of "democratic" discipline, feeling that the children should not be in charge of the family. A better term might be an *authoritative approach*, in which the parents maintain authority but allow some discussion and input from the children in certain areas, particularly as they grow older. This approach allows children to learn positive ways of dealing with authority and to increase their self-esteem.

In sum, parents should love and respect their children, respond to individual needs and skills, and set clear limits. Family patterns have clear implications for children's self-esteem, as shown in Table 7.4.

Children need rules and expectations for their behavior. But this need for limits changes as they grow and develop. When children are little, they need more sense of direction. As they get older, through the school years and adolescence, they still require stability on the part of their parents, but they need a lot more freedom to explore and to make mistakes. Parents today seem to go in the

TABLE 7.4
Parenting Styles and Children's Behavior

Parental Type	Children's Behavior
Permissive-indulgent parent	**Impulsive-aggressive children**
Rules not enforced	Resistive, noncompliant to adults
Rules not clearly communicated	Low in self-reliance
Yields to coercion, whining, nagging, crying by the child	Low in achievement orientation
Inconsistent discipline	Lacking in self-control
Few demands or expectations for mature, independent behavior	Aggressive
Ignores or accepts bad behavior	Quick to anger but fast to recover cheerful mood
Hides impatience, anger, and annoyance	Impulsive
Moderate warmth	Aimless, low in goal-directed activities
Glorification if importance of free expression of impulses and desires	Domineering
Authoritarian parent	**Conflicted-irritable children**
Rigid enforcement of rules	Fearful, apprehensive
Confronts and punishes bad behavior	Moody, unhappy
Shows anger and displeasure	Easily annoyed
Rules not clearly explained	Passively hostile and guileful
View of child as dominated by uncontrolled antisocial impulses	Vulnerable to stress
Child's desires and opinions not considered or solicited	Alternates between aggressive unfriendly behavior and sulky withdrawal
Persistent enforcement of rules in the face of opposition and coercion	Aimless
Harsh, punitive discipline	
Low in warmth and positive involvement	
No cultural events or mutual activities planned	

Table 7.4. Continued.

No educational demands or standards	
Authoritative Parent	**Energetic-friendly children**
Firm enforcement of rules	Self-reliant
Does not yield to child coercion	Self-controlled
Confronts disobedient child	High energy level
Shows displeasure and annoyance in response to child's bad behavior	Cheerful
Shows pleasure and support of child's constructive behavior	Friendly relations with peers
Rules clearly communicated	Copes well with stress
Considers child's wishes and solicits child's opinions	Interest and curiosity in novel situations
Alternatives offered	Cooperative with adults
Warm, involved, responsive	Tractable
Expects mature, independent behavior appropriate for the child's age	Purposive
Cultural events and joint activities planned	Achievement-oriented
Educational standards set and enforced	

Note: From Baumrind (1967).

opposite direction: They give more freedom when children are little and less when they are older. This tendency may stem from our anxiety about what our teenagers might do–they might make mistakes that will reflect poorly on us as parents or, worse still, be disastrous to their well being. However, having room for mistakes is an important part of the learning process.

Fathers and Self-Esteem

Fathers can be quite influential in the achievement motivation of their children. Girls have the advantage of higher achievement if their fathers are more active in the child-rearing process, especially if they encourage independence and performance (Hoffman, 1977). Many fathers seem at a loss as to how to relate to their teenage daughters. If only they would realize the importance of their interest and efforts. *Where there's a will, they will find a way.* Fathers also have a vital effect on the self-esteem of their sons. A close father-son relationship is associated with higher self-esteem (Coopersmith, 1967). Although fathers often enjoy guiding their sons in athletics or other "masculine" pursuits, a problem can emerge if and when fathers feel disappointed in the quality or quantity of their sons' efforts. Men need to examine their own ego needs before embarking on a negative cycle of anger and rejection toward their sons.

FRIENDSHIPS

Self-esteem is influenced strongly by one's ability to relate to other people successfully. Friendship is a wonderful, spontaneous experience of creativity and self-affirmation. No one in a position of authority can dictate the meaning of friendship. It occurs between peers or equals. Friendship is an inner experience of one's very own. It is influenced by our ability to communicate as well as sharing common interests, playing well together, and avoiding conflict.

At young ages, the ability to play together is most important, while in middle childhood acceptance by peers is central. In adolescence, the focus of friendship is on self-disclosure and self-understanding (Hetherington & Parke, 1975, p. 572).

Peer acceptance is influenced by children's names, physical characteristics and attractiveness, as well as sex and age. Children who are attractive and tall or physically mature tend to be more popular. Birth order is influential in that youngest children in a family often are more socially successful than first-born children. Academic skill and ability at sports or other activities valued by the peer group offer social advantages as well. Finally, the social behavior of children who are well liked in elementary school includes friendliness, outgoingness, and self-control. These behaviors can be taught in small counseling groups, giving children some control and choice over their social interactions and increasing their self-esteem (see Activities 7.1 through 7.10).

Social skills are important in building friendships. As described by Hetherington and Parke (1975), children who get along well with others show prosocial behaviors. Rejected children often are overly active and aggressive. Children who are neglected by their peers tend to be quiet and withdrawn. There are strategies, however (such as coaching), for teaching children social skills. Parents also play a large role in help their children develop friendships. Many children no longer live in established neighborhoods where playmates are available right outside the front door. Parents who set up play times with one other child or a small group provide opportunities for social interaction. They set the stage for interaction by encouraging invitations and modeling how they want their child to be.

Some children are not naturally outgoing, such as those with slow-to-warm-up temperaments (Chess, Thomas, & Birch, 1980). If parents back off totally, these children are likely to become couch potatoes. If they push and coerce, however, the children will certainly resist–quietly or maybe not so peacefully. (Children can learn passive-aggressive techniques as well as anyone.) Instead, parents should develop a list of options with their children and allow them to choose. This gives the children choice–but not the option of doing nothing.

It is important to help children foster self-esteem and learn good social skills at an early age. Rosenberg (1965, 1979) performed a survey of 5,000 adolescents and found that social isolation is associated with low self-esteem. Almost two-thirds of the teenagers with low self-esteem said they felt lonely. Because of their low self-esteem, they did not reach out to others, compounding the problem and creating a self-defeating cycle.

EARLY AND LATE BLOOMERS

The experience of puberty strongly influences the development of self-esteem. Boys who mature early in puberty show some social advantages, some of which follow them into adulthood (Peskin, 1973). Early-maturing males may be more successful in their careers as well as more socially astute and concerned about making a good impression. They also may be more cautious or anxious. The results for girls are not as clear, but Peskin (1973) concluded that early maturing was not such an advantage during adolescence, although early-maturing girls might have some advantages in adulthood.

Other studies (e.g., Jaquish & Savin-Williams, 1981) have produced contradictory findings. Bee and Mitchell (1984) concluded that youth who mature physically during the normative period show the most advantageous levels of self-esteem. Those youth who mature before or after the normative period, such as early-maturing girls or late-maturing boys, seem to have more difficulty with self-esteem.

In sum, individuals of either sex whose pattern of development is outside the norm are more likely to have difficulties. Early or late development may be a negative experience for both boys and girls, whereas development within the norm is optimal for the development of self-esteem.

Since we cannot influence the timing of puberty, we need to help our teenagers understand how these changes influence their feelings about themselves during adolescence and in adulthood. We all know boys who are small and not interested in sports. We can encourage them to set up their own circle of friends around other common interests or activities, such as art. Girls often get side-tracked from achievement in adolescence when their physical development leads to attention from boys. Some girls as young as 12 and 13 are completely dependent on such attention for feelings of self-worth. Make sure your daughter has other areas of interest and accomplishment. Fathers are important here in spending time and showing an interest in their daughters' activities.

The Importance of Self-View

How can we apply the findings of developmental studies in our efforts to improve our children's self-esteem? According to Moshman, Glover, and Bruning (1984), it is important to consider how children understand and view themselves as we foster self-esteem. Children vary as to what qualities they value and see as important in themselves as individuals. We must let individual interests and talents–and not gender stereotypes–steer our children's decisions. We must teach our children how to think about sex-role messages and stereotypes. It also is important to ask questions and help children see the larger picture, teaching them not to make decisions too early about their life goals. We should consider mutuality of goals and needs in choosing our children's teachers, as well. Further, we must teach our children to recognize both similarities and differences between themselves and others as they develop. Finally, we must learn to view adults (including ourselves) as well as children in developmental terms, since they change and grow as well.

BUILDING SKILLS FOR SOCIAL SUCCESS

McWhirter, McWhirter, McWhirter, and McWhirter (1994) listed five basic skills that are relevant for social success during the teenage years: school competency, concept of self and self-esteem, communication skills, coping ability, and control. High-risk teens may have weaknesses in one or more areas that can lead to self-destructive behaviors. These authors maintained that both basic academic skills and academic survival skills are essential for success. By academic survival skills, they meant work habits or behaviors that aid in learning, such as attending to task, following directions, raising one's hand to ask or answer questions, and writing clearly. "One of the common denominators among high-risk youth is biased attributions that result in alienation (e.g., beliefs that they cannot learn, that they are not responsible at school)" (McWhirter et al., 1994, p. 190). Low achievement in school leads to low self-esteem (Harter & Connell, 1982).

Communication skills to build and maintain positive relationships with others include:

- beginning and maintaining friendships,

- engaging in laughter and joking with peers,
- effectively joining a group activity,
- ending a conversation appropriately, and
- effectively relating to different types of people.

Other skills that contribute to social success and high self-esteem include the ability to deal with stress, a sense of control over decisions and directions for the future, decision-making skills, the ability to delay gratification, and the ability to set realizable goals.

Counseling Intervention

Counselors in both elementary and middle schools can help students develop these five skill areas (McWhirter et al., 1994). Classroom strategies might include cooperative learning groups, which "can be useful in teaching both basic academic skills and academic survival skills (Johnson & Johnson, 1986; Slavin, 1983). Counselors can help teachers to use cooperative learning groups in the classroom (McWhirter, Bourgard, & Bassett, 1991). They also can work with students who demonstrate skill deficits.

In individual counseling sessions or in small groups, counselors can help such students improve their self-concepts, communication skills, coping skills, and self-control. Social skills training in groups is effective in working on all five areas, as skills can be taught directly. Relaxation and imagery training are helpful to students in these areas as well. Counselors can be coordinators and trainers in the school district as a whole. School peer mediation, peer tutoring, and peer facilitation are also useful strategies.

Classroom Approaches

In an effort to prevent youth suicides, Stivers (1990) proposed several techniques for building self-esteem in the classroom, including suggestions for improving self-concept in youth. Stivers stressed that teachers should not withhold praise or affection until the task is completed. Children need acceptance for who they are. Teachers who reflect self-esteem will enhance its development in their students. Socially acceptable self-expression is fundamental to the development of self-esteem. Stivers (1990) listed resources for self-esteem curricula and materials for the classroom, including information on the National Association for Self-Esteem (1776 Lincoln St., Suite 1012, Denver, CO 80203).

Skillstreaming, developed by McGinnis and Goldstein (1984), is an approach that advocates teaching prosocial skills as a part of all mainstream and special education programs. This approach asks teachers to teach constructive behavioral alternatives and to set limits on unacceptable behaviors. Skillstreaming teaches prosocial behaviors and facilitates the actual use of these alternatives. Students learn through modeling and role-play, evaluating each others' performances in positive terms. (Later in this chapter I will discuss the application of this approach to small groups of ADHD children.)

Camp and Bush (1985) designed the *Think Aloud* curriculum for use in elementary classrooms to enhance self-esteem and problem-solving skills. In this approach, Ralph the Bear teaches the steps of problem solving, as shown in Figure 7.1:

1. What am I supposed to do?
2. What are some plans?
3. How is my plan working?
4. How did I do?

Teachers who use the *Think Aloud* curriculum must be able to accept noise in the classroom as a sign of constructive activity. Given time, students can respond to most questions. The training involves cognitive modeling of the four self-instruction questions. Children need time to formulate their own answers. They are taught to evaluate their own behavior, asking themselves about its safety, how it makes them and others feel, its fairness, and its effectiveness.

Classroom activities also can include cooperative tasks in small groups. Children typically are taught to function as individuals in our schools. We focus on grades and efficiency of production. As we move into the 21st century, however, group-work skills will be ever more vital. These can be encouraged through peer tutoring classroom activities, such as *The Missing Dragon* (see Activity 7.11). In these activities, small groups of students work together to master the material. Each member of the group learns part of the material and teaches it to the others (Aronson, Stephan, Sikes, Blaney, & Snapp, 1978). When there is diversity, the students also learn how to relate to differences in others, which has a positive impact on self-esteem (Minuchin & Shapiro, 1983).

> When I was in graduate school, I attended a lecture on the nature of human behavior, which concluded that we are all motivated by human greed and the desire to acquire wealth. I found the comments interesting in light of a course I was taking on the philosophy of Karl Marx. What I remember from that course is the idea that the political system we live in determines our ideas on the nature of man and what motivates us. Being in a capitalist society means we view people as out to gain as much for themselves as possible.

How to Solve a Problem

Say the problem.
Ask yourself detective questions (who, what, where, when, why).
Think of some new ideas that will help.
Think how you can use the new ideas.
Solve your problem using your new ideas.

1
What am I supposed to do?
2
What are some plans?
3
PLAN
How is my plan working?
4
How did I do?

Figure 7.1. How to solve a problem.

Note: Illustrations from *Think Aloud: Increasing Social and Cognitive Skills—A Problem-Solving Program for Children* (primary level, p. 56) by B. W. Camp and M. A. S. Bash (1981). Champaign, IL: Research Press. Copyright 1981 by the authors. Reprinted by permission.

These views of human behavior shape our educational system in many ways. For example, students are graded on their performance as individuals. They are asked to work on their own. Talking to neighbors or soliciting opinions from classmates is considered disruptive or even cheating. We emphasize capital gain as the ultimate outcome of the educational process. And we value speed, as evidenced by timed math tasks like the "Mad Minute." Even classroom projects are competitive, such as math races between two groups. The group that responds most quickly gets the points, even if the other team has the answer seconds later. The emphasis is on the product or "the answer," rather than the process of thought.

Our culture is highly competitive. Cross-cultural research has demonstrated that the attitudes of Anglo-American children interfere with their ability to cooperate with others in problem solving, even when such cooperation is to their advantage. Children raised in cultures that place less value on self-sufficiency and competition, such as Mexican or Black families, are better able to work cooperatively for common goals. In some societies, such as in Russia or on the Israeli Kibbutz, the norm of cooperation and an orientation to group goals are systematically inculcated into the educational system. Children in these societies show more cooperative behavior than Anglo-American children. The self-concern generated by a competitive orientation and the focus on status needs and self-sufficiency interfere with behaviors such as giving and sharing with others. There is less inclination to consider the needs and feelings of others.

How do variations in the American classroom relate to the degree of cooperation children show? Schools using the open classroom concept offer one contrasting view. Children in open classrooms engage in more prosocial behavior and more imaginative play, although they also tend to be more aggressive than children in highly structured environments. But for many children the open classroom is not the most efficient way to learn.

The style of the teacher–authoritarian, democratic, or laissez-faire–is one of the strongest influences of children's social behavior. Democratic leadership produces productive, happier students with less hostility. Laissez-faire leadership leads to disorganization, whereas the authoritarian style leads to passivity or rebelliousness, aggressive peer interaction, and inefficient work habits.

Teaching cooperation has not been valued in the past. However, *we are beginning to recognize that the secret to success in the future may lie in our ability to cooperate.* Cetron & O'Toole (1982) gave a fascinating forecast of life in the 21st century in which they maintained that social skills will be even more vital to our way of life. In fact, learning cooperation and social skills will be, according to Cetron and O'Toole (1982), the most important product of education in the future. Children will need these skills to function in the workforce as well as for global survival. This means that teachers will need to learn new skills and new ways of approaching the socioeconomic realm. Classrooms will need to allow for different styles of learning, to promote group-oriented functioning, and to teach ways of getting along. After we move into the 21st century, children will need a myriad of social skills and communication approaches to help them solve enormously complex problems.

Physical Activity

As parents and teachers, we must recognize the psychological benefits of physical activity and exercise for children. According to Biddle (1993, p. 212), "quality experiences for children in sports and exercise can have beneficial emotional effects in terms of reduced negative affect and increases in self-esteem and feelings of well-being." Even children who are not strong athletes can benefit from the camaraderie of peer interaction, learning the rules of the game, and experiencing the success of rising to the challenge. I remember a 6-year-old boy with a supportive coach and team who overcame his social phobia and avoidance of others during the baseball season and came to feel like "one of the guys." Coaches need special skills in handling this type of situation, and children will respond accordingly.

Sports can affect children's social growth, friendships, motivation, and self-esteem (Roberts & Treasure, 1992). When children are overly concerned with social comparisons, however, they may experience negative consequences from participation. Roberts and Treasure (1992) maintained that it is important to establish "mastery climates" for children participating in sports, so that the experience is positive for all children. They called on the coach, parents, and teacher to teach sports through positive methods that build self-esteem. Coaches can emphasize learning skills, enjoyment of the game, and personal improvement rather than winning at all costs. Gifted athletes should be recognized, and team members should understand the importance of their contributions; but they also must learn that not all players can be stars. Coaches should be able to situate their players for maximum team performance.

OPTIMISM AND DEPRESSION

Many people do not realize that children can experience depression or a deep sense of helplessness and hopelessness. Some children may show perfectionism, with its all-or-nothing thinking. Perfectionists overgeneralize and tend to jump to the conclusion that a negative event will be repeated endlessly. They think in terms of "shoulds." Perfectionists also incorrectly believe that people who are successful do not have to put forth maximum effort, make few mistakes, and are supremely self-confident and calm (Burns, 1980).

How do children learn to be perfectionists? If children make mistakes or fall short of the mark and their parents respond with anxiety, they may perceive that anxiety as a withdrawal of love. This leads children to believe that, in order to be loved, they must not make mistakes. The tragedy is that taking risks and making mistakes is part and parcel of the learning process.

In his book *The Optimistic Child,* Seligman (1995) maintained that the self-esteem movement, in advocating "unconditional positive feedback" to help children feel better about themselves, overemphasized the "feel good" side of the equation. In spite of this movement, he observed, depression is more common in children today than ever before. Self-esteem is a feeling state based in successful interactions with the real world. Thus, "doing well" is a pivotal part of developing high self-esteem. According to Seligman (1995), there is no formula for teaching children how to feel good if they do not know how to perform well. Good feelings about oneself are based on actual performance.

There is no question that feeling high self-esteem is a delightful state, but trying to achieve the feeling side before achieving good commerce with the world profoundly confuses the means and the end (Seligman, 1995, p. 33). Self-esteem does not cause success. Rather, success builds self-esteem.

Seligman (1995) also maintained that how children think about failure is an important aspect of their self-esteem. Feeling bad about the self does not *cause* failure. The belief that problems will last forever and undermine everything, in contrast, causes children to stop trying. Giving up leads to more failure, which then undermines feelings of self-esteem (Seligman, 1995, p. 35).

Optimism and *pessimism* are the explanatory styles children use to explain events that happen to them. There are three crucial dimensions to these styles: permanence, pervasiveness, and personalization.

Permanence: Pessimists view bad events as permanent, whereas optimists view them as temporary.

Pervasiveness: Children with a pessimistic style think about their failures in terms of "always" and "never." Optimists can see a failure as a one-time event.

Personalization: This is the style of deciding who is at fault. "When bad things happen, children can blame themselves (internal) or they can blame other people or circumstances (external)" (Seligman, 1995, p. 57).

Pessimists blame both themselves and others in a general way. We must help our children take *realistic* responsibility for their actions. We also must teach them to use behavioral rather than general self-blame. In addition, there is a "right way" to criticize a child. Instead of implying a permanent fault, such as "What's wrong with you?", we must affirm that the child can change: "You are acting up. I don't like it." Instead of ascribing a global defect, such as "You're bad," we must be specific about the behavior: "You're teasing your brother." Instead of imputing passive traits, such as "You're lazy," we should emphasize behavioral solutions: "You could spend more time on studying for tests." When parents, teachers, and coaches criticize, they influence the child's theory of the way the world works. A child soon "begins to criticize himself using the explanatory style of the criticism he gets from respected mentors" (Seligman, 1995, p. 105). (To practice optimistic criticism, see Activity 7.12.)

Teachers sometimes are biased in how they criticize their students. Girls often receive disparagement of their ability, whereas boys are chastised for "lack of effort, rowdiness, and not paying attention" (Seligman, 1995, p. 107). This leads girls to view failure at work as permanent, while boys learn to work harder.

It is important for us to teach our children curiosity about their feelings and thoughts on a day-to-day basis. Working with the idea of an internal dialogue is helpful. "After your child is tuned into his internal dialogue, it is time to explain the ABC (adversity-belief-consequence) model to him" (Seligman, 1995, p. 152). In this model, adversity triggers beliefs and self-talk that lead to the experience of certain feelings. Matching thoughts to feelings is an important skill in applying the ABC model to real-life situations. To teach explanatory style to your child, begin by explaining the concepts of optimism and pessimism and then explain the accuracy of beliefs.

Personal responsibility is a cornerstone of optimism. You cannot successfully maintain an optimistic attitude and avoid responsibility. But simply "repeating positive statements to yourself does not change mood or achievement very much, if at all" (Seligman, 1995, p. 168). Children need to learn to accurately assess what went wrong. We must teach them to apply the ABC model in real-life situations, to distinguish between permanent and temporary and personal and impersonal behaviors.

In teaching our children optimism, we give them an invaluable skill for achieving goals and meeting challenges. They learn the importance of gathering data, generating alternatives, assessing outcomes, and developing a plan. In teaching them the five steps to problem solving (Seligman, 1995)–slowing down, taking perspectives, setting goals, choosing a path, and evaluating how it went–we can help our children to acquire "the powerful tool" of optimism.

SPECIAL NEEDS CHILDREN

Special circumstances can affect the development of self-esteem in children. For example, gifted girls may feel different and alone when they do not fit feminine stereotypes. Divorce produces negative effects on the life choices of millions of children. Another problem for large numbers of children today is

Attention Deficit Hyperactivity Disorder (ADHD). ADHD greatly affects children's perceptions of themselves. Finally, it is indisputable that minority youth experience a "double whammy" in today's culture. In the following sections, we'll look at each of these special cases.

Gifted Girls and Self-Esteem

Kerr (1985) studied a small group of gifted women and found several patterns of adjustment:

The Happy Homemaker focuses her energies on the life of her family. "She has given so much to others that she isn't very good at giving to herself" (p. 28).

The Disposable Career Woman has a limited career that she sacrifices as needed for her husband and children.

The Lone Achiever says she wants to stay single, investing primarily in her profession.

Fulfilled but exhausted, **the Dual-Career Coupler** is a workaholic who wants to be the best mother possible.

None of the women in Kerr's sample was the primary breadwinner, with a stay-at-home husband. Further, "[m]any of the women in this group had learned to deny their gifts in the same way others denied them; they had learned to lower their sights and adjust to 'reality'" (Kerr, 1985, p. 32).

In the 1960s, some gifted women participated in the counterculture and were successful in nontraditional careers. But they were not reimbursed financially at the same rate as gifted males. Further, those woman invested in careers were less likely to be married or to have children. It also appears that girls are taught to view their failures, but not their successes, as related to ability. Boys, in contrast, perceive success as a reward for their efforts but failure as resulting from bad luck. Therefore, girls lose confidence in their ability to achieve through their own estimation of what they have accomplished. Further, women in traditional roles may have difficulty finding time for achievement-related concerns.

Kerr also noted that, typically, marriage and parenthood drastically reduce the time and energy women invest in education and in the workplace. By contrast, men traditionally have less conflict between family responsibilities and their investment in education and work (Kerr, 1985, p. 81).

Clearly, marriage and childbirth strongly affect women's achievement, particularly for those with the highest potential. In addition, the more children a woman has, the greater the negative effect on her career status. Gifted girls experience a conflict between their capabilities and gender expectations. Can they combine careers and homemaking successfully, and how?

Many girls seem achievement-oriented and high in self-esteem until early adolescence. What happens then? Powerful forces dissuade girls of the notion that their accomplishments matter. Their desires for love, affection, and social approval become paramount. Women tend to continue showing this intense need until their 40s, when they may have the opportunity to focus again on their own self-esteem–if they have any left after years of catering to others.

In Kerr's (1985) study, most of the gifted women had not fulfilled their potential. Our society tends to view female achievement negatively. *Fear of success* may have led the most feminine of Kerr's group to underachieve. The *Cinderella complex* may have encouraged others to search for someone to take care of them. The *impostor phenomenon* may have created self-doubts, blocking achievement. In fact, most of the women studied "were hurt by their tendencies to be well-adjusted, easygoing, and accommodating" (p. 166).

Advice for Parents. Kerr (1985) maintained that we must make a better effort to identify gifted girls–not an easy task, given "their social camouflage." Then we must nourish them and give them opportunities to develop their gifts. Finally, we must guide them in an active way. We must love and appreciate our gifted daughters and give them room to grow.

> Parents and teachers can also augment gifted girls' needs for personal and career guidance by shaping their adventurousness, seeking information about future alternatives in their areas of interests, and always challenging them to be more and do more than they thought they could (Kerr, 1985, p. 168).

While emotional support is nice, sometimes just the expectation of performance by a significant person, such as one's father, is highly influential. On my return home from college each summer, my father's first question was always, "So what are you going to do for a living?" (He was not pleased when I answered, "modern dance.") I generally felt nervous when he asked me that question, because I did not have a real answer yet. But the fact that he asked focused my thoughts in this area and certainly affirmed my capability.

Gifted girls need a belief in their ability and a sense of urgency about their achievement. They also need real-life assistance and support in combining family and career goals.

Divorce and Children's Self-Esteem

Given that the frequency of divorce is growing astronomically and currently affects nearly one of every two children in this country, there has been a great deal of concern in recent year about its effects on the self-esteem of children. Wallerstein and Kelly (1980) and Francke (1983) provided a comprehensive overview of the emotional issues of divorce, which vary depending on the child's age:

Infants experience a sense of helplessness.

Preschoolers struggle with guilt.

Children 6 to 8 years old face sadness.

Children 9 to 12 years old must cope with anger.

Teenagers face the dilemma of false maturity.

These feelings exist at all ages in reaction to divorce, but different emotions predominate at different ages. The child's first reaction most likely includes a combination of anger, fear, depression, and guilt and is affected by the child's age, personality, and sex (Kurdek & Berg, 1987).

Even babies show reactions to divorce in the form of disruptions in their eating or sleeping patterns. Toddlers ages 2 and 3 may regress in their behavior, show bewilderment, and cling in the presence of strangers. In some cases, development continues to be delayed in the following year. Preschoolers show less self-confidence and lowered self-esteem; they also exhibit a tendency to take responsibility for the absence of the parent who has left. Neal (1983) discussed how preschoolers believe that a parent *has left them*, because they have done something "bad." Children ages 5 and 6 tend to continue believing that the absent parent will come back. Seven and 8-year-olds are saddened and scared by divorce, many of them missing the absent parent all the time. Some of these children are afraid that if they make the other parent upset, he or she might leave as well. Nine and 10-year-olds may initially react calmly, but they still have to cope with inner feelings of anger and shame.

A year after the divorce, half of these children will have adjusted with resignation and some remaining sadness. The other half will experience depression, low self-esteem, poor school performance, and poor relationships with peers. Young adolescents show a deeper understanding of their parents' divorces. Unlike younger children, they are much less likely to harbor feelings of guilt about the divorce or hostility toward their parents. Divorce has a tremendous impact on children. These problems may be manifested later at school, with peers, or with adults.

There has been concern that younger children may be more vulnerable to divorce because they tend to develop misconceptions and have fewer coping skills. However, Wallerstein (1984) found that children 2½ to 6 years old were better adjusted later. Younger children have not had as much time to experience the nuclear family, and so feel less sense of loss and grief overall. They are more flexible in adjusting to alternative family structures.

Boys tend to be more vulnerable to divorce and show more divorce-related problems. This may be because they have less opportunity following divorce to identify with their fathers, since mothers often have custody. Santrock and Warshak (1979) found that children in cross-sex custody arrangements were less well-adjusted. To counteract this effect, a mother with custody of her son should promote regular contact between son and father. If this is not feasible, the mother can set up a special relationship for her son with a male friend, such as a "big brother," godfather, grandfather, coach, or minister.

Divorce is a long-term process with many subsequent adjustments. Some effects shown in adulthood include a reduced sense of psychological well-being and a more difficult adjustment to parental and marital roles (Wallerstein, 1984). It may be useful to conceptualize divorce as a framework for organizing later experiences (Kulka & Weingarten, 1979).

Therapy and counseling efforts can help children and their families adjust to their new family status. Group intervention is particularly effective. Pedro-Carroll and Cowen (1985) adapted a children's group to a school environment and found improvements in problem behaviors and adjustment. Most group intervention efforts have been set in elementary schools and have focused on the children's needs. One group program has been offered in the Court of Domestic Relations for both children and their parents (see Bergman-Meador & Cordell, 1987). Youngsters continue to deal with the issues of divorce for many years (Kalter, Picker, & Lesowitz, 1984); therapists and counselors need to be aware of this, as divorce issues may not be the presenting problem.

Children ages 4 to 7 are particularly interested in divorce-related activities and seem to benefit a great deal from group intervention. I highly recommend the following books for this age group (see the reference list at the end of this chapter for full cites):

How Does It Feel When Your Parents Get Divorced? by T. Berger

Dinosaurs Divorce: A Guide for Changing Families, by L. K. Brown and M. Brown

The Boys' and Girls' Book About Divorce, by R. A. Gardner

Talking About Divorce and Separation: A Dialogue Between Parent and Child, by E. A. Grollman

When Mom and Dad Separate: Children Can Learn to Cope with Grief from Divorce, by M. Heegaard

Will Dad Ever Move Back Home? by P. Z. Hogan

The Divorce Workbook: A Guide for Kids and Families, by S. B. Ives, D. Fassler, and M. Lash

What's Going to Happen to Me? When Parents Separate or Divorce, by E. LeShan

Divorce Is ... A Kids' Coloring Book, by K. Magid and W. Schriebman

Bernard, by B. Waber

I Love My Mother, by P. Zindel

A Father Like That, by C. Zolotow

Children in counseling group programs for issues of divorce can learn to be less alienated from their parents, especially the absent parent. Given the large numbers of children experiencing divorce, we need to make such programs widely available to both children and parents.

Advice for Parents. If you are going through a divorce yourself, there is a lot you can do to minimize the pain your children experience. First, you must avoid at all costs putting your children in the middle of the conflict or setting up loyalty conflicts. Try to separate your feelings toward your ex-spouse from your responsibilities as a parent. Ideally, you should talk to your ex-spouse about parenting issues, trying to put your dissatisfaction with each other aside. You should also make an extra effort to recognize your children's emotions and to talk with them about their feelings.

ADHD and Learning Disabilities

Children with learning disabilities are "at risk for having low self-esteem" (Searcy, 1988, p. 456). Since a learning disability affects a child's sense of competence, it significantly influences his or her feelings of self-worth. Children's levels of self-esteem rise and fall depending on their assessment of how they are measuring up to their own expectations or the expectations of others. By adolescence, children's self-esteem is less likely to shift depending on what others think. Searcy (1988) maintained that an infant with LD responds differently to his or her mother than a normal baby, as there may be difficulty localizing and responding to the mother's voice or playing games together. Thus, an effect on self-esteem may arise even before the child enters school.

Those who have learning disabilities tend to have an overall feeling of inadequacy. They often feel they cannot perform well enough to meet the expectations of others. They tend to carry this belief with them even in the face of success experiences.

Recently, it was estimated that more than 2 million school-age children in the country have ADHD (Barkley, 1995). These are children who show significant behavior problems that are very stressful for family life. Families of ADHD children often experience conflict over chores, homework, and getting along with siblings, with the ADHD child showing antagonistic behavior at school and in the neighborhood. Further, ADHD children typically have trouble making friends. They often are not invited to birthday parties or sleep-overs. It compounds the problem that nothing seems wrong physically. ADHD children may be moody and emotionally overreactive. They tend to be upset, disorganized, unhappy, and isolated and to perceive themselves as powerless. They often are angry and defensive. They tend to be uncommunicative about their feelings and internal experiences.

ADHD children are resistant to social demands, overly "independent" for their age, and domineering in their behavior (Wender, 1987). They may be friendly and enthusiastic in play, with a high energy level, as well as zestful and reckless with problems in unstructured activities. They lack subtle social skills and often are described as bossy, selfish, or immature. They may be more successful playing with younger children, who better accept their dominant behavior. Their social problems are central and pervasive (Whalen & Henker, 1985).

The peers of an ADHD boy, for example, are likely to be put off by his impulsiveness and poor self-control. They dislike his rough, grabby behavior, his bossiness, and his inability to await his turn or abide by the rules of a game. They know him to be a poor loser, and they view his emotional outbursts with disdain. If he blows up or bursts into tears over minor upsets, other children are likely to ridicule him as a crybaby and may even take malicious pleasure in trying to provoke an outburst (Ingersoll, 1988 p. 151-152).

ADHD children do not have insight into how their behavior affects others. They seldom see the connection between their behavior and the outcome. They do not detect subtle social cues–or even obvious ones. These children view themselves as victims, although those around them are, in fact, inadvertently "victimized" by their behavior. The problem goes to the very core of these children's interactions with others. They experience low self-esteem due to the negative reactions of others. Specific social skills lacking in ADHD children are shown in Table 7.5.

The good news is that there has been a great deal of interest in developing procedures for enhancing children's interpersonal relationships with their peers. We know that popular children behave in specific ways, initiate interactions,

TABLE 7.5
ADHD/Communication Skills

Specific social skills are missing

- formulating useful descriptions
- repairing communication breakdown
- taking an assertive position

Difficulty understanding "who can say what, in what way, where, when and by what means, and to whom"

More hostile communication

- less complex speech
- difficulty adjusting to the listener
- unassertive

Functions okay when given adequate messages and feedback not required

- difficulty assuming responsibility for communication

smile often, and make positive comments. Children can be taught these social skills. This approach has been applied to a wide variety of problems, including ADHD.

Several intervention strategies have been used to teach social skills effectively, including contingent positive reinforcement, modeling, coaching and behavioral rehearsal, and peer initiation strategies.

In **contingent positive reinforcement**, children are encouraged and rewarded for taking behavioral steps that are appropriate socially. Here we have to know what is appropriate for a child's age level and social context. We also need to notice the appropriate "pieces" of the behavioral sequences and reinforce those efforts, even though other aspects of the sequence may be nonexistent, inappropriate, or extremely aggravating.

In **modeling**, the adult or model behaves as we wish the child would. Children learn from this method, but some of that learning is latent or in "deep freeze" and not immediately apparent.

In **coaching and behavioral rehearsal**, we teach the specific behavioral steps through practice and role-play.

Peer initiation strategies are very effective as peers model desired behaviors and provide rewards.

In our ADHD/social skills group program (at Cordell & Associates in Dayton, Ohio), we use the steps of *Skillstreaming* (McGinnis & Goldstein, 1984) for eight behaviors. We have developed role-plays for use in groups of 6 to 10 ADHD children of similar ages (see Activity 7.18). We have found that groups balanced evenly between boys and girls work best. The role-plays are initially done by the adult group leaders. The students assess the adult models for the presence of each behavioral step, then develop their own scripts and volunteer to be main and support actors. The role play is videotaped, and students assess the actors' performance of the behavioral steps. Watching the videotape of their role play reinforces learning the steps of appropriate behavior.

Examples of specific skills that can be taught from the Skillstreaming curriculum are listed here:

Controlling Myself

Listening

1. Look at the person who is talking.
2. Sit quietly.
3. Think about what is being said.
4. Say "yes" or nod your head.
5. Ask a question.

Expressing Your Feelings

1. Stop and think how you feel.
2. Decide what it is you are feeling.
3. Think about your choices.
4. Act out your best choice.

Getting Along With Friends

Understanding the Feelings of Others

1. Watch the other person.
2. Listen to what the person is saying.

3. Figure out what the other person might be feeling.
4. Think about ways to show you understand what he or she is feeling.
5. Decide on the best way and do it.

Responding to Teasing

1. Decide if you are being teased.
2. Think about ways to deal with the teasing.
3. Choose the best way and do it.

Getting Along With Adults

Making a Complaint

1. Decide what your complaint is.
2. Decide who to complain to.
3. Tell that person your complaint.

Dealing with Another's Anger

1. Listen to the person
2. Think about your choices:
   A. Keep listening
   B. Ask why he is angry
   C. Offer a solution
   D. Walk away
3. Act out your best choice.

Getting My Duties Done

Arranging Problems by Importance

1. Think about the problems that are bothering you.
2. List these problems from most to least important.
3. Do what you can to hold off on your less important problems.
4. Go to work on your most important problems.

Getting Ready for a Difficult Conversation

1. Think about how you will feel during the conversation
2. Think about how the other person will feel.

3. Think about different ways you could say what you want to say.
4. Think about what the other person might say back to you.
5. Think about any other things that might happen during the conversation.
6. Choose the best approach you can think of and try it.

Below are some books that can be very helpful for ADHD children:

Eagle Eyes: A Child's Guide to Paying Attention, by J. Gehret

What to Do? by K. T. Hegeman

Shelley, The Hyperactive Turtle, by D. M. Moss

Putting on the Brakes: Young People's Guide to Understanding Attention Deficit Hyperactivity Disorder (ADHD), by P. O. Quinn and J. M. Stern

Advice for Parents. Parenting involves many complex changes and adjustments. Most parents today are well-prepared for labor and delivery, but later may feel lost and overwhelmed. No sooner do we figure out our new baby than we discover we have a toddler, and the nature of what we need to do has changed drastically. We may feel more confident with our second child (having been trained by our first), but then our second probably has a very different personality and set of needs. And if the family expands further, we discover we are outnumbered. The discovery that one of our children has ADHD is incredibly stressful: It certainly means that our job just got a lot bigger.

Children with ADHD have trouble paying attention. This affects their behavior at home as well as their work in the classroom. They may go from one activity to another too quickly or be overly engrossed in one activity and have trouble shifting their attention. They present a challenge for parents and teachers alike with their high activity level and difficulty following rules.

Often the usual approaches to child-rearing are not effective with hyperactive children, and alternatives are needed. Parents may feel a high level of frustration. You may find yourself gravitating to more punitive methods than you want to be using. It helps to know that other mothers and fathers have been there, too.

Having an ADHD child poses challenges for all families, especially in several areas of vulnerability for the child. As parents, we often feel incompetent; we also may feel guilt and ambivalence about the child's ADHD characteristics. Our self-control may be severely tested. But our capacity for emotional control in the face of the child's difficulties is critical. The importance of consistency and follow-through with behavior management procedures cannot be overstated. Structured routines are also needed. We must model a high level of frustration tolerance, and we will need it to set realistic behavioral and educational goals, deal with intensified sibling rivalry and fighting, and help our children deal with social miscommunications.

ADHD children should be given opportunities to function with non-ADHD children and supported in developing their own forms of compensation and adaptation (Ziegler & Holden, 1988). Compensation efforts in learning and self-control should be reinforced. As parents we must understand that ADHD is medically based and that we are not to blame; we also must realize that *we cannot control all aspects of the problem*. We can learn to feel competent, committed, and concerned but detach ourselves in dealing with ADHD-related problems. Both parents need to work together in raising the ADHD child, sharing responsibilities, and providing mutual support.

There are successful ways of coping with hyperactivity in your child. *There are solutions*. Support groups for parents and specific social skills training for children can be quite helpful. A group of parents of ADHD children generated the following list of methods for coping:

Try to relax

- deep breathing
- muscle relaxation
- guided imagery

Detach from the situation

- think of your child as someone else's
- set priorities of what to be excited about
- find social outlets; get support from friends

Engage in regular physical exercise and other physical outlets

- gardening, housework, etc.
- take turns between spouses
- have a sense of humor
- verbalize your feelings
- leave the room

Allow yourself to feel the anger

Parents also can learn helpful attitudes, such as these:

Helpful	Not Helpful
Cool/calm/even-tempered/ "step back"	Emotional
Positive (I-messages)	Negative (You ...)
Distinguish behavior vs. self	Blaming
Long view/consistency	Nagging/not following through on consequences
Parents together as a team	Parents argue/disagree on basics

Barkley (1995) listed several helpful suggestions for parents of ADHD children, including his ten guiding principles:

- Give your child more immediate feedback and consequences
- Give your child more frequent feedback
- Use larger and more powerful consequences
- Use incentives before punishment
- Strive for consistency
- Act, don't yak!
- Plan ahead for problem situations
- Keep a disability perspective
- Don't personalize your child's problems or disorder
- Practice forgiveness

Communication skills for adolescents are listed in Table 7.6.

African-American Issues

Extensive research has been done on the social development of African-American children and the role of self-esteem in that development. Early studies looked at the beneficial effects of integration for minority youth. Research

Table 7.6
Negative Communication Habits

Check if people in your family do this:	More positive way to do it:
1. ____ Call each other names.	Express anger without hurtful words.
2. ____ Put each other down.	"I am angry that you did ______."
3. ____ Interrupt each other.	Take turns; keep it short.
4. ____ Criticize all the time.	Point out the good and bad.
5. ____ Get defensive when attacked.	Listen carefully and check out what you heard–then disagree calmly.
6. ____ Give a lecture/big words.	Tell it straight and short.
7. ____ Look away, not at speaker.	Make good eye contact.
8. ____ Slouch or slide to floor.	Sit up and look attentive.
9. ____ Talk in sarcastic tone.	Talk in a normal tone.
10.____ Get off the topic.	Finish one topic, then go on.
11.____ Think the worst.	Keep an open mind. Don't jump to conclusions.
12.____ Dredge up the past.	Stick to the present.
13.____ Read each other's minds.	Ask the other's opinion.
14.____ Command, order.	Ask nicely.
15.____ Give the silent treatment.	Say it if you feel it.
16.____ Throw tantrums, "lose it."	Count to 10; take a hike; do relaxation exercises; leave the room.
17.____ Make light of something serious.	Take it seriously, even if it is minor to you.
18.____ Deny responsibility.	Admit you did it, but say you were accused.
19.____ Nag about small mistakes	Admit no one is perfect; overlook small things.

Your "Zap score" (total number of checks) ___

Note: From Robin (1990). Reprinted by permission.

has found that relationships between the races improve when high school students work together and play together on teams (Minuchin & Shapiro, 1983). The balance of Black and White children in school also is important. If the balance is not equal, the students in the minority feel accepted by their own group but rejected by the larger group (Edwards, Miller, McCormack, Mitchell, & Robinson, 1983).

How is self-esteem affected by integration in the school system? "Some reported increased self-esteem among Black students, while others reported no effect or decreases in self-esteem especially in academic self-concept" (St. John, 1975). The assumption that Black children have a low self-image has been challenged by several studies that show that Black children's self-esteem is equivalent to that of White children. Desegregation does not necessarily improve the self-esteem of Black children. Further, when there are gains in self-esteem, it is unclear why they have occurred.

The effect of desegregation on academic improvement varies, with increases in verbal test scores more likely than in math test scores (Miller, 1983). Overall, researchers have found that the earlier the desegregation occurs, the more benefit there is for the students in terms of test scores. However, Stephan (1983) noted that Black children in integrated schools made greater achievement gains in the 1960s than in the 1970s . While there have been some gains in recent years, there still is an achievement gap between Black and White children after integration (Miller, 1984). A major concern among sociologists is that many Black children in integrated schools seem to suffer in academic status. They also may experience less acceptance by new peers and teachers. Some have argued that desegregation is actually detrimental to the academic and psychological well-being of African-American students. In any case, studies on the self-esteem of African-American children have found vast improvements since the Civil Rights Movement (Spurlock, 1986).

Early studies found what was termed "White preference behavior" among African-American children; researchers assumed that this indicated low self-esteem. In the last decade, researchers have once again found White preference behavior prevalent among African-American preschool children. The results, however, have been interpreted in different ways. Some consider it an indication of low self-esteem, while others claim that the relationship between such behavior and self-esteem is unclear. Still other studies have indicated that White preference behavior is not a reflection of low self-esteem. For example, Spencer (1985) found that African-American children have positive self-concepts even when they show White preference behavior. In addition, there is no evidence that African-American children actually have a lower sense of self-esteem than White children. In sum, research has not shown a real relationship between African-American children's racial attitudes or preferences and their self-esteem.

Play therapists now often have both Black and White dolls available for play. This allows an exploration of racial attitudes. Children may make comments or show preferences in their choices.

> I remember working with a 5-year-old Black girl in play therapy at the local child welfare agency 25 years ago. She was a bright, beautiful child in the care of her loving aunt. She was eager to play. I tried to understand her feelings and to provide "unconditional positive regard." However, she would never take off her knit cap, saying that her hair was "nappy." I never saw her hair, and I knew she was keeping part of herself from me. In every other way, she seemed competent and happy.

There is evidence that self-esteem and cultural identity are "independent and differentially related to other areas of psychosocial functioning in African-American children, with the latter being more important" (Whaley, 1993, p. 418). Whaley (1993) concluded that self-esteem and cultural identity are separate aspects of identity formation influenced by cognitive-developmental processes. For African-American children, the sense of cultural identity appears to be highly relevant for their sense of psychosocial adjustment. Thus, intervention should target the developing sense of cultural identity.

We need to study the self-esteem of African-American children in the social context in which it develops to truly understand the resiliency and capability of this group of young people (Spurlock, 1986).

One suggestion is to do a better job teaching African-American children that science and math are not culture-bound or strictly fields for Whites. Another approach is to learn more about how African-American students cope when they are academically successful and popular. We also must provide increased opportunities for educational and occupational experiences and success in the mainstream culture. These suggestions are useful for educators and counselors alike.

Thompson (1995) found that Black self-hatred leads to behaviors that are destructive to self, including violence and homicide. In African-American youth, the sense of self-esteem is generally positive, but racial pride is low. African-American youth need identification with positive role models. In terms of academic achievement, children may have a positive assessment of their abilities but choose not to achieve, as this is viewed as a White value and not relevant. There may be no support from the community. Intervention should focus on cultural identity, not self-esteem. Culturally sensitive churches can be helpful in counteracting the negative attitudes and low expectation that are communicated both consciously and unconsciously when, for example, good students are accused of being "White." Thus, the major role of importance is teaching self-efficacy, not self-esteem. The concept should be how to earn status and not be the recipient of help from others.

It is vital to the developing self-concept of African-American children that family and peers provide positive role models (Walker, Taylor, McElroy, Phillip, & Wilson, 1995). The extended family system is particularly beneficial to children's positive self-esteem. African-American children must acknowledge and transcend negative social stereotypes as they develop their identities. They need to "devise mechanisms to ward off threats to self-esteem" (Spurlock, 1986, p. 66). Social isolation, denial, rejection of negative societal attitudes, and focusing on specific talents can all be useful. Projection–as in blaming "them" and channeling rage–are also coping strategies.

Advice for Parents. African-American parents can give their children powerful tools by:

negating social stereotypes that undermine their competence and sense of self-worth,

stressing unique talents and abilities,

teaching strategies for coping with racism, and

fostering ways to deal with discrimination (Miller & Miller, 1990).

Black parents will find good advice for nurturing their children and enhancing their self-esteem in *Raising Black Children* by Comer and Poussaint (1992). In addition, Hopson and Hopson (1990) listed suggestions for African-American parents raising their children in a race-conscious society. The authors stated that "racism is a direct assault" (p. 43) upon our children's sense of self-esteem. They provided ideas on anticipatory role-playing for dealing with a variety of situations, such as, "What if Whites make fun of your hair?"

In addition to positive modeling, parents can emphasize the accomplishments of historical and political figures. Many libraries have special collections of Black literature from the time of slavery. Some museums show the contributions of African-Americans to U.S. history. Encourage your children to keep journals of their family history, following the model provided by Alex Haley. Asking questions of family members about previous generations can lead to an appreciation of the role of the family in the flow of historical events.

Recently, a CNN television program maintained that there is a great deal of separation between the races in our nation's churches. However, some churches make a special effort to be integrated. Their diversity is deliberate. Seeking out and visiting such churches provides a powerful lesson in cooperative living.

Biracial Children. The needs of biracial youngsters are seldom addressed. Yet, their numbers are growing faster than ever before. Biracial children have some special needs, related to the fact that their ethnic identity is ambiguous "in a society where race has always been a significant social dimension" (Gibbs, 1991, p. 322). They are faced with the daunting task of combining two ethnic and cultural backgrounds with no real reference group. According to Gibbs (1991, p. 328), "Empirical studies of biracial children indicate that their racial attitudes and self-concept develop differently than those of either Black or White children."

Studies of self-esteem have found conflicting findings, from a negative self-concept to higher self-esteem compared to nonmixed peers. Gibbs (1991) proposed that these children have difficulties resolving several psychological tasks, including these:

Conflicts with their dual racial/ethnic identity

Conflicts about their social position

Conflicts about their sexuality and choice of sexual partners

Conflicts about separation from their parents

Conflicts about both school and work

The biracial child must acquire skills for coping with minority status and may not find complete acceptance in either community. Parents should encourage the child to integrate aspects of both cultures (Miller & Miller, 1990). Books such as *Interracial Dating and Marriage,* by Elaine Landau (1993), may be helpful in helping children cope with racial and sexual identity issues.

> A young biracial boy came to me with a problem that distressed him greatly. He lived in a community of diversity with integration of the races and many mixed-race children. However, he was hurt one day at school that White children on the playground did not believe he was Black. The next day he explained to them that there is a broad range of color among Black people. He drew a picture of Black people in a continuum of color. The White children said, "Oh, we didn't know that!"

Hopson and Hopson (1990, pp. 68-69) dealt directly with this dilemma:

> It might indeed be more accurate or even desirable to tell mixed-race children that they are Brown, as a way of acknowledging their dual heritage. However, open, honest communication requires that

> they be told how the world around them will see them–as Black–and that their Blackness is beautiful.

McGoldrick, Pearce, and Giordano (1982) pointed to the bicultural experience of African-Americans in our country generally. This can be adaptive when families are clear about their own values. However, identity confusion can exist as the legacy of the victim system. The more racism and poverty a family has experienced, the greater will be the effect on its overall coping ability. Families that have achieved middle-class status often experience the stress of helping others less fortunate or face an emotional cutoff from their roots (McAdoo, 1978).

> If we are to teach our children how to fight racism, we must first create an atmosphere suitable to the open communication of honest feelings–nothing can be off-limits in our communication with them. We must tell them what we want them to know and be willing to listen calmly to what they want us to know (Hopson & Hopson, 1990, p. 69).

A wide range of books is available for building self-esteem and cultural awareness in children, including these:

My Black Me: A Beginning Book of Black Poetry, by A. Adoff

All the Colors of the Race, by A. Adoff

Black Is Brown Is Tan, by A. Adoff

The Fortune Tellers, by L. Alexander

Abby, by J. Caines

Stencils–West Africa: Nigeria, edited by R. Dempsey

Her Stories: African-American Folktales, Fairy Tales, and True Tales, by V. Hamilton

Many Thousand Gone: African-Americans from Slavery to Freedom, by V. Hamilton

Together, by G. W. Lyon

You Be Me, I'll Be You, by P. Mandelbaum

Octopus Hug, by L. Pringle

Self-Esteem and Homelessness

A creative approach is needed in helping homeless children deal with such major blows to their self-esteem. Hunter (1993) outlined one such approach: A social worker provides services to parents and children in a shelter for high-risk families. Play therapy can help to increase self-esteem and improve interpersonal skills. One benefit is teaching siblings to accept and nurture each other.

CONCLUSION

Children with high self-esteem have persistence and determination to tackle problems as well as to feel good about themselves as individuals. Self-esteem comes from struggle, hard work, and adversity; it cannot be "given." Children need to feel competent and effective in interacting with the environment. Even during infancy, parents have a major effect on how children develop in this respect. We know that the use of play and imagination should be valued and cherished during childhood, as it teaches children the rules of social interaction and enhances their sense of mastery.

Self-esteem also enhances moral development. Those who value themselves treat others with respect. Morality is learned both in interaction with peers and also from the values of parents within the family.

There are several ways parents and counselors can enhance self-esteem in children. One of the best is by nurturing their own self-esteem. Another is to form authoritative families, in which parents exercise moderate control, but children are given choices. We have also seen that fathers play a special role in encouraging the self-esteem of both sons and daughters.

There are many specific ways we can help children to become more optimistic in their approach to solving problems. It is important for our children to know how to feel good about themselves, but it is vital for them to know how to solve problems and handle failure.

ACTIVITIES FOR GROUPS

ACTIVITY 7.1 INTERVIEWING AND REMEMBERING

Introduction: Children learn how to ask each other questions and to remember the answers.

Time required: 10 minutes

Participants: Children ages 5 to 10

Materials: A 3 x 5 card per child

Procedure: Ask the children these questions: What is something you like to eat? What is something you like to do? What is something you like to play with? Where is someplace you would like to go?

Write down each child's responses on a 3 x 5 card.

Now ask the children to make up riddles and questions relating to the statements on their cards. Have the other children try to guess whose card it is as riddles or questions are read.

Outcomes: Encourages children to take more interest in each other.

Note: From Cannon and Cordell (1996).

ACTIVITY 7.2 EXPRESSING FEELINGS

Introduction: Children learn to recognize and to express their feelings.

Time required: 20 minutes

Participants: Children ages 5 to 10

Materials: Poster board, markers, scissors, a copy of Polland (1975)

Procedure: Read the book and discuss various feelings we all have and their expressions, both verbal and nonverbal.

Have each child make a "Spin-a-Feeling" wheel, then pantomime the feelings that are indicated as they spin the arrow on the wheel.

An alternative is to play "Statues," in which one or more children stay in continuous motion until you call out the name of a feeling.

Then the children "freeze" in a position that expresses that feeling.

Outcomes: Teaches children to recognize their own and others' feelings.

Note: From Cannon and Cordell (1996).

ACTIVITY 7.3 WORRY WART

Introduction: Children learn to cope with their worries and to share with each other.

Time required: 30 minutes

Participants: Children ages 5 to 10

Materials: a 5 x 5 folder booklet and a copy of Hargreaves (1980)

Procedure: Ready *Mr. Worry* by Roger Hargreaves. Each child may share what he or she worries about the most.

Give each child a small folder booklet (5 x 5) of blank paper and ask them to create a new "Mr." book describing their biggest worry. When they have finished, let them share their books with the group.

Outcomes: Gives children mastery over their fears.

Note: From Cannon and Cordell (1996).

ACTIVITY 7.4 EXPLORING SELF-CONTROL AND RELAXATION

Introduction: Children learn self control and body awareness.

Time required: 15 minutes

Participants: Children ages 5 to 10

Materials: None

Procedure: Ask the children to pretend they are turtles and walk very slowly. Then have them sing and move vigorously to an energizing, fast song. Finally, have them pretend to be rag dolls and relax each part of their bodies.

Now ask the children to share how they controlled their bodies in the different situations, and how this could be applied to other situations with family and friends.

Outcomes: Helps children improve their self control.

Note: From Cannon and Cordell (1996).

ACTIVITY 7.5 MY OWN SPECIAL PLACE

Introduction: This activity teaches children to imagine their own special place as a way of coping with stress.

Time required: 30 minutes

Participants: Children ages 5 to 18

Materials: Paper, pencils, and markers

Procedure: Ask the children where they go to think when they want to be alone. Have them visualize their special place, using creative visualization techniques.

When you have finished, have the children draw their special places and share their drawings with the group. They also can make books of their drawings and activities to take home.

Outcomes: Teaches children to expand the use of their minds and inner resources.

Note: From Cannon and Cordell (1996).

ACTIVITY 7.6 AESOP'S FABLES

Introduction: Participants develop self-confidence; learn moral lessons.

Time required: 60 minutes

Participants: All ages

Materials: A copy of *Aesop's Fables* (Spriggs, 1975)

Procedure: Read several of the fables out loud to the children.

Tell the children to find a partner. Each pair will present a very short play based on a fable. Allow them time to practice their plays.

Have the children take turns presenting their plays and discussing some morals expressed.

Outcomes: Teaches children refinements of social skills and morality.

Note: From Cannon and Cordell (1996).

ACTIVITY 7.7 MAKING FRIENDS

Introduction: Children learn how to build friendships.

Time required: 30 minutes

Participants: Children ages 8 to 12

Materials: Paper and pencils

Procedure: Ask each child to share something he or she likes about a special friend. Record their responses on a chart.

Now ask the children to select the most important characteristics.

Have the children either draw a cartoon strip showing how to make a friend or role-play situations to demonstrate their understanding. For example, you might say, "A new child enters your classroom and is ignored by most of the other children in the class. Show what you would do."

Outcomes: Teaches children to think more critically about the qualities that make a good friend.

Note: From Cannon and Cordell (1996).

ACTIVITY 7.8 COMMUNICATION SKILLS ARE TOUGH!

Introduction: Children learn the use of questions and verbal descriptions in the communication process.

Time required: 30 minutes

Participants: Children ages 6 to 10

Materials: Pattern blocks

Procedure: Allow the children time to play with a set of pattern blocks.

Now ask the children to sit back to back and give each child seven blocks. Have one child create a pattern and the partner copy it.

Then have the first child create another pattern, while the partner keeps his or her back turned. When the pattern is complete, the partner has 30 seconds to look at it before it is covered. The partner then tries to reproduce the pattern. He or she may question and ask for information, but cannot look at the pattern until his or her own pattern is completed.

After each child tries this activity, have them sit back to back and ask one child to communicate a direction for placement of the blocks while the other tries to copy the pattern without looking.

Outcomes: Teaches children that communication skills are necessary in producing a product.

Note: From Cannon and Cordell (1996).

ACTIVITY 7.9 EENSY WEENSY SPIDER

Introduction: Children learn creative ways to solve a problem.

Time required: 20 minutes

Participants: Children ages 5 to 8

Materials: Paper and pen for group leader only

Procedure: Sing "The Eensy Weensy Spider" and work together through problem solving to figure out a way to get the spider up the spout. Write a new verse to the song using the new idea.

Outcomes: Encourages group cohesiveness and creativity.

Note: From Cannon and Cordell (1996).

ACTIVITY 7.10 MOTHER GOOSE RHYMES

Introduction: Children learn group problem-solving skills using familiar material.

Time required: 10 minutes

Participants: Children ages 5 to 8

Materials: Easel paper

Procedure: Ask the children to recite several of their favorite nursery rhymes. Then choose three of four rhymes, and ask the children to try and solve the character's problems or change the outcome of the rhyme. For example, "How can we keep Mary's lamb at home?" or "How can we help Little Boy Blue from losing his job?" Write their ideas on a group chart.

Outcomes: Teaches children to think creatively.

Note: From Cannon and Cordell (1996).

ACTIVITY 7.11 THE MISSING DRAGON

Introduction: Children learn to work cooperatively in pairs or small groups.

Time required: 50 minutes

Participants: Children ages 5 to 10

Materials: "The Missing Dragon" story (see Wayman & Plum, 1977, pp. 11 & 12) and a picture of a dragon to color (see Figure 7.2 for an example)

Procedure: First, tell the children the story about the missing dragon. Then, in pairs or groups of three, have each group member color in an outline of a dragon given to them by the leader.

The catch is that the children in each small group must complete the coloring the same way within their small group. This requires the children to notice, talk, negotiate, and agree on what they are doing. This task involves creativity but also group cooperation, communication, and problem-solving skills.

Discuss the activity from the point of view of how each pair or small group worked together to accomplish a goal.

Outcomes: Teaches children about group dynamics and how to work together.

Note: From Cannon and Cordell (1996).

ACTIVITY 7.12 OPTIMISTIC CRITICISM

Introduction: Parents and children practice the skills of optimistic criticism.

Time required: 15 minutes

Participants: Parents and children ages 5 and up

Materials: "Worksheet for Optimistic Criticism" (see page 340)

Procedure: Ask parents and children to respond to the worksheet, either individually or in discussion with each other.

Outcomes: Teaches parents and children how to use the skills of optimistic criticism.

Figure 7.2. Example of dragon coloring sheet.

Worksheet for Optimistic Criticism

Criticism	Optimist	Pessimistic
Situation: *Your child accidentally spills a glass of milk on the kitchen floor.*		
You are very careless.	____	____
You need to be more careful.	____	____
You never do things right.	____	____
Situation: *Your child (age 3) goes into the refrigerator and throws eggs on the floor.*		
I can't believe what a devil you are.	____	____
Please do not do that again. It makes a big mess.	____	____
There are other things here that you can throw.	____	____
Situation: *Your child throws wet towels on the bedroom floor.*		
You will probably be a slob all your life.	____	____
You should pick this towel up without having to be told.	____	____
Kids just make more work for their mothers.	____	____
Situation: *Your child (age 10) arrives home 10 minutes late.*		
It's okay. Your dad is always late too.	____	____
I would like you to be home on time.	____	____
This is an important job for you to learn to do what you are asked.	____	____

Situation: *You have given your teenage boy permission to drive your car on a date. He was told to be home at 1:00 a.m. He shows up at 1:45 a.m.*

How Would You Criticize Optimistically?

Changeable:____

____

Specific:____

____

Internal/Behavioral:____

____

ACTIVITY 7.13 DIVORCE PUPPET SHOW

Introduction: Children learn about the typical situations of divorce and how to problem solve.

Time required: 30 minutes

Participants: Children ages 4 to 12

Materials: Puppets and script

Procedure: Present the puppet show to the children. Then ask about their feelings and reactions.

Let the children make their own puppets out of brown paper bags, glue, colored paper, and markers. They can use these to devise their own plays.

For teens, the graphing of family trees is useful. This activity makes clear the difference between the last generation of parents who rarely divorced and our present circumstances.

Outcomes: Teaches children about the typical situations of divorce with ideas about solutions to problems.

Puppet Show

Girl: This puppet show is about divorce. Every family's divorce is different. This is about one brother and sister. Some things might be different. But there are some good ideas here for you to learn from.

Scene 1 (Boy and Girl)
Whose Fault Is It?

Should We Blame Mom or Dad?

Boy: Dad said last weekend that the divorce is Mom's fault. He doesn't want a divorce–she does.

Girl: Well, you know they were always fighting. Seems to me they were both part of the problem.

Boy: No way–not my Dad! He is a great guy.

Girl: Well, I love him too, Brother, but no one, not even a grown-up, is perfect.

Boy: Well, Mom says that Dad started all the fights, she said she always tried to be a good mom. But he always came home too late–even after we were in bed. I get so confused about whose fault it is!

Girl: Well, Mom wasn't very patient with him. He was working so hard.

Boy: That isn't what Mom says. She said he was out with the boys playing cards and partying.

Girl: Well, if Mom would have cooked his favorite dinner, Dad would have come home on time!

Boy: You know, I think you were right in the first place. Maybe they were both part of the problem. Dad was gone too much, and Mom wasn't very patient.

Girl: And maybe they both tried to make it work. Dad was good to us kids when he was home. And sometimes Mom did make his favorite meals.

Boy: Maybe Mom and Dad are both just people like everyone else–not perfect but not all to blame either.

Girl: I love them both so much–I just can't pick who to blame!

Boy: Me either.

Girl: They both shared in trying to make things work out–and they both caused some of the problems between them.

Boy: It really helps to realize that. Thanks Sis!

Is It Our Fault?

Girl: I keep worrying. Maybe if we had been better kids, Mom and Dad would have been happier and not always fighting with each other.

Boy: Oh, you're a worry wart!

Girl: Mom is always mad when we don't clean our rooms. Do you think Daddy got so tired of the mess he left because the house was a wreck?

Boy: Nah, he made a lot of mess! Remember all his dirty socks piled up in the middle of the bedroom?

Girl: If only I had gotten better grades in school. That's the cause of all these problem, I know it! I heard them fighting once about my school work.

Boy: No, I'm sure they were fighting over me.

Girl: I just get this heavy, unhappy feeling like a big, dark cloud over me–like this divorce was my fault or something.

Boy: No, No, No. It couldn't be your fault.

Girl: How do you know?

Boy: Because I'm sure it was my fault! I've felt this way since the night they told us.

Girl: What? That's amazing! You were always so good and happy. And you get good grades. No, Brother, you're not to blame.

Boy: (*laughing*) I just realized something. We've both been blaming ourselves!

Girl: But I can see it's not your fault. (*laughing*) And why am I blaming myself? It wasn't my fault either.

Boy: No, Sis, it really wasn't. (*to himself*) Even though she is a brat!

Girl: No more black clouds hanging over me! Kids shouldn't blame themselves!

Boy: So what can you do, Sis?

Girl: I've already done it. I just made up my mind. I'm not blaming myself anymore for the problems Mom and Dad had with each other. I feel free!

Boy: (*to himself*) Yeah, but she's still a brat!

Scene 2 (Boy and Girl)
Who Will We Live With?

Who Wants Us?

Girl: Who do you want to live with, Mom or Dad?

Boy: I guess we have to live with Mom. Dad left, and he doesn't want us anymore.

Girl: That's not true! Dad told me that he's going to fight for us in court.

Boy: What do you mean?

Girl: Well, Dad and Mom both said that the judge is going to decide who we'll live with. I guess they can't agree.

Boy: How will the judge know which one we should live with?

Girl: Well, she gets as much information as she can and tries to make the best decision.

Boy: So Mom and Dad both want us?

Girl: Yes, of course. And whoever we live with, we'll still visit the other parent. I like that idea! So we won't lose either one.

Boy: But some parents might not both fight for custody.

Girl: That's right. Sometimes the parents can decide themselves. That's nice. Sometimes both parents want the children, but they decide not to fight about it.

Boy: So we know both of our parents want us, but we still don't know where we'll be.

Who Can Take Care of Us?

Boy: Well, you know, Mom knows how to cook and things, but she doesn't know how to fix my bike.

Girl: I know, but Dad doesn't know how to take care of us. He doesn't know how to fix my hair right. And he doesn't know how to make banana bread.

Boy: What if robbers try to get in at night? Dad could beat them up, but Mom would be scared like us. I guess I'll have to protect us if we live with Mom. But I don't know if I'm big enough. You'll have to help.

Girl: (*crying*) I'm scared. I can't even see if it's dark. What if the robbers came in my room?

Boy: (*hugging her*) Don't worry. I'll call the police and Mr. Johnson next door.

Girl: You know, Mom can learn how to be brave! And Dad can learn how to cook!

Boy: Hey, you're right! Things are going to be different, that's for sure.

Girl: But maybe not as bad as we think!

What if Dad Goes Away?

Girl: What if Dad goes away? Mom says he doesn't like Dayton and wants to get as far away as he can. Do you know where China is? Mom says she wishes he would go to China.

Boy: Dad won't go away! He loves us and, besides, he promised to help me build a race car this summer. Mom was mad the other day, though, because Dad didn't send the support money. She said that he can't have his cake and eat it too. She said if he doesn't pay, we can't visit him.

Girl: Why does dad have to pay to visit us? What if he doesn't have enough money? He hardly has any furniture in his new apartment. And there's almost no food in his refrigerator. I bet he won't be able to pay for everything. Maybe eating will be more important than visiting.

Boy: I told Mom about all that, but she just got mad and said that Dad is eating in fancy restaurants instead of paying her the support.

Girl: I wish those two would stop fighting.

Boy: Me too. But even though they fight, I know they won't forget us.

Maybe We Can Get Them Back Together

Girl: Wouldn't it be better if we all lived together again? We wouldn't have to be scared any more.

Boy: Yeah. And there would be enough money for all of us again. Do you think if we got Mom and Dad together and explained everything they would understand, and Dad would come home?

Girl: I don't know. Maybe we should be *real* good–clean up at home and do well in school. Then they would both see what a happy family we could have if we were all together again.

Boy: But remember we decided that these problems grown-ups have are not our fault.

Girl: Yeah. Maybe I could teach Mom and Dad about not fighting–we're learning in school about how to express anger without fighting. It works real well when my teacher helps. Maybe she could come over and help Mom and Dad.

Boy: You know what–when my friend broke her leg at school on the jungle gym, both of her parents left work and went to the hospital. I wonder what would happen if ...

Girl: Come on, Brother! That won't help anything. You can't get Mom and Dad back together that way. And besides that wouldn't be much fun for you.

Boy: A boy in my class ran away once and both of his parents went out to look for him. Maybe ...

Girl: Now that's another hare-brained scheme! You sure can come up with some lemons!

Scene 3 (Mother and Son)
Being in the Middle

Spying Missions

Mother: Well, how was your visit with your father? I bet he didn't make you any breakfast.

Boy: It was fine Mom. He made a real good breakfast–you know, toast and cereal.

Mother: Well ... how is your father these days? Losing weight? Looking pale?

Boy: Well, no Mom. He looks terrific. Just bought a new car–real jazzy–it's fast ... a sports car.

Mother: What? How could he afford that? You mean he's enjoying himself? When I have to work everyday and do all this laundry! I wonder ...

Boy: Can I go play with Jason?

Mother: Hold on, Son. I have a few more ... well, questions. Did you ... have you noticed any sign of ... well ...

Boy: Yes, Mom, he has a girlfriend. Her name is Kathy.

Mother: That's his business. I'm not interested in the least. Say, son, how long has he known Kathy?

Boy: Mom, come on! You're making me feel like a spy!

Mother: Oh I'm sorry, Son. I shouldn't put you in the middle. ... A month or so then? Has he known Kathy ... well, how long would you say?

Boy: About as long as you've known your friend Doug!

Mother: Well, that's not the same. Say, Son, could you maybe keep your eyes open over at your father's–just check out this Kathy and let me know more about this.

Boy: How much?

Mother: How much what?

Boy: Well, Dad might give me $1 for information on Doug. If I'm going to have to be a spy, it should at least be profitable.

Mother: (*to herself*) Maybe this spying business has gone too far!

Playing One Against the Other (Father and Son)

Boy: Hi Dad. It's great to be back. Really missed you.

Father: Me too Son! (*kisses boy*) Well, time to get to the yard–chores you know.

Boy: But Dad, I shouldn't have to work here! This is my visiting time.

Father: Visiting time is not all playtime, my boy.

Boy: (*thinking fast*) But mom says I shouldn't have to do yardwork.

Father: Huh? What?

Boy: Yes, she says that's too much for a boy my age. In fact, she doesn't think I should do chores at all.

Father: (*to himself*) Well, maybe that's right. I hadn't looked at it that way.

***Later That Weekend* (Mother and Son)**

Boy: Hi Mom. Good to be home.

Mother: Yes, Son, those dishes you left are growing mold.

Boy: (*more confidently*) Well, Dad said a boy shouldn't do dishes. It isn't right for a boy.

Mother: Oh?

Boy: He doesn't make me do chores.

Mother: (*to herself*) Well, I don't want to be too hard on the boy.

Boy: (*to himself*) This could work out nicely. I never have to do chores anymore. But, you know, I'm not sure that's the answer either. It sounds great, but Mom and Dad work really hard all week, and if I don't help, they will have to do all the chores, too. That would make me feel really bad. Maybe if I helped with some of the chores for each of them ...

Bribery (Father and Son)

Father: Want to go shopping?

Boy: Sure!

Father: I sure miss you. Want me to buy you a car?

Boy: Yeah!

Father: How about some candy?

Boy: Dad, I love you! You don't have to buy me all this stuff.

Father: I guess I have been overdoing it. I'm unsure of your love anymore since I don't see you every day. So here I am, almost trying to buy your love. Boy, I get unsure of myself!

Boy: You're okay the way you are, Dad! Don't sweat it! Say, in two weeks my buddy Jason asked me to spend the night.

Father: But that's my time! ... Say, Son, would you like a new castle and action knight figures?

Boy: (*to himself*) Oh no! There he goes again. I'll just have to keep telling and showing Dad how much I love him. He's had a bad time with the divorce, just like Mom and I have. But if I just quietly let him know I love him, he'll feel good about letting me be with my friends sometimes too.

Being Used as a Weapon (Father, Mother, and Son)

Father: Well bye, Son. See in you two weeks. I know it will be hard for you with your mom on your case all the time.

Boy: It's okay, Dad.

Mother: Hi Son. Well how was it? Kind of boring as usual?

Boy: Fine Mom, just fine.

Father: Don't let her hassle you, Son. She's a nag. I know how you really feel.

Boy: I love you, Dad.

Mother: He probably let you slide out of doing your homework–he never was very responsible.

Boy: Aw, come on, Mom–you're talking about my father.

Father: She never was a good mother.

Boy: But she's the only one I have. Don't hurt her!

Mother: I know how you dread those visits with your father.

Boy: (*to himself*) I can't win coming or going. They're using me to get back at each other. I'm like a new weapon–the new deadly XKE missile! I keep hoping for peace and disarmament. Maybe I better stop just hoping and do something about this situation. Maybe they don't even realize what they are doing and how sad it makes me feel. Maybe I ought to tell them how hard it is for me when they talk that way, because I love them both.

Scene 4 (Boy and Girl)
Sometimes I Feel Down

Boy: Hey Sis, your nose is so big–I'm going to tweak it.

Girl: Leave me alone, twerp.

Boy: I'm going to jump on your pumpkin face.

Girl: Boy, brothers!

Boy: I'm going to pinch you.

Girl: You know, Brother, I get the feeling you're picking a fight.

Boy: Who? Me? Nah–it's you. It's all your fault!

Girl: You know, I think you're feeling downright rock-bottom down in the dumps.

Boy: Gee, Sis, how could you tell?

Scene 5 (Boy and Girl)
What Can I Do About Being Down?

Boy: Okay, Sis, you were right. I feel down about Mom and Dad's divorce. I just want my family together, and it isn't.

Girl: Well at least you know how you feel. That's good.

Boy: But what else can I do?

Girl: Well, for starters, why don't you think about me–how I feel? Now I could use a loan, Brother–$5 could really change my mental outlook.

Boy: You know this isn't helping me much.

Girl: Okay, Okay. Let's start by deciding once and for all that it wasn't our fault. We just have to go on with a new way of being a family.

Boy: Right! Let's not make ourselves feel worse by playing "If Only" or "What If."

Girl: This divorce is adult business. Let's realize how important and special we still are–that hasn't changed. I can still be a good student in school–my lessons do matter.

Boy: And I can still try even if I do get Cs. It's okay–we can't all be brains like you!

Girl: You could join the track team.

Boy: Yeah–I'll get to do all that running. What a great idea! I feel better already.

Girl: Let's not give up just because the going gets tough!

Boy: I know! When I get mad and frustrated, I can run around the block.

Girl: How 'bout punching your punching bag instead of me, Brother?

Boy: Oh, okay Sis. You know you're a regular guy!

Scene 6 (Boy and Friend)
Talking with a Friend

Friend: How ya doing?

Boy: Fine–just great. (*to himself, sarcastically*) Yeah, just super.

Friend: What's new? (*to himself*) I know his parents got divorced, just like mine.

Boy: Nothing. (*to himself*) I'd like to tell him about my parents, but how could he ever understand? I'm the only one around this has happened to.

Friend: So ... how's tricks?

Boy: How 'bout by you?

Friend: Well ... great. Say you want to play some basketball?

Boy: Yeah, except my ball ... I left it at my dad's house ... well, you see ...

Friend: Yeah I know. I've been though all that. I write notes to myself to keep me and my stuff organized.

Boy: No you don't know at all–you couldn't.

Friend: Well sure I do. My mom and dad got divorced last year.

Boy: Gee, I didn't know that.

Friend: Well, maybe I was too embarrassed to say. But I know it does help to talk about it.

Boy: It help me to know I'm not the only one!

Friend: You know, there is something that's still hard for me to tell.

Boy: What is it? Tell me!

Friend: No, it's too hard to tell.

Boy: Well, okay then.

Friend: My Dad's getting remarried. Oh, this is so embarrassing.

Boy: Don't feel that way! Guess what? My mom lives with her boyfriend now. So you see, it's not that bad. It's just hard to get used to at first.

Friend: Like you said–it helps to know I'm not the only one!

ACTIVITY 7.14 THE DIVORCE GAME

Introduction: Children play a divorce game with a small group of peers or with their family. The game highlights feelings, situations, and solutions related to divorce and emphasizes that children are not alone in facing the difficulties of divorce.

Time required: Approximately 30 minutes

Participants: Children ages 4 to 18

Materials: One piece of posterboard made as shown, markers, dice, and cards as shown (see Figure 7.3)

Procedure: Decide the order of play, roll the dice, move your marker, pick and answer your card, and receive a chip.

Outcomes: Children learn about feelings, situations, and "solutions" related to divorce. They also realize that they are not alone in experiencing divorce in their family.

Note: Older children and teens might enjoy playing *The Changing Family Game* (Berg, 1982).

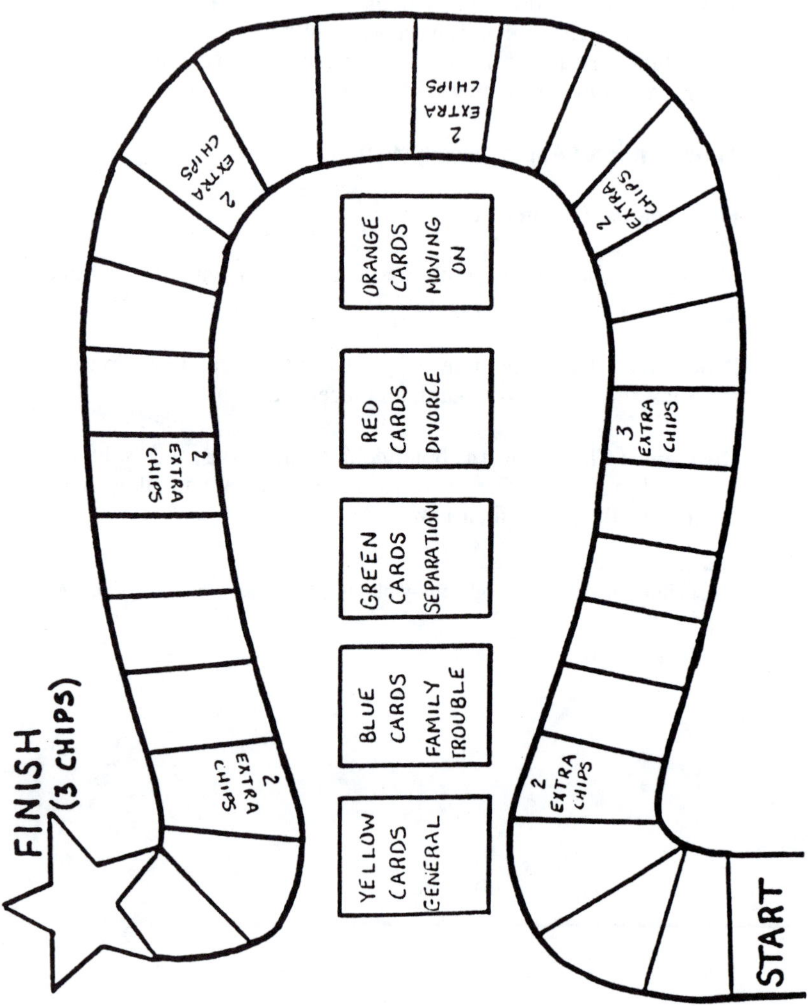

Figure 7.3. Example of the divorce game.

Note: The five colors are distributed along the path of spaces with more yellow and blue initially, then green spaces added, and finally red and orange spaces added more frequently as the path moves toward the finish.

The Divorce Game

Yellow Cards (General)

What makes you mad?

Who are you close to in your family?

What would you like to be when you grow up?

What do you like most about your mother?

Is it best to have one close friend or many friends you do not know as well?

What do you like most about your father?

What do you do well?

What mistake have you made?

What is your greatest strength?

What is your favorite thing to do?

Tell something that is confusing to kids.

What is your favorite season of the year? Why?

Name a hobby you have.

If you could have one wish, what would it be?

What is hard for you to do?

What should your mother learn?

Which feeling do you like the most?

What makes you happy?

Blue Cards (Family Trouble)

Jack's mother has gone back to school. How do you think Jack feels about this?

Ryan misbehaves and then his parents argue about what to do. Is this Ryan's fault?

Why do parents become unhappy with each other?

Katie's parents do not do things together. Is this a problem?

John's mother has decided to get her own apartment. What should John do?

Sharon's mother drinks a lot and burns dinner. What can Sharon do?

Dan's parents argue often. How does that make Dan feel?

Angela is shocked to learn that her father has a girlfriend. What does Angela want to say to him?

Megan's father begins drinking too much. Why does this happen?

One day Michael's mother had a black eye. Do men ever hit their wives?

Paige's mother scowls a lot and complains. How is she making her family feel?

Arthur's father always criticizes his mother. Is this a good idea?

Is it a good idea to never argue or never disagree?

What makes a family unhappy?

Heather's father seldom comes home now after work. Does Heather feel confused?

Paul's father screams and hits his wife. What should he do instead?

Green Cards (Separation)

What did you think when your parent left home?

Do you know any other kids whose parents have separated?

Who can you talk to about your parents' separation?

Does your dad seem different since the separation?

Sometimes kids are happier after their parents' separation; were you?

What is the worst thing about parents separating?

What does separation mean?

Do you ever worry about how your mother is doing?

Would you like your parents to be back together again?

Does your mom seem different since the separation?

Do you ever worry about how your father is doing?

What makes you the saddest?

Is there anything good about your parents' separation?

How do kids feel when their parents separate?

Children are usually pretty surprised when a parent moves out. Were you?

Red Cards (Divorce)

Sometimes grandparents takes sides in a divorce. Have yours?

How does your mother feel about the divorce?

What does divorce mean?

Do you have any friends whose parents have divorced?

Terry's parents are getting divorced. How should she handle it?

Can friends help you when your parents get divorced?

Do brothers and sisters fight more when their parents divorce?

What can you do when your parents say bad things about each other?

How do you feel when your parents say bad things about each other?

What is a dissolution?

Have you told your friends that your parents have divorced?

Adjusting to divorce takes time. What are the steps in getting used to divorce?

What can you do when you miss the parent you don't live with?

How did you find out that your parents are getting divorce? How did you feel?

Janet is still angry that her parents have divorced. What can she do?

Todd wonders why no one asked him if the family should break up. Did anyone ask you?

Kayla feels ashamed that her parents have divorced. Should she feel this way?

Do you think divorce is harder for an only child?

Pink Cards (Moving On)

Is it harder for a little child or a teen when their parents divorce?

Jim will soon have a stepbrother. How does he feel?

How long does it take a child to adjust to divorce?

What is a blended family?

What is a stepmother?

Do you have regular visits with the parent you don't live with?

How do you feel when the parent you visit forgets to pick you up?

How would you feel about your father dating?

Does a child still miss the parent who moved out a year after a divorce?

Have you experienced anything worse than divorce?

Do you think you might get divorced when you grow up?

Is it confusing to kids if their divorced parents are friendly with each other?

Do you think your parents might make up?

Do you still hope your parents will get back together?

Would you get married when you grow up?

What's a child's biggest worry in divorce?

ACTIVITY 7.15 DIVORCE DRAWINGS

Introduction: In a court-run program, we asked children of all ages to draw pictures of their families divorcing. We found the drawings extremely expressive of the emotions associated with the divorce and how the children were coping. Some children denied the divorce altogether and drew unrelated family pictures, whereas others clearly acknowledged the divorce in their drawings. Some displayed emotion and others showed no emotional content.

Findings from our study indicated that children who made drawings exhibiting emotionality feared abandonment less than those who depicted no emotion (Cordell & Bergman-Meador, 1991). And children whose drawings were characterized as nonaggressive feared abandonment less than those whose drawings showed fighting or conflict.

Time required: Varies, but averages 10 minutes

Participants: Children ages 4 to 18

Materials: Paper and pencil

Procedure: Ask the children to "draw a picture of your family divorcing." They can include people in their drawings or use abstractions.

Outcomes: Enables children to express their deeper feelings about their parents' divorce.

ACTIVITY 7.16 INSIGHTS INTO FRIENDSHIP

Introduction: Parents get in touch with the value and special qualities of friendships.

Time required: 10 minutes

Participants: Parents' group

Materials: None

Procedure: Have the group practice a simple relaxation procedure. Then ask them to picture a friendship they experienced during childhood and the interactions and feelings that occurred.

Finally, ask the parents to discuss what their friendships during childhood meant to them.

Outcomes: Sharpens parents' awareness of the qualities needed to build friendships. This enables them to better teach their children.

ACTIVITY 7.17 KEEP A SMILE ON YOUR FACE

Introduction: Children learn self-control by playing a game of resisting teasing.

Time required: 10 minutes

Participants: Children ages 7 to 12

Materials: Stopwatch, pencil, and paper

Procedure: Explain the rules of the game to the children: One child maintains a steady smile while another one makes jokes or acts silly in an effort to provoke him or her.

Keep track of the number of seconds the child can maintain the smile without losing control.

Outcomes: Helps children gain mastery over their reactions to others.

ACTIVITY 7.18 EXPRESSING YOUR FEELINGS

Introduction: Children learn specific social skills, such as how to express their feelings appropriately.

Time required: 45 minutes

Participants: Children ages 7 to 14

Materials: The "Kids' Script" shown on the following pages

Procedure: Ask the children to volunteer for roles in a play.

Allow time for the actors to rehearse their parts. Then let them present the play.

Have one of the children who is not in the play videotape the performance.

Ask the audience to critique the performance, reminding them to make all comments in positive terms.

Finally, show the videotape of the play (which is of great interest and reinforces what they have learned).

Outcomes: Teaches children to improve their skills for handling potentially volatile situations.

Note: The "Kids' Script" was developed by Oakes (1996).

Kids' Script

Expressing Your Feelings

Narrator: Ted overhears his friends Billy and Sam talking in the lunch line about getting together on Saturday to go bowling and then to the video arcade. Ted is feeling jealous and lonely and would like to get invited along. After lunch, he walks up to Billy and asks about making plans for Saturday.

Ted: Hey Billy! I've got no plans for Saturday. I'd love to do something with you in the afternoon.

Narrator: Billy, in a shy mood, says:

Billy: Sorry Ted. My mom told me we'd be spending the whole weekend cleaning the basement. I'm grounded because of the mess I made building my castle for the Social Studies fair, and I have to stay home this weekend and get it all cleaned up.

Narrator: Ted seems very surprised by Billy's answer and says:

Ted: Oh Wow! That's no fun. So you have to be home all weekend with no time for friends?

Billy: Yeah. It was a big mess and I didn't keep my promise to clean it up by Tuesday, so I have to get it done on the weekend.

Narrator: Ted is feeling confused and a bit angry. He really likes Billy and he does not want to ruin the friendship. He is feeling mad because he thinks the story that Billy has told him is different from what Billy and Sam were talking about earlier, and he feels angry because he thinks he was lied to. He doesn't know what to say. At this point, Ted has to make a choice. His choices are:

1. To tell Billy how he is feeling
2. To end the conversation and walk away
3. To get involved with another activity and forget about playing with Billy on Saturday.

What should Ted do? Ted decides to be honest with Billy and tell him how he feels.

Ted: Billy, I'm confused and a little bit angry. I heard you and Sam talking in the lunch line about getting together for bowling and the video arcade. I would really like to join you. And that's why I asked about Saturday.

Narrator: Billy is embarrassed.

Billy: I'm sorry Ted. I made up that story about the basement. I really do have to get it cleaned up, but I made up the story about being grounded. Sam invited me and it wasn't fair for me to invite you along because he invited me. You're my friend. I didn't want to hurt your feelings, so I felt it was better to tell a little story because I didn't know what else to do.

Narrator: Ted feels a little bit different now and says,

Ted: I guess I understand that Billy. You can't invite me when it's Sam's mom who's going to be taking you. I guess I really just wanted to go and maybe even I wanted you to tell the truth, too. I would be sad if I couldn't go with you, but I would feel even worse if I thought you were lying to me–because if you were lying to me it would make me feel you weren't my friend, and you're important to me.

Narrator: Billy says:

Billy: Ted, you are my friend. I didn't want to hurt you. I just felt trapped. Maybe I made a bad choice. I've got an idea. What about if I go over to Sam and suggest to him that it would be really good to invite you along? We could really be a great threesome! What do you think?

Ted: Gee! That would be great Billy. I would really appreciate that. And if he says "No," I'll understand. I won't hold it against you. Things like that happen. Maybe if we can't do it this Saturday, we could make plans for another Saturday. How about that?

Billy: I would really like that, Ted. That would be great. I'm going to go see Sam now, and I'll let you know what he says before we get on the bus. Okay?

Ted: Thanks, Billy.

Narrator: Ted heads off to shoot some baskets on the court, while Billy goes off looking for Sam to ask if Ted can join them on Saturday.

ACTIVITY 7.19 VISITING A MUSEUM OF AFRICAN-AMERICAN HISTORY

Introduction: Children learn to value African-American history.

Time required: Several hours

Participants: Children ages 7 to 18

Materials: Field trip permission slips and transportation

Procedure: Take the children on a prearranged field trip to a museum that has a display about African-Americans.

Ask the children to discuss these questions: What have you learned about African-American history? What did you find surprising?

Mention how African-Americans have contributed in positive ways to this country.

Outcomes: Fosters a greater understanding and appreciation of African-American history.

ACTIVITY 7.20 LIFE JOURNALS

Introduction: Children learn to appreciate their own family history.

Time required: Varies

Participants: Children ages 10 to 18

Materials: Journals and pencils

Procedure: Have the children interview family members, take notes, and then write or dictate their own family story. Make sure you ask them to answer these questions: What is special about your family? What are your family themes? What have you learned from your family? How has your family become part of you?

Let the children share their family journals with one another, if they want to.

Outcomes: Enhances children's sense of identity and self-esteem.

ACTIVITY 7.21 VISITING A CHURCH

Introduction: Children learn to appreciate the cultural aspects of identity.

Time required: Varies

Participants: Children of any age

Materials: Parental permission slips and transportation

Procedure: Choose a church, and take the children to visit during a worship service.

Afterward, ask the children to discuss these questions: How is this church the same as others you have attended? How is it different? How does this church build a sense of identity?

Outcomes: Enhances children's understanding of themselves and others.

REFERENCES

Adoff, A. (1973). *Black is brown is tan.* New York: HarperCollins.

Adoff, A. (1982). *All the colors of the race.* New York: Beech Tree.

Adoff, A. (Editor). (1994). *My Black me: A beginning book of Black poetry.* New York: Puffin Books.

Alexander, L. (1992). *The fortune tellers.* New York: Dutton Children's Books.

Aronson, E., Stephan, C., Sikes, J., Blaney, N., & Snapp, M. (1978). *The jigsaw classroom.* Thousand Oaks, CA: Sage.

Barkley, R. A. (1995). *Taking charge of ADHD.* New York: Guilford.

Baumrind, D. (1967). Child care practices anteceding three patterns of preschool behavior. *Genetic Psychology Monographs, 75,* 43-88.

Baumrind, D. (1971). Current patterns of parental authority. *Developmental Psychology Monographs, 1,* 1-103.

Bee, H. L., & Mitchell, S. K. (1984). *The developing person: A life-span approach.* New York: Harper & Row.

Berg, B. (1982). *The changing family game: Cognitive-behavioral intervention for children of divorce.* Dayton, OH: University of Dayton.

Berger, T. (1977). *How does it feel when your parents get divorced?* New York: Julian Messner.

Bergman-Meador, B., & Cordell, A. S. (1987). Divorce counseling groups for parents and children. *Innovations in Clinical Practice: A Source Book, 7,* 361-372.

Biddle, S. (1993). Children, exercise, and mental health. *International Journal of Sport Psychology, 24,* 200-216.

Briggs, D. C. (1975). *Your child's self-esteem.* New York, Doubleday.

Brown, L. K., & Brown, M. (1986). *Dinosaurs divorce: A guide for changing families.* Boston: Little, Brown.

Burns, D. (1980, November). The perfectionist's script for self-defeat. *Psychology Today,* 34-52.

Caines, J. (1973). *Abby.* New York: Harper & Row.

Camp, B. W., & Bash, M. A. (1985). *Think aloud: Increasing social and cognitive skills–A problem-solving program for children.* Champaign, IL: Research Press.

Cannon, T., & Cordell, A. S. (1996). *Social skills program activities.* Unpublished manuscript.

Cetron, M., & O'Toole, T. (1982). *Encounters with the future: A forecast of life into the 21st century.* New York: McGraw-Hill.

Cherry, C. (1985). *Parents, please don't sit on your kids: A parent's guide to nonpunitive discipline.* Carthage, IL: Fearon Teacher Aids.

Chess, S., Thomas, A., & Birch, H. G. (1980). *Your child is a person.* New York: Penguin.

Comer, J. P., & Poussaint, A. F. (1992). *Raising black children.* New York: Plume.

Coopersmith, S. (1967). *The antecedents of self-esteem.* San Francisco: Freeman.

Cordell, A. S., & Bergman-Meador, B. (1991). The use of drawings in group intervention for children of divorce. *Journal of Divorce and Remarriage, 17*(1/2), 139-155.

Covitz, J. (1986). *The family curse: Emotional child abuse.* Boston: Sigo.

Dempsey, R. (Editor). (1994). *Stencils—West Africa: Nigeria.* Glenview, IL: Good Year Books.

DiLeo, J. H. (1983). *Interpreting children's drawings.* New York: Brunner/Mazel.

Edwards, K., Miller, N., McCormack, M., Mitchell, C., & Robinson, C. (1983). *Effects of individuation, status, and threat on in-group bias.* Paper presented at the meeting of the American Psychological Association, Anaheim, CA.

Elkind, D. (1981). *The hurried child.* Reading, MA: Addison Wesley.

Erikson, E. H. (1968). *Childhood and society.* New York: Norton.

Finkelstein, N. W., & Ramey, C. T. (1977). Learning to control the environment in infancy. *Child Development, 48,* 806-819.

Francke, L. B. (1983). *Growing up divorced.* New York: Simon & Schuster.

Gardner, R. A. (1970). *The boys' and girls' book about divorce.* New York: Science Home.

Gardner, R. A. (1992). *Self-esteem problems of children: Psychodynamics and psychotherapy.* Cresskill, NJ: Creative Therapeutics.

Gehret, J. (1991). *Eagle eyes: A child's guide to paying attention.* Fairport, NY: Verbal Images Press.

Gibbs, J. T. (1991). Biracial adolescents. In J. T. Gibbs & L. N. Huang (Eds.), *Children of color: Psychological interventions with minority youth.* San Francisco: Jossey-Bass.

Grollman, E. A. (1975). *Talking about divorce and separation: A dialogue between parent and child.* Boston: Beacon Press.

Hamilton, V. (1993). *Many thousand gone: African-Americans from slavery to freedom.* New York: Knopf.

Hamilton, V. (1995). *Her stories: African-American folktales, fairy tales, and true tales.* New York: Blue Sky.

Hargreaves, R. (1980). *Mr. Worry.* Los Angeles: Price/Stern/Sloan.

Harter, S. (1978). Effective motivation reconsidered: Toward a developmental model. *Human Development, 21,* 34-64.

Harter, S. (1983). Competence as a dimension of self-evaluation: Toward a comprehensive model of self-worth. In R. Leahy (Ed.), *The development of self* (pp. 51-121). New York: Academic.

Harter, S., & Connell, J. P. (1982). A comparison of alternative models of the relationships between academic achievement and children's perceptions of competence, control, and motivational orientation. In J. Nicholls (Ed.), *The development of achievement-related cognitions and behaviors* (pp. 179-221). New York: Academic.

Heegaard, M. (1990). *When mom and dad separate: Children can learn to cope with grief from divorce*. Minneapolis, MN: Woodland Press.

Hegeman, K. T. (1982). *What to do?* New York: Trillium.

Hetherington, E. M., & Parke, R. D. (1993). *Child psychology: A contemporary viewpoint.* New York: McGraw-Hill.

Hopson, D. P., & Hopson, D. S. (1990). *Different and wonderful: Raising black children in a race-conscious society.* New York: Simon & Schuster.

Hoffman, L. W. (1977). Fear of success in 1965 and 1974: A follow-up study. *Journal of Consulting and Clinical Psychology, 45*(2), 310-321.

Hogan, P. Z. (1980). *Will Dad ever move back home?* Milwaukee, WI: Raintree Children's Books.

Huizenga, J. N. (1983). The relationship of self-esteem and narcissism. In J. E. Mack & S. L. Albon (Eds.), *The development and sustenance of self-esteem in childhood* (pp. 151-162). New York: International Press.

Hunter, L. B. (1993). Sibling play therapy with homeless children: An opportunity in the crisis. *Child Welfare, 72*(1), 65-75.

Ingersoll, B. (1988). *Your hyperactive child.* New York: Doubleday.

Ives, S. B., Fassler, D., & Lash, M. (1985). *The divorce workbook: A guide for kids and families.* Burlington, VT: Waterfront Books.

Jaquish, G. A., & Savin-Williams, R. C. (1981). Biological and ecological factors in the expression of adolescent self-esteem. *Journal of Youth and Adolescence, 10*, 473-486.

Johnson, D. W., & Johnson, R. (1986). *Learning together and alone: Cooperative, competitive, and individualistic learning*. Englewood Cliffs, NJ: Prentice-Hall.

Kalter, N., Picker, J., & Lesowitz, M. (1984). Developmental facilitation groups for children of divorce: A preventive intervention. *American Journal of Orthopsychiatry, 54*, 613-623.

Kerr, B. A. (1985) *Smart girls: Gifted women.* Columbus: Ohio Psychology Press.

Kohlberg, L. (1985). *The psychology of moral development.* New York: Harper & Row.

Kulka, R. A., & Weingarten, H. (1979). The long-term effects of parental divorce childhood on adult adjustment. *Journal of Social Issues, 35,* 50-78.

Kurdek, L. A., & Berg, B. (1987). The Children's Beliefs About Parental Divorce Scale: Psychometric characteristics and concurrent validity. *Journal of Consulting and Clinical Psychology, 55,* 712-718.

Lamb, M. E., & Easterbrooks, M. A. (1981). The relationship between quality of infant-mother attachment and infant competence in initial encounters with peers. *Child Development, 50,* 380-387.

Landau, E. (1993). *Interracial dating and marriage.* New York: Julian Messner.

Lefrancois, G. R. (1986). *Of children.* Belmont, CA: Wadsworth.

LeShan, E. (1978). *What's going to happen to me? When parents separate or divorce.* New York: Four Winds.

Lyon, G. W. (1989). *Together.* New York: Orchard.

Magid, K., & Schriebman, W. (1980). *Divorce is ... A kids' coloring book.* Gretna, LA: Pelican Publishing.

Mandelbaum, P. (1990). *You be me, I'll be you.* Brooklyn, NY: Kane/Miller.

McAdoo, H. (1978). Factors related to stability in upwardly mobile Black families. *Journal of Marriage and the Family, 40,* 761-776.

McGinnis, E., & Goldstein, A. P. (1984). *Skillstreaming the elementary school child: A guide for teaching prosocial skills.* Champaign, IL: Research Press.

McGoldrick, M., Pearce, J. K., & Giordano, J. (Editors). (1982). *Ethnicity and family therapy.* New York: Guilford.

McGraw, K. (1987). *Developmental psychology.* New York: Harcourt Brace Jovanovich.

McWhirter, J. J., Bourgard, L. L., & Bassett, C. (1991, April). *Counselors and cooperative learning groups*. Paper presented at the annual convention of the American Association for Counseling and Development, Reno, NV.

McWhirter, J. J., McWhirter, B. T., McWhirter, A. M., & McWhirter, E. H. (1994). High- and low-risk characteristics of youth: The five Cs of competency. *Elementary School Guidance & Counseling, 28*(3), 188-196.

Miller, N. (1983). *The effect of school desegregation on Black academic achievement: A meta-analysis*. Paper commissioned by the National Institute of Education.

Miller, N. (1984). Israel and the United States: Comparisons and commonalities in school desegregation. In Y. Amir & S. Sharan (Eds.), *School desegregation cross-cultural comparisons* (pp. 237-252). Hillsdale, NJ: Erlbaum.

Miller, R. L., & Miller, B. (1990). Mothering the biracial child: Bridging the gaps between African-American and white parenting styles. *Women and Therapy, 10*(1/2), 169-179.

Minuchin, P. P., & Shapiro, E. K. (1983). The school as a context for social development. In P. H. Mussen (Ed.), *Handbook of child psychology* (vol. 4). New York: Wiley.

Moshman, D., Glover, J. A., & Bruning, R. H. (1984). *Developmental psychology: A topical approach.* Boston: Little, Brown.

Moss, D. M. (1989). *Shelley, the hyperactive turtle*. Kensington, MD: Woodbine House.

Neal, J. A. (1983). Children's understanding of their parents' divorce. In L. A. Kurdek (Ed.), *Children and divorce: New directions for child development* (pp. 3-14). San Francisco: Jossey-Bass.

Oakes, R. (1996). *Social skills program activities*. Unpublished manuscript.

Parten, M. B. (1932). Social participation among preschool children. *Journal of Abnormal Social Psychology, 27,* 243-270.

Pedro-Carroll, J. L., & Cowen, E. L. (1985). The children of divorce intervention program: An investigation of the efficacy of a school-based prevention program. *Journal of Consulting and Clinical Psychology, 53,* 603-611.

Peskin, H. (1973). Influence of the developmental schedule of puberty on learning and ego functioning. *Journal of Youth and Adolescence, 2,* 272-290.

Piaget, J. (1932). *The moral judgment of the child.* New York: Harcourt Brace.

Polland, B. K. (1975). *Feelings inside you and out loud too.* Berkeley, CA: Celestial Arts.

Pringle, L. (1993). *Octopus hug.* Honesdale, PA: Caroline House.

Quinn, P. O., & Stern, J. M. (1991). *Putting on the brakes: Young people's guide to understanding attention deficit hyperactivity disorder (ADHD).* New York: Magination Press.

Roberts, G. C., & Treasure, D. C. (1992). Children in sport. *Sport Science Review, 1*(2), 46-64.

Robin, A. L. (1990). Training families with ADHD adolescents. In R. A. Barkley (Ed.), *Attention-deficit hyperactivity disorder: A handbook for diagnosis and treatment* (pp. 462-497). New York: Guilford.

Rosenberg, M. (1965). *Society and the adolescent: Self-image.* Princeton, NJ: Princeton University Press.

Rosenberg, M. (1979). *Conceiving the self.* New York: Basic Books.

Santrock, J. W., & Warshak, R. (1979). Father custody and social development in boys and girls. *Journal of Social Issues, 4,* 112-125.

Searcy, S. (1988). Developing self-esteem. *Academic Therapy, 23*(5), 453-460.

Seligman, M. P. (1975). *Helplessness: On depression, development, and death.* San Francisco: Freeman.

Seligman, M. P. (1995). *The optimistic child.* Boston: Houghton Mifflin.

Selman, R. L. (1976). Social-cognitive understanding: A guide to educational and clinical practice. In T. Lickona (Ed.), *Moral development and behavior: Theory, research, and social issues* (p. 309). New York: Holt, Rinehart & Winston.

Selman, R. L. (1980). *The growth of interpersonal understanding: Developmental and clinical analysis.* New York: Academic.

Selman, R. L., & Byrne, D. F. (1974). A structural-developmental analysis of levels of role taking in middle childhood. *Child Development, 45*, 803-806.

Singer, J. L. (1973). *The child's world of make-believe: Experimental studies of imaginative play.* New York: Academic.

Slavin, R. (1983). *Cooperative learning*. New York: Longman.

Spencer, M. B. (1985). Cultural cognition and social cognition as identity correlates of black children's personal-social development. In M. B. Spencer, G. K. Brookins, & W. R. Allen (Eds.), *Beginnings: The social and affective development of black children* (pp. 215-230). Hillsdale, NJ: Erlbaum.

Spriggs, R. (Editor), (1975). *The fables of Aesop*. New York: Rand McNally.

Spurlock, J. (1986). Development of self-concept in Afro-American children. *Hospital and Community Psychiatry, 37*(1), 66-70.

St. John, N. H. (1975). *School desegregation*. New York: Wiley.

Stephan, W. G. (1983). *Blacks and Brown: The effects of school desegregation on black students*. Paper commissioned by the National Institute of Education.

Stivers, C. (1990). Promotion of self-esteem in the prevention of suicide. *Death Studies, 14*, 303-327.

Thompson, S. (1995). *The role of racial identity*. Unpublished doctoral dissertation, Wright State University, Dayton, OH.

Waber, B. (1982). *Bernard*. Boston: Houghton Mifflin.

Walker, K., Taylor, E., McElroy, A., Phillip, D., & Wilson, M. N. (1995). Familial and ecological correlates of self-esteem in African-American children. *New Directions for Child Development, 68,* 23-34.

Wallerstein, J. S. (1984). Children of divorce: Preliminary report of a ten-year follow-up of young children. *American Journal of Orthopsychiatry, 54,* 444-458.

Wallerstein, J. S., & Kelly, J. (1980). *Surviving the breakup: How children and parents cope with divorce*. New York: Basic Books.

Wayman, J., & Plum, L. (1977). *Secrets and surprises.* Carthage, IL: Good Apple.

Wender, P. H. (1987). *The hyperactive child, adolescent, and adult.* New York: Oxford University Press.

Whalen, C. K., & Henker, B. (1985). The social worlds of hyperactive (ADHD) children. *Clinical Psychology Review, 5,* 447-478.

Whaley, A. L. (1993). Self-esteem, cultural identity, and psychological adjustment in African-American children. *Journal of Black Psychology, 19*(4), 406-422.

White, R. (1959). Motivation reconsidered: The concept of competence. *Psychological Review, 66,* 297-333.

Zeigler, R., & Holden, L. (1988). Family therapy for learning disabled and attention-deficit disordered children. *American Journal of Orthopsychiatry, 58*(2), 196-210.

Zindel, P. (1975). *I love my mother*. New York: Harper & Row.

Zolotow, C. (1971). *A father like that.* New York: Harper & Row.

BIBLIOGRAPHY

Adderholdt-Elliott, M. (1987). *Perfectionism: What's bad about being too good?* Minneapolis: Free Spirit.

Battle, J. (1981). *Culture-free SEI: Self-esteem inventories for children and adults.* Seattle: Special Child Publications.

Bean, R. (1992a). *Positive risks, challenges, and other paths: Four conditions of self-esteem in elementary and middle school.* Santa Cruz, CA: ETR Associates.

Bean, R. (1992b). *Cooperation, social responsibility, and other skills.* Santa Cruz, CA: ETR Associates.

Berg, B. (1990). *The social skills workbook: Exercises to improve social skills.* Dayton, OH: Cognitive Counseling Resources.

Bessell, H. (1972). *The magic circle. Human development program: Level IV. Activity guide*. San Diego, CA: Human Development Training Institute.

Borba, M. (1989). *Esteem builders: Student achievement, behavior, and school climate (K-9).* Carson, CA: Jalmar.

Cartledge, G., & Milburn, J. F. (1980). *Teaching social skills to children: Innovative approaches.* New York: Pergamon.

Cetron, M., & Davies, O. (1989). *American renaissance*. New York: St. Martin's.

DeBono, E. (1974). *Children solve problems*. New York: Harper & Row.

DeMille, R. (1982). *Put your mother on the ceiling: Children's imagination games*. New York: Penguin.

Dinkmeyer, D. (1973). *Developing understanding of self and others.* Circle Pines, MN: American Guidance Service.

Dossick, J., & Shea, E. (1988). *Creative therapy: 52 exercises for group.* Sarasota, FL: Professional Resource Exchange.

Forman, S. G. (1993). *Coping skills interventions for children and adolescents.* San Francisco: Jossey-Bass.

Freed, A. (1973). *T. A. for tots*. Carson, CA: Jalmar.

Friedman, B., & Brooks, C. (Editors). (1990). *On base! The step-by-step self-esteem program for children from birth to 18.* Kansas City, MO: Westport.

Galbraith, J. (1983). *Gifted kids' survival guide.* Minneapolis: Free Spirit.

Glenn, H. S., & Nelson, J. (1987). *Raising children for success.* Fair Oaks, CA: Sunrise Press.

Goldstein, A. P. (1988). *The prepare curriculum: Teaching prosocial competencies*. Champaign, IL: Research Press.

Good, T., & Brophy, J. (1971). Analyzing classroom interaction: A more powerful alternative. *Educational Technology, 11*, 36-41.

Good, T., & Brophy, J. (1973). *Looking in classrooms*. New York: Harper & Row.

Hargreaves, R. (1972). *Mr. Messy*. Los Angeles: Price/Stern/Sloan.

Hattie, J. (1992). *Self-concept*. Hillsdale, NJ: Erlbaum.

Holt, J. C. (1970). *How children fail*. NY: Dell.

Johnson, N. L. (1990). *Learning how to learn: Strategies and activities to stimulate high-level thinking in the K-8 classroom* [video]. Dayton, OH: Creative Learning Consultants.

Keating, K. (1983). *The hug therapy book*. Minneapolis: CompCare Publications.

Kerman, S., & Martin, M. (1980). *Teacher expectations and student achievement*. Bloomington, IN: Phi Delta Kappa.

Kincher, J. (1990). *Psychology for kids: Fun tests that help you learn about yourself*. Minneapolis: Free Spirit.

Korb, K. L., Azok, S. D., & Leutenberg, E. A. (1992). *S.E.A.L.S. + plus: Self-esteem and life skills*. Beachwood, OH: Wellness Reproductions.

Krans, R. L. (1971). *The late bloomer*. New York: Dutton.

Krewer, J. (1979). *Future think: Planning for tomorrow's world in today's classroom*. Carthage, IL: Good Apple.

Limbacher, W. J. (1977). *Here I am*. Fairfield, NJ: Cebco Standard Publishing.

Mack, J. E., & Ablon, S. L. (Editors). (1983). *The development and sustenance of self-esteem in childhood*. New York: International Universities Press.

McDaniel, S., & Bielen, P. (1990). *Project self-esteem: A parent involvement program for improving self-esteem and preventing drug and alcohol abuse, K-6*. Carson, CA: Jalmar.

McGuire, J. V., & Heuss, B. (1995). *Bridges: A self-esteem activity book for students in grades 4-6*. Boston: Allyn & Bacon.

McPhail, P. (1975). *Points of view*. Allen, TX: DLM.

Murphy, J. F., Weil, M., Hallinger, P., & Mitman, A. (1982, December). Academic press: Translating high expectations into school policies and classroom practices. *Educational Leadership, 40*, 22-26.

Owens, K. (1995). *Raising your child's inner self-esteem: The authoritative guide from infancy to teen years.* New York: Plenum.

Plum, L. (1980). *Flights of fantasy*. Carthage, IL: Good Apple.

Podesta, C. (1990). *Self-esteem and the six-second secret.* Thousand Oaks, CA: Sage.

Pope, A. W., McHalen, S. M., & Craighead, W. E. (1988). *Self-esteem enhancement with children and adolescents.* New York: Pergamon.

Purkey, W. (1978). *Inviting school success*. Belmont, CA: Wadsworth.

Radl, S. (1979). *New mother's survival guide*. Champaign, IL: Research Press.

Reasoner, R. W. (1982). *Building self-esteem.* Palo Alto, CA: Consulting Psychologists Press.

Redfield, D. L., & Rousseau, E. W. (1981). A meta-analysis of experimental research on teacher questioning behavior. *Review of Educational Research, 51,* 237-245.

Rimm, S. B. (1990). *How to parent so children will learn.* Watertown, WI: Apple.

Sapon-Shevin, M. (1981). Teaching cooperation in early childhood settings. In G. Cartledge & J. F. Milburn (Eds.), *Teaching social skills to children: Innovative approaches* (pp. 229-248). New York: Pergamon.

Silvernail, D. L. (1981). *Developing positive student self-concept.* Washington, DC: National Education Association.

Simon, N. (1974). *I was so mad!* Chicago: Albert Whitman.

Stanish, B. (1979). *I believe in unicorns*. Carthage, IL: Good Apple.

Stanish, B. (1979). *Sunflowering*. Carthage, IL: Good Apple.

Striker, S. (1980). *The anti-coloring book of exploring space on earth.* New York: Holt, Rinehart & Winston.

Tuchscherer, P. (1988). *TV-interactive toys: The new high-tech threat to children*. Mt. Ranier, MD: Pinnaroos.

Vernon, A. (1989). *Thinking, feeling, behaving: An emotional education curriculum for children.* Champaign, IL: Research Press.

Wallerstein, J. S., & Blakeslee, S. (1989). *Second chances.* New York: Ticknor & Fields.

Wallis, L. (1985). *Stories for the third ear*. New York: Norton.

Walz, G. R., & Bleur, J. C. (1992). *Student self-esteem: A vital element of school success.* Ann Arbor, MI: Counseling and Personnel Services.

Wayman, J., & Plum, L. (1977). *Secrets & surprises*. Carthage: IL: Good Apple.

Wegscheider-Cruse, S. (1987). *Learning to love yourself.* Deerfield Beach, FL: Health Communications.

Wilen, W. (1987). *Questioning skills for teachers*. Washington, DC: National Education Association.

Wilt, J. (1978). *Saying what you mean: A children's book about communication skills*. Waco, TX: Word.

Youngs, B. B. (1992). *The six vital ingredients of self-esteem: How to develop them in your students: A comprehensive guide for educators, 1-12*. Carson, CA: Jalmar.

Chapter 8

PARENTING AND SELF-ESTEEM

Nancy Hastings King

Nancy Hastings King, M.S., L.P.C., N.C.C., has worked in counseling for 12 years. She holds a master's degree in Mental Health Counseling from Wright State University, and completed two years of post-graduate study at the Gestalt Institute of Central Ohio. Nancy is a frequent presenter and consultant to several local and regional institutions and organizations in the area of personal effectiveness, relationship building, parenting, and self-esteem. She is married and the mother of two sons, and has been active in parent organizations and school volunteer work for many years.

A large part of a parent's identity as a loving, worthwhile person is determined by his or her ability to provide for his or her children's physical and psychological well-being. In interviews with 97 adults, Whitbourne (1986) found that the vast majority rated family as the "most important area of my life." The deep emotional involvement with family has multiple effects on self-esteem. The parenting experience can result in perspective changes, often causing parents to see matters in a new light. Generalized feelings of competence and con-

I want to acknowledge the contribution of Antoinette Cordelle, Ph.D., who provided helpful information on special and adoptive parenting for this chapter.

fidence come from lessons learned (Erikson & Erikson, 1997). This chapter reviews the effects of parenting on self-esteem.

THE SELF-IMAGE OF THE BEGINNING PARENT

From the onset of pregnancy, prospective parents form rudimentary images of their child-to-be and of themselves as parents. Embedded in these images are hopes and dreams for the future. An unplanned pregnancy may present fears or obstacles that dominate the parent's emotional landscape. When the parents are unprepared and must make major adjustments in work, living space, lifestyle, and finances, it certainly affects their attitudes and emotions toward the pregnancy and the child. Even with planning and preparation, most parents experience anxiety about impending changes.

As the pregnancy progresses and physical changes occur in the mother's body, the reality of the impending event hits home and the growing self-identity as parents deepens. This self-identity may include a new life-meaning and purpose and acceptance of a meaningful adult role in society. Conscious and unconscious issues during this time may include an anticipation of vicariously living life over again, but with the advantage of experience and knowledge; a deep desire to correct, control, and heal old wounds; and a strong drive to pass down closely held values or to express a legacy. Often expectant parents have an image of "the perfect family" and spend significant energy trying to create this state. This drive may facilitate the energy and tolerance necessary to deal with the intense demands of a newborn.

When a newborn enters the world, different realities raise new issues for self-perception. Beginning with the delivery experience itself, parents interpret the meaning of each successive event. The birth may be interpreted as victorious, difficult, traumatic, a disappointing letdown, or something completely different. The good health of a newborn often is interpreted as a good omen, while health problems may be a source of immediate worry and self-blame. Good health does provide the parents with relief and a comfort zone great enough to move on to a new focus–perhaps an emphasis on sleep patterns, feeding, or temperament issues.

Health Problems and Handicapping Conditions

Initial health problems usually evoke fear and can be tremendously destabilizing, which has a serious negative impact on the family (Fortier & Wanlass, 1984). Examples of this destabilization include self-blame; anxiety resulting from inadequate information; self-doubt about one's ability to provide adequately for the needs of the child; hurt, anger, and a sense of unfairness; and feelings of personal defectiveness. The physical demands of a special-needs child, coupled with the parents' own anxiety, can leave new parents feeling perpetually tired, discouraged, and frustrated with the professionals and systems on which they depend (Ambert, 1992; Schneider, 1983).

Several factors influence a parent's response to a handicapped child, including these:

The severity of the handicapping condition

How the parent was informed of the condition

The age of the child at diagnosis

The socioeconomic level of the family

The visibility of the handicap

The degree of perceived social acceptability of the condition (Schell, 1981)

The response of family and friends has a significant impact on new parents who are experiencing profound disappointment and confusion (Ablon, 1988; Schneider, 1983). Support and sensitivity are invaluable at this time, because the parents are intensely attuned to cues of support or rejection. During crisis events, the strength of acceptance, availability, and tangible aid are invaluable to most families. An offer to baby-sit an older child while the parent takes the infant to the doctor can give the message that the people who care will provide assistance and not abandon the family.

Silver, Bauman, and Ireys (1995) addressed the many aspects of psychological distress experienced by parents of children with chronic physical illnesses and how that distress affects parents' self-esteem. The features of a chronic illness may induce fear and dread in a parent who doubts personal ability to make qualified decisions about care in the absence of professionals. Parents can feel hurt and isolated, especially when their children are excluded from the activities of other children. It is difficult for parents to deal with their children's hurt and disappointment, and this can impact self-esteem. An example of this is when parents plan a special outing and their child doesn't feel well enough to go. Parents may be caught between wanting something for the child to look forward to and yet not wanting expectations to be let down. There can be self-blame either way.

It is important for parents to feel that they are doing their best. This is affirming and gives some comfort. Educating themselves about the illness, finding supportive environments and individuals, and having some time for healthy diversion are ways for parents to take care of themselves. It is especially helpful when parents of children with special conditions find others who observe and appreciate the uniqueness and special gifts that their child brings.

THE NEWBORN AND PARENTS' ADJUSTMENT

Temperament and Appearance

The temperament and appearance of a newborn both affect the new parent's self-esteem (Langlois, Ritter, Casey, & Sawin, 1995). Donley (1993) referred to the infant as "constantly influencing and being influenced." Most new parents immediately evaluate similarities between their babies and themselves. And most feel an intense desire to become familiar quickly.

New parents must learn quickly to distinguish their newborn's cries of hunger from other cries, which can be difficult with an irritable baby. Most parents judge their success in determining their baby's needs by his or her restful, quiet responses, especially during waking times. There seems to be an "I-feed-you-you-feed-me" expectation on the part of most parents–that is, if you are doing the right thing (feeding your baby), the baby will demonstrate contented cues of well-being. When this does not happen, as in the case of a "colicky baby," the parents may feel helpless, ineffectual, and incompetent. Family and societal pressures regarding "feeding on demand" versus feeding on a schedule and breast-feeding versus bottle-feeding also affect the parents' self-concept.

Sleep patterns can set in motion the same kinds of expectations and frustrations, but with larger consequences for the parent. If the baby's sleep patterns develop as anticipated and he or she begins sleeping through the night, the parents may believe that development is on track and progressing well. However, if the infant is "getting days and nights mixed up," or waking for feedings every two to three hours, the parents may begin to question what they are doing wrong. This confusion often is worsened by disorientation and irritability stemming from their own sleep deprivation.

A related issue is general infant irritability, which has strong effects on the mother-infant interaction. "Visual and physical contact, effective stimulation, soothing, noninvolvement, and responsiveness to positive infant signals are the interactive behaviors in which mothers of irritable infants differ from those of non-irritable infants" (van den Boom & Holksma, 1994). The demand cues of these infants greatly affect the responses of their mothers. Parents often assume that irritability suggests that the baby has a need that is not being addressed. Distress signals such as crying (especially prolonged crying) can generate deep feelings of distress and incompetence in parents.

Varied degrees of success in effectively comforting the infant leave parents with varied emotional reactions. Because a newborn cannot communicate with words, parents often interpret prolonged crying as evidence that they are not good enough parents. Traditional wisdom holds that a baby is irritable because of something the parent is doing or not doing. Recently, research has broadened the scope of infant irritability to include more attention to direction-of-effect issues (Seifer, Schiller, Resnick, Riordan, & Sameroff, 1996). We have traditionally assumed that the parents' anxiety somehow causes the infant's irritability, but we may also safely assume that irritable babies can produce anxious parents! Because people tend to project their anxieties into the future, parents may fear that the stress of daily life with an irritable baby sets the stage for the rest of the life of the family.

External Feedback

The onset of parenting brings new expectations for all current relationships, and this may well affect the self-identity of the new parent. Parents receive feedback from one another (if one is absent, that is also feedback), from parents and friends, and from bystanders. Positive support or negative feedback between the mother and father can be a source of positive or negative self-esteem during this fragile time (Pistole, 1994). Feelings of partnership can ease the stress, while negative feedback imposes feelings of isolation, loneliness, and despair.

New parents are especially vulnerable to messages of approval or disapproval from their own parents at this time. They also have very specific expectations of the new grandparents and their close friends during this important transitional time, but these expectations often are not communicated. How you as a new parent perceive your parents' or friends' support or disapproval deeply affects your self-esteem. For example, you might want your parents' help in the beginning and interpret this as support. If your parents do not offer this help, you may feel abandoned and rejected. Or you may need and expect privacy in the beginning, while your newly expanded family does its bonding and adjustment. If your parents offer assistance, you may then see that as intrusive. Worse, you may even interpret such offers of help as a sign that your parents lack confidence in your abilities. These difficulties can be avoided if new parents and grandparents demonstrate a clear desire to be considerate.

The observations of casual acquaintances and bystanders also affect your new identity as a parent. We tend to perceive these observations as "true" because of their objectivity. We may perceive that these statements reflect the perception of the world-at-large. For example, the father of a newborn son who hears, "Isn't she cute!" may experience distress if he thinks the world perceives his son as feminine. Comments like "Why don't they do something with that crying baby?" can reinforce a new mother's fears that she is not an adequate caregiver. We experience the bystander's critical judgment of ourselves and our child at this point. Conversely if the comments are positive (such as "What a good baby!" when the baby is quiet), we may feel proud and effective; but such comments also reinforce that quiet babies are more acceptable in society. General comments from bystanders set the stage for society's expectations.

Parents of special-needs babies can experience difficulty in the newborn attachment process. Infants in the early months of life commonly learn to distinguish and prefer their parents' faces, as evidenced by the smiling response. This reinforces and supports parent-child interaction and provides for emotional bonding. In this way, the infant affects the emotional and responsive needs of the parent. This was demonstrated in research by Fraiberg (1974), who found that parents of nonsighted infants used high-intensity, gross tactile stimulation (such as bouncing, jiggling, tickling, and nuzzling) to ensure a stimulus for smiling responses. Parents need feedback from their infants, as this reciprocity boosts the attachment process.

THE DEVELOPING CHILD AND PARENTAL SELF-ESTEEM

Interaction and Interpretation

As your newborn grows and changes, so does your parental identity. Relationship patterns influence both your self-concept and your image of the developing family. Your ability to evoke a positive response from your baby produces pleasure and is self-reinforcing. The opposite is true, as well: If parents feel ineffective in their efforts to elicit a positive response from their baby, they feel discouraged and inadequate. A socially withdrawn infant may spark fears in the parents that their own social inadequacy may be repeated through their child. This pattern is repeated many times in various ways with regard to attributes that are of concern to the parents.

Even during the earliest days of a baby's life, parents look to compare and then interpret the comparisons. The nonverbal cues from the infant sometimes are interpreted in the context of personality: For example, "She doesn't like to be held. She's going to be very independent." These interpretations are based both on the subjective history of the parents and on heavy doses of desires for the future.

Because a parent's identification with his or her child is so strong, there is a heightened sensitivity about such observations. Comparisons are made with close scrutiny, and judgments are reached accordingly. The attempts to distinguish and differentiate are exercises in identity formation. However, rather than simply observing and allowing differences, many parents go on to the next step of evaluating, rating, and prioritizing–all of which happens in the context of the parents' own experiences and priorities. Some parents, for instance, perceive extroversion as being socially competent, while others judge extroverts to be pushy and obnoxious. Accordingly, parents may feel competent and proud or embarrassed and frustrated by a child's outgoing nature. How the parents interpret their child's temperament affects their feelings about the child and themselves.

There also is an intrapsychic component that affects the self-esteem of new parents: *how the new parents interpret and experience their own behaviors*. If they perceive their personal responses to the child as appropriate (such as in allowing the child to cry for a few moments to help achieve a certain sleeping schedule), they maintain feelings about themselves as "good parents," even if the child's reactions are not pleasant. However, when a parent acts impulsively out of anger or confusion, he or she often experiences regrets and feelings of inadequacy, especially if these experiences continue and are reinforced.

We do not start out with all the information we need to be effective parents. But parenting resources and personal experience can help us at every developmental stage. Support groups for new parents are helpful in reinforcing choices and levels of confidence. You can locate these groups through local hospitals, newspapers, and parent organizations. It is a sign of competence for parents to seek help or information when they feel confused or frustrated. Finding the best resources available can help you develop confidence in your own skills.

Skill Development

Your child's skill development can enhance or inhibit your self-esteem, especially if you believe that the skill reflects genetic or parental influence. A child's ability to walk or talk at a certain age may be a source of pride or concern. Other developmental tasks–such as toilet training, learning colors and numbers, or reading–may result in pride or anguish, depending on how you interpret what is age-appropriate or socially acceptable. Although you may experience loss and some sadness as your child matures and leaves behind cute (and dependent) modes of behavior, your relief and respect will grow as the child individuates and achieves new levels of personhood.

When there is delayed or stunted development, however, parents face special issues that affect their self-concept. They may experience unfounded guilt and hidden sorrow. The way the parents frame and interpret the situation is tremendously important for their healthy emotional development. For example, strong "if only" thoughts exacerbate feelings of hopelessness and depression; feeling unequipped and uncertain about the future can lead to chronic anxiety and depression. Parents can either withdraw and become divisive or strengthen their bonds to support one another. If parents believe and reinforce feelings that they are equipped to deal with their circumstances, they can strengthen their feelings of confidence and self-worth.

Most parents are interested in and experience some anxiety about skill development, and they measure progress in several ways. For example, most pay attention to their children's academic achievement, as measured by letter grades, exam scores, and IQ tests. As achievement occurs, parents grade themselves accordingly.

Some parents try to correct their own former (and present) mistakes and failings through the accomplishments of their children. We see this pattern at work when parents turn fun and leisure activities into competitive events. Increasingly, sports activities result in tournaments. Music, dance, and cultural activities develop into competitions. Science fairs produce winners and losers. Too often winning or placing is the only acceptable outcome, which can leave both children and parents feeling discouraged and defeated. This places the pressure to excel at the heart of self-concept for both parent and child.

Socialization

Your child's socialization is one of the greatest areas of impact on your self-esteem. Parental desires and expectations are strong in this area because socialization is an expression of the child's personality and adjustment in the world. There is constant feedback and judgment not only of your child but of you (Ambert, 1992; Casey & Fuller, 1994; Donley, 1993). Many parenting books focus heavily on the actions parents must take to obtain certain behavioral results from their children. The resulting conclusion for many parents is that if their children make social (or other) mistakes or inappropriate choices, it is their fault. While it is true that some parents do not instill appropriate societal values and behaviors in their children, *it also happens that children may choose to ignore what they are taught.* Society frequently judges our effectiveness by our children's behavior, even though we may have worked hard to establish appropriate values and behaviors in our children. This creates great anxiety, which can lead to anger or withdrawal. Because we all want to change or avoid what is painful, we may become overly firm (or abusive) or may helplessly acquiesce and avoid situations in which the child's acting out is likely to occur.

We can see a common example in the battle of needs between parent and child at the grocery store. The parent needs to accomplish a task, and the child has a need to explore. Both want their needs to be fulfilled. However, the parent also needs not to be embarrassed or distressed while getting the job done. If this need is great, the child quickly learns that difficult behavior is more powerful under these conditions. This, of course, is self-reinforcing, and negative patterns may develop as a result.

Parenting books often stress that a parent's voice should be calm and firm when a child is out of control. This is as important for the parent as it is for the child, because a parent begins to feel more confident and calm as the sound of his or her voice reflects this state. Parents often are surprised that their actions do not reflect their general sense of themselves. The parent in the grocery store might say, "I've always thought of myself as a very patient person. What is wrong with me? I don't feel patient at all!" Likewise, parents who think of themselves as good listeners may come home from work and scoot the children out of the room, preferring some quiet time for themselves. These parents often feel guilty and confused for not living up to their own expectations of themselves.

All of these experiences affect your self-esteem, so it is important to do some reflection. Maybe quiet time and listening are both important and can happen in the same evening at different times. Or maybe tonight is an exception. No one makes perfect choices consistently. It is important to balance your needs and expectations and learn to forgive yourself for not measuring up occasionally. Parental demands sometimes exceed our need to follow our own sense of who we are (e.g., "I thought I was a person who could set appropriate boundaries, but my toddler is out of bed for the fifth time!").

"Experts" can be helpful, of course, and it is important to gather knowledge; but each child, parent, and situation has its own variables. Sometimes perfect answers don't come, and we are left to do the best we can with the resources we have. At such times, we can benefit from reminding ourselves that parenting is only a part (an important part, to be sure) of the total person. This perspective is important across the life span for healthy parent development.

The Shy Child. The shy child may evoke difficult feelings in his or her parents, and with those feelings, certain types of reactions and behaviors (Richman & Davidson, 1994). An inhibited, socially fearful child often elicits parental feelings of helplessness and self-doubt. We may react to these feelings by taking on certain roles and patterns, such as the protector/defender role. In this case, we blame others or a specific situation for our child's social anxiety and we see the child as defenseless and helpless. We then may take actions to rescue or defend the child. There certainly are times when this type of intervention is appropriate, but it can set in motion harmful patterns if used routinely.

Confusion and withdrawal are typical reactions to the feelings of helplessness generated by a shy child. Not knowing what to do can lead us to feel inept and to have doubts about our parenting abilities. Because of our confusion, we may look for advice from "experts" such as teachers, counselors, self-help books, and friends. We may even begin to look for ways to avoid socially distressing situations. Repeated ineffectiveness heightens anxiety for us as well as for our child. If social avoidance becomes a way of life, it can set in motion chronic depression for both child and parent. Helplessness and depression are correlated in parent-child relationships (Nolen-Hoeksema, Wolfson, Mumme, & Guskin, 1995).

Some people view shyness as a self-limiting condition that can be remedied with appropriate measures. Parents who believe this may feel a strong need to change their child's condition. They may be motivated by two strong needs: They want their child to experience the benefits of being socially acceptable, and they want to alleviate their own discomfort, establishing a sense of mastery in their lives. Feelings of frustration can lead to anger and the desire for a "quick fix." The parents may push or cajole the child to be more outgoing, using shaming, bribery, or various other means. But even gentle, appropriate encouragement can feel like pressure to the child. In a society that says every question has an answer, parents may come to the conclusion that if one solution does not work, another must. Therefore, if appropriate encouragement does not seem to be working, negative alternatives may be used.

Most parents suffer when their children suffer. Sometimes parents try to force children to be more sociable, believing that it is better than their suffering long-term social anxiety. In fact, parental fear of a negative, painful future for the child may lead to an intense need to transform the child's behavior. New research (Rubin & Asendorph, 1993) has indicated possible genetic origins of shyness, as well as how to build anxiety tolerance, which may be helpful to both children and parents. Calm encouragement combined with frequent social experiences seem to help develop social hardiness for some children. Regardless of the results, parents need to remember that their children are unique individuals with their own needs and fears.

The Aggressive Child. Parents' responses to aggressive behaviors in children are based largely on their interpretation of the event and on their values regarding aggression (Bugental & Shennum, 1984). If the aggressive behavior is seen as representing drive and ambition, parents may be tolerant, showing subtle (or not-so-subtle) encouragement. Aggressive behavior may be viewed as an appropriate expression of power, in which case the parents' reaction might be one of justification, defensiveness, and support. Either of these interpretations may be entirely appropriate in a specific situation, depending on the value system. Some parents, however, encourage inappropriate behavior patterns because they want their children to be more powerful than they were as children.

Aggressive behavior also may be viewed as an inappropriate use of power, in which case the parents may feel shamed and angry or helpless and confused. Often parents respond to such behavior with increased use of directives, commands, and threats to try to reduce the negative behavior (Ambert, 1992). They may fear how the child's behavior reflects on them or what such behaviors indicate about the child's future. Because parents have such an profound investment in their children, they may experience significant anxiety and worry over such behaviors.

Immaturity. The immature child may elicit varied reactions in parents. Infantile behaviors may seem "cute" to parents or other observers and bring positive attention. This may elicit a desire to overindulge, laugh, or show off the child even more. For other parents and observers, however, the same behaviors–such as "baby talk" or inappropriate demands for attention–elicit embarrassment and irritation. This can lead to criticism, irritation, and over-teaching.

Regardless of which interpretation or response they experience, the parents will have residual feelings about themselves in relation to the child's behavior.

The "Perfect" Child. The socially skilled child may seem "perfect" to parents whose children are experiencing social problems. Struggling parents sometimes believe that other parents have it easy. But parents of socially skilled children have their own difficulties. A child adept at discerning subtle social cues may become a successful manipulator. Because society rewards those who use successful means of communicating, the child might learn how to avoid necessary consequences, how to get out of work, and other unhealthy lessons.

To explore a common example, imagine a teacher at the end of a long, tiring day asking the students to turn in their assignments.

> Kelly does not have the assignment prepared. She is painfully shy and avoids the teacher's gaze. When prompted for her assignment, she mutters a response in fear and embarrassment. The teacher interprets this as a sullen, uncooperative attitude and responds with consequences.
>
> April has excellent social intuition and good communication skills, and she has a completely different experience. April does not have the assignment prepared either, but she picks up verbal and nonverbal mood cues from the teacher. She does not wait until the teacher requests the assignment in front of the whole class. Instead, April chooses a time when the teacher is fresh, relaxed, and alone. She approaches the teacher proactively, establishes rapport, and explains her situation in a confident but apologetic tone. She says she will submit her assignment before class the next day.
>
> The teacher, though not necessarily happy with the missed assignment, is impressed by April's "cooperative attitude" and lets the infraction slide, convinced that April has nothing to learn from a penalty.

Thus, the socially adept student learns how to set up conditions to avoid consequences. The teacher (and others) might label Kelly "lazy and uncooperative" and April "cooperative but scattered," when the reverse may be true. Kelly's parents may be struck by the teacher's unfairness and lack of understanding and by Kelly's and their own powerlessness. April's parents, on the other hand, are proud that their child knows how to "handle her own affairs."

But a socially competent child who has learned to manipulate well often is confusing to parents. Trust and questions regarding power and control can result in the parents feeling powerless and confused about "what they did wrong."

The reality is that humans like and seek a sense of personal power. There is power in any action or trait performed well. There is even passive power in withdrawal and dependency. When children find a source of power, it often gets reinforced and developed, regardless of the setting or people involved. This can result in the parents, teachers, and other primary adults feeling powerless. *Power is not the same as self-esteem.* Children seem to have a better sense of self-esteem when their parents exercise appropriate authority and control. They sense the limitations of their knowledge and experience and are most secure and content when the alignment of power is appropriate and when parents see themselves as benevolent but authoritative.

We all have greater self-esteem when we feel effective in our attempts to establish and maintain appropriate norms of behaviors for our children. This is not to say that there is an absolute and perfect measurement of how power should be balanced: Ideally, this is a fluid process, accounting for the shifts in development of the family over time.

School is an important source of new information and identity feedback not only for the student but for parents, as well. Parents compare the behavior, personalities, and knowledge skills of their children's classmates as evidence of personal success or failure. And they are aware that other parents are doing the same. The plunge into the school experience exposes a child's knowledge, behavior, and personality to outsiders. The child is evaluated on an ongoing basis, away from the protection, supervision, and instruction of the parents. Parents may seek approval or disapproval cues from the child's teacher and may be quite vulnerable, especially the first time around. (Erikson & Erikson, 1997).

Differentiation

Differentiation represents an exciting transition, one that is both stressful and rewarding. It occurs in a gradual, constant progression, but there are rites of passage that celebrate this process of development of the self as a separate unit. Religious groups celebrate with confirmations and bar mitzvahs. In the educational world, we celebrate entry into kindergarten, grade promotions, recognition of talent and achievement, proms or other major events, and graduations. As this process continues, we can learn about our children's unique traits and characteristics and support those differences as special and important.

An appreciation of similarities and differences is an important developmental task for both child and parent. As we accept these similarities and differences, it becomes easier to experience our children as separate beings with separate lives. If differences in interests and preferences are not accepted, however, resentments and conflict often occur. The father must relinquish his dream of a baseball star son when it becomes clear that his son's primary interest is art.

Letting go is difficult, given the strong bonds between parent and child and the investment of so much time, emotion, and effort, but the process is essential for both child and parent. It is a paradox that both attachment and differentiation are necessary in the process of healthy parenting.

A good way to develop and maintain a broad perspective on differentiation is to collect family comics from local newspapers. These constantly express dilemmas encountered by parents with a humorous twist and can normalize your fears and frustrations (see Activity 8.6).

A few circumstances can complicate the progress of differentiation, including mutual dependence and balance of time spent with the child.

Mutual Dependence. Mutual dependence patterns between parent and child can generate resistance to change. When one ventures toward independence, the other balks. The first day of school often brings this issue to the fore, when the child expresses reluctance to leave the parent and enter this new world. What is not so obvious is that the parent experiences a shift in identity as well, and this shift calls for some searching and decision making.

We all make ongoing choices about how much to be involved and absorbed in our children's lives. It is important, of course, to be involved to the point that our children feel important and valued. It also is necessary for our self-esteem to experience being a caring and involved parent. However, we should not focus on our children to the point of excluding the needs of others, even our own. It is important to children's *sense of other* to learn that others (including their parents) have needs, interests, and demands that extend beyond them. Through this our children gain a perspective of an appropriate personal place in a social context.

It is the parent who must learn to establish this balance. It is certainly difficult when friends, school, work, self-help books, and society are communicating varied and conflicting messages about the appropriate balance. These messages feed programming into our self-worth. It is a difficult task indeed to discover the right mix, given that the needs and values vary greatly from person to person and from family to family.

Balance of Time. Another issue in the differentiation process is the balance of time we spend with our children. A parent's employment situation can affect both the quantity and quality of time he or she spends with the child. Spending time away while the child is in daycare (or home alone at older ages) can cause tremendous anxiety and guilt for parents. If the parent feels satisfaction with his or her work situation and with the development of the child, he or she typically experiences less guilt. However, if the child is having problems at school or daycare, the parent may feel that time away is a strong, contributing factor to these problems. Parents who are unemployed or who choose to stay at home, on the other hand, may look for evidence of their success with the child and measure this by achievement. If the child does not have superior grades or extracurricular accomplishments, the stay-at-home parent may personalize a sense of failure.

When you are feeling anxiety and guilt, you need to examine the situation closely. It could be that you do need more time with your child. Or your child may need to be held accountable for his or her actions. Or maybe your overall expectations are too high. Often, identifying strategies to improve the situation can help immediately. Just having a plan establishes a sense of direction and confidence to tackle the problem.

Differentiation is a process that children and parents face on an ongoing basis. A fun and beneficial way to view the process is to take a real or pretend situation and imagine trading places. Try to stay away from the "blame game" and instead imagine what your child would like or need in certain situations (e.g., an outing, a special event, or a disappointment), while he or she does the same for you. Then compare and learn from each other.

Low Self-Esteem in Parents

Researchers have noted that it is critical for parents to meet their own needs and not depend on their children as their sole sources of emotional support. "The more fulfilled you are as a person, the less you will use your children as your personal security blankets" (Briggs, 1975, p. 55). So it is important for us to experience parenting as only one of many facets of our adult lives.

Parents need emotional strength to withstand the effects of raising children on their marriage and overall stress levels. Having children may increase marital stability, but it can decrease marital satisfaction (Belsky, 1990). Children simply require a lot of time, energy, and money. It is difficult to be fully prepared for the onslaught of demands that children bring.

Therapists who work with children often see parents who allow their children to "run over" or even abuse them. These parents do not set limits, perhaps because they are afraid their children will not love them or meet their needs for personal fulfillment. Sometimes the parents were abused as children, adolescents, or adults. In the worst-case scenario, a pattern of emotional abuse is set in motion, in which the child fills the role of abuser. More often, parents have difficulty providing guidelines and setting expectations for their children. It may be hard for them to set limits, a *sine qua non* of parenting. As parents, we need to know more about what will help us strengthen ourselves emotionally to build our own self-esteem. The remainder of this chapter suggests how we can do just that.

ADOLESCENTS AND PARENTAL SELF-ESTEEM

During adolescence we see new challenges to the parent-child relationship, and these affect parental self-esteem. There are numerous mutual influences on parents and children during this time (Ge, Conger, Lorenz, Shanahan, & Elder, 1995). This discussion will center on the emerging needs of parent and child, communication in the relationship, values, and special challenges.

Physical Needs

Parents of adolescents usually are beginning to address the start of their own physical decline. Even physically fit middle-agers may experience hair loss or a reduction in their normal stamina. Weight gain can be a distressing accompaniment to the aging process, along with changing sleep patterns. All of this comes at a time when the child is gaining adult height and strength, seems to need no sleep, and requires voluminous amounts of food! Hormonal changes are occurring in both parent and child, and the physical changes can be tumultuous. How these needs differ is an apt metaphor for the many opposites occurring simultaneously for parents and adolescent.

Social Needs

As adolescents mature, peers become more prominent in their lives. There is a heightened intensity of peer socialization. Adolescents enter into more differentiation from their parents, and avoidance behaviors are common. The parents of a teenager may experience this transition with confusion. The child who once enjoyed spending time with the family now seems distant and embarrassed to be seen with them. The child may feel "chaperoned," while the adults may feel rebuffed and rejected. Most parents understand their children are growing up, but the turbulence of this developmental period finds many unprepared.

Friends. A common issue is the teen's choice of friends. An inexperienced teen may choose friends by default. Your disapproval of your child's friends can bring on major conflicts. You may feel threatened by the unhealthy influences on your daughter, while she resents your "meddling" and the implications of her incompetence.

One way to lessen the conflict over your child's friends is to get to know them (without being intrusive). Making this effort gives you more credibility with your child and provides avenues for influence. You might ask a simple, casual question such as, "So, what do you like *best* about Jenny?" This is not judgmental or "teachy" but might prompt your child to reflect on what is appealing or not about a friend. This lays excellent groundwork for evaluation of friends in light of personal values. This kind of dialogue also helps parents feel effective.

Dating. Struggles over your teenager's dating and other social activities may trigger unfinished business from your own adolescence. Stop to check the intensity of your feelings over your child's struggles. Intense feelings may be clues to parallel struggles you experienced long ago. If so, it is helpful to sort out the issues. It is important for parents and teens to share their difficult times with one another. However, not every instance is a teachable moment. Sometimes quiet listening is best.

The Parents' Needs. The monitoring and supervision necessary during this time can interfere with your own social and occupational needs. Support and contact with other parents of teenagers is important during this volatile time. However, just when you need contact the most, you are tied up actively monitoring your teen! Social functions and events for adults tend to be held at the same times teenagers have their social gatherings. Your best solution may seem to be staying home and falling asleep on the couch. This does not provide for the social support you need, but at times there may be few alternatives. Many parents give up on their own social needs in order to have peace of mind, but it is important to nurture your own identity as more than just "a parent."

Emotional Needs

Both adolescents and their parents can feel fragile at this difficult time of change. The volatility of emotions can become a way of life, and it is a major task in some families to avoid conflict at all costs. This can lead to reduced contact overall and influence patterns of inhibition. For instance, because mothers are better predictors of their children's inner experience than their outward expressions of emotions (Casey & Fuller, 1994), they may experience anxiety due to the unpredictable outbursts and emotionality of their adolescents. In other words, a mother may predict that her child will be angry but not anticipate the behavior associated with the anger. This uncertainty and misinterpretation can cause much confusion and volatility. During times of transition, we all need a sense of control and to be able to obtain comfort. So we often are struggling at cross-purposes with our children, each of us needing the same emotional support, perhaps for different reasons.

Parents are bombarded with literature on adolescent development. But it would undoubtedly be helpful for adolescents to learn about "parental development" during this time of life, perhaps in health classes. Since both are tied so closely to one another's experience of the self, this could lead to greater tolerance and more positive relationships.

Developmental Needs

Adolescents have a strong developmental need to become more autonomous; unfortunately, this need emerges just as parents are attempting a last-ditch effort to pass on values and life lessons. The child often is not interested and wants to acquire his or her own values and wisdom. For parents the process of letting go is a challenge. There are no assured outcomes. But new opportunities, roles, and relationships can emerge from this process of letting go. Taking time to reflect on hopes and dreams for a new phase of life can reap renewed interest and energy.

Communication: Content and Context

Teen-parent communication has a definite impact on self-esteem. Relevant variables of the communication process are content and context, style, and nonverbal messages.

Context. The most highly charged variable in many cases is the *context of the communication* and how it is presented and interpreted. Since the parent-child relationship has a long and broad contextual base, it is not hard for either child or parent to identify contextual examples and settings that are highly irritating. For example, if a parent wants correct grammatical use in the home, it is irritating for the child to use "ain't" and double negatives. The larger message is, "I am aware of your preferences and choose not to comply." These messages tend to become internalized and generalized to other situations.

> Shara and her son Marcus recently had an argument about the condition of the house when Marcus had friends over. They tracked in dirt and left crumbs on the floor from snacks. Shara cited new rules about the types of snacks allowed in certain rooms. Two weeks later, Marcus informed his mother, "We're all going over to Jerome's house. We all like it over there. His parents are cool. They aren't picky about their house at all. I think they like having us around."
>
> Shara felt angry and unappreciated, but she wasn't sure why. Marcus was not nasty; he did not say anything that was disrespectful or hurtful. Given the context, however, Marcus said a lot more than his words might indicate. His praise of Jerome's parents seemed like direct criticism of Shara's rules and values. Communication patterns can indicate subtle (and not-so-subtle) power struggles between parent and child. When this occurs, each may suspect some hidden agenda from the other.

Another tactic teens sometimes use to facilitate their parents' helplessness is making comments based on shock value. While the teen may be trying to explore and assert personal identity, the parent may feel a disturbing sense of general opposition from the child.

> Mary said to her father, "What do you think about the legalization of marijuana? I support it. Everybody uses it and it's not that harmful, so what's the big deal?!"

Her father's emotional reaction was highly charged. Was Mary asking him for his honest opinion, or was she baiting him to deliver a values lesson so she could discount him or leave him to worry about her choices and behavior?

At such times parents may feel they are in no-win situations. These feelings of ineffectiveness (in communicating and in parenting) fuel anxiety, depression, and a sense of inadequacy.

Because our relationships with our children are charged with emotional experience, it may be difficult to detach from the immediate circumstances and offer a calm, detached response. But we can achieve a greater level of competence in communication by focusing less on the content of the conversation and more on the process. This helps us prevent getting "hooked" emotionally.

When Mary finished with her hook, "so what's the big deal?" her father responded, "Why do you think so many people oppose legalization?"

When she continued to bait him, saying, "Because they're stupid and they just don't know the facts," he responded with a noncommittal, "Oh."

This left her nothing to push against, and Mary ended up with the issue in her lap. If she had responded to his first question in earnest, a sincere and important discussion might have followed. Mary's father felt less dragged around by his teenage daughter. He was in a more proactive position. These differences in communication patterns contribute to how family members perceive themselves and their family as a whole.

Adolescents also evoke feelings of warmth, pride, and high self-esteem in parents. A teen who confides in you or requests advice is acknowledging your wisdom and ability to listen. At these times, it is important to be aware of protective feelings that may prompt intervention on behalf of the child. The feelings of worth for both of you will be greater if your child can find solutions to his or her own problems. This inspires confidence in both of you. If your child remembers you on holidays or special events, or expresses gratitude in some way, you may feel honored and valued. Once again the adolescent has a significant impact on how the you feel as a person and as a parent.

Ellen was tired from a long day working at the grocery store. She had been on her feet all day and was not looking forward to coming home. She knew she would be late (having been caught in traffic) to pick up her 8-year-old son at the latch-key program, and matters

> had not been going well with her teen-age daughter, Lucy. As Ellen entered the house, she noticed that Lucy had picked up the clutter in the living room.

Lucy's gesture is an overture of helpfulness. Moments like these happen with adolescents, often at unexpected times or places. These times give the teen a feeling of contribution and a sense of making a difference (positive power). Teens especially like the thrill of surprising their parents. Ellen's response of delight or appreciation will be important for herself and Lucy both and will reinforce Lucy's actions.

Humor. Humor is an important element in parent-teen interactions. However, it must be used in a context that everyone understands to be affection. Humor can be a way to connect even when a teen is being avoidant. It encourages fun within the home. This environment benefits both parents and teen and lightens the atmosphere. Note, however, that *humor is not sarcasm.* Sarcasm often has a mean edge, covering issues of conflict. It leads to deterioration in communication and should be avoided.

Communication Style and Nonverbals

Most people want warm, supportive social interactions, especially in their family relationships. These patterns support positive self-esteem. Donley (1993) found that the parent-child relationship is repeatedly influenced by patterns and social forces within the family relationship system. Donley discovered that relationships in families can look completely different under calm conditions than they do under stressful conditions.

If one child is having feelings of sibling jealousy, it affects the whole family system. The stress of one family member frequently permeates throughout the family system. (This has implications for how churches, organizations, and schools deal with students and parents.) The conclusion, then, can be made that external forces and events–such as school performance, discrimination, and changes in employment status–may be significant contributors to a family's interaction style. It also follows that a dispute or resentment between two family members will be felt throughout the entire family system, affecting subsequent interactions between other family members.

The good news, of course, is that positive social forces within the family are pervasive as well. When supportive interactions are demonstrated, others will want to join in for their share of the bounty. Negative communications often occur out of intense emotional reactions, discouragement, or unfulfilled needs. Positive communication requires more of an intentional initiative.

Especially in the teen years, competing emotional and developmental needs between parents and children drive different types of interactions. As children enter early adolescence, they exhibit increased avoidance behaviors. Kahlbaugh and Haviland (1994) found that as adolescents grow older, they and their parents both demonstrate greater avoidance behavior, as evidenced by reciprocated contempt. Often experienced as negative, this phenomenon may actually facilitate individuation. The avoidance behaviors cited in this study were as follow:

- Covering face with hand
- Averting face
- Self-manipulation (soothing and regulating behaviors, including tapping and rhythmic motions)
- Self-inspection
- Facial and body signals of contempt (eye rolls, head tosses, shrugs)
- Disgusted facial expressions (nose wrinkles, constricted mouth, extended eyebrow raised showing skepticism)
- Closed arm position
- Backward lean

When we are on the receiving end of this behavior, we may have highly charged emotional reactions but not be able to clarify them, which contributes to even greater feelings of powerlessness. These nonverbal behaviors can have a tremendous impact on the communication process, especially when combined with sarcasm, muttering, and physical distancing, such as excessive time in the room or out of the home. Because these behaviors have such an emotional impact on us, our adolescent experiences increased power and effectiveness in getting what he or she wants or making us uncomfortable. It may serve us well to study this list of adolescent behaviors so that we can be more emotionally objective and ready to respond when we meet them. This also may help us to feel less emotionally bruised.

It is surprising to note that approach behaviors by adolescents remain static and constant over time (Kahlbaugh & Haviland, 1994). These behaviors include smiling, head nods, face and body orientation in the direction of the other, symmetry of body position, and touching. With the increase in contempt behaviors, we may not realize that approach behaviors have not actually diminished. Although the child is increasing differentiation, the need for connection and security remains strong. Often, the negative signals do not replace the positive, but are added to them.

Parental behaviors of contempt likewise increase during this period, especially for fathers (Kahlbaugh & Haviland, 1994). The way we respond to our teenagers influences the images we have of ourselves as parents and of our families in general. If we interpret our own contempt behaviors as appropriate attempts to demonstrate power and authority and as necessary in setting boundaries, it has a different effect on our self-image than if we believe our behaviors are shameful and out of control.

Tonality and context of communication count for a lot when it comes to interpreting meaning. The question, "Why?" may take on a completely different meaning, depending on the tone and context.

"Why don't you study more?"

"Why don't you clean your room better?"

These are not questions; they are observations and judgments. Much has been written about how this affects the child. But it also works in reverse. A mother reminds her adolescent son to come home at curfew. When the teen responds with, "Why?" he may not be seeking information, but posing resistance. The "Why?" question, far from asking clarification, may be a challenge to perceived unfairness. Pat answers, accusatory and defensive tones, and "over-talk" are some ways communication can be negative during this stage.

As children resist our influence, we may push hard to over-explain and over-teach as a way to stress the importance of our values. This seldom is effective, as teens often block perceived attempts to over-control. As our children become more autonomous and self-regulated, we should strive to redefine what is appropriate and necessary and to release outdated norms in our relationship. Effective redefinition usually is accompanied by feelings of growth and an expanded self-identity.

Values

Most parents want and need to extend a legacy that expresses their identity into the future. This need, combined with a conviction about what is important in life, drives us to emphasize our own value systems to our children. If our children adopt the values most important to us, we feel successful. We may consider it as validation of the directions we have taken and the choices we have made.

Success is measured in many ways. Some generally accepted measures of success include commitment to family, performance and recognition at work, financial achievement, and general life satisfaction. Individuals have different opinions about how to achieve success and what values are necessary to do so.

Parents may encourage diligence or patience, risk-taking or caution. Because it is a teaching process, parenting can encourage life review and reflection. However, children often hit adolescence just as their parents hit mid-life, a time when they are confused themselves and looking for alternative avenues.

Shared interests or leisure activities provide opportunities for bonding and reciprocal validation for parent and child. Again, context is critical. A fiercely competitive sports match or debate may leave more scars than mutual appreciation. It helps to have a mutual interpretation of the activity and its goal. This can be as simple as saying, "Let's go outside and shoot a few baskets. I need some relaxation before I go back to work tomorrow." Comfortable expectations need to be maintained and reinforced daily. Because of the image identification between adolescent and parent, each is vulnerable to the judgment of and wants respect from the other.

Helping your teen learn to encourage and support you is a benefit to both of you. "I have a career decision to make. Here are the issues. I'd like to hear your thoughts on it," gives your child the feeling that his or her ideas and contributions are valued and important. It also encourages behaviors of generosity and a focus on the needs of others. This sets the stage for further positive interaction.

Passing morality and ethics to our children is a highly charged process. Some generally accepted values in our society are honesty, responsibility, perseverance, generosity, fairness, and altruism. Most of us want our children to learn these values, especially honesty and responsibility. We have a great stake in this, since society measures our parenting success in these terms. To have reared an honest, responsible child is an honor; to have reared a dishonest, irresponsible child is a failure of the highest magnitude. Because society judges parents so harshly for the behavior and values of their children, we have a vested interest in teaching our children the values that are highly regarded by society. This influence is helpful in maintaining societal standards and keeping order.

Whether just or not, the press, schools, popular literature, and our judicial system hold parents accountable for the actions and values expressed by their children. New research on the circularity and reciprocity of influence between parents and children may help to change attitudes of condemnation of parents whose children do not conform to expectations, and may encourage efforts toward supportive networks for families.

Special Challenges

Juvenile Delinquency. Special parenting challenges can cause anxiety, heartache, and self-reproach. One such challenge is juvenile delinquency. Much has been written about the family's impact and influence on juvenile delinquent, but little has been written on the impact the juvenile delinquent has on the family unit.

Ambert (1992) explored the view that parents of juvenile delinquents might have ineffective coping skills because of the burnout and stress of living with a difficult child. She found a definite bias in the literature toward assuming that parent behavior is *causal* in juvenile delinquency. However, it is difficult to assess whether parental ineffectiveness is the cause or an effect of the child's behavior. Ambert (1992) suggested that parental blame may be reinforced by probation officers and social workers who believe the parents "caused" the problem. This excuses the delinquent for the criminal behavior and throws in extra attention for good measure. Thankfully, a few researchers are beginning to explore the reciprocity and circularity of effect related to juvenile delinquents and their families.

The following are suggestions for parents of children exhibiting juvenile delinquent behavior:

- Be clear with social workers, teachers, courts, counselors, and other professionals about the nature and scope of problems you are dealing with.
- Ask those helpers to do some role-playing with you of typical scenarios that you experience with your teen. You might get some fresh ideas from them, and they may gain perspective from your experiences and insight.
- Take some time out to have fun and laugh, to be with other supportive adults, and to work on being a healthy person.
- Try something new during a crisis or difficult time when distress occurs—a different reaction, a different tone, a different behavioral response, or different decisions or consequences. You might be more effective.
- Remember that the fact that your child is acting out does not mean that you are a bad person. If you could change your child's behavior, you would, right?
- Find some spiritual nourishment that can provide you with a feeling of being grounded.

Death of a Loved One. Many mid-lifers experience the death of a close friend or parent during this time of life. Such a loss shakes our security and forces us to face the instability of life and our personal mortality. It can force introspection and reflection on issues we have avoided before. We must contemplate the passage of time and our own aging. And we can begin to interpret and evaluate life in the context of events, achievements, relationships, and values. Based on this evaluation, we may feel satisfaction, regret, confusion, or a mixture of feelings. The experience of this reflection itself may affect the self-esteem of the parent who is evaluating everything in light of eventual death. A loss can add perspective and intensity to the living of life. This has implications for how we deal with minor conflicts, how we handle relationships, and how we resolve problems. The results of this process influence our self-image.

> Patricia's friend–who was only five years younger than Patricia–died recently from a terminal disease. Patricia felt alternately numb, tearful, and confused. Gradually, she began to acknowledge the passage of time in her own life. She realized she had not called her parents lately and that it had been awhile since she organized a family gathering. She also realized that her children would be out of the nest soon and that she wanted to spend time with them before they left. Come to think of it, she thought, she had better get a health checkup. Patricia decided to set aside some time to take care of matters she had been neglecting.

This kind of experience is common during the mid-life years and has a strong influence on self-image.

Work Transitions. A change in work conditions is another common experience for mid-life adults. Such transitions may mean our job security and way of life are threatened–and that translates into stress. Another way our children affect our lives is when their needs come first, at the expense of job promotions. You may forego a better job offer or promotion because you don't want to move your family. You may feel satisfied with this decision if positive results occur. But you also may feel resentful, unappreciated, and exploited if your sacrifices do not reap positive rewards. Any type of destabilization at this vulnerable time adds to the pool of pressure.

To bolster your self-esteem during a career transition, try developing a "transition plan" including activities, time lines, potential personal and family impacts, and decisions that need to be made. Follow it, allowing and expecting that the transition plan will not completely eliminate the volatility and chaos. The plan *will,* however, help you be more in control and anticipate problems more effectively. Ask for family support when you need it, particularly from teens. This is a message of respect to them, and they are more likely to be cooperative when they understand that their parents struggle with change and fears too.

Teen Sexuality. The emerging sexuality of teens adds to the stress and anxiety of the parent-child relationship. Parents often are ambivalent about their teens' sexuality because of their religious or ethical values; because they are not ready to see the child move toward leaving home; or because they fear irresponsible behavior. No one wants a child to experience an unwanted pregnancy, disease, or a generally reckless lifestyle. Parents are aware of the significant life consequences of choices in sexual behavior, and they often have the burden of worry without the controls to limit certain behaviors. The teen's impact on the parents' marriage also is significant. Adolescents are cited as the most frequent sources of marital disagreement (Ambert, 1992). This stress on the marital relationship can be a major inhibitor of self-esteem.

When parents experience these fears, often they rush ahead in their thinking to devastating outcomes. Although it is important to prepare teens for responsible choices and address irresponsible choices, it is also important for parents to accept that they cannot control all of their children's choices. It may be important for parents to remind themselves that their parenting role, though vitally important, is one of many roles that they play in their lives. This perspective may help parents be appropriately responsible and supervisory without being in a perpetual state of alarm. During this time, parents could seek opportunities to be with other parents of teens who are dealing with similar issues. This can help normalize their experiences. Parenting support groups and parent volunteer organizations are ways of meeting other parents of teens. Married parents need to spend some "spouse only" time in order to nurture the health of their marriage and to affirm their partnership.

Gay Teens. As gay and lesbian youth discover their sexuality, the dynamics between parents and child can be quite strained. Many families establish a "demilitarized zone," placing certain topics–such as marriage, dating, and future plans–off-limits for a time (Boxer, Cook, & Herdt, 1991). Most families report improved relations following disclosure, particularly if open and honest dialogue results. After the initial disappointment and adjustment, parents of gay and lesbian teens tend to focus on the "loss" of grandchildren (although that is changing); concerns about safety, health, and discrimination; and care in old age (Boxer et al., 1991). Parents also worry about others' reactions and their own need to restructure their expectations for their child's future. Parents who find themselves asking, "Where did we go wrong?" might focus instead on what they did right–as evidenced by their child's decision to be open with them.

Parents of gay and lesbian youth, who may be feeling a sense of crisis, may be advised to consider that the time of a child's disclosure is a vulnerable time and an opportunity for parental love. Part of our legacy as parents is how our children remember us at critical moments in their lives. If support is not an immediate option, honesty and dialogue can provide a bridge to continued interchange between parent and child. Parents' self-esteem is usually enhanced when they believe that they have dealt well with difficult issues with their children. The group Parents and Friends of Gays and Lesbians can be very helpful.

Single-Parent Families. The vast majority (86% in 1994) of single-parent households are maintained by women (Taylor, 1997). Single-parent families can be created by divorce, separation, out-of-wedlock births, death of a parent, or adoption. "Para-parenting" is an informal arrangement with friends or relatives to provide care, supervision, and support to a single-parent family situation, and the frequency of this arrangement is growing as single parents try to balance employment and parenting roles (Taylor, 1997).

Much has been written about the effects of family structure on the child, but family structure also affects the parent. The single parent often struggles with limited time, stress, fatigue, conflict over work hours, financial restrictions, and many other concerns (Yawkey & Cornelius, 1990). However, children in single-parent homes seem to be included more in decision-making and may be a part of more adult discussions.

Because of the intense demands of work and child care, single parents can feel overwhelmed. When we feel overwhelmed, we can feel incompetent due to beliefs that we are not managing our lives well enough. These feelings are part of the reason good support groups of others wrestling with similar issues can be so vital (for example, Parents Without Partners). Sharing frustrations and solutions can help single parents feel grounded, hopeful, and rejuvenated, and can lessen feelings of isolation. Another possibility is to team with another single parent to trade baby-sitting time in order to take breaks or to get caught up, a variation of the "para-parenting" described above.

Divorced Parents. Divorced parents face some important issues that can affect their self-esteem. Their children's reactions to the divorce can cause great distress and guilt. Custody arrangements often are highly charged emotional issues, and parent-child alignment or alienation affects parents greatly (Johnston, 1993). There are significant costs to both the residential and the nonresidential parent. The residential parent experiences daily living routines with the child, the majority of the parenting decisions, and (in some cases) more societal approval. He or she also has less leisure time, more ongoing responsibility, more work conflicts, and less time for peer contact. The nonresidential parent often experiences the pain and awkwardness of visitation, financial and time costs, ongoing anger and conflict with the residential parent (the most often cited reason for infrequent visits), and negative feedback from others (Braver, Wolchik, Sandler, & Sheets, 1993). Both parents can benefit from the relationship with the child, societal approval, and feelings of self-worth at doing what is best for the child.

Whenever possible, it is helpful in the process of divorce for parents to develop a parenting plan, customized for the situation, to best meet the needs of the children and parents. A plan that deals with the division and sharing of responsibilities and expectations can ease the transition for everyone and support self-esteem at a vulnerable time. Sample issues that could be covered in the plan include attendance at special functions, supervision of homework, parent-teacher conferences, grandparent relationships, privacy issues, responses to sensitive questions and problems, scheduling for children's activities, monetary issues, etc. It is easier to deal with these issues before problems arise than during times when emotions are running high and there is conflict.

Blended Families. Parents in blended families are particularly vulnerable to the impact of the children. In one study, "adolescent children in stepfamilies were more effective in altering behavior of parents than parents were in shaping children's behavior in the early stages of remarriage" (Booth & Dunn, 1994). This certainly points to the influence children have on parents. Booth and Dunn also found that stepchildren are more likely to leave home early because of conflict. It is difficult to fully appreciate what kind of long-term impact such a departure has on the parents and their relationship.

For blended families, a family plan can provide a secure foundation and a working structure to support rules and norms for everyday family living. Set up in advance of problems, a family plan is a resource that can be referenced to help foster fairness and good will. A plan such as this might include how space and chores are shared, scheduling needs, manners, etc.

With or without a written family plan, a common understanding of values and goals for the family is particularly crucial between the parents of a blended family. Stepparents' initiative toward forging kin-like relationships with stepchildren is the primary influence on the character of the blended parent-child relationship, although it is true this relationship cannot be attained without the cooperation of the child (Arendell, 1997). When adolescents are part of the blended family, it can be noted that they are at a developmental age when they are looking for more flexibility in relationships and are likely to be resistant to more restrictions in their lives. That said, many are more adaptable to change at this age than younger children. Finally, the quality of the spousal relationship has probably the greatest impact on adjustment for everyone involved.

In summary, to achieve positive self-esteem during these transition times, planning and preparation can help blended families with optimal adjustment.

ADOPTION AND SELF-ESTEEM

Adoptive parents face many difficult issues. They may worry that their child will be reclaimed by or want to seek the birth parents. They may feel particularly vulnerable and need their friends and relatives to verbally recognize and reinforce their parenthood status.

Parents who adopt older "high-risk" children and those who provide foster care need special parenting skills. Because these children often have experienced abuse or neglect in prior relationships, they are adept at disruptive behaviors and creating chaos. So they trigger strong emotional reactions in their adoptive parents. These parents can benefit greatly from classes that teach them how to handle these reactions and reinforce their emotional fortitude.

Researchers have recognized that older children experience intense emotional reactions to adoption. Chapman (1991) discussed the developmental issues in adoption, including grieving losses, establishing control, loyalty conflicts, fears of rejection and abandonment, dealing with blows to self-esteem, difficulties establishing trust,; and struggling for identity. These themes become prominent issues for adoptive parents as well.

Parry (1983) analyzed the stages of grief as they apply to parents who adopt older children. These parents often experience shock, denial, the need for emotional release, physical symptoms, depression, isolation, a sense of helplessness, guilt, anger, and idealization. They must establish new patterns of living. In short, they must cope with the loss of their ideal family. The complexity of adoption also has a strong effect on children's self-esteem. Parents need to be flexible in distinguishing the differences of adoption as they bond with their child and set the stage for establishing a firm sense of belonging and self-value (Kaye, 1990). Adoptive parents clearly need better preparation as well as long-term support.

How can parents cope with such intense grief and emotional reaction? No one really knows until the time approaches, but preparation can help. Here are some ideas for parents:

You may need to dig down deep and use emotional resources you did not know you had.

Sometimes, denial is necessary–as facing every aspect of reality can be too painful all at once.

Recognize that your anger may give you energy and spur you on to better solutions.

When facing depression and defeat, it is important to remember that *it will be better later*.

Often we believe we should be able to solve problems easily–that it should not be so hard. But what is hard for us is hard, period. Sometimes time rushes by and does not give us an opportunity to reflect. Other times, time stands still. When we are depleted of strength, we must simply go on. We may not be able to control the outcome, but we can endure. In an effort to maintain a healthy perspective, we should engage in sharing with others. From active coping, we learn that nothing stays the same–that life is change.

What follows is advice from four special parents:

> We try not to feel guilty, to recognize that the problems are not our fault. We realize now that it is best not to hide the problem, as keeping it from other people makes it hard to work out solutions.

****

> [A] key concept is unconditional love. It is important to be able to overlook the little things, not to hold grudges, to walk away when you are too angry to discuss it. Still, it is hard to handle intentional destructive behavior. Be direct about your feelings: "I love you, but I don't like what you're doing."

****

> It takes a lot of nerve or *chutzpa*. You have to stay in there even when the kids say they hate you. You need patience and to adapt to nonadaptable situations. You tolerate, not necessarily accept. The problems don't go away just because there has been an adoption. You have to distinguish what you are responsible for and what you can't control. Refusing to ask for help means not allowing others to be helpful. Every kid is different, so discussions have to be tailor-made. These kids have no dreams.

****

> The tolerance thing is a big one. Trying to still put up with her. You know you love the child, but you can only put up with so much abuse. Trying to get her to fit in, a juggling thing. There is so much more work involved than with a normal child. You have to be able to put up with a lot. Half the time you feel guilty that you are not doing enough. I don't like coming off as cold-hearted, but I try to distance myself from being constantly hurt.

Katz (1986) listed nine qualities that are important for successful adoption of older children:

1. Tolerance for one's own ambivalence or strong negative feelings
2. A refusal to be rejected by the child and an ability to successfully delay gratification of parental needs

3. The ability to find happiness in small increments of improvement
4. Parental role flexibility
5. A systems view of their family
6. Firm entitlement
7. Intrusive and controlling qualities
8. Humor and self-care
9. An open versus closed family system

Katz (1986) explained that there may be surges of rage or unpredictable changes in affection for the child due to the stress of conflicts and difficult behavior. Here are some points to remember in the daily grind of child-rearing:

- Don't judge yourself too harshly. You can feel intense emotion without acting on it.
- Try not to equate lack of gratification in parenting with failure.
- Instead of trying to remake the child, help the child achieve success in small daily tasks.
- Learn to rely on your partner. For example, fathers who perceive that their wives are burned out can take over part of the care-taking role.
- Look to the family system to find answers for problem solving rather than blaming one person.
- Learn how to incorporate differences and recognize that sameness is not an essential ingredient.
- It may be necessary to use intrusive and controlling ways to show caring.
- Assume control; try to anticipate behaviors; interrupt behavior spirals early; and provide a great deal of praise, positive reinforcement, and physical affection.
- Use humor and self-care.
- Refuse to accept martyrdom as the price of parenting.
- Turn to respite care on a regular basis.

- Be receptive to seeking and accepting help, and be willing to reveal weaknesses and discouragement.

- Finally, recognize that special emotional qualities are necessary in parenting the older adopted child.

More research on these special qualities is needed, along with information on how parents can refine these skills. We also need to put more effort into developing a curriculum to prepare parents for the emotional tasks they will face. It is important to be able to encourage parents toward success in this difficult endeavor, as their happiness and the welfare of their children are at stake.

OTHER SPECIAL PARENTING ISSUES

Discrimination

Parents who belong to special ethnic or other groups in society face unique issues. Parents whose race, economic status, sexual orientation, family structure, immigrant status, language, or religious affiliation are in the minority face additional problems in the parenting experience. Discrimination certainly can extend to the school system, service networks, and any child-related resource organization on which parents must rely. Parents can realistically fear the social, academic, and emotional effects for their children, and this can affect parental behavior. For example, if parents believe their "differences" will negatively affect their child, they might reduce contact levels with the teacher or school. They also might avoid this contact because of prior painful experiences with other parents or professionals. As a result, educational systems might assume a lack of interest on the part of the parents, and a cycle of misperception begins.

These parents find themselves having to rely on institutions and individuals they otherwise would have been able to avoid (Cardenas & Zamora, 1980). Immigrant parents have the special problems of language differences, societal attitudes about immigrant status, and seeing their children adapt quickly to the society, sometimes only to reject their parents' cultural attitudes and values. This can create fear and confusion for the parents (Ambert, 1992).

Chronic Illness, Mental Illness, and Special Needs

As noted earlier, parenting a child with a chronic illness or handicaps involves special concerns. Many parents of such children face restrictions on their freedom, social avoidance, high child-care costs, energy drain, dealing with ongoing disappointment, and encountering professional scrutiny (Ambert, 1992; Schneider, 1983).

The impact of mental illness on families can be severe and difficult on many levels. Both the behaviors of the child (which may include argumentativeness, withdrawal, verbal or physical abuse, and other signs of distress) and the disruption of other areas of life (including missed work, financial stress, isolation, and reduction of social and leisure activities) cause stress to family members (Gubman & Tessler, 1987).

Children with special needs may pose many concerns for parents. Parents may have questions about living arrangements; autonomy and independence; education, training, or career opportunities, financial issues; and special care arrangements. They have to grapple with questions of what is a "responsible parent" and what is an "overprotective parent." Often they are hurt badly by "labeling." Parents need support in making appropriate decisions. They often have to struggle through this process with little guidance. They may also have to face the reality that the parenting process may not end for them when the child turns 18, or 21, or 50, or ever, depending on the severity of the problem.

One study found two major impacts on mothers of technology-dependent children: Out of necessity, they grew more assertive with health care professionals; and they felt chronically tired (Ambert, 1992). Parents of disturbed children may find that pathology interferes with mutual pleasure and satisfaction in the relationship (Schneider, 1983). It may be difficult for these parents to see other parents experiencing greater freedom.

With each challenge, a parent needs to feel a sense of control and effectiveness. It is important to take time to reflect on accomplishments and to acknowledge what a big job parenting is. Support groups, religious and educational affiliations, therapy or consultations, extended family, and trusted friends are all resources for reducing stress, providing insights and ideas, and supporting and reinforcing the struggling parent.

PARENTING THE YOUNG ADULT

People with secure attachments "emphasize the importance of openness and closeness in their relationships, while at the same time seeking to retain their individual identity" (Feeney & Noller, 1990). Although Feeney and Noller were discussing romantic relationships, the same is true of adult child-parent relationships. The transition to young adulthood requires new definitions for the roles of and expectations for parent and adult child (Cohler & Boxer, 1984).

Many parents seem to enjoy giving up the role of disciplinarian as their children leave home (Erikson & Erikson, 1997). This seems to take much of the stress and pressure out of the parent-child relationship. Most parents welcome the end of this responsibility and look forward to a less taxing role. Others may resist the process of letting go and cling to means of continued control. It is clear that a sense of security and accomplishment in the second half of adulthood depends heavily on the knowledge that offspring have "turned out okay" in their adult life. This feeling helps to advance parents' own development as adults (Offer & Sabshin, 1984).

There seems to be a time of distance between parents and their adult children as the developmental tasks of each take them into more intense self-development. Rosenfarb, Becker, and Khan (1994) found that in nonpsychiatric controls, women reported decreased attachment to their parents over time, but a renewed development of closeness with their mothers in adulthood. (Moderately depressed individuals reported the same reduction of attachment during adolescence, but no resumption of closeness during adulthood.) Both parents and children are in an intense differentiation mode and heavily involved with school, friends, pursuit of new interests, and careers. The parent usually experiences fewer financial and time demands and more freedom. As one woman put it, "You have the freedom of a 20-year-old with the experience and financial resources to be able to enjoy it!" These are generally peak earning years and many people focus on travel, hobbies, and retirement planning.

For many others, however, more difficult circumstances arise. An unexpected pregnancy at this age can bring on panic and disappointment or elation at another chance at parenting. The unexpected pregnancy of a child or child's girlfriend can generate anger and hurt and cause the parents to feel guilt, shame, remorse, and resentment. The same is true for an adult child's involvement with drugs or criminal activity and problems with employment or job retention. Problems between parent and young adult child can crop up over choices of lifestyle or primary friends or mates.

Any of these situations can complicate the differentiation process, especially if the grown child moves back in with the parent. Today's financial realities sometimes make this prudent, but expectations must be clearly negotiated if it is to be successful. Many parents are motivated to help their children get a "hand up," but they generally feel better about it if they have a choice about it. Observe the case of Diana:

> After earning her baccalaureate degree, Diana moved back in with her parents and began looking for a position in the community. Unable to find a job in her field, she worked odd hours at a fast-food restaurant to earn some money. Since she was grown, Diana expected to set her own rules and standards.
>
> Diana's parents were glad to have her move back in, under the circumstances. They assumed she would be considerate of their needs for quiet at night and help with chores around the house. They expected Diana to pull her own weight as an adult.

> But this was not Diana's prior experience in her parent's home. She remembered her childhood home as a place of comfort and acceptance. She was insulted when her parents asked her when she would be in at night. She did not need supervision, she told them. Furthermore, she did not have time to do extra chores when she was busy working and looking for a real job.

As Diana's case illustrates, parents and their adult children need to spell out clearly their expectations and needs *before problems arise*.

Attachment behavior appears to continue throughout life, especially when adult children are distressed, ill, or threatened in some way (Bowlby, 1979). It also appears in the grief at the loss of a parent or when a parent is seriously ill (Cicirelli, 1991). These feelings go both ways. Parents are profoundly affected by the lives of their adult children.

Parents and their adult children sometimes experience renewed closeness following the birth of a grandchild. However, the relationship at this time may be vulnerable due to the new roles and identities being formed: The adult child is working to form a new "parent identity" and often wants parental validation and approval for new choices and decisions.

New grandparents have their own identity issues to deal with. Most find satisfaction in the continuation of another generation and another opportunity to pass down wisdom and values. Grandparents may struggle with the dilemma of how much to be involved and how to mention helpful ideas without seeming judgmental. Grandparents still want their children to benefit from their own experiences, but they may fear rejection and hurt feelings.

> Mariko was delighted to become a grandmother. She was proud of and impressed by the way her daughter and son-in-law had organized and planned their lives and with how hard they were working to provide for their new baby.
>
> Watching her daughter struggle with sleep deprivation, Mariko was tempted to offer tips from her own experience. She wanted to share with her frazzled daughter how she had handled the same situation, what she learned and changed the second time around. Despite this desire to help, Mariko said nothing. She did not want her exhausted daughter to feel criticized and incompetent.

Grandparents make various decisions in response to this dilemma, and they evaluate their success as both parents and grandparents by the outcomes. This generates either positive or negative feelings.

As grandchildren grow older, grandparents have important decisions to make about appropriate levels of involvement. Grandparents often want to spend time with their children and grandchildren but also want separate lives. Saying "no" to baby-sitting requests may be difficult but important in establishing limits and boundaries. Size and number of gifts are another decision that may be interpreted in various ways. Gifts can be signs of love and support or overindulgence and competition. Because interpretations vary from person to person and there are no universally accepted standards, clarity and sensitivity in communication becomes absolutely essential to avoid problems.

THE SENIOR PARENT

Life experiences, both positive and negative, bring maturity and wisdom to the senior individual. Seniors sometimes find that their peers are much more tolerant and accepting and less competitive than they were at younger ages. By this time, most people have experienced hardship and are less likely to judge and criticize the difficult circumstances of others.

Issues around children, grandchildren, and family in general are still at the forefront for seniors. In any continuing care facility, one will find evidence of this: The residents show pictures and talk of the activities of their children and grandchildren. Socially, they still present their identities as parents–evidence of how strong this self-concept continues over time. Seniors, especially older seniors, measure the love their children feel for them in time spent together and time devoted to their needs. Time becomes a more precious commodity. Seniors often are wrestling with estate planning, which also represents future expressions of themselves in the world. Their children's attitudes regarding the parents' possessions or plans for the parents' future care will make them feel either important or insignificant. Obviously, this is another important issue in the realm of self-esteem.

There is some evidence that the attachment of adult child to elderly parent may lead to protective behavior, as in the case of caregiving (Cicirelli, 1991). Obligatory feelings also may lead to these behaviors, but this motivation often prompts very different attitudes. Caregiving needs can be stressful for both the adult child and the elderly parent. Our society tends to give more support for the caregiver's "heroic efforts" and less understanding and empathy for the feelings of guilt, shame, and anxiety that those receiving such care sometimes experience. The elderly receiving such care can feel guilt and embarrassment about loss of privacy, being a burden, and helplessness that others might fail to recognize. Sensitivity and validation can support self-esteem at these times.

The affects on the elderly parent are less noted but can include financial and emotional distress and feelings of isolation and helplessness (Pillemer &

Suitor, 1991). Parents may not share these feelings because of shame, fear of becoming a burden, or fear of rejection and abandonment. Elderly parents often have a diminished peer network and increasingly must depend on family members, which can increase their feelings of vulnerability. This vulnerability may lead to a reduction in general trust (Hansson & Carpenter, 1994) and feelings of low self-esteem.

CONCLUSION

From the very beginning of parenthood until the very end of life, parenting plays a large role in a person's life. The impacts of the child, both positive and negative, are felt by the parent throughout his or her life. These influences are substantial and affect the parent's self-esteem.

As we have seen, perceptions of events and struggles in the parent-child relationship are relevant concerns. This relationship goes through many cycles and changes over the course of a lifetime. Core issues of authority and control, needs and values, and communication styles may shape the relationship differently in various developmental periods. Self-esteem is influenced in a variety of ways. Each parenting experience is different from another, because each parent and child is unique. Parents will enhance their own sense of self-worth if they learn how to evaluate their parenting in ways that encompass several factors, not solely the child's response.

You can explore a broader spectrum of "self as parent" by completing the activities that follow. As you learn more about the reciprocal nature of the parent-child relationship, you can develop better strategies for building the self-esteem of your child and yourself.

ACTIVITIES YOU CAN DO

ACTIVITY 8.1 SPLITTING IMAGES

Introduction: Given the multidimensional, multifaceted nature of self-esteem, an individual's general self-esteem and parental self-esteem can vary greatly. This activity helps you sort out the variances in attitude and behavior between the roles of adult-in-the-world and adult-as-parent.

Time required: 30 minutes

Participants: Any number: parents

Setting: Homework, classroom, group, or office

Materials: Paper and pen

Procedure: Draw a line down the center of a blank piece of paper. At the top of the first column write "In General." At the top of the second column write "As a Parent." Now write down answers to the following questions, using the words you have written at the top as the end of each question.

1. What are my feelings about how I communicate (in general and as a parent)?
2. How am I perceived?
3. How do I express my sense of humor?
4. How do I display my kindness, generosity, and tolerance?
5. How would I describe my attitudes and optimism?
6. How would I describe my effectiveness?
7. What are my feelings about the success of my relationships?
8. How do I measure the control I have in my life?
9. What are the physical and emotional demands of my life?
10. How do I feel about the future of the world?

Outcomes: Comparing and contrasting roles helps you to broaden your perspective and create paths for growth.

ACTIVITY 8.2 COMPASSIONATE LETTER TO A "FRIEND"

Introduction: The parenting process involves significant stress. Although social supports are important, sometimes they are unavailable or insufficient. It is important to learn skills of self-support that will help you get through the tough times.

Time required: 45 minutes

Participants: Any number: parents

Setting: Classroom, office, homework

Materials: Paper and pen

Procedure: Think of a parent you know who has experienced a lot of heartache over his or her children. Jot down some notes about events, disappointments, and hurts he or she has experienced. Using this list, write a compassionate, supportive, warm letter you believe the parent would find healing. After writing the letter, tuck it away someplace safe. The next time you are feeling hurt or discouraged as a parent, get the letter out and read it to comfort yourself.

Outcomes: Parents learn self-support techniques and develop empathy for other parents in the process.

ACTIVITY 8.3 FAMILY PORTRAIT

Introduction: Symbols and images can be powerful for expressing and describing who we are. In this activity, you will look at the family as a dynamic web of individuals who come together as a unit and form a unique system that affects each member.

Time required: 60 minutes

Participants: Family members

Setting: Retreat, camp, home, any comfortable setting with facilities to do artwork

Materials: Poster board, markers, crayons, construction paper, scissors, magazines, glue, stickers, and other art supplies

Procedure: Each family member creates a page of art representing him- or herself, including activities, interests, personality, and so on.

Each person then puts his or her name on a second sheet of paper and passes it around for other family members to create artwork representing the person's role and contribution to the family.

Finally, the family works together to create a third piece of art that represents the family as a whole, including interests, memories, and values.

Attach all of these pages to the poster-board. Keep this as a family treasure and get it out occasionally to remember your importance to one another and how your lives are intimately intertwined.

Outcomes: This exercise provides a concrete representation of how your family perceives itself and affirms individual family members as well as the family system.

ACTIVITY 8.4 THE ROAD NOT TAKEN

Introduction: Parents sometimes view themselves only in the parent role. Although it is important to feel the necessary responsibility of this role, it also is important to consider yourself as an individual. Otherwise you may find yourself "living through your children" or have trouble letting them live their own lives.

Time required: 20 minutes

Participants: Parents

Setting: Classroom, office, homework

Materials: Paper and pen

Procedure: Sometimes as parents, we have little control over our children's choices of behavior. Imagine, just for a moment, that you never had children or that your children are grown and live far away. Think about you, as an individual–your own accomplishments, talents, abilities, and dreams. Focus on how you want to be and those aspects that are under your control. Observe the differences in your self-perception as an individual only.

Resolve to pursue the development of your own separate identity and develop an action plan accordingly.

Outcomes: This activity tickles the untapped or neglected potential of the individual.

ACTIVITY 8.5 DIRECTED JOURNALING

Introduction: This activity invites you to do some serious reflection over the span of a month. Because it is drawn out it may facilitate the continuation of introspection and get you into the habit of regular journal writing.

Time required: 20 minutes daily for 30 days

Participants: Any number; parents

Setting: Homework

Materials: Journal, notebook or paper, and pen

Procedure: Use the following statements to get you started on reflection. Then write your thoughts and feelings down for 20 minutes. When you finish, read what you have written and appreciate the value of getting to know yourself better.

1. One characteristic I really enjoy about my child is ...
2. One characteristic I am pleased I developed as a child is ...
3. I remember a time that I made a mistake as a parent. Next time I will ...
4. I have decided to look for special, peaceful moments with my child. My ideas of where to look are ...
5. I want to explore how my own voice tone and that of my child affect our feelings. What I am aware of in this regard is ...
6. I know I have some regrets in my parenting role. I will release them by ...
7. I know I have some strengths in my parenting role. They are ...
8. This is something from my childhood I want to share with my child ...

9. Today I will reflect on my general tastes and preferences. They are ...

10. Today I will reflect on the general tastes and preferences of members of my family. They are ...

11. To feel a sense of satisfaction, I need ...

12. This is how I contribute to the world ...

13. Probably most parents experience ...

14. I want to be remembered as someone who ...

15. For friends, I prefer people who ...

16. For a general life mentor I would choose (*fill-in*) because ...

17. Next year I hope ...

18. Tomorrow I hope ...

19. What I have learned about worry is ...

20. What I have learned about joy is ...

21. What I hope for my child is ...

22. What I believe my child hopes for me is ...

23. I trust my child to ...

24. I trust myself to ...

25. In my life I am looking forward to ...

26. The way I deal with the things I can't control is ...

27. The way I deal with the things I can control is ...

28. What I know about love is ...

29. These are the types of special events I enjoy ...

30. I hope that in my lifetime I ...

Outcomes: Participants encounter and appreciate more aspects of their preferences and values.

ACTIVITY 8.6 MY LIFE AS A COMIC

Introduction: Many newspaper comic strips are based on humorous and trying experiences in family life. They owe their success to their universal appeal. This exercise will help you normalize your parenting experiences and dilemmas, explore the humor and universality of those situations, and gain perspective in sharing similar personal experiences. In addition to sharing experiences and observations, you will gain from hearing about others' difficulties and solutions that worked for them.

Time required: 30 minutes minimum, depends on the size of the group

Participants: 6 to 8 participants

Setting: Retreat, meeting room, any group meeting place that is quiet, private, and conducive to sharing

Materials: A collection of newspaper clippings of family comics dealing with a wide range of parenting issues; a basket or dish in which to place them

Procedure: As the basket of comics is passed around, choose one from the container. Take turns reading your comics. Now share a personal story evoked by the comic or some personal observations about the message of the comic.

Outcomes: Participants can share observations, experiences, and humor with other parents. This helps to support the parenting role and provides an opportunity to gain perspective on universal themes.

ACTIVITY 8.7 TAKING INVENTORY AND MOVING FORWARD

Introduction: This exercise is especially helpful for parents with unique concerns (exceptional children, minority issues, adoption, social skills problems, economic issues, single parenting, etc.), although any parent can benefit from it. The activity also can help parents who feel frustrated or stuck, and those having trouble sorting out what direction to take in their parenting process.

People tend to feel their strongest motivation based on their core beliefs and values. This exercise will help parents to set directives for themselves that they are likely to carry out.

Time required: 60 minutes

Participants: Any number of parents; best done alone or with your parenting partner

Setting: Any quitc, private setting

Materials: Paper and pen or pencil

Procedure: The first part of this exercise is an inventory. Answer these four questions. The answers can take the form of a narrative essay, a simple list, or any other form.

1. What are my unique circumstances as a person and a parent, and how do they affect my self-esteem?

2. What are my specific parenting problems, and how do they affect my self-esteem?

3. Which affects my self-esteem more: my child's responses to my decisions or my beliefs about the need for my decisions? Do I self-support unpopular decisions I feel need to be made?

4. What are my unique resources as a parent (e.g., insight, creativity, personality traits, extended family, spirituality)?

Next, turn the sheet of paper over to the back side. Divide the paper into one narrow column and two wide columns. In the first column, list your most firmly held *value* and *beliefs* (e.g., honesty, generosity, and hard work).

Title the second column, "How I have shown these as a parent." Note that you are not measuring the result, only the behaviors of demonstrating these values and beliefs.

Title the third column, "How I will act on these as a parent."

Now begin to carry these plans out immediately and to pursue them because you believe in them–regardless of apparent outcomes. Sometimes outcomes are not immediate.

Outcomes: This exercise helps participants to ground themselves in their values and beliefs and to develop consequent action plans.

REFERENCES

Ablon, J. (1988). *Living with difference: Families with dwarf children.* New York: Praeger.

Ambert, A.-M. (1992). *The effect of children on parents.* New York: Haworth.

Arendell, T. (1997). Divorce and remarriage. In T. Arendell (Ed.), *Contemporary parenting: Challenges and issues* (pp. 154-195). Thousand Oaks, CA: Sage.

Belsky, J. (1990). Children and marriage. In J. Fincham & T. Bradbury (Eds.), *The psychology of marriage* (pp. 172-200). New York: Guilford.

Booth, A., & Dun, J. (Editors). (1994). *Stepfamilies: Who benefits? Who does not?* Hillsdale, NJ: Erlbaum.

Bowlby, J. (1979). *The making and breaking of affectional bonds.* London: Tavistock.

Boxer, A. M., Cook, J. A., & Herdt, G. (1991). Double jeopardy: Identity transitions and parent-child relations among gay and lesbian youth. In K. Pillemer & K. McCartney(Eds.), *Parent-child relations throughout life* (pp. 59-92). Hillsdale, NJ: Erlbaum.

Braver, S. L., Wolchik, S. A., Sandler, I. N., & Sheets, V. L. (1993). A social exchange model of nonresidential parent involvement. In C. E. Depner & J. H. Bray (Eds.), *Nonresidential parenting: New vistas in family living* (pp. 87-108). Thousand Oaks, CA: Sage.

Briggs, D. D. (1975). *Your child's self-esteem.* Garden City, NY: Doubleday.

Bugental, D. B., & Shennum, W. A. (1984). "Difficult" children as elicitors and targets of adult communication patterns: An attributional-behavioral transactional analysis. *Monographs of the Society for Research in Child Development, 49*(1), 205.

Cardenas, J. A., & Zamora, G. (1980). The early education of minority children. In M. D. Fantini & R. Cardenas (Eds.), *Parenting in a multicultural society* (pp. 187-206). New York: Longman.

Casey, R. J., & Fuller, L. L. (1994). Maternal regulation of children's emotions. *Journal of Nonverbal Behavior, 18*(1), 57-89.

Chapman, S. F. (1991). Attachment and adolescent adjustment to parental remarriage. *Family Relations, 40,* 232-237.

Cicirelli, V. (1991). Attachment theory in old age: Protection of the attachment figure. In K. Pillemer & K. McCartney (Eds.), *Parent-child relations throughout life* (pp. 25-42). Hillsdale, NJ: Erlbaum.

Cohler, B. J., & Boxer, A. M. (1984). Settling into the world: Person, time, and context. In D. Offer & M. Sabshin (Eds.), *Normality and the life cycle* (pp. 145-203). New York: Basic Books.

Donley, M. G. (1993). Attachment and the emotional unit. *Family Process, 32,* 3-20.

Erikson, E. H., & Erikson, J. M. (1997). *The life cycle completed* (2nd ed.). New York: Norton.

Feeney, J. A., & Noller, P. (1990). Attachment style as a predictor of adult romantic relationships. *Journal of Personality and Social Psychology 58*, 281-291.

Fortier, L. M., & Wanlass, R. L. (1984). Family crisis following the diagnosis of a handicapped child. *Family Relations, 33,* 13-24.

Fraiberg, S. (1974).Blind infants and their mothers: An examination of the sign system. In M. Lewis & L. A. Rosenblum (Eds.), *The effect of the infant on its caregiver* (pp. 215-232). New York: Wiley.

Ge, X., Conger, R. D., Lorenz, F. O., Shanahan, M., & Elder, G. H. (1995). Mutual influences in parent and adolescent psychological distress. *Developmental Psychology, 31*(3), 406-419.

Gubman, G., & Tessler, R. (1987). The impact of mental illness on families. *Journal of Family Issues, 8,* 226-245.

Hansson, R. O., & Carpenter, B. N. (1994). *Relationships in old age: Coping with the challenge of transition.* New York: Guilford.

Johnston, J. R. (1993). Children of divorce who refuse visitation. In C. E. Depner & J. H. Bray (Eds.), *Nonresidential parenting: New vistas in family living* (pp. 109-135). Thousand Oaks, CA: Sage.

Kahlbaugh, P. E., & Haviland, J. M. (1994). Nonverbal communication between parents and adolescents: A study of approach and avoidance behaviors. *Journal of Nonverbal Behavior, 18*(1), 91-113.

Katz, L. (1986). Parental stress and factors for success in older-child adoption. *Child Welfare, 65*(6), 569-578.

Kaye, J. (1990). Acknowledgment or rejection of differences. In D. M. Brodzinsky & M. D. Schechter (Eds.), *The psychology of adoption* (pp. 121-143). New York: Oxford University Press.

Langlois, J. H., Ritter, J. M., Casey, R. J., & Sawin, D. B. (1995). Infant attractiveness predicts maternal behaviors and attitudes. *Developmental Psychology, 31*(3), 464-472.

Nolen-Hoeksema, S., Wolfson, A., Mumme, D., & Guskin, K. (1995). Helplessness in children of depressed and nondepressed mothers. *Developmental Psychology, 31*(3), 377-387.

Offer, D., & Sabshin, M. (1984). *Normality and the life cycle.* New York: Basic Books.

Parry, L. (1983). *Growing through grief: A parent's perspective on adopting older children.* New York: New York State Citizens' Coalition for Children.

Pillemer, K., & Suitor, J. J. (1991). Relationships with children and distress in the elderly. In K. Pillemer & K. McCartney (Eds.), *Parent-child relations throughout life* (pp. 163-178). Hillsdale, NJ: Erlbaum.

Pistole, M. C. (1994). Adult attachment styles: Some thoughts on closeness-distance struggles. *Family Process, 33,* 147-159.

Richman, M. D., & Davidson, R. J. (1994). Personality and behavior in parents of temperamentally inhibited and uninhibited children. *Developmental Psychology, 30*(3), 346-354.

Rosenfarb, I. S., Becker, J., & Khan, A. (1994). Perceptions of parental and peer attachments by women with mood disorders. *Journal of Abnormal Psychology, 103*(4), 637-644.

Rubin, K., & Asendorph, J. (1993). *Social withdrawal, inhibition, and shyness in children.* Hillsdale, NJ: Erlbaum.

Schell, G. C. (1981). The young handicapped child: A family perspective. *Topics in Early Childhood Special Education, 1*, 21-27.

Schneider, P. (1983). Self-esteem of parents of disturbed children and the self-esteem of their children. In J. E. Mack & S. L. Albon (Eds.), *The development and sustenance of self-esteem in childhood* (pp. 270-284). New York: International Universities Press.

Seifer, R., Schiller, M., Resnick, S., Riordan, K., & Sameroff, A. J. (1996). Attachment, maternal sensitivity, and infant temperament during the first year of life. *Developmental Psychology, 32*(1), 12-25.

Silver, E. J., Bauman, L. J., & Ireys, H. T. (1995). Relationships of self-esteem and efficacy to psychological distress in mothers of children with chronic physical illnesses. *Health Psychology, 14*(4), 325-332.

Taylor, R. L. (1997). Who's parenting? Trends and patterns. In T. Arendell (Ed.), *Contemporary parenting: Challenges and issues* (pp. 68-91). Thousand Oaks, CA: Sage.

van den Boom, D. C., & Holksma, J. B. (1994). The effect of infant irritability on mother-infant interaction: A growth-curve analysis. *Developmental Psychology, 30*(4), 581-590.

Whitbourne, S. K. (1986). *The me I know: A study of adult identity.* New York: Springer-Verlag.

Yawkey, T. D., & Cornelius, G. M. (Editors). (1990). *The single-parent family.* Lancaster, PA: Technomic.

Chapter 9

TRANSITIONS AND SELF-ESTEEM

C. Jesse Carlock

Transitions are inevitable in today's rapidly changing culture. Our ability to manage these transitions is inextricably related to our attitudes about ourselves. The higher our self-esteem, the better we are able to cope with changes of all types. The more positive our self-esteem, the more likely we are to take risks and initiate transitions that result in self-expansion and self-improvement, and the more likely we are to adequately cope with the inevitable rhythms of change. With positive self-esteem we can move from looking at change as an unwelcome intruder to seeing it as a welcome guest; for with change comes not only loss but opportunity for growth.

THE RELATIONSHIP OF SELF-ESTEEM TO TRANSITIONS

Some changes result in diminished choice. People with high self-esteem tend to be more flexible and better able to shift sources of esteem in response to diminished choice. Their self-esteem does not rest so heavily on external factors. Take, for example, a tennis professional whose self-esteem is based on personally valued psychological traits. Faced with an accident or illness that renders her unable to play tennis, she will be able to adjust and recoup her high self-esteem. If people are confident, they are able to weather changes and make necessary adjustments—unless those changes are multiple, occur within a short time span, or disrupt core concepts on which their self-concept has been built. Such conditions may result in a temporary disruption in self-esteem. Nonetheless, the higher our self-esteem, the more resilient we are.

People with low self-esteem, on the other hand, face more precarious transitions. Often such individuals unconsciously precipitate negative changes or crises. For example, a woman with low self-esteem might allow a financially irresponsible man to move in with her and destroy her financial stability. People with low self-esteem also tend to hold themselves responsible for negative changes over which they have no control. For example, a man with low self-esteem might feel like a failure if he is laid off from work—even if the lay-off is related to an economic downturn. Unless intervention occurs, his self-esteem may plummet. People with low or unstable self-esteem lack the resources (internal or external) and self-confidence necessary for negotiating transitions adequately.

The Inevitability of Change

While ours is an age of rapid change, change always has been a part of human existence. Throughout history, we can see broad swings in the nation's economic, social, and political climate that reverberated down to the level of every individual. Some changes occur in big swings and with breathtaking speed: for example, high inflation, high unemployment, fast-moving technological changes, or striking political changes like the fall of the Berlin Wall.

Yet, many people do not expect change. They expect the world to remain the same, that life will always run smoothly. These people perceive natural ups and downs as major catastrophes. They don't anticipate the downs (mistakes, accidents, losses, illnesses) and accept them as a part of life, so they are less able to roll with the punches—less able to cope. People with low self-esteem tend to take too much responsibility for some changes and not enough for others. They also tend to turn everything into life-or-death matters: saying, for example, "I'll just die if we have to move."

We are affected not only by our own actions and attitudes but also by external forces. Like dominoes toppling, changes at higher levels reverberate to the lowest levels of system (see chapter 10). On the other hand, internally generated changes have far less dramatic effects on higher levels (see Figure 9.1). Effects of individual changes on higher levels of a system rapidly diminish, except in rare circumstances in which an individual's influence is far-reaching.

We must continually deal with situations over which we have little control. The stress of change, internal pressures, and restricted coping capacities often combine to undermine our adaptive functioning. But most people can learn to

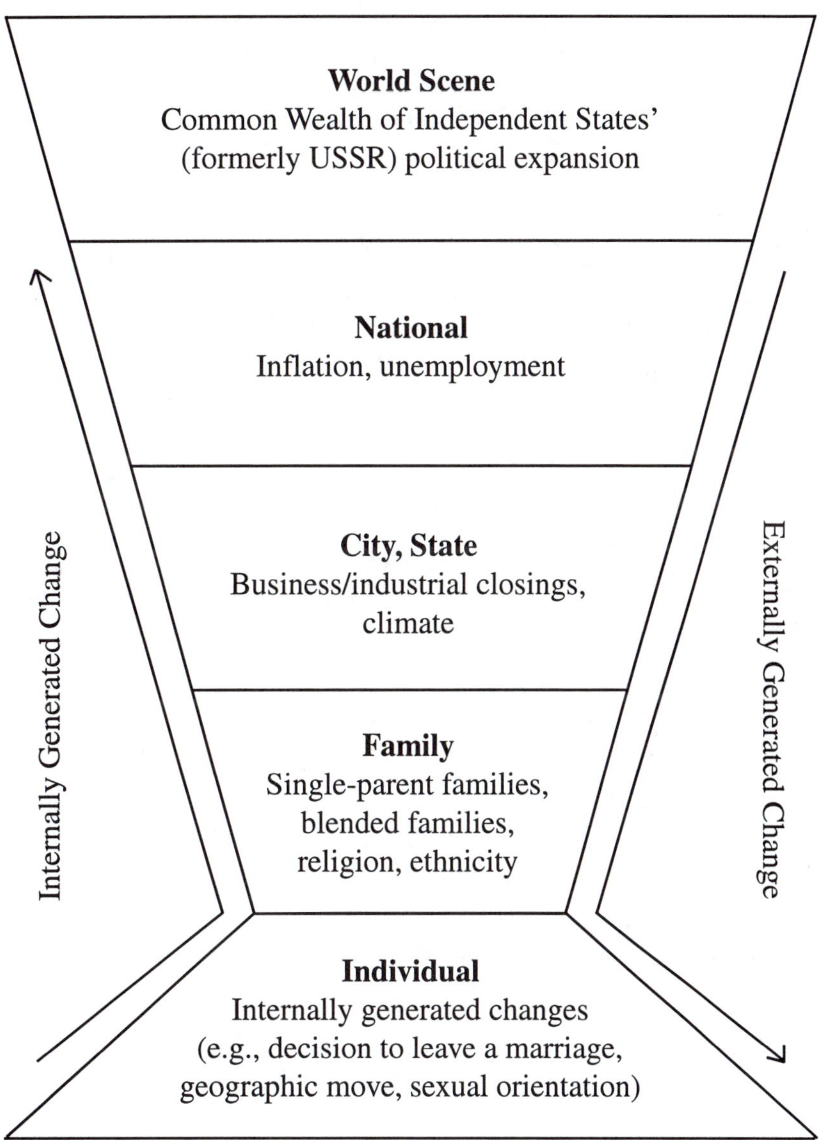

Figure 9.1. Effects of internal and external change.

be strong and resilient, if they are given the proper skills early in life. Childhood is the best time to start teaching these skills.

When children learn that change is a natural part of life and develop positive attitudes toward change early in life, they have an easier time adjusting to change. Skills for coping with change can and should be introduced at early ages. With enough support, children can learn to adjust to change without being overwhelmed.

Some people lack the resilience that comes from having solid coping skills. This is evidenced in a variety of ways: depression, anxiety, behavioral problems, psychosomatic complaints, and addictions, to name just a few. Such problems are signs of inadequate coping; they signal that a person's coping system has been overwhelmed by an inordinate amount of stress. People need more effective coping strategies to preserve their esteem through the inevitable ups and downs of life.

Self-Parts and Transitions

All of us have a number of different personality parts or ego states that we activate in response to the demands of a situation. When I'm in urban New Jersey, for example, I activate my "aggressive driver part." In this context, I value my ability to be aggressive. By focusing on the positive value of each personal trait, we can use our resources to manage life transitions.

Each part of us can be a resource. Even our worst flaws have applications that are positive or can be transformed into resources, with modifications. For example, the energy of a fiery temper can be channeled into a charismatic style of leadership. There are valuable ingredients in all of our parts. These aspects are easier to see and accept in parts that are favored and acceptable to others. We may have to search out the positive aspects of our less acceptable parts. These parts inevitably get in the way in transitions if they are not modified, transformed, or used in appropriate contexts. For example, if one of my self-parts is passive and unintrusive, it may inhibit my ability to build a resource network if I must make a geographic move.

Whenever we face a transition, we must assess what resources we need to deal with it and develop a plan to use our internal resources and help from others to meet the demands of the new situation. As in all transitions, we also must find ways to deal with the myriad of feelings that will emerge.

Types of Transitions

Transitions are turning points in life that are either internally generated or externally induced. They involve passing from one condition, stage, or place to another and have within them dimensions of differentness. Transitions mark points of growth for individuals and larger systems (e.g., families or organizations). They require people to reorganize their way of experiencing and perceiving the world (Parkes, 1971).

Transitions are times of incredible possibilities: Even in changes that might be viewed as negative, positive outcomes can occur, as the following case study reveals:

> Rebecca had a very stressful job. While she was going through a divorce, she found that she had to lower some of her expectations of herself at work. She could not continue business as usual. Her tendency to take too much responsibility and her self-demanding attitude had been her hallmarks at work. The stress of the divorce forced her to reduce her pace. She would not have risked this voluntarily but, to her amazement, she was not called on the carpet by her supervisors. In fact, she found herself producing almost as much work as she ever had.

Transitions can be bittersweet. Sometimes the road gets bumpy and rocky; at those times we need to create our own benches to sit down, rest, and absorb our progress. Other times the road seems so dark we almost believe we will never see the light again. At those times we must remember this: As painful as transitions can be, they are opportunities for growth. We have all heard someone in pain say something like this: "All right, already! I've had enough opportunities for growth for now. Give me a rest!" Or, "They say God only gives people as much as they can handle. I hope He knows I'm at my limit!" Humor is an indispensable release valve when we're dealing with transitions.

As Satir (1987) pointed out, there are two types of internal transitions: automatic and conscious. *Automatic change* is a natural part of living: Our hair and fingernails grow; our skin ages, wrinkles, and begins to sag. *Conscious change* involves an effort to develop a different outcome. Conscious change is always possible, given the right attitude, willingness, hope, timing, and circumstances. When she worked with people, Satir often planted this presupposition: "It isn't a question of *will* you change. It's a question of *when*."

According to Satir (1987), conscious change is fueled by a clear picture of what you want, *not by what you don't want*. In order for people to get in touch with what they want, they must identify the impediments to realizing those wants—impediments such as these:

I can't have that.

This is too much to ask for.

Girls can't do that.

Each turning point in the life journey is a landmark of possibilities—a time of loss and a time of beginnings. If we view the next leg of our journey negatively or see only the losses—thinking, for example, "Old age means I'm useless" or, "Starting college means I have to leave my friends"—our spirits will wither and we will miss the excitement, challenges, and rewards of the new period. But if we believe that each new phase of life presents both losses and opportunities, we will find creative ways to learn and get all we can from life.

Some circumstances fall outside our control and precipitate change: These include loss of a partner, family member, or pet through death or divorce, loss of a job due to recession, hereditary medical problems, or forced retirement. Such transitions are hard on our self-esteem. They put us in touch with our powerlessness, our utter vulnerability. But we can cushion the jolt of such transitions by taking preventive measures when things are going well: Such measures include doing adequate financial planning, building a good support network, developing leisure-time interests, and maintaining a program of exercise and good nutrition. We always have some control. Even when the transition is not self-chosen, we can take control and choose how we will handle the change. However, if a no-choice/unplanned transition occurs during an off-time (for example, the death of a parent early in life) when other facets of our lives are shaken, the repercussions may be magnified and high self-esteem may be more difficult to maintain.

Schlossberg (1989) described another type of transition: the "sleeper transition." Such a transition does not have a clear beginning and creeps up on us over time: For example, a health problem might develop slowly or a job may become increasingly dissatisfying. When we find identifying clear precipitants more difficult, we tend to blame ourselves, and our ability to mobilize coping resources often is compromised.

Phases of Transitions

According to Keleman (1979), each transition involves three distinct phases: *endings* (something ends or changes in life), *middle ground* (a time of disorganization), and beginnings or *new formations* (a time for trying out new behaviors). These phases appear in all transitions and provide a common base of experience.

Before the endings phase is the state of *status quo*. According to Satir (1987), at this time individuals hold a set of expectations and validations on which they can count. For example, "On Tuesdays, I drive 15 minutes to work, see several clients, and meet my women's group." These expectations are clear and repeatedly reinforced. As they are reinforced, they gain power. If, for some reason, I am not able to drive, this familiar pattern is disrupted. If I become permanently unable to drive (for example, due to a visual disability), the disruption will be even greater and my reaction will be more severe.

Satir (1987) explained that we grow to believe the familiar way is the only way for us to be; we then connect these expectations with our survival. According to Satir, "changing is like a whole new birth; it is hard." If a young man is continually told, "You're no good—just like your father. You'll never amount to anything," making the shift to a new identity is no easy task. Most change is initiated in response to threat (Satir, 1987). Few of us move voluntarily toward change with greater comfort as a motivator, although this kind of proactive stance to change can be learned.

Endings. Endings involve leaving behind a particular way of doing things. An ending is an indication that some part of the person, some way of being, some circumstance has outlived its usefulness. It usually involves the introduction of a foreign element or an intervention (Satir, 1987). Given that people are continually dealing with endings, Bridges (1980) and Scott and Jaffe (1989) contended that a person's first response to an ending is often minimizing, denying, ignoring, or catastrophizing. This phase is a time of unbounding, withdrawing, and self-collecting, during which a person feels great conflict between staying and going. Sickness is a clue that an ending is occurring: for example, headaches, intestinal problems, or even heart attacks. Brammer (1991) said that people often are aware of constriction (i.e., feeling boxed in, trapped, or squeezed). The more energy we have invested in a pattern, the more an ending of that pattern poses a threat to our identity. Our expectations are disrupted, our security is threatened, and we feel awkward and out of control (Scott & Jaffe, 1989). According to Keleman (1979), in order to survive endings, we must confront situations in a state of emerging helplessness and resist falling back on automatic, counter-productive (yet comfortingly familiar) responses. For example, a person attempting to let go of a pattern of over-work may become anxious with new blocks of free time and impulsively refill the time with work.

Bridges (1980) outlined four different aspects of endings: disengagement, disidentification, disenchantment, and disorientation, describing them as follows:

> **Disengagement** involves separating ourselves from the context in which we have known ourselves; our identity is shaken. For example, a newly divorced, middle-aged woman might move from the home she shared with her husband for 30 years.
>
> **Disidentification** involves doing away with the outward signs of the former identity. Continuing the previous example, the divorcee might buy new furniture and change her hairstyle and wardrobe.
>
> Often people make changes but continue to identify with their former self-images. In such cases, disidentification has not been completed. It takes some time for our self-perceptions to catch up with our

changes in behavior. The divorced woman described above may have a difficult time viewing herself as a free agent, able to make a wide range of choices now that she does not have to consider the impact on her spouse.

Disenchantment involves the discovery that what we believed and expected are no longer real. We discover that a significant part of our expectation was fantasy. Disenchantment also is a sign that we are entering a transition. For example, a growing feeling of dissatisfaction with one's job usually precedes a job change or career move and may increase through the actual ending as disengagement occurs.

Disorientation results when our reality—our way of orienting ourselves—has been shaken. Confusion, emptiness, and resulting fears abound. Our senses of space and time are altered. For example, parents whose son leaves for college might find themselves wandering into his room or missing the sounds him bounding up the stairs.

We must pass through each of these four phases before the ending is complete. Incomplete endings may negatively affect our self-esteem.

Individual growth can become arrested between endings and the middle ground. A person may refuse to go on when something ends, because giving up ritualized patterns can feel like death itself. New interactions are inhibited, new learnings are avoided, and the growth process is slowed down, eventually leading to distress. An example would be a man who is laid-off from a corporation and then shuts down his feelings, lays around idly, and is unable to mobilize, restructure his career goals, and productively organize his free time.

Middle Ground. The middle ground, according to Keleman (1979), is a time of chaos, a period of being unformed, of feeling lost or overwhelmed. It's easy to see why we often avoid this phase. A flood of emotion occurs, and what evolves seems crazy, illogical, irrational. The system has been shaken and a state of confusion reverberates throughout our lives. Satir (1979) compared the process of moving through this disequilibrium to driving through fog. It is a scary process because we cannot see very far ahead; we must trust ourselves and use whatever data we have available to negotiate the passage, waiting for the fog to lift.

According to Bridges (1980), in ancient societies people learned to call on spirit guides to help light the way through this phase. This is the time when people "hang hats on" (project onto) others. Strong, often unjustified emotional reactions appear. Images and feelings dominate. People project their familiarity from the past onto the present (Satir, 1981). If a person is in this chaos period and additional changes are introduced, the chaos period will be prolonged and accommodation to the change is likely to be slower and less reliable.

Safety and trust are crucial in this stage. Therapists and other helping professionals can help provide this safety by taking charge of the process, setting boundaries that prohibit harmful interactions, responding honestly and congruently, and looking ahead to anticipate needs (Satir, 1987). Satir emphasized that this chaos period is necessary, that no real change can happen until chaos appears. Superficial changes do not stick. Many therapists become frightened when clients begin to experience this chaos. Some may be tempted to medicate the client to relieve the chaos (or to relieve their own anxiety). This should be avoided if clinically possible.

Some clients will self-medicate in this phase with alcohol, drugs, food, other substances, or destructive behaviors. According to Satir (1987), the change agent (the therapist) holds total responsibility for the process in this phase. She emphasized that during the chaos stage the change agent must be:

- in control of the process (creating safety and trust);
- devoid of judgment;
- very creative;
- observant by the second; and
- straight-talking, congruent, and loving.

Therapists must avoid getting caught up in the chaos, which would render them ineffective. The more they are flexible and unbiased, the more effective they will be guiding their clients.

Satir (1987) warned that when the going gets tough in the chaos period, people often want to retreat to the familiar. Through the therapist's centeredness—which is conveyed through eyes, touch, and tone of voice—clients can be helped to move forward instead of back to what is familiar. No lasting change can occur until the desire to "go back" is acknowledged and the chaos is passed.

A number of survival skills can help us negotiate this phase. The mature person learns to pause, wait, and inhibit impulsiveness. Many people find getting away and being alone for awhile is helpful in this phase, so they can attend to their inner selves (Bridges, 1980). At other times, they may need encouragement from friends to stay with the experience. It is an in-between time—a time of discovering how we want to live, the needs we want to satisfy, how we want to satisfy those needs, and how we want to be in the world. It is a time of grasping certain truths about ourselves. Bridges (1980) described this period as a time of gestation, when a new self is growing. We must learn to surrender to the emptiness, which requires a great deal of courage. Many people run away or try to fill it up with social activities, business, precipitous relationships, and other diversions. But the tasks involved in a sturdy reconstruction cannot be completed until this chaos period is acknowledged.

Satir (1981) called the chaos period a time of active patience (waiting, moving, but not always knowing what we are doing), a time when we must be able to say and think what we feel *and be heard*. This middle ground is a time of formlessness, a primal experience, a state of pure energy from which every new beginning develops (Bridges, 1980). Many people reevaluate their lives during the chaos state, reworking their priorities and changing their life goals and course.

But, according to Satir (1987), we cannot move on until we have enough experience with the new beginning. We must form a clear picture of the desired change and try on that behavior, so our bodies have the experience of behaving differently, letting new words pass through our mouths, and so on. Identifying the body cues that go along with both the old experience and the new behavior will help facilitate the process of change. All of this, Satir (1987) explained, gives us an experience in rewiring. Heightened awareness facilitates the change process.

New Formations. This is a period of trying out new behaviors and reinforcing changes. Repetition and a symbol of the desired change can help us at this stage. At this stage of integration and practice, we are better able to handle the introduction of additional change, unless the changes are multiple. As a new status quo is achieved, further changes are more easily tolerated.

During this period of new formations, we experience spurts of outgrowth; now a new birthing begins. We make commitments to truths learned about ourselves. An internal alignment occurs that allows us to get in touch with our deep wants and become amazingly motivated, even overcoming difficult obstacles (Bridges, 1980). This is a time of getting ourselves ready to do something, gathering information, focusing our inner resources, mobilizing our images, even changing our muscular patterns to form another shape (Keleman, 1979).

Often through adult transitions, people begin anew, making dramatic changes in their lives (Bridges, 1980). Gandhi, Lincoln, F. D. Roosevelt, and Walt Whitman are a few famous figures who turned their lives around through adult transitions. Through transitions many people begin to make their lives their own, beginning a path to their own dreams rather than rebelling against or living out someone else's. The fertile ground turned during a transition provides a more nurturing environment for dormant seeds to grow. This growth can enhance our self-esteem if we acknowledge to ourselves and to others the process of that growth. Artwork, movement, and other expressive forms can help us to fully take in our growing experience.

Depending on how central or how peripheral the change is, movement through this cycle can be rapid or gradual. It is critical that we be willing to look at our lives and our patterns, to learn how we prevent ourselves from achieving complete endings. Keleman (1979) stressed that in order to end something, we must see how we are immersed in a particular pattern. Many endings involve a change of form rather than a total obliteration of connections. According to Keleman (1979), unbounding, unforming, and destructuring are all parts of the inescapable rhythms of life. He pointed out that to experience living as a process is to see the possibility for living and forming one's life, not as a slave or victim but as a pioneer.

The psychological journey cannot be ignored as we move from point A to point B (Satir, 1981). For example, with the addition of a new baby, a family cannot proceed with business as usual—though many people try. The family must make room for the new person, physically and emotionally. Members must learn to deal with the inevitable losses and gains that result from such an addition and to let their feelings surface—their anger or jealousy, their wish to be taken care of, whatever feelings arise—without expecting anyone else to do something about those feelings (Satir, 1981).

Time is not the relevant factor in change; awareness is. According to Satir (1981), time only provides the opportunity.

Approaching a desired change with joy and exhilaration means repeated cycling through the phases of change until we achieve a high comfort level and our anxiety is diminished. As we go through even more cycles, we may learn to look forward to change and welcome it with excitement and ease.

NEGOTIATING TRANSITIONS

Identify Real Need

In order to negotiate transitions well, we must learn to be aware of what we really need to change. Many people, when they are feeling discontented, are prone to change external aspects of their lives—jobs, geographic location, marital partners—when their *internal life* might be a more fitting focus of change. People who repeatedly make external changes are thinking, "There must be a place where life will be better." Their focus is outside themselves rather than on their communication patterns (Satir, 1981), life patterns, or other internal patterns (see chapter 3).

Examine the Situation

Schlossberg (1989) emphasized evaluating a transition by asking a few questions. Is it good or bad in your eyes? How pervasively has the transition affected your life (your roles, relationships, routines, beliefs, and self-image)? Were you able to plan the transition? Is the timing good or bad? Can you exert control over some aspects of the transition? Can you draw upon past experiences to better cope with it? Is the change time-limited or enduring? Are you experiencing other transitions that complicate your ability to cope with this transition? By evaluating a transition we can, in those transitions that allow it, make choices about when to schedule a change and mobilize our internal and external resources to better manage the transition. Evaluating the context, nature, extent, and impact of the transition can help us be more patient and less demanding with ourselves, enabling us to ride the transition more easily.

Know Yourself

If you know yourself, you increase the number of coping strategies available (Schlossberg, 1989). What are your strengths (e.g., fighting spirit, resilience, perspective, humor, optimism, or persistence)?

If you are aware of what kinds of stresses are overwhelming or challenging you, you can learn and practice coping skills that can increase your ability to pace yourself and successfully negotiate these difficult situations. By logging stressful moments and examining your experiences (your behavior, cognition, and feelings), you may begin to see patterns. Identifying problematic patterns clears the way for change.

Identify Supports

Identify who in your life can give you emotional support, respect, and love (Schlossberg, 1989). Who is affirming? Who can provide tangible assistance and aid? Support people might include personal friends, family, hired help, institutions, or organizations. Having a wide range of support in all these areas increases your strength and lengthens your endurance (see chapter 4).

Recognize Common Transition Points

Transitions occur around characteristic developmental points, such as the first day of school, the growth of facial hair or breasts, the onset of menstruation, a first date, a first serious illness, marriage, childbirth, the loss of parents, retirement, and significant losses of all types.

Sometimes these transition points are marked by changes in behavior (e.g., driving for the first time), specific events (e.g., childbirth), or rituals (e.g., marriage). At other times they are marked by a less obvious internal shift that eventually shows itself in one's feelings and behavior (e.g., a search for spirituality, "coming out," a shift from giving to a "what about me?" attitude). Often these internal shifts are attempts to bring greater balance to one's personality or life (e.g., less focus on work and more on play, less focus on the intellect and more on the physical body). Developmental transitions can be both automatic and conscious. Some are inevitable changes we experience as we grow and age; others are clearly self-chosen.

Some people choose to see such transitions as times for character building; times when they can discover the depth of others' support, love, and caring; times of blossoming or balancing; or joyous rites of passage. But transitions often mark times of excruciatingly difficult value clashes. Sometimes these clashes can be resolved; sometimes we must learn to live with the disquiet. Transitions can be gut-wrenching when they involve losses of roles (as in retirement) or key relationships (as in death).

Although developmental transitions are natural and expected, they are not always welcomed. This is particularly true if the transition involves loss, constriction of normal functions, or sudden changes that disrupt daily rituals. If we are not prepared to master increasing demands (e.g., leaving home and assuming independent functioning or assuming the tasks of parenting), these transitions may be delayed or rocky.

Identify Your Attitude Toward Change

Another important factor in negotiating transitions is your attitude toward change. Those who resist change experience physical and psychological symptoms. Those who view change as an opportunity for growth and approach change actively fare better than those who experience change as helpless victims. Those who view change as a challenge thrive better in times of high stress (Scott & Jaffe, 1989). Our attitudes affect whether we can go with the new flow or try to keep the status quo (Satir, 1981). Trying to maintain the status quo when we are always changing is like trying to stay at the same level on a moving escalator (Satir, 1981).

Trying to change, on the other hand, can be as counterproductive as trying to stop it. Trying to change yourself or somebody else means interrupting what is already happening. We might say that people do not change; rather, more of them is made available. People simply discover more of themselves. In the process of uncovering ourselves, we create change.

Responses to change—to disruption—fall between two polarities:

overbounded |____|____|____|____| underbounded

Overbounded people are rigid and unyielding (Keleman, 1979) and resist change. Their energy is constricted and they do not allow their excitement to expand and grow. Such persons press life in and ward off the world, reaching out as little as possible. They have no springs to absorb the shock of inevitable change (Keleman, 1979).

Underbounded people, on the other hand, are victims, surrendering to every impulse. Their shapes are weak and toneless. Such persons let their process leak out; they erupt and expel life, vacillating and caving in. To be healthy, we must find a place in the middle, a place of firmness and centeredness, yet still flexible.

In Satir's (1981) view, transitions are never the problem—it is coping with the transitions that is the problem. We must learn to make room for the psychological journey. Those who are committed to growth and are effective managers of change see change as a challenge and opportunity, focus their attention on what they can control through the change process, and reach out for help and support (Scott & Jaffe, 1989).

Recognize Your Personal Filters

All of us approach change differently, based on the personal filters that affect how we experience the world. Such factors as personal history (losses, traumas, experience with change, how our family of origin coped with change), gender, ethnic background, and life phase affect our personal filters. For example, a man who suffered several unresolved major losses in childhood (such as early parental deaths or repeated abandonment) may approach losses in adulthood (such as a friend moving out of state) from a helpless, defeatist position. A man who had a more secure childhood might possess greater internal resources to approach such changes with a more positive attitude. He might be better able to process feelings of loss, reach out for support, and actively seek out ways to remain connected as opposed to sinking into depression.

But we can change our filters by examining our survival rules and challenging our conclusions. In the example above, the first man learned, "You can never count on anyone. People always leave you. No one cares about your feelings." So his survival rules might be, "Don't express your feelings. Don't ask for what you need." As he challenges these conclusions and rules, he can develop better coping strategies.

Discover a New Picture and Release the Old One

Our present situation consists of life as we know it (see Figure 9.2). Regardless of how uncomfortable it may be, at least it is familiar. When we decide to make a change, or when a change is forced upon us, the system is disrupted

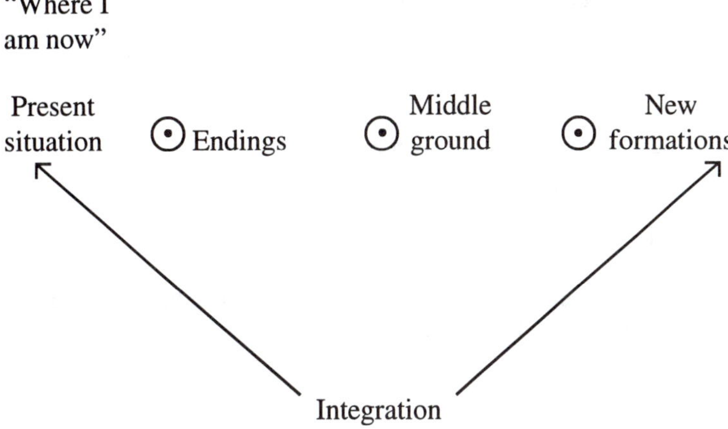

Figure 9.2 Phases of transition.

and we must make room for the feelings that go along with the inevitable endings that are to come (Satir, 1981). Even when something positive is added, the old picture is lost. Acknowledging our feelings in the various phases of a transition helps us to manage the shift. Other factors affect how we cope with change, including these:

- Our ability to accept that we are changing and moving
- Our willingness to meet strangers (people, places, and objects that are alien)
- Our ability to look forward and picture the ultimate integration of our new parts (which involves faith in the process of life)
- Our attitude toward risking, exploring, and discovering

Identify Coping Strategies

A variety of coping skills can help ease transitions. O'Grady (1992), Schlossberg (1989), and Scott and Jaffe (1989) identified these:

- Relaxation and other self-regulatory skills
- Seeking new information or advice from others
- Assertiveness

- Empowering beliefs, such as these:

  I can change.

  I can learn from this.

  Change is normal and natural.

  I can find a solution.

  The future will be better.

- Getting adequate rest (including sleep, relaxation, and meditation time)
- Exercising
- Understanding the process and phases of transitions so you have a kind of map to use in experiencing and viewing your change process
- Rehearsing the transition and using your imagination to practice more effective behaviors
- Creating a ritual to mark the transition
- Redefining your priorities
- Making positive comparisons between your situation and the situations of others
- Relabeling or redefining the transition (for example, amplifying the good parts of the transition and downplaying the negative effects)
- Using humor to distance yourself and gain perspective or a sense of control
- Relying on faith
- Developing avenues for release, such as play, sports, reading, counseling and support groups, hobbies, and the like
- Eating a balanced diet

Parts and Transitions

If we experience difficulty negotiating a transition, it often is helpful to identify the various parts of ourselves that are touched by or involved in the change. Let's look at Larry's case for an example:

> Larry, aged 56, had become dissatisfied with his marriage. He was involved in an affair with a woman who was stimulating in a variety of ways: sexually, emotionally, and intellectually. He believed he had only two choices: He could end the affair—but he found the relationship so satisfying he couldn't bring himself to end it and recommit to his wife—or he could surface his feelings and end his relationship with his wife. He was in a dilemma.
>
> As Larry looked back at his marriage, he realized he had experienced reservations about the relationship from the start. He had wanted to call the wedding off, but he couldn't bring himself to disappoint and hurt his wife-to-be. Besides, Larry's wife was close to his family, and he had believed they would be angry with him—and perhaps reject him—if he broke off the relationship.
>
> Larry had continued for years in a marriage he saw as distant and void of passion. He saw no hope for the marriage and did not even want to try to strengthen it. So he remained stuck, with one foot in the marriage and one foot out.

What parts of Larry seem to be at work here? For example:

Caring	Rebel	Passionate
"Good Boy"	Dutiful	Selfish
Self-Sacrificing	Intellectual	Angry
Lonely	Deceitful	Sad

What rules and introjects seem to be at play? For example:

"Your needs don't count."

"You are responsible for others' feelings."

"Commitments should not be broken."

Once you've identified the parts of yourself involved in a transition, you can begin to give these parts more voice; identify and explore the parts in conflict—those that are holding back and those charging forward; identify values, rules, and introjects; evaluate and revise these as necessary; and work toward greater harmony and balance among the parts. Once you have done this, you may find your choices are clearer, although the decision will probably not be any less painful. Each option involves loss and gain.

FACTORS INFLUENCING ADAPTATION TO CHANGE

Schlossberg and Kent (1979), and later Schlossberg (1989), identified a number of factors that influence an individual's adaptation to change, including these:

- The significance of the transition
- Whether the source is internally based or externally induced
- Whether the stress occurs on-time or off-time (This is an application of Neugarten's (1976) "social clock" principle, which posits that there are social penalties for blooming early or blooming late. For example, it is less stressful to lose a job at 25 than to lose one at 50; and it is more stressful for a parent to die at 30 when a child's needs are much greater
- Whether the transition is perceived as essentially positive (job promotion) or negative (death of spouse)
- Whether the transition necessitates a permanent or a temporary change (a permanent disability as opposed to a temporary handicap due to broken bone)

Brammer (1991) outlined several factors that affect the length and severity of your responses to transitions:

- The meaning you attach to the transition
- The degree to which you allow yourself to experience and express the feelings that bubble up throughout the transition
- The extent of your previous experiences with transitions and your ability to learn from these
- The strength of your social support system (Satir [1981] noted that one's pattern of communicating is crucial as well.)
- The degree to which you are a hardy "coper" (Scott and Jaffe [1989] discussed this also.)
- The extent to which you know your own values, have goals and pursue them, feel empowered, and feel a sense of control
- Your ability to view change as one of life's challenges

Schlossberg (1989) added other factors that affect the length and severity of a transition:

- The significance of the transition to you
- Whether the transition results in a change in roles; relationships; routines; and your beliefs about yourself, others, and the world

Major transitions affects us in all of these ways.

Characteristics of the Environment

People generally do not exist in isolation. We need other people. We enhance the quality of each other's lives, help each other become more whole, and steady each other through changes. Objects—such as books and financial resources—also can enhance our existence, as can our geographic location or the season of the year. Many aspects of our environment affect our ability to cope with change. Analyze your environment by considering the following questions:

- How strong is your interpersonal support system?
- Are intimate relationships available to you?
- What community resources are available?
- How cohesive and adaptable are your family members?

Degree of Change Required

Goodman (1979) highlighted another factor that may influence change: To understand why one person changes and another does not, we must look at the degree to which a particular change threatens the *meaning of the person's life.* Goodman (1979) and Schlossberg (1989) explained that this kind of threat might jeopardize a person's experience of attachment, how he comes to understand his life, where she invests a commitment, what he values, or on what she hangs her self-esteem.

Take, for instance, a woman who centers her life around caring for her family while her husband works. She has few, if any, friends or outside interests. She is likely to be highly invested in her husband and children. Her family is her sole source of meaning and, therefore, of self-esteem. Now imagine this woman begins thinking about a return to school. If her husband strongly disapproves, his disapproval—combined with her own guilt over decreasing her availability—may make it difficult for her to pursue her school plans. On the other hand, adding a new piece of furniture to her home is a much lower-risk change, because such a change does not threaten a central belief or a source of meaning (see Figure 9.3).

Goodman (1979) and Schlossberg (1989) stressed that people are more likely to make changes that "conserve" the meaning of their lives and to avoid those that threaten to disrupt their roles, relationships, and routines. They also distinguished between people's reactions to different degrees of change:

Change: becoming distinctly different

Alter: partially changing

Modify: producing a minor change

Modifications clearly are easier to handle than more central changes. Schlossberg (1989) also pointed out that changes arising from expanded choices are easier to incorporate than changes involving a diminished number of choices: Living with a raise is an easier adjustment than living with a pay cut.

CHILDREN, ADOLESCENTS, AND TRANSITIONS

Obviously, adults are not the only ones who experience transitions. Transitions begin early in life and continue until we die. The concepts presented in this chapter apply to children and adolescents as well as to adults.

Low-Risk Change	**Growth**	**High-Risk Change**
<------------------	------------------	------------------>
Adding a new piece of furniture	Graduation or receiving a promotion	Quitting a job or moving to another part of the country involves a significant loss.
Changing a schedule to accommodate children	More mixed feelings start occurring at this point.	

Figure 9.3. Relationship of risk to change.

Many of the transitions children and adolescents face are initiated by others and are outside their control: These might include the birth of a sibling, a parent's decision to move, enrollment in daycare or a new school, the death of a family member or a pet, the loss of a friend, and changes in voice and body as they mature (Lewis & Lewis, 1996). Adults should remember that "children are people, too," and be aware that children have feelings about transitions that need tending. Parents can help their children adjust to change by adequately preparing them for upcoming events. It is important to tell children ahead of time what is going to happen, when, and why, and to provide support through transitions. Sudden changes create fear and anxiety, and can destroy trust.

Other-initiated transitions continue throughout life, of course. But as children grow older, they also begin to initiate changes themselves. For example, a child might decide, with his or her parents' permission, to become involved in a new activity, to take on newspaper route or a baby-sitting job, or to make a new friend. Allowing children and adolescents to make age-appropriate decisions, and helping them think through the effects of their decisions, gives them good practice in important life skills.

By teaching our children early to anticipate change and giving them skills to manage change, we equip them for transitions and help ensure that they will adjust more readily. Stress management techniques (such as those presented in activities below and in chapter 5) can help children learn to manage their feelings. Teaching our children to view change as a positive, and emphasizing their resourcefulness in dealing with change, increases their self-confidence and self-efficacy (Kersey, 1986). What better time to learn than at the beginning? Successfully negotiating early transitions lays the groundwork for their future.

CONCLUSION

Transitions are inevitable. Anyone who is alive and growing goes through transitions. Having even a general sketch of the territory ahead can ease our movement through life's changes. Other factors that may ease the passage are our attitudes and beliefs about change, our ability to be flexible and to operate more from an internal locus of control, and our ability to let go of past images and form clear images of what we are moving toward. In all transitions, we must leave room for the emotional journey, from the initial ending through the reintegration of new beginnings. Transitions are times of great opportunity, bringing the possibility of renewal and growth.

Our self-esteem is both affected by and affects transitions. We can learn new skills to better negotiate transitions and so preserve our self-esteem. Some of these skills involve active behaviors, others involve attitudinal changes. The activities that follow will help you develop the skills you need to navigate your own transitions.

ACTIVITIES YOU CAN DO

ACTIVITY 9.1 RISKING

Introduction: This activity helps you begin to identify and evaluate specific behaviors you consider risky.

Time required: 15 minutes

Participants: Any number; adults

Setting: Classroom or office

Materials: Pencil and paper

Procedure: Read the following statements and rate each on this 5-point scale according to your assessment of the degree of risk involved.

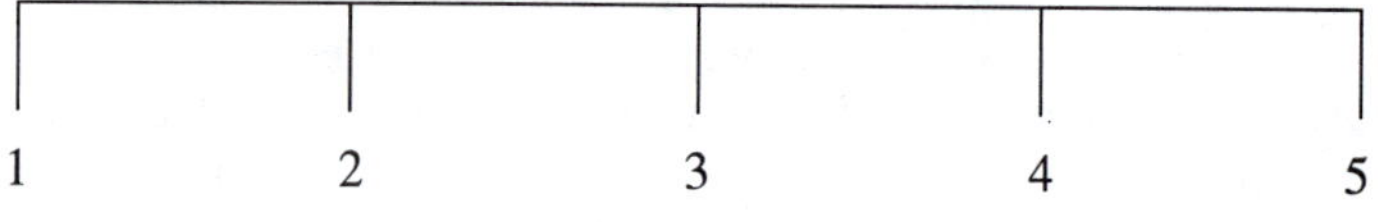

Low Risk ***High Risk***

1. Start a new project at work.
2. Visit a city where you've never been.
3. Express anger at someone.
4. Ask someone for a personal favor.
5. Admit you're wrong about something.
6. Ask directly for attention.
7. Wear something that would be different for you.
8. Ask someone for feedback on how he or she sees you.
9. Go to dinner or a movie alone.
10. Initiate a social engagement with someone you would like to know better.
11. Try a new hobby or sport.
12. Fill in another suggestion of your own.

Now choose an item you rated 2 or 3 and carry it out. Make a record of your feelings and thoughts throughout the process as well as how you supported yourself.

Outcomes: Expands your self-concept through modulated risk-taking.

Note: Activity is original. Idea initiated by Pfeiffer and Jones (1973).

ACTIVITY 9.2 VISUALIZATION: COPING

Introduction: This activity lets you create models of ways to cope with situations you find difficult.

Time required: 15 minutes

Participants: Any number; adolescents or adults

Setting: Classroom, office, or homework

Materials: Paper and pen

Procedure: Identify something you find difficult to do. Think of someone you know or have seen who performs this activity well.

Now picture this person coping easily with the situation. Imagine yourself imitating these actions. Repeat this imagery again and again.

Reflect on the image and identify the attitudes and the behavior traits you value and want to have as your own. Record your thoughts. Now observe people who possess those traits.

Imagine one of these people reacting to a situation you find difficult. How would he or she deal with it? See it in your mind's eye. Now imitate him or her.

Practice this behavior regularly.

Outcomes: Expands your behavioral repertoire.

Note: Activity is original. Idea initiated by Lazarus (1977).

ACTIVITY 9.3 NEGOTIATING A TRANSITION

Introduction: This activity helps you assess external resources available to you in managing a change.

Time required: 20 minutes

Participants: Any number; adolescents or adults

Setting: Classroom or office

Materials: Paper and pen

Procedure: Identify a change you want to make. Describe the change on paper.

Now, on a separate sheet of paper, respond to the following questions.

1. What institutional supports are available that can help you make this change? For example, can you use libraries, churches, schools, spiritual directors, community mental health agencies, or women's centers (Schlossberg & Kent, 1979)?

2. What particular people might be helpful to you? List their names and the resources they could offer.

3. What services do these supports offer that can help with this transition?

4. What environmental changes will occur as a result of this transition? For example, will you encounter climate differences, a rural area as opposed to a big city, a small school as opposed to a large school (Schlossberg & Kent, 1979)?

5. What changes, as you view them, are in a positive or negative direction?

6. How much weight do you assign to each of those changes?

7. How can you cope with what you assign negative value? Can you look at these factors differently?

Outcomes: Facilitates smoother transitions and anticipates a degree of disruption in transitions.

ACTIVITY 9.4 TRANSITION POINTS

Introduction: By reflecting on your patterns of approaching and coping with transitions, you can set new goals and ease the process of change.

Time required: 60 minutes

Participants: Any number; adults

Setting: Homework, classroom, group, or office

Materials: Paper and pen

Procedure: Outline the transition points of your life (include ages and pertinent facts). Next, come up with images or metaphors that symbolize each of these transitions (your feelings, how you coped, etc.). Now answer these questions:

1. What did you feel at the beginning of each transition?

2. What patterns do you see in your transitions: for example, strength in adversity, helplessness and defeat, resistance and rigidity, or isolation and retreat?

3. What actions did you take to cope with each transition (Herek, Levy, Maddi, Taylor, & Wertlieb, 1990):

   Social support and direct problem solving: Reaching out for emotional and informational support

   Distancing: Trying to cushion yourself from the problem by shifting attention to other matters

   Positive focus: Attempting to find meaning in the situation by asking, for example, "What am I to learn from this?"

   Cognitive escape/avoidance: Engaging in wishful thinking; pretending the crisis is not happening

   Behavioral escape/avoidance: Taking illegal drugs or medications, drinking alcohol, eating excessively, smoking, over-working, engaging in compulsive activity

4. Which actions raised your self-esteem? Which hurt your self-esteem?

5. What were the high points and low points of each transition?

6. What are your current feelings about the transition?

7. How did you respond to relationship, role, or routine changes?

8. As you reflect on what you have written, are there any changes you want to make in your coping behaviors, attitudes, and feelings?

Outcomes: Improves your coping ability during transitions.

ACTIVITY 9.5 TAKING RISKS

Introduction: Growth necessitates taking risks. Are you a reckless risker, or do you habitually opt for the safety and security of the familiar? Where do you place yourself on this continuum?

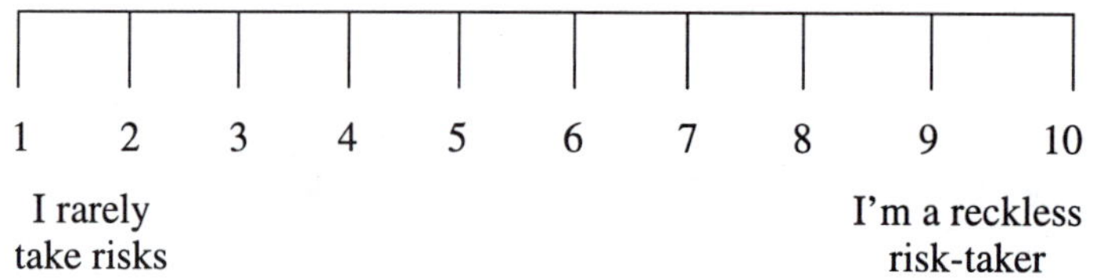

Time required: 45 minutes

Participants: Any number; adolescents or adults

Setting: Classroom, office, homework

Materials: Paper and pen

Procedure: Successful people report that they frequently take risks. Think about the different periods of your life. Describe the significant risks you took in each period. What was the outcome of your risk? What did you learn?

- Childhood
- Adolescence
- Young adulthood
- Middle years
- Older adult years

Now answer the following questions for each period:

1. What impact did these risks have on you?
2. Did any of these risks increase your personal power?
3. Are there any risks you could take today to increase your personal power? What are they?
4. Rank order them according to level of difficulty.

Consider setting a goal to take a risk that would be moderately challenging for you.

Outcomes: Expands your skills, increases your sense of self, develops your courage and judgment.

ACTIVITIES FOR GROUPS

ACTIVITY 9.6 HOLIDAYS

Introduction: This activity helps children explore their thoughts and feelings about holidays. This may be especially helpful for children who have experienced a family transition (such as a death in the family, divorce, or the chronic or life-threatening illness of a parent) or for those who experience other hardships around holidays (such as poverty or dysfunctional families).

Time required: 30 minutes

Participants: Children ages 8 to 12

Setting: Classroom, group, individual therapy

Materials: Drawing paper, crayons or markers, and a box filled with items of different textures: soft, rough, hard, smooth, etc.

Procedure: Use this activity for any holiday (e.g., Easter, Hanukkah, Christmas, Thanksgiving). Ask the children to answer these questions: When you think of this holiday,

- What colors come to mind?
- What feelings come to mind?
- What shapes come to mind?
- What memories come to mind?
- What textures come to mind?
- What thoughts come to mind?

Ask the children to draw a symbol for each of the holidays on a large sheet of paper. Under the symbol, have them draw shapes with colors that remind them of the holiday and how it feels to them.

Have children choose one or more textured pieces to convey their feelings associated with the particular holiday and paste these under the holiday. You might want to show the children a couple of different examples.

Invite the children to describe what they have produced.

Work with the children to write a song (using a familiar tune) that might help them cope with the holiday if it is problematic or refocus the holiday in a more positive way.

An example (set to the tune of "Hark the Herald Angels Sing") is shown below:

> You are my favorite boy.
> You sure bring me loads of joy.
>
> Your sweet smile and big brown eyes . . .
> To be with you, I'd cross miles.
>
> Joyful for the love we share,
> I will hold you when you're scared.
>
> Ease you pain and comfort too,
> All you need do is just be you.
>
> You miss Mom, I know it's true.
> It's okay to if you are blue.
>
> You'll see her another day.
> Wish it could be some other way.

This example highlights the skills of expressing one's real feelings and seeking physical comfort.

Ask the children what would happen if they sang this song in their heads when they felt troubled over the holiday.

Outcomes: Helps children express their feelings about holidays and teaches coping skills.

ACTIVITY 9.7 THE CHANGE MACHINE

Introduction: Change involves a number of phases. This activity introduces the stages of change and gives children a total body experience of each phase.

Time required: 30 to 45 minutes

Participants: 8 or more children, ages 10 to 12

Setting: Any setting large enough for movement

Materials: Blackboard and chalk or easel with markers

Procedure: Briefly introduce the stages of change using examples familiar to your age group. Examples might include:

- The birth of a sibling
- Older sibling leaving home
- Going to camp for the first time
- Starting at a new school
- The death of a grandparent
- Divorce of parents
- Moving
- Losing a best friend
- The death of a pet
- Sharing a room with a sibling
- Someone moving into your household (e.g., a grandparent, cousin, international student, or foster child)

Ask for a volunteer from the group—someone who is currently going through or has recently gone through a transition. This person will be the star of the show.

Ask for a show of hands from those who have gone through any of the changes you listed above. Most or all of the children probably will raise their hands.

Talk about how change is a part of life. Describe how learning to cope with transitions effectively is important.

Ask children to volunteer to act out (using movement and sounds) each of the following stages of transition.

- **Status quo:** The way it is or the way it was before a recent change. Whatever is familiar is strong here. The *status quo* wants things to stay exactly as they are or were.

- **Foreign elements:** A change that disrupts the way things are. These might include a parent's job transfer that leads to a family move; parents talking about divorce; a transfer to a new school; the death of a pet, family member, or friend; starting high school; getting a driver's license; graduating; and starting a part-time job. Some foreign elements (such as age or graduation) may be welcome; others are obviously unwelcome.

- **Chaos:** Because everything has been shaken up, confusion abounds. Lots of different emotions surface, including fear, anger, excitement, sadness, and frustration. Sometimes people have headaches, stomachaches, or other physical symptoms. The pull to the familiar is strong. Remind children of the five freedoms (see chapter 4) and the resources in their self-maintenance kits (see activity 3.15). Several children will be needed to play chaos.

- **Practice and integration:** During this phase, emotions have subsided and people begin finding ways to adjust to the new situation. The pull to the familiar subsides. A new order is established, new behaviors are learned, perspectives change, and support is garnered.

- **New status quo:** Change often spurs dreams and helps fertilize our lives, making the new status quo more lively and opening up new opportunities. Even more dramatic changes can occur during this stage, sparked by the new order.

Note: You may have to give suggestions on how to portray each stage and gather ideas from entire group.

Help the children find a physical way to express what each stage might look like, using movement and sound.

Direct the star to move through the phases of change silently.

Then walk the star through each phase, asking what he or she feels, thinks, and needs. Use the five freedoms when needed as well as tools from the self-esteem maintenance kit.

Help the children process what it was like to play each of the parts. Talk about what they learned from the experience.

Outcomes: Gives children an understanding of the inevitability of change through life; teaches the phases of change so they can prepare for them; and helps them learn to view change more positively.

REFERENCES

Brammer, L. (1991). *How to cope with life transitions: The challenge of personal change*. New York: Hemisphere.

Bridges, W. (1980). *Transitions*. Reading, MA: Addison Wesley.

Goodman, E. (1979). *Turning points*. New York: Fawcett Columbine.

Herek, G., Levy, S., Maddi, S., Taylor, S., & Wertlieb, D. (1990). *Psychological aspects of serious illness: Chronic conditions, fatal diseases, and clinical care.* Washington, DC: American Psychological Association.

Keleman, S. (1979). *Somatic reality*. Berkeley, CA: Center Press.

Kersey, K. C. (1986). *Helping your child handle stress: The parent's guide to recognizing and solving childhood problems*. New York: Berkley Books.

Lazarus, A. (1977). *In the mind's eye: The power of imagery for personal enrichment*. New York: Rawson Associates.

Lewis, S., & Lewis, S. K. (1996). *Stress-proofing your child: Mind-body exercises to enhance your child's health*. New York: Bantam Books.

Neugarten, B. L. (1976). Adaptation and the life cycle. *Counseling Psychologist, 6*(1), 16-20.

O'Grady, D. (1992). *Taking the fear out of changing*. Dayton, OH: New Insights Press.

Parkes, C. M. (1971, April). Psycho-social transitions: A field for study. *Social Science and Medicine, 5*(2), 101-115.

Pfeiffer, J. W., & Jones, J. (Editors). (1973). *A handbook of structured experiences for human relations training: Vol. 4.* Iowa City: University Associates.

Satir, V. (1979, August). Presentation at Avanta/Process Community. Park City, UT.

Satir, V. (1981). *Communication in families*. South Bend, IN: Family Institute.

Satir, V. (1987). *Process of change*. Presentation at Avanta meeting. Crested Butte, CO.

Schlossberg, N. (1989). *Overwhelmed: Coping with life's ups and downs.* Lexington, MA: Lexington Books.

Schlossberg, N., & Kent, L. (1979). Effective helping with women. In S. Eisenberg & L. Patterson (Eds.), *Helping clients with special concerns.* Skokie, IL: Rand McNally.

Scott, C. D., & Jaffe, D. T. (1989). *Managing personal change: A primer for today's world.* Menlo Park, CA: Crisp Publications.

Chapter 10

MEASURING SELF-ESTEEM

Kathleen Glaus

Kathleen D. Glaus, Ph.D., Psy.D., is Professor and Dean of Academic Affairs at the School of Professional Psychology, Wright State University, Dayton, Ohio. Her clinical specialties include assessment of self-esteem as well as assessment and treatment issues in depression, chemical dependency, and health psychology. She is the author of numerous articles on health psychology and chemical dependency, and she currently serves as consulting editor for Professional Psychology: Research and Practice.

The authors of preceding chapters in this book have made a convincing case that self-esteem is an important construct that underlies and often helps to explain human thoughts, feelings, and behavior. Moreover, the authors have displayed a general consensus that high self-esteem is good, because it is associated with higher levels of psychological health and functioning, and that low self-esteem is undesirable, because it is associated with lower levels of psychological health and functioning. Having established the importance of self-esteem to the understanding of human behavior, it is fitting that we now turn to the question of measurement. How do we measure self-esteem? How might we determine whether a person's self-esteem is high or low?

This chapter will give an overview of the issues involved in measuring or assessing self-esteem. At the risk of beginning on a negative note, I will first review the problems we encounter in measuring self-esteem. Next, I will review some of the self-esteem tests and measures currently in use. Finally, I will discuss some special issues, including sociocultural and gender issues, as they relate to the measurement of self-esteem.

PROBLEMS IN MEASURING SELF-ESTEEM

Both conceptual and methodological problems arise when we attempt to measure self-esteem. Many of these problems are not unique to this issue, but are encountered when we try to measure other human attributes: for example, intelligence or empathy. It is important that we understand these fundamental problems and how they arise, however, as they influence the development, use, and interpretation of self-esteem tests and measures.

Conceptual Problems

Definition Problems. The first conceptual problem we encounter when we set out to measure self-esteem is defining the concept itself. What exactly do we mean by *self-esteem*? Although the term is commonly used in everyday language and in scientific or scholarly discourse, there is no universally accepted, precise definition of self-esteem. In ordinary terms, self-esteem may be defined as the extent to which one prizes, values, approves of, or likes oneself. In more esoteric, scholarly terms, self-esteem is defined as the overall affective evaluation of one's worth, value, or importance (Blascovich & Tomaka, 1991). The lack of consensus on how self-esteem should be defined has created considerable confusion, as differing definitions have led researchers and clinicians down different paths in their search for a means to accurately assess or measure the construct.

Competing Constructs. A second conceptual problem is the relationship between self-esteem and other "self" constructs. If self-esteem is imprecisely defined, the same can be said for the myriad other self constructs, such as self-concept, self-regard, self-acceptance, and self-respect. Is there merit in distinguishing among these constructs? For example, should a distinction be drawn between self-esteem and self-acceptance? Between self-esteem and self-regard? Many people accustomed to using these terms in daily language would argue that there are at least shades of difference in meaning, but do the terms really denote separate and distinct constructs? Answers to these questions will emerge as self-esteem and each of these other self constructs is more precisely defined. In the absence of clarity around these fundamental, conceptual issues, however, many of these terms have been and still are used interchangeably, which has only added to the confusion.

Self-Esteem Versus Self-Concept. An issue that has considerable significance in measuring self-esteem is the distinction between *self-esteem* and *self-concept*. The relationship of self-esteem to self-concept has been a controversial issue and the subject of considerable debate among scholars and clinicians alike (e.g., Blascovich & Tomaka, 1991; Byrne, 1996; Hattie, 1992). Although the issue is far from settled, there is some consensus that self-esteem and self-concept represent two aspects of the self-system, and that self-concept is a broader, more-inclusive term. Specifically, self-concept includes cognitive and behavioral components as well as affective ones. The affective components of self-concept, on the other hand, are subsumed by self-esteem. Self-esteem, then, relates to part of but not all of one's self-concept.

The relationship between the broad notion of self-concept and the more limited, affective view of self-esteem is complex, but understanding it is crucial for anyone attempting to measure or assess self-esteem. Were the relationship simple and straightforward, thoughts or beliefs about the self (the cognitive components of self-concept) would always and predictably influence self-esteem (the affective component of self-concept).

Certainly there are times when a person's self-concept is directly related to his or her self-esteem. For example, a man believes he is intelligent (cognitive component), and this belief enhances his self-esteem (affective component). A young woman who believes she is lazy, on the other hand, might experience diminished self-esteem. But not all beliefs that are part of our self-concept affect our self-esteem. For example, a man believes he is inept when it comes to mechanical abilities, and the belief has no effect on his feelings of self-esteem. Sometimes aspects of our self-concept interact with our feelings of self-esteem in ways that seem, at least on the surface, paradoxical or counterintuitive. For example, a woman believes she is abrasive and domineering in her relations with others, yet this belief increases her feelings of self-esteem. Another woman believes she is a competent housekeeper, and it lowers her feelings of self-esteem.

If self-concept can be distinguished from self-esteem, and if beliefs about the self do not always or predictably affect self-esteem, then measuring self-esteem becomes complicated (as do any efforts to change or enhance self-esteem). The researcher who sets out to measure self-esteem is immediately confronted with a number of questions–questions about all the beliefs a person holds about the self; about which ones will influence self-esteem and which will have no effect. Which particular beliefs will raise self-esteem; which will lower it?

Byrne (1996) suggested that these issues can be clarified by considering which attributes are important to the person whose self-esteem is at issue. It stands to reason that those attributes judged unimportant will have little impact on self-esteem, whether they are evaluated positively or negatively. On the other hand, personal attributes that are judged important may profoundly effect self-esteem in a positive or negative direction. Whether a person judges any personal attribute as important or trivial, good or bad, depends on his or her beliefs, values, and views of the self and world, which are shaped by social and cultural processes. Later in this chapter, we will look at sociocultural and gender influences on self-esteem and their implications for measurement. At this point, I simply want to point out the conceptual distinction between self-concept and self-esteem and the complexities this introduces to the measurement of self-esteem.

Global Versus Multidimensional Nature of Self-Esteem. A final conceptual issue relates the very nature of self-esteem. Is self-esteem best conceptualized as a global, one-dimensional entity? For example, is it the overall affective evaluation of one's worth, value, or importance in the broadest sense? Or should self-esteem be conceptualized as multidimensional? Is overall self-esteem related to discrete facets of a person's life (social standing, family, school, etc.)? This issue has been the subject of controversy among scholars for some time.

Moreover, since measures of self-esteem grow out of particular theoretical frames of reference, this controversy has direct implications for the way tests and measures of self-esteem are developed. Not surprisingly, there are scales that measure only a global sense of self-esteem (e.g., the Rosenberg Self-Esteem Scale, Rosenberg, 1987) and scales that measure self-esteem associated with several discrete areas of functioning (e.g., the Tennessee Self-Concept Scale, Roid & Fitts, 1994). Although there is some evidence that multidimensional models of self-esteem have greater empirical construct validity (Byrne, 1996), there is conceptual simplicity in taking a one-dimensional view as well. Clinicians and researchers choosing an instrument should do so based on the level of detail or specificity best suited to their needs.

Methodological Problems

Reliability. This is the extent to which scores on a test or assessment instrument are consistent and free from measurement error. For any test or measure, several reliability coefficients may be calculated, including *internal consistency reliability* (the extent to which test items are consistent in measuring the same construct), *interrater reliability* (the extent to which different observers of the same phenomenon are consistent in their scoring), and *test-retest reliability* (the extent to which the same individual obtains consistent scores on the same test given on two different occasions). These different forms of reliability are discussed in detail by Anastasi (1988) and the American Psychological Association (1985).

Generally, reliability is expressed as a correlation coefficient. The closer the coefficient is to 1.00, the higher the reliability of the test and the greater the consistency of scores resulting from its use. Although there are a number of views on the minimum acceptable level of reliability (Thorndike, Cunningham, Thorndike, & Haen, 1991), Hammill, Brown, and Bryant (1992) suggested .80 as the minimum. They further urged that clinicians and researchers make every attempt to choose instruments with reliability coefficients of .90 or greater.

Validity. The validity of an instrument is the extent to which appropriate, meaningful, and useful inferences can be made from the scores or results it yields. There are several indices of validity (APA, 1985), including *content validity* (the extent to which behaviors demonstrated in the testing situation accurately reflect behaviors exhibited in the real world), *criterion validity* (the extent to which scores correlate with some other outcome criterion score or measure), and *construct validity* (the extent to which the test measures the attribute it was intended to).

Researchers have questioned the validity of several self-esteem measures for some time (Demo, 1985; Wylie, 1968). This criticism has led to several studies of the validity issue (Byrne, 1996). Given the problem we have even defining self-esteem, it is no wonder we face problems with the validity of self-esteem tests and measures.

In the absence of strong empirical evidence of validity, we must be guided in choosing an appropriate measure by a careful analysis of inferences to be made based on the test results and a close review of the characteristics of the groups on which the assessment instrument was normed. Test reviews and critiques also are informative when test validity is at issue (Hammill et al., 1992; Keyser & Sweetland, 1992).

Response Bias. The measurement of self-esteem is nearly always based on a person's self-report, whether that self-reporting is done in a clinical interview or on a paper-and-pencil test. Any such self-reports are subject to response bias, particularly when test items or interview questions have a high degree of face-validity (i.e., when it is fairly obvious what attribute is being assessed). Although there are several types of response bias, attempts to measure self-esteem have been most affected by social desirability.

Social desirability is the tendency for people to respond in a socially approved or acceptable manner, regardless of what they actually believe to be true. Since high self-esteem is generally viewed as desirable, it is more socially desirable to present oneself as high rather than low in self-esteem. As a result, scores of self-esteem tests and measures tend to be inflated, which reduces their validity and sometimes leads either to a "ceiling effect" or to gross overestimates. This response bias also may be present when self-esteem is assessed using a clinical interview or observation by others, including trained observers (Blascovich & Tomaka, 1991). Respondents may not be aware that social desirability is influencing their self-reporting, and they may not intentionally be inflating their reports.

In addition, Blascovich and Tomaka (1991) suggested that individuals may present themselves as high in self-esteem as a defense method, either consciously or unconsciously. Doing this protects the individual from rejection, criticism, or other threats to the self. Paulhus (1986, 1991) provided useful analyses of various response biases that can inform both clinicians and researchers. However, there are no easy solutions to the problem of report bias on self-esteem measures. Inflated self-esteem scores should be expected, and this inflation should be taken into account in interpreting or drawing inferences from all measures of self-esteem.

SELF-ESTEEM TESTS AND MEASURES

We can choose several tests and instruments for measuring self-esteem in adults, adolescents, and children. Reviewing some of the commonly used ones will illustrate some of their characteristics. All measures of self-esteem are subject to the conceptual and methodological problems discussed above. When selecting a measure, you should consider the clinical decisions or inferences you want to make and the characteristics of the individuals or groups you are testing. Generally, measures are distinguished by their target populations (e.g., adults versus children), whether they purport to measure global self-esteem or specific facets of self-esteem, and whether they measure self-esteem broadly or in terms of narrow constructs such as self-confidence or body esteem.

The self-esteem measures listed here were chosen for their demonstrated popularity, psychometric soundness, and utility for clinicians. Some–for example the Rosenberg Self-Esteem Scale (Rosenberg, 1987)–were designed to measure global self-esteem, while others–for example the Personal Evaluation Inventory (Shrauger) and the Body Esteem Scale (Franzio & Shields, 1984)–focus on narrow dimensions of self-esteem. I have included measures for adults, adolescents, and children.

Anyone using self-esteem measures (or any psychological tests or measures) should be aware of the strengths and limitations of the measures they are using, and should also be familiar with the *Standards for Educational and Psychological Testing* (APA, 1985).

Adult-Adolescent Scales

The Rosenberg Self-Esteem Scale (SES). The Rosenberg Self-Esteem Scale (Rosenberg, 1987) is one of the most widely used measures of self-esteem for adolescents and adults (Blascovich & Tomaka, 1991). Rosenberg viewed self-esteem as a one-dimensional concept that reflects a person's experience of general self-worth and that transcends evaluations of discrete characteristics of the self. Thus, the SES measures global self-esteem as a one-dimensional entity. In this respect, it differs from instruments like the Tennessee Self-Concept Scale (Roid & Fitts, 1994), which considers global self-esteem as a sum of self-evaluations across several areas of personal functioning. Consisting of only 10 items, the SES is brief, easily scored, and useful in many clinical or counseling settings where a global index of self-esteem is desired.

The Tennessee Self-Concept Scale (TSCS). The TSCS (Roid & Fitts, 1994) is another widely used measure for adolescents and adults. In contrast to the SES, the TSCS was constructed on the premise that a general sense of self-esteem derives from positive self-evaluations across a number of areas of functioning. Thus the TSCS provides a total score that may serve as an index of general or global self-esteem and also separate indices of self-esteem in five major domains: physical self, moral-ethical self, personal self, family self, and social self. Providing a multidimensional approach to self-esteem, the TSCS may have particular applicability in clinical settings, where counselors are interested in a specific breakdown of those areas of functioning or attributes contributing to high or low self-esteem. In addition, the TSCS may be the most appropriate self-esteem instrument for individuals exhibiting psychopathology, as it provides special scales measuring response biases, defensiveness, maladjustment, psychosis, neurosis, and personality disorder. The test consists of 100 items and yields 29 subscale scores.

The Feelings of Inadequacy Scale (FIS). The FIS (Janis & Field, in Blascovich & Tomaka, 1991) asks respondents to indicate the extent to which they feel bad about themselves. This scale has been revised several times since it was first published and now provides an overall index of self-esteem along with subscales addressing social confidence, school abilities, self-regard, physical appearance, and physical ability. The FIS is brief, with only 36 items, but it provides measures of both specific facets of self-esteem and global self-esteem.

Children's Scales

Piers-Harris Children's Self-Concept Scale (PHCSCS). The PHCSCS (see also Piers, 1984) was designed to measure self-esteem in children and adolescents ages 8 to 18. The test yields a total score reflecting global self-esteem and subscale scores for six areas of functioning: behavior, intellectual and school functioning, appearance, anxiety, popularity, and happiness. As is true for other scales that tap both global and domain-specific self-esteem, the PHCSCS may be useful for the clinician interested in identifying functional domains that contribute to either high or low global self-esteem.

Although this scale can be used with adolescents, response biases (in the form of socially desirable response sets) may be more problematic for adolescents than for children in the 8- to 12-year range. The PHCSCS is easily and quickly administered to children individually or in small groups. Because of the amount of empirical support for the PHCSCS, it may be the measure of choice for children 8 to 12 years old (Hughes, 1984).

Self-Esteem Inventory (SEI). The SEI (Coopersmith) was developed for use with children and adolescents ages 9 to 15. It measures self-esteem as it relates to social, academic, family, and personal areas of functioning. Although the SEI has been used widely in clinical, counseling, and school settings, it has been criticized as susceptible to social desirability bias and for its lack of a stable internal factor structure (Hughes, 1984).

Clinicians contemplating the SEI should consult technical information to determine its utility for their particular application. The fact that the SEI has been used in several research studies (Blascovich & Tomaka, 1991) might argue for its use in a clinical setting, as the scores obtained in a clinical setting can be compared with published research results. The SEI comes in two forms. The short form (Form B) can be administered quickly in a clinical setting.

Self-Perception Profile for Children (SPPC). The SPPC (see also Harter, 1985) measures both global self-esteem and five domain-specific self-esteems in preadolescents: scholastic competence, athletic competence, social acceptance, physical appearance, and behavioral conduct. Because the skills and attributes that indicate competence and acceptance change significantly as children develop, there are several versions of the SPPC. Two versions–one for kindergartners and one for first- and second-graders (ages 6 to 7 years)–use a unique pictorial format in which children choose between pairs of pictures (one positive, the other negative).

A third version of the SPCC, developed for children ages 8 to 12 years, uses words rather than pictures, as does a new instrument Harter developed for use with adolescents: the Self-Perception Profile for Adolescents (SPPA) (see also Harter, 1988). Currently, the SPPC is among the most widely used instruments for assessing self-esteem in preadolescents, particularly with children in the 5- to 7-year age range. Similarly, the SPPA is becoming more widely used with adolescents. These instruments are well constructed and, because they span a considerable age range, they may be useful for tracking changes in children's self-esteem across developmental periods.

Special Scales

Body Esteem Scale (BES). The BES (Franzio & Shields, 1984) measures the extent to which men and women are satisfied or dissatisfied with various body parts or processes. The BES is based on an earlier instrument, the

Body-Cathexis Scale (Secord & Jourard, 1953), and is appropriate for use with adults of college age and older. Separate, gender-specific scales are yielded for men and women. Specifically, for men the BES provides subscales for physical attractiveness, upper-body strength, and physical condition. For women, it provides subscales for sexual attractiveness, weight concern, and physical condition. Overall, the BES has proved itself a psychometrically sound index of body esteem in adults and may prove useful in clinical or research settings that deal with eating disorders or other disturbances of bodily satisfaction.

Personal Evaluation Inventory (PEI). The PEI (Shrauger, 1995) taps a narrowly defined aspect of self-esteem: self-confidence. Specifically, the PEI provides a measure of general confidence and subscales that measure self-confidence in six domains: academic performance, athletics, physical appearance, romantic relationships, social interactions, and speaking with people. Because the PEI is new, information on its psychometric properties is limited. However, the inventory has been shown to correlate moderately with global measures of self-esteem and to be minimally influenced by social desirability, socioeconomic status, or religious affiliation (Shrauger, 1995). Based on these preliminary data, the PEI may be useful in clinical or consulting settings in which an index on both general and domain-specific self-confidence is needed. Since most of what we know about the PEI's validity and reliability is based on normative groups of college students, it is most appropriately used with these or similar groups.

Sources of Additional Tests and Measures

If you are interested in additional measures of self-esteem or related personality attributes (or in detailed psychometric data for specific instruments), consult the reviews by Blascovich and Tomaka (1991) and Byrne (1996), and an earlier review by Hughes (1984). Blascovich and Tomaka will be particularly useful if you want to review the actual items included in self-esteem instruments, as many of the tests and scales were reprinted in whole or part.

In addition, you will find several resources invaluable when the time comes to select an appropriate measure for clinical or research application, including Kramer and Conoley (1992), Keyser and Sweetland (1992), Hammill et al. (1992), and Corcoran and Fischer (1987).

SPECIAL ISSUES IN MEASURING SELF-ESTEEM

Sociocultural Issues

I noted before that sociocultural issues are integrally related to self-esteem because they provide the beliefs, values, and views of the self that serve as the underpinnings of esteem, for a number of reasons. First, they influence which attributes or aspects of the self we rate important. In addition, they influence the affective component of self-evaluation; that is, whether we evaluate any particular attribute positively (i.e., self-esteem enhancing) or negatively (i.e., self-esteem diminishing).

In this section, I will elaborate on these ideas and provide some perspectives on the measurement of self-esteem from cross-cultural studies. My treatment of these issues will be brief, as a great deal has been written in recent years on the sociocultural nature of both emotion and concepts of the self (e.g., Kitayama & Marcus, 1994; Marcus & Kitayama, 1991, 1994; Marsella, DeVos, & Hsu, 1985; Ortony & Turner, 1990; Oyserman & Marcus, 1993; Shweder, 1991, 1993; Triandis, 1990). It is important to note at the outset that in this discussion, I make broad characterizations of cultures with the full realization that such characterizations are not equally true for all members of the cultural group. These characterizations are meant to describe only general traits or tendencies that emerge when members of a cultural group are considered as a whole. With this final caveat in mind, let us turn to a consideration of self-esteem in sociocultural context.

Each person can be viewed as embedded in a complex array of sociocultural contexts associated with, for example, country or region of origin, ethnicity, religion, family, and economic level. Each of these sociocultural contexts, in turn, shapes beliefs and values about what it means to be a good person or a bad person and to feel good or bad about oneself, which is the fundamental issue in self-esteem. Sociocultural influences are so profound, in fact, that they determine what we meant when we say *the self.*

Differences in how cultures construe *self* can be illustrated by comparing the Western (i.e., North American and Western European) view of the self with that of other cultural frameworks. In the West, the self is viewed as an independent, autonomous, self-contained entity composed of a unique set of attributes (traits, feelings, values, etc.). Westerners generally believe that these attributes determine and explain a person's behavior (Marcus & Kitayama, 1991). This Western cultural perspective has been termed the *independent view of the self.* From this perspective, an explicit social goal is to separate oneself from others, to be independent and unique, to prevent others from unduly influencing us.

This view of the self contrasts sharply with the cultural framework of *interdependence* that characterizes many Oriental, African, and Hispanic cultures (Triandis, 1994). From the perspective of an interdependent cultural frame, the self is not and cannot be separate from others and the surrounding social context. Thus the self-in-relation is focal, and the culturally prescribed goal is not to become separate and autonomous but to fit in with others. From this perspective, the person's behavior is determined and explained by social context and relations with others (Marcus & Kitayama, 1991).

What implications does this have for self-esteem? Self-esteem, or feeling good about oneself, depends in part on realizing the approach to selfhood required by the cultural framework (Marcus & Kitayama, 1994). In an independent culture, high self-esteem derives from evidence that one has distinguished oneself from others, that one is different or unique in some positive sense. Thus, for people socialized in Western cultures, there is a powerful drive to see themselves as somewhat better than their peers. Not surprisingly, these people frequently exhibit a phenomenon termed the *false-uniqueness effect*, or the tendency to view oneself as better than one's peers and to underestimate the commonality of one's desirable attributes (Mullen & Riordan, 1988).

By contrast, in an interdependent culture, high self-esteem is a function of good social relationships, a sense of fitting in, belonging, and occupying one's proper place. The cultural press is to see oneself as *like others* in terms of attributes that are important, to accentuate the commonality of one's desirable behaviors, and to minimize any sense of uniqueness or distinction. Rather than exhibiting a false uniqueness effect, individuals from interdependent cultures may exhibit a *self-effacement effect* (Marcus & Kitayama, 1994).

The impact of cultural frames and their implications for self-esteem measurement are illustrated in studies comparing people from independent cultures (e.g., Americans) with those from interdependent cultures (e.g., Oriental). For example, Marcus and Kitayama (1991, 1994) reviewed cross-cultural studies on child-rearing and educational practices. They found that the notion of building children's self-esteem was not emphasized or viewed as particularly important by Chinese and Japanese parents and educators. This was illustrated by Chao's finding (in Marcus & Kitayama, 1994) that only 8% of Chinese mothers stressed building self-esteem as an important goal of child-rearing. This contrasts sharply with Chao's finding that fully 64% of American mothers (of European-American descent) believed that building self-esteem was important in child-rearing (Chao, cited in Marcus & Kitayama, 1994). Moreover, Marcus and Kitayama (1991, 1994) noted that Americans often encourage their children to identify and selectively attend to attributes of the self that are unique in a positive sense, to assert themselves, to stand up for their rights, and to express their individual thoughts and feelings. Japanese children are taught to value relationships as ends in themselves, whereas American children are taught to value relationships as means of self-expression, personal growth, or some other end. Unlike Americans, many Japanese parents viewed children's asserting or expressing themselves as a sign of immaturity.

The dramatic differences that emerged in Marcus and Kitayama's (1991, 1994) research underline the importance of taking into account sociocultural factors in any attempt to measure self-esteem. As the comparison of American and Japanese child-rearing practices suggests, a particular attribute or belief about the self may give rise to feelings of high self-esteem in one culture and low self-esteem in another. One might wonder, for example, how American and Japanese children would respond to the following items from the SEI, and how their responses might be interpreted:

- I give in very easily.
- I can usually take care of myself.
- If I have something to say I usually say it.

In a broader sense, cross-cultural work has called into question the very importance of self-esteem, however it is measured, for many cultures. While Americans and other Westerners place great value on self-esteem, believing it is important for good psychological health and functioning, this perspective is culture-bound and anything but universal. Indeed, in their comparison of independent and interdependent cultural views of the self, Marcus and Kitayama (1991) suggested that esteeming the self is primarily a Western phenomenon.

The profound effects of sociocultural influences on self-esteem should serve as a cautionary note to anyone using standardized tests and measures of self-esteem, as these have been developed within a Western cultural frame. They may or may not be appropriate or useful for assessing self-esteem in people from non-Western cultural groups.

By the same token, they may have limited utility for assessing self-esteem in certain subcultural groups in the United States, Canada, and other Western cultures, including members of racial and ethnic minority groups such as African-Americans, Hispanic-Americans, Latinos, and Native Americans (Dana, 1993). Although members of these groups may be "Westernized" to a large degree, they may also retain many of the beliefs, values, and views of the self of the interdependent cultures they or their forebears left behind.

Thus, anyone proposing to measure self-esteem in the many ethnic and racial subgroups in the United States (and other Western countries) should be aware that members of these groups may not be fully Westernized–that they may exhibit many non-Western cultural characteristics. If standardized tests and measures are used with members of these groups, results should be interpreted cautiously. For clinicians and researchers acculturated within a Western framework, the assessment of self-esteem in people from ethnic and racial minority groups may prove a significant challenge.

Gender Issues

Do men and women differ in self-esteem? Should self-esteem be assessed differently in men and women? These are important questions, particularly in view of the many gender differences that have been documented to date. This section will deal with gender issues as they affect the measurement of self-esteem. Gender issues affecting self-esteem therapy are discussed in chapter 6.

According to Josephs, Marcus, and Tafarodi (1992), men and women score quite similarly on measures of self-esteem, although not much research has been devoted to this issue and the work that has been done has been limited to Western sociocultural groups. However, the findings to date suggest that men and women do not differ significantly in the levels of self-esteem they exhibit on standardized tests. This is not to say, however, that men and women do not differ in self-esteem; indeed, different approaches may be needed to adequately assess self-esteem in men and women.

Increasingly, gender is viewed as a sociocultural construction; gender differences are being analyzed and explained in terms of the differing sociocultural prescriptions for men and women (Josephs et al.,1992). In light of this, gender issues represent an extension of the sociocultural issues discussed in the previous section. Even within a predominately Western cultural framework, men and women encounter from birth different social and cultural pressures and expectations. As a consequence, they may develop very different beliefs, values, and views of the self that have important implications for the measurement of self-esteem.

For example, it has been argued that women develop an *interdependent* sense of self, while men develop an *independent* sense of self (Gilligan, 1982; Josephs et al., 1992; Miller, 1986), although various authors have used different terms to describe men's and women's relational styles. (The distinction between independent and interdependent cultural frames has a great deal of relevance in the context of gender issues.) As a result, women experience the self in relation to others, and they emphasize and value connections to and relationships with others. Men, on the other hand, experience the self as an autonomous, self-contained entity and emphasize and value difference and individuality (Miller, 1986; Jordan & Surrey, 1986; Jordan, Kaplan, Miller, Stiver, & Surrey, 1991).

Because of the differing values placed on relations with others, it follows that different personal attributes would be valued by men and women. The personal attributes valued by and for women (i.e., the attributes of a "good woman") include those important for connecting with others: empathy, warmth, intuition, constraint of personal wants or needs in deference to those of others, and so on. In contrast, the attributes valued by and for men (i.e., the attributes of a "good man") include those important for maintaining autonomy and distance from others: a proclivity to focus on the self and its unique attributes, selective inattention to the emotions or needs of others and to social cues of strain or rupture in an interpersonal relationship, assertion of personal wants or needs, resistance to deferring to the wants or needs of others, and so on.

Differences in what it means to be a "good woman" or a "good man" and related gender differences have important implications for self-esteem in men and women. Generally, men derive self-esteem from evidence that they have distinguished themselves from others and achieved autonomy and independence. For women, the picture is more complicated. To a large extent, women derive self-esteem from evidence that they have achieved and maintained solid connections and relationships with others. However, because of recent dramatic changes in women's roles (at least in the United States), women may experience sociocultural pressures to individuate, to become autonomous and assertive, and to be less influenced by others. Josephs et al. (1992) defined this cultural press as a *pressure to be a good person–American style.*

For women in the United States (and perhaps in other Western countries), the result is something of a culture clash, in that the cultural prescription for being a good woman is at odds with that for being a good person, at least under some circumstances (Joseph et al., 1992). Unfortunately, many women caught in this dilemma experience themselves as failures in both roles and, as a result, experience a double dose of low self-esteem.

Efforts to assess self-esteem in men and women must be tempered by an awareness of gender differences and the unique situation of women in the United States and other Westernized countries. Standardized measures of self-esteem should be reviewed in terms of their appropriateness for use with men and women, especially since women's roles have changed and the research showing that men and women score similarly on measures of self-esteem is now somewhat dated.

Measuring Self-Esteem via the Clinical Interview

So far, I have focused on standardized tests and measures of self-esteem and some of the issues involved in their use and interpretation. Although standardized tests and measures offer a number of advantages, the clinical interview also can be used to assess self-esteem.

The clinical interview offers the advantage of being open-ended. Thus, the clinician can access information that allows him or her to evaluate self-esteem while taking into account sociocultural, subcultural (e.g., racial, ethnic), and gender issues. Through careful listening and the use of interviewing techniques, the clinician can directly access a client's beliefs, values, and view of the self and how these factors interact with the client's experience of high or low self-esteem.

Assessing self-esteem through a clinical interview is most effective if the clinician is aware of the conceptual, sociocultural, and gender issues discussed above. For example, response biases related to social desirability, ego defense mechanisms, false-uniqueness effects, or self-effacement effects appear as reliably in clinical interviews as they do on standardized tests of self-esteem.

The validity of any conclusions or interpretations resulting from a clinical interview also will depend on the ability of the clinician to adjust his or her conceptual and sociocultural frameworks to coincide with those of the client. This is no small task for some clinicians who have been both socialized and educated within a Western cultural frame.

Many American clinicians, for example, have been led to believe (if not explicitly taught) that American (or Western) beliefs, values, and views of self are universal, or are reflections of some sort of universal human nature. Because of the combined effects of acculturation and educational experiences that neglect to emphasize different sociocultural issues, some clinicians have difficulty shifting sociocultural perspectives. However, the success of any self-esteem assessment made via a clinical interview will depend on the clinician's ability to join with the client's frame of reference.

Given its flexibility, the clinical interview might be the most appropriate choice for assessing self-esteem when significant sociocultural or gender issues threaten to render a standardized test inappropriate.

CONCLUSION

Self-esteem is the foundation on which much of human thought and behavior is based. As is true for many human attributes, measuring self-esteem is complicated by a number of conceptual and methodological issues. Nonetheless, these issues are being addressed, and several tests and measures available are both methodologically sound and clinically useful. As we understand more about how self-esteem is shaped by sociocultural influences, current tests and measures will be refined and new measures of self-esteem will be developed. Advances in the measurement of self-esteem will both lead and follow progress in theoretical formulation and clinical understanding of this important human attribute.

REFERENCES

American Psychological Association. (1985). *Standards for educational and psychological testing*. Washington, DC: Author.

Anastasi, A. (1988). *Psychological testing*. New York: Macmillan.

Blascovich, J., & Tomaka, J. (1991). Measures of self-esteem. In J. P. Robinson, P. R. Shaver, & L. S. Wrightsman (Eds.), *Measures of personality and social psychological attitudes.* San Diego: Academic Press.

Byrne, B. M. (1996). *Measuring self-concept across the lifespan: Issues and instrumentation.* Washington, DC: American Psychological Association.

Coopersmith, S. (1967). *The antecedents of self-esteem.* San Francisco: Freeman.

Coopersmith, S. *Self-Esteem Inventory* (SEI). Consulting Psychologists Press, 3803 E. Bayshore Road, Palo Alto, CA 94303; 800-624-1765.

Corcoran, K., & Fischer, J. (1987). *Measures for clinical practice.* New York: Free Press.

Dana, R. H. (1993). *Multicultural assessment perspectives for professional psychology.* Boston: Allyn & Bacon.

Demo, D. H. (1985). The measurement of self-esteem: Refining our methods. *Journal of Personality and Social Psychology, 48,* 1490-1502.

Franzio, S. L., & Shields, S. A. (1984). The Body Esteem Scale: Multidimensional structure and sex differences in a college population. *Journal of Personality Assessment, 48,* 173-178. (Scale also available through: Blascovich, J., & Tomaka, J. (1991). Measures of self-esteem. In J. P. Robinson, P. R. Shaver, & L. S. Wrightsman (Eds.), *Measures of personality and social psychological attitudes* (pp. 153). San Diego: Academic Press.)

Gilligan, C. (1982). *In a different voice: Psychological theory and women's development.* Cambridge, MA: Harvard University Press.

Hammill, D. D., Brown, L., & Bryant, B. R. (1992). *A consumer's guide to tests in print.* Austin, TX: Pro-Ed.

Harter, S. *Self-Perception Profile for Children* (SPPC) and *Self-Perception Profile for Adolescents* (SPPA). Susan Harter, Department of Psychology, University of Denver, 2155 Race Street, Denver, CO 80208.

Harter, S. (1985). *Manual for the Self-Perception Profile for Children.* Denver: University of Denver.

Harter, S. (1988). *Manual for the Self-Perception Profile for Adolescents.* Denver: University of Denver.

Hattie, J. (1992). *Self-concept.* Hillsdale, NJ: Erlbaum.

Hughes, H. M. (1984). Measures of self-concept and self-esteem for children ages 3 to 12 years: A review and recommendations. *Clinical Psychology Review, 4,* 657-692.

Janis, I. S., & Field, P. B. (1959). A behavioral assessment of persuasibility: Consistency of individual differences. In C. I. Houland & I. L. Janis (Eds.), *Personality and persuasibility.* New Haven, CT: Yale University Press.

Jordan, J. V., Kaplan, A. G., Miller, J. B., Stiver, I. P., & Surrey, J. L. (1991). *Women's growth in connection.* New York: Guilford.

Jordan, J. V., & Surrey, J. L. (1986) The self-in-relation: Empathy and the mother-daughter relationship. In T. Bernay & D. W. Cantor (Eds.), *The psychology of today's women* (pp. 81-104). Cambridge, MA: Harvard University Press.

Josephs, R. A., Marcus, H. R., & Tafarodi, R. W. (1992). Gender and self-esteem. *Journal of Personality and Social Psychology, 63,* 391-402.

Keyser, D. J., & Sweetland, R. C. (Editors). (1992). *Test critiques: Vol. 9.* Austin, TX: Pro-Ed.

Kitayama, S., & Marcus, H. R. (1994). *Emotion and culture: Empirical studies of mutual influence.* Washington, DC: American Psychological Association.

Kramer, J. J., & Conoley, J. C. (Editors). (1992). *The eleventh mental measurements yearbook.* Lincoln, NE: Buros Institute of Mental Measurements.

Marcus, H. R., & Kitayama, S. (1991) Culture and the self: Implications for cognition, motivation, and emotion. *Psychological Review, 98,* 224-253.

Marcus, H. R., & Kitayama, S. (1994). The cultural construction of the self and emotion: Implications for social behavior. In S. Kitayama & H. R. Marcus (Eds.), *Emotion and culture: Empirical studies of mutual influence.* Washington, DC: American Psychological Association.

Marsella, A., DeVos, G., & Hsu, F. (1985). *Culture and self.* London: Tavistock.

Miller, J. B. (1986). *Toward a new psychology of women* (2nd ed.). Boston: Beacon.

Mullen, B., & Riordan, C. A. (1988). Self-serving attributions in naturalistic settings: A meta-analytic review. *Journal of Applied Social Psychology, 18,* 3-22.

Ortony, A., & Turner, T. J. (1990). What's basic about basic emotions? *Psychological Review, 97,* 315-331.

Oyserman, D., & Marcus, H. R. (1993). The sociocultural self. In J. Suls (Ed.), *Psychological perspectives on the self: The self in social perspective* (pp. 187-220). Hillsdale, NJ: Erlbaum.

Paulhus, D. L. (1986). Self-deception and impression management in test responses. In A. Angleutner & J. S. Wiggins (Eds.), *Personality assessment via questionnaire* (pp. 134-156). New York: Springer-Verlag.

Paulhus, D. L. (1991). Measurement control of response bias. In J. P. Robinson, P. R. Shaver, & L. S. Wrightsman (Eds.), *Measurement of social psychological attitudes: Vol. 1. Measures of personality and social psychological attitudes* (pp. 17-59). San Diego: Academic.

Piers, E. V. *Piers-Harris Children's Self Concept Scale* (PHCSCS). Los Angeles: Western Psychological Services.

Piers, E. V. (1984). *Piers-Harris Children's Self-Concept Scale: Revised manual.* Los Angeles: Western Psychological Services.

Roid, G. H., & Fitts, W. H. (1994). *Tennessee Self-Concept Scale* (TSCS). Los Angeles: Western Psychological Services.

Rosenberg, M. (1987). *Rosenberg Self-Esteem Scale (The)* (SES). In K. Corcoran & J. Fischer. *Measures for clinical practice* (pp. 408-409). New York: Free Press.

Rosenberg, M. (1989). *Society and the adolescent self-image.* Middletown, CT: Wesleyan University Press.

Secord, P. E., & Jourard, S. M. (1953). The appraisal of body cathexis: Body cathexis and the self. *Journal of Consulting Psychology, 17,* 343-347.

Shrauger, J. S. *Personal Evaluation Inventory* (PEI). Sidney Shrauger, Psychology Department, Park Hall, State University of New York at Buffalo, Buffalo, NY 14260.

Shrauger, J. S. (1995). Self-confidence in college students: Conceptualization, measurement, and behavioral implications. *Assessment, 2,* 255-278.

Shweder, R. A. (1991). *Thinking through cultures: Expeditions in cultural psychology.* Cambridge, MA: Harvard University Press.

Shweder, R. A. (1993). The cultural psychology of the emotions. In M. Lewis & J. M. Haviland (Eds.), *Handbook of emotions* (pp. 417-431). New York: Guilford.

Thorndike, R. M., Cunningham, G. K., Thorndike, R. L., & Haen, E. P. (1991). *Measurement and evaluation in education and psychology.* New York: Macmillan.

Triandis, H. C. (1990). Cross-cultural studies of individualism and collectivism. In J. Berman (Ed.), *Nebraska symposium on motivation, 1989* (pp. 41-133). Lincoln: University of Nebraska Press.

Triandis, H. C. (1994). Major cultural syndromes and emotion. In S. Kitayama & H. R. Marcus (Eds.), *Emotions and culture: Empirical studies of mutual influence.* Washington, DC: American Psychological Association.

Wylie, R. C. (1968) The present status of self theory. In E. A. Borgatta & W. W. Lambert (Eds.), *Handbook of personality theory and research* (pp. 728-787). Skokie, IL: Rand McNally.

EPILOGUE

C. Jesse Carlock

From the first time I was invited to reflect on myself (in a personal growth group in graduate school), I have enjoyed the excitement of learning about myself. I yearned to be more in touch with myself, to know why I behaved as I did and how others experienced me, to discover hidden parts of myself, and to feel better about myself. I became hooked on self-awareness. I was hungry to know myself. But expanding my awareness often has been painful and challenging as well as exciting. Early on I wished I could turn back, could diminish my growing awareness. But there was no turning back for me. Though I have taken respite along the way, to this day (and I hope every day of my life) I look for ways to hone my awareness and, in so doing, to nourish my self-esteem.

I know I am not alone in this hunger for self-awareness and improvement. Each generation tries to improve upon the last. Most people want to feel better about themselves and to help their children, employees, friends, family, and colleagues feel better about themselves as well. In that pursuit, some become lost and discouraged, but we all do the best we can with what we know. Some begin their self-search early, some later (there is no time limit, no "too late" in my way of thinking). Some search with guides, flashlights, maps, and compasses; others struggle along in darkness with no navigational aides.

I was not raised in a family aware enough to provide an accurate and detailed mirror of my strengths, to teach me how to remedy my deficits, to recognize my talents and encourage me to develop them, or to teach me how to build support. Had they been aware and known how, my parents and family members would have. They were good people and wanted the best for me. They gave me what they could. But there are always gaps in the knowing. Each day of my life I fill in missing pieces.

I hope this book will ignite your interest in self-discovery or inspire you to take steps to feel better about yourself and to help others as well. The tools are here. Use them. Reading is only the first step. Devoting time to the activities contained here is another important step. Many of the activities can be completed more than once. Practicing in your everyday life the skills and attitudes described and teaching them to others will propel you even further in the directions you choose to go.

Once you are aware of your options and tools, you have a choice. This is your life. You are the architect now. Inviting others to work with you on improving your self-esteem can help keep you on task and motivated, provide a source for feedback and encouragement, and ensure a check point for goals you set. I saw a sign once that read: "Goals are the stepladders to your dreams." Without dreams, there is no hope. Without some sense of progress, dreams die. You can be each others' listening ears and cheering squads. Most of us can use a chorus of support to keep us going when we come to those difficult knots in the change process.

It is never too late to start improving your self-esteem. Children through older adults can change how they feel about themselves. I am always delighted when people in their 70s seek me out for psychotherapy, some for the first time in their lives. But there are thousands of others, young and old, who do not believe change is possible. "I'm too old to change. It's too much trouble to change. I'm too scared to change. I've tried and I can't." Lack of direction, lack of adequate support, and negative attitudes impede change. The most frequent person to stand in the way of making change is you. You can change. Experience tells me that you already have the basic resources to realize your dreams. You need only breathe and turn your fear into excitement, lift the lid, and look underneath. Will you dare?

If you decide to commit to this process of enhancing your self-esteem, I have some recommendations that may help you:

1. Find a partner, therapist, or group of people with whom you can work on self-esteem enhancement. Meet with these growth partners on a regular basis.

2. Read the text carefully, a chapter at a time, and discuss it with them.

3. Complete each activity independently at least once, then review each with your partner or group. Some activities you might want to complete more than once at various intervals in order to review skills, expand learnings, or check your programs.

4. Set clear, measurable, and realistic goals for yourself. Use your growth partners to help formulate these goals and to develop strategies for achieving them. Check in with your partners regularly to review your progress. Your partners also can help you deal with obstacles you encounter. Use personal journaling, graphs, and other tools to chart your progress.

5. If you get stuck along the way, find a psychologist or professional to help you. A professional's expertise often is necessary at some point.

6. Remember that it is not uncommon to experience a relapse into feelings of low self-esteem. Look at these relapses as indicators that

   - you have overlooked something you need to address,

   - you have not developed enough time to assimilating new traits, behaviors, skills, and attitudes (you can now zero in on these newly identified vulnerable areas),

   - your support network needs to be shored up, or

   - you need to revise your ongoing self-maintenance plan to reinforce core learnings. Integration requires practice over time.

Almost everything in our lives requires ongoing maintenance: our cars, homes, bodies, appliances, the list goes on and on. Why would we think our self-esteem is any different? As part of my self-maintenance plan, I attend a support group weekly. Close friends and family are important to me, so I also spend quite a bit of time nurturing those relationships, which I see as vital to my emotional health. I read books and watch films that guide me in self-reflection. I also attend some kind of workshop that helps inspire me a couple of times a year. Meditating, journaling, recording my dreams, and writing are therapeutic for me. Every now and then, if something continues to trouble me that I can't resolve with my regular resources, I schedule time with a therapist. I also build exercise, good nutrition, sufficient sleep, and leisure into my maintenance plan.

If you will review the self-mandala in chapter 1 and address each of its elements with structured, specific, personalized, ongoing goals, you will develop a fairly complete plan to maintain your own high self-esteem. You may need time and trial and error before you find a plan that works for you, and you may have to revise your plan now and then as your priorities and needs change, but the self-mandala is a good tool to use in your planning. Periodic check-ins with your growth partners also will help keep you on track with your commitment to yourself.

If you allow it to, self-neglect will eventually lead to a breakdown in self-esteem. With the challenges we face in this complex world, a sound maintenance policy is well worth the effort. After all, you deserve it.

APPENDICES

A. Children's Books

B. Videography

C. Educational Audio and Video Cassettes

Appendix A

CHILDREN'S BOOKS

BODY

Aliki. (1989). *My five senses.* New York: HarperCollins.

Carlson, Nancy. (1991). *Take time to relax.* New York: Viking.

Erson, R. (1993). *Courageous pacers: The complete guide to running, walking, and fitness for kids.* Corpus Christi, TX: Proactive Publications.

Nelson, Nigel. (1989). *Body talk.* New York: Thomson Learning.

O'Neill, Catherine. (1993). *Relax.* New York: Child's Play International.

Parry, Linda, & Parry, Alan. (1992). *Wonderful you!* Nashville, TN: Nelson.

INTERNAL DYNAMICS

Frasier, Debra. (1991). *On the day you were born.* New York: Harcourt Brace.

Himmelman, John. (1994). *I'm not scared.* New York: Scholastic.

Modesitt, Jeanne. (1992). *Sometimes I feel like a mouse: A book about feelings.* New York: Scholastic.

Decision Making

Lionni, Leo. (1993). *A color of his own*. New York: Knopf Books for Young Readers.

Ness, Evaline. (1971). *Sam, bangs, and moonshine*. New York: Henry Holt.

Polacco, Patricia. (1992). *Chicken Sunday*. New York: Putman.

Feelings

Fassler, Joan. (1983). *My grandpa died today*. New York: Human Science Press.

Gackenback, D. (1977). *Harry and the terrible whatzit*. Boston: Houghton Mifflin.

Rosenberg, Maxine. (1985). *Being a twin, having a twin*. New York: Lothrup, Lee & Shepard.

Rosenberg, Maxine. (1989). *Growing up adopted*. New York: Simon & Schuster.

Sharmat, Marjorie, & Sharmat, Marjorie W. (1984). *My mother never listens to me*. Morton Grove, IL: Albert Whitman.

SELF-ESTEEM

Byars, B. (1970). *The summer of the swans*. New York: Puffin.

Carlson, Nancy. (1988). *I like me!* New York: Viking.

Galdone, Paul. (1985). *The little red hen*. New York: Clarion.

Hutchins, Pat. (1993). *Titch*. New York: Aladdin Paperbacks.

Klassen, Allison. (1994). *I did it!* Austin, TX: Bright Books.

Little, Lessie Jones, & Greenfield, Eloise. (1978). *I can do it myself*. New York: Crowell Junior.

Pallerson, Claire, & Quilter, Lindsay. (1988). *It's OK to be you*. Berkeley, CA: Tricycle Press.

Paulus, T. (1963). *Hope for the flowers*. New York: Paulist Press.

Paulus, T. (1972). *The pinkish, purplish, bluish egg*. Boston: Houghton Mifflin.

Payne, Lauren Murphy. (1994). *Just because I am: A children's book of affirmations*. Minneapolis, MN: Free Spirit.

Piper, W. (1961). *The little engine that could*. New York: Platt.

Ross, Dave. (1980). *A book of hugs*. New York: HarperCollins.

Sharmat, Marjorie. (1992). *I'm terrific*. New York: Holiday.

Waber, Bernard. (1973). *Ira sleeps over*. Boston: Houghton Mifflin.

Waber, Bernard. (1991). *Nobody is perfick*. Boston: Houghton Mifflin.

SOCIAL

Carlson, Nancy. (1990). *Arne and the new kid*. New York: Viking.

Carlson, Nancy, (1994). *How to lose all of your friends*. New York: Viking.

Hutchings, P. (1993). *My best friend*. New York: Green Willow.

Lester, Helen. (1990). *Tacky, the penguin*. Boston: Houghton Mifflin.

Petty, Kate, & Firmin, Charlotte. (1991). *Feeling left out*. New York: Aladdin Books.

Polacco, Patricia. (1992). *Mrs. Katz and Tush*. New York: Bantam.

Powell, Richard. (1990). *How to deal with friends. A child's practical guide*. Mahwah, NJ: Watermill Press.

Rosenberg, Maxine. (1992). *Living with a single parent*. New York: Simon & Schuster.

Surat, Michele Maria. (1989). *Angel child, dragon child*. New York: Scholastic.

Waber, Bernard. (1976). *But names will never hurt me*. Boston: Houghton Mifflin.

DISABILITIES

Auditory Disabilities

Ancona, G., & Miller, M. B. (1989). *Handtalk zoo.* New York: Simon & Schuster.

Charlip, R., & Miller, M. B. (1987). *Handtalk.* New York: Aladdin Paperbacks.

Levine, E. (1974). *Lisa and her soundless world.* New York: Human Science Press.

Litchfield, A. B. (1976). *A button in her ear.* Morton Grove, IL: Albert Whitman.

Physical Disabilities

Fassler, Joan. (1975). *Howie helps himself.* Morton Grove, IL: Albert Whitman.

Lasher, J. (1980). *Nick joins in.* Morton Grove, IL: Albert Whitman.

Rosenberg, Maxine. (1983). *My friend Leslie: The story of a handicapped child.* New York: Lothrup, Lee & Shepherd.

Schwie, M. (1992). *Edward's different day.* San Luis Obispo, CA: Impact.

TRANSITIONS

Burton, V. (1978). *The little house.* Boston: Houghton Mifflin.

Risom, O. (1963). *I am a bunny.* New York: Golden Books.

GENERAL RESOURCES

Childswork/childsplay. (annual catalog). King of Prussia, PA: Center for Applied Psychology. A catalog addressing the mental health needs of children and their families through play. Includes posters, books, workbooks, and games on a variety of topics.

Kidsrights. (annual catalog). Charlotte, NC: Author. A catalog of games, books, activities, videos, toys, puppets, posters, therapy tools for elementary, middle school, and high school on topics related to self-esteem, life skills/management, feelings, social skills, parenting, grief, sexual abuse, rape, batterings, and multicultural issues.

Lipson, E. (1991). New York Times *parent's guide to the best books for children*. New York: Random House.

Westridge young writers workshop. (1994). Santa Fe, NM: John Muir. Kids explore the gifts of children with special needs.

Appendix B

VIDEOGRAPHY

By Linda Rauch, Fall, 1995
Whipp Road, Suite A-1,
Kettering, Ohio 45440
(937) 434-6217

SUBJECT	VIDEO
Addiction/Codependency	
Blue Sky	In this drama a husband is codependent on his bipolar wife, while their children are able to see the dysfunctional dynamics.
Parenthood	A supposed comedy that has important drama within it, this film clearly shows the family dynamics and pain of compulsive gambling.

*Movies that may not yet have been released on video.

When a Man Loves a Woman	A drama about an alcoholic wife, her codependent husband, and two small children. This can be useful in breaking through denial and delusion in children being affected.

AIDS

Common Threads: Stories from the Quilt	A stirring documentary narrated by Dustin Hoffman which can help parents, lovers, friends, and those living and dying with AIDS deal constructively with the disease.
Longtime Companion	An ensemble piece that depicts how AIDS came to affect the lives of nine gay men and a woman friend over a nine-year period, showing how ignorance of the disease decimates lives.
Philadelphia	A drama about an AIDS-infected employee's victory over discrimination. This can be useful in empowering HIV- and AIDS-affected persons.

Empowerment of the Aged

Harry and Tonto	A delightful story of a senior citizen who refuses to be told where he and his cat will live.
The Trip to Bountiful	An elderly woman runs away from her son's home to her old hometown and has a grand adventure.

Empowerment of Persons

Driving Miss Daisy	A gentle drama of an unlikely friendship in an environment of discrimination.
The Power of One	A powerful drama of victory over various forms of bigotry, including anti-Semitism and racism, set in South Africa.

Empowerment of Women

Fried Green Tomatoes	The friendships between women in this drama empower them to make choices outside their role expectations.

Shirley Valentine This film is helpful for stuck, middle-aged women. The heroine stops taking care of her husband to go on an adventure, and in the process finds herself.

Grief/Loss

The Accidental Tourist A father is emotionally immobilized by the death of his son in this drama.

Da A dramatic and beautiful film in which a son relives his life while in dialogue with his recently deceased father's spirit.

Dad A son tries to make a connection with his aging father before it is too late.

Corrina, Corrina A young girl loses her mother and is unable to communicate her grief. This film can be helpful in showing how deeply affected children are by the loss of a parent.

Fried Green Tomatoes A number of losses occur to the main characters in this film, including the loss of a brother and life companion.

The Lion King This film is especially helpful for men who have lost their fathers at an early age and who feel responsible for the death.

My Life A career-obsessed young man spends his last months making peace with his parents and recording a video for his unborn son. This drama can facilitate feelings for either a father or a son.

Shadowlands An intellectual man out of touch with feelings learns the importance of expressing love during his wife's terminal illness.

Sleepless in Seattle A young boy helps his father rejoin the living after the death of the child's mother.

Unstrung Heroes* A young boy is losing his mother and runs to the apartment of two mentally ill uncles for refuge.

Homophobia/Homosexuality

Desert Hearts	A woman struggles with accepting her feelings for another woman. This film can be helpful to clients facing the same struggle. (Contains explicit sex scenes).
Philadelphia	The family of the gay main character is lovingly supportive of him and his lover. His employer and attorney epitomize the struggle with homophobia.
Common Threads: Stories from the Quilt	This documentary contains respectful examples of a number of gay men and their lovers, friends, and families.
The Sum of Us	A father and his gay son have a wonderful relationship in this Australian film. The father's mother has had a same-sex relationship, which is also lovingly depicted.
Torch-Song Trilogy	Homophobia is depicted in this film on the part of a gay man, society, and a mother. This film also includes the adoption of a child by a single gay man.

Impotence

Coming Home	A paraplegic makes love to a woman in an erotic, explicit love scene.

Mentally Challenged

Dominic and Eugene	A "slow" fraternal twin works to support himself and his twin brother, who is in medical school.
Forest Gump	The importance of a determined mother and good friends, and the difference they can make in a mentally challenged person's life, are central to this film. Also, we are reminded of how much can be learned from a simple person.
Rain Man	Another film about brothers. In this one, the "able" brother learns from his interaction with autistic savant older brother how to love.

Unstrung Heroes*	Two mentally ill brothers are supportive of their nephew as his mother is dying. The boy's father is an eccentric genius and unable to connect with him.

Parenting

Parenthood	This film is wonderful for uptight parents who need to lighten up and laugh at themselves.
Uncle Buck	This film shows how an unlikely family member can bring a family together.

Physically Challenged

Coming Home	Paraplegic Vietnam veteran is instrumental in teaching a woman about tenderness.
The Doctor	An aloof surgeon learn through his own cancer about patient rights.
The Elephant Man	A severely deformed man struggles for dignity in this black-and-white film. (Not suggested for clients who are depressed.)
Gaby, A True Story	Parents struggle to accept their infant daughter's cerebral palsy. The film also deals frankly with the sexuality of physically challenged young people.
The Mask	A mother helps her son brave a disfiguring disease.
My Left Foot	Another true story, this time with siblings rallying around their brother, who has cerebral palsy. As an adult, he becomes a writer-artist.
Passion Fish	An embittered, paralyzed actress learns to live again through her friendship with her nurse.
Regarding Henry	Through a head injury, a successful, self-centered attorney becomes a gentle, childlike man who slowly recovers his memory but not his self-centeredness.

Spirituality

Dances with Wolves	A disillusioned Union soldier finds inner peace in harmony with nature and Native Americans.
The Priest*	A young priest struggles with his homosexuality, his associate priest's affair with the housekeeper, and the issue of the seal of confession (a young girl shares in confession that her father is being sexual with her).
Shadowlands	Writer C. S. Lewis changes his beliefs about suffering through his beloved wife's illness and death.

Appendix C

EDUCATIONAL AUDIO AND VIDEO CASSETTES

BODY

The body image trap: Taking control of how you see your body [video]. (1993). Center City, MN: Hazelden.

Ebbitt, Joan. (1988). *Compulsive eating: When does it become an illness* [video]? Center City, MN: Hazelden.

Ebbitt, Joan. (1989). *Eating disorders and sexuality* [video]. Center City, MN: Hazelden.

Hay, Louise. (1989a). *Love your body* [audio cassette]. Santa Monica, CA: Hay House.

Hay, Louise. (1989b). *Heal your body* [audio cassette]. Santa Monica, CA: Hay House.

Hollis, Judi. (1986). *Hope for compulsive eaters* [12 audio cassettes]. Center City, MN: Hazeldon.

Warwick, Shakti (Writer), & Francis, Richard (Producer). (1990). *Meditation* [video]. New York: Meditation.

BODY IMAGE/AWARENESS

Niemi, Earl (Producer), & Walher, Arnold (Director). (1977). *Body image, disability, and sexuality* [video]. Minneapolis: University of Minnesota Program in Human Sexuality (Distributed by Multimedia Resource Center, San Francisco).

Stroebel, Charles. (1983). *Quieting reflex training for adults* [narrated by Judith Proctor; 4 audio cassettes]. New York: BMA Audio Cassette.

INTERNAL DYNAMICS

Braza, Kathleen (1994). *To touch a grieving heart* [video]. Salt Lake City, UT: Pancom Video.

Human Race Club. (1989). *The lean machine: A story about handling emotions* [based on books by Joy Berry; video]. St. Louis: Kids' Media.

Cognitive

RET video library. Produces videos, workbooks, and booklets on anger, shame, depression, anxiety and worry, perfectionism, self-esteem, grief, and guilt. A facilitator's video (1993) is also available. Center City, MN: Hazelden.

Cognitive Techniques

Burns, David. (1983). *Feeling good about yourself* [audio cassette]. Washington, DC: Psychology Today.

Ellis, Albert. (1978). *Rational emotive cognitive therapy in the treatment of dysfunctional habits* [audio cassette]. New York: BMA Audio Cassettes.

Emery, Gary. (1982). *Controlling depression through cognitive therapy* [3 audio cassettes]. New York: BMA Audio Cassettes.

Coping

Lazarus, Arnold. (1970). *Daily living: Coping with tensions and anxieties* [audio cassette]. Chicago: Human Development Institute.

Imagery

Elliott, James. (1977). *Personal growth through guided imagery* [audio cassette]. Berkeley, CA: Explorations Institute.

Lazarus, Arnold. (1986). *Personal enrichment through imagery* [3 audio cassettes]. New York: BMA Audio Cassettes.

Self-Awareness

Miller, Emmett. (1980). *Tools for taking charge* [audio cassette] Stanford, CA: Source.

Relaxation

Cohen, Ken. (1996). *Healthy breathing* (audio cassette). Boulder, CO: Sound True.

McKay, M., & Fanning, P. (1977). *Calm your mind* (audio cassette). Oakland, CA: New Harbinger.

McKay, M., & Fanning, P. (1997). *Relax your body* (audio cassette). Oakland, CA: New Harbinger.

Meditation

Goleman, David. (1989). *The art of meditation* [audio cassette]. Los Angeles: Audio Renaissance Tapes.

Hanh, Thich Nhat. (1994). *The miracle of mindfulness: A manual of meditation* [audio cassette]. New York: HarperCollins.

LeShan, Lawrence. (1987). *How to meditate* [audio cassette]. Los Angeles: Audio Renaissance Tapes.

Mulry, Ray. (1976). *Tension management and relaxation: An approach to a balanced way of living* [audio cassette]. WSU Media Services BF 575575M842.

Tubesing, Donald. (1976). *Spiritual centering* [music by Steven Halpern; audio cassette]. Duluth, MN: Whole Person Associates.

SELF-CONCEPT

Felker, David. (1976). *Positive self-concept* [audio cassette]. San Jose, CA: Lansford.

Seldin, Ruth. (1982). *Self-concept: How do I know who I am* [video]? Pleasantville, NY: Sunburst Communications.

SELF-ESTEEM

Am I worthwhile [video]? (1989). Mount Kisco, NY: Guidance Associates.

Beattie, Melodie. (1989). *Caring for ourselves* (video). Center City, MN: Hazeldon.

Branden, Nathanial. (1980). *Building self-esteem* [audio cassette]. New York: Ziff-David Publishing.

Branden, Nathanial. (1985a). *The art of self-acceptance* [audio cassette]. Beverly Hills, CA: Biocentric Institute.

Branden, Nathanial. (1985b). *Self-esteem enhancement through hypnosis: A lecture* [audio cassette]. Beverly Hills, CA: Biocentric Institute.

Branden, Nathanial. (1986a). *The psychology of high self-esteem* [6 audio cassettes]. Chicago: Nightingale-Conant.

Branden, Nathanial. (1986b). *Raising your self-esteem* [audio cassette]. Beverly Hills, CA: Biocentric Institute.

Branden, Nathanial. (1986c). *Self-esteem enhancement through hypnosis* [audio cassette]. Beverly Hills, CA: Biocentric Institute.

Burns, David. (1983). *Feeling good about yourself* [audio cassette]. Washington, DC: Psychology Today.

Dobson, James. (1985). *Preparing for adolescence: The origins of self-doubt* [video]. Waco, TX: Word Lifeware.

Felker, David. (1976). *Positive self-concept* [4 audio cassettes]. San Jose, CA: Lansford.

Image in a mirror [video]. (1968). New Brunswick, NJ: Holt Rinehart Winston.

Larsen, Earnie. (1989). *Dealing with discouragement* [video]. Center City, MN: Hazelden.

Larsen, Earnie. (1989). *Overcoming fear* [video]. Center City, MN: Hazelden.

Larsen, Earnie. (1991). *Building self-confidence* [video]. Center City, MN: Hazelden.

Larsen, Earnie. (1992). *Believing in yourself* [video]. Center City, MN: Hazelden.

Parker, Jonathan. (1985). *Building a positive self-image* [3 audio cassettes]. Ojai, CA: Gateways Research Institute.

Pritchard, Michael. (1993). *Big changes, big choices video series* [videos]. Center City, MN: Hazelden.

Rogers, Cosby, S. (Writer), Rogers, Cosby S. (Producer), & Dalton, Jeff (Director). (1988). *Self-esteem in school-age children* [video]. Blacksburg: Virginia Polytechnic Institute and State University, Department of Family and Child Development.

Williamson, Marianne. (1992). *On self-esteem* [audio cassette]. New York: HarperCollins.

SOCIAL

Black, Claudia, & Gorski, Terry. (1989). *The addictive relationship series* [3 videos]. Center City, MN: Hazelden.

Ellis, Albert. (1986). *Effective self-assertion* [audio cassette]. Washington, DC: American Psychological Association.

Guerra, Julio J. (1986). *Assertion training series: A guide to self-dignity* (4 cassettes). Champaign, IL: Research Press.

Jakubowski-Spector, Patricia, Perlman, Joan, & Coburn, Karen. (1973). *Assertiveness training for women* [video]. Washington, DC: American Personnel and Guidance Association (in cooperation with KEC, Channel 9, St. Louis).

Keller, Kay. (1994). *Powerful communication skills for women* [video]. Shawnee Mission, KS: National Business Women's Leadership Association.

Marcum, Howard. (1991). *Fighting for your marriage* (2 videos). Denver: PREP Educational Videos.

Parker, Jonathan. (1984). *Assertiveness* [audio cassette]. Ojai, CA: Institute of Human Development.

Smith, Manuel. (1975). *When I say no I feel guilty*. [audio cassette]. Los Angeles: Pacifica Foundation.

Wegscheider-Cruse, Sharon. (1985). *The family trap* [video]. Center City, MN: Hazelden.

You can choose series [videos] (1992). Center City, MN: Hazelden. (cooperation, being responsible, dealing with feelings, saying no, doing the right thing, dealing with disappointment, appreciating yourself, asking for help, being friends, and resolving conflicts).

INTERPERSONAL COMMUNICATION

Mayo, Kathleen (Producer, Writer). (1981). *Listening skills: The art of active listening* [3 filmstrips, 3 audio cassettes, and teacher's guide]. Pleasantville, NY: Human Relations Media.

Nebraska Educational Television Council for Higher Education. (1987). *The trained ear* [video]. Lincoln: Metche.

Ratliffe, Sharon, & Hudson, David. (1989). *Interpersonal competence* [3 videos]. Belmont, CA: Wadsworth.

Zimbardo, Philip. (1978). *Shyness clinic* [audio cassette]. New York: Bio Mounting Applications.

Zimbardo, Philip. (1985). *Overcoming shyness* [audio cassette]. Washington, DC: American Psychological Association.

CONFLICT

Cooper, Ken (Writer, Narrator). (1985). *Conflict management* [video]. Santa Monica, CA: The Program Source.

Piaget, Gerald, & Brinkley, Barbara. (1981). *How to deal with difficult people* [audio cassette]. New York: Psychology Today.

Gottman, John, & Stockton, Phil. (1976). *Three styles of marital conflict* [video]. Clear Creek, IN: Behavioral Images.

TRANSITIONS

Andreas, Connirae, & Andreas, Steve (Producers). (1985). *Changing beliefs* [video]. Boulder: NLF of Colorado.

Flack, Frederic. (1977). *Coping with change* [audio cassette]. Washington, DC: Psychology Today.

Metcalf, C. W. (1990). *Humor, risk, and change* [video]. Des Moines, IA: American Media.

Mead, Margaret. (1968). *How people change* [audio cassette]. New York: McGraw Hill.

Rees, John (producer). (1989). *How to set and achieve goals* [2 videos]. Boulder, CO: Career Track Publications.

WILL Radio, University of Illinois at Urbana-Champaign. (1983). *Transitions: Gaining through losing* [audio cassette]. Arlington, VA: Soundworks.

Woods, Jim, Lyons, Joan, & Carroll, Richard (Writers); Bent, Quincey, & Bransfield, Barry (Producers). (1981). *Transitions* [video]. Highland Park, IL: Perennial Education.

Index

G

Q – R

S

ABOUT THE EDITOR

C. JESSE CARLOCK

Dr. C. Jesse Carlock has been a psychologist and therapist in private practice in Dayton, Ohio, for more than 20 years. After completing three years of postgraduate training at the Gestalt Institute of Cleveland, she studied extensively with Virginia Satir. She has been a member of Satir's Avanta Network for 15 years.

Jesse is a member of the Association for the Advancement of Gestalt Therapy and the International Society for the Study of Dissociative Disorders. She is certified in clinical hypnosis by the American Society of Clinical Hypnosis.

Jesse is coauthor of *Practical Techniques for Enhancing Self-Esteem* and *Bridges to Intimacy* and has written articles on couples, group work, alcoholism, gay and lesbian issues, and Satir methodology.

Currently Jesse is Clinical Professor with the School of Professional Psychology at Wright State University. She also is training coordinator for first year students at the Gestalt Institute of Central Ohio in Columbus, Ohio.

In her free time, she enjoys playing with her dogs, Harley and Roxie, scuba-diving, cross-country skiing, antiqueing, underwater photography, and just "being a kid."